DATE DUE

Demco, Inc. 38-293

THE METRICS OF SCIENCE AND TECHNOLOGY

THE METRICS OF SCIENCE AND TECHNOLOGY

Eliezer Geisler

QUORUM BOOKS
Westport, Connecticut • London

For Betsy, my wife and soulmate

Library of Congress Cataloging-in-Publication Data

Geisler, Eliezer, 1942–
    The metrics of science and technology / Eliezer Geisler.
        p. cm.
    Includes bibliographical references and index.
    ISBN 1–56720–213–6 (alk. paper)
    1. Science—Social aspects. 2. Technology—Social aspects. I. Title.
Q175.5.G43 2000
    303.48′3—dc21   00–026230

British Library Cataloguing in Publication Data is available.

Library of Congress Catalog Card Number: 00–026230
ISBN: 1–56720–213–6

First published in 2000

Quorum Books, 88 Post Road West, Westport, CT 06881
An imprint of Greenwood Publishing Group, Inc.
www.quorumbooks.com

Printed in the United States of America

The paper used in this book complies with the
Permanent Paper Standard issued by the National
Information Standards Organization (Z39.48–1984).

10 9 8 7 6 5 4 3 2 1

CONTENTS

List of Figures   vii
Preface   xi

Part I . Historical Overview   1

Chapter 1.   A Short History   3
Chapter 2.   The Emergence of Institutions   17

Part II.   Metrics: Approaches, Methods, Techniques   31

Chapter 3.   Measurement: Concepts and Issues   33
Chapter 4.   Selecting a Metric   69
Chapter 5.   Inputs to Science and Technology   97
Chapter 6.   Outputs from Science and Technology:
             Categories and Metrics   113
Chapter 7.   Economic and Financial Metrics   129
Chapter 8.   Bibliometric Measures: Publications and Citations   153

Chapter 9.	Co-word Analysis and Mapping of Science and Technology	179
Chapter 10.	The Metric of Patents	201
Chapter 11.	The Metric of Peer Review	217
Chapter 12.	The Metric of Process Outcomes	243
Chapter 13.	Performance of Science and Technology	267

Part III. Applications: The Value, in Practice, of Science and Technology — **281**

Chapter 14.	Metrics and Evaluation of Academic Science and Technology	283
Chapter 15.	Metrics and Evaluation of Industrial Science and Technology	299
Chapter 16.	Science, Technology, and Strategy	317
Chapter 17.	Metrics and Evaluation of Public-Sector Science and Technology	329
Chapter 18.	Metrics and Evaluation of National Innovation Systems	349
Chapter 19.	Values, Ethics, and Implications	359

Epilogue	367
Selected Bibliography	371
Index	377

LIST OF FIGURES

FIGURE

2.1	Factors That Contributed to and Facilitated the Institutionalization of American Science and Technology	20
2.2	Federal and Industrial Support for R&D Performed by American Universities, 1960-1993	22
2.3	Enrollment in U.S. Higher Education: 1967-1991	23
3.1	Classification Scheme for Measurement Instruments	36
3.2	Characteristics of Measurement Instruments	39
3.3	Categories of S&T Metrics and Characteristics of Measurement	42
3.4	The Abstraction Ladder in Capturing Critical Aspects of Complex Phenomena	43
3.5	Issues in the Use of Indicators to Measure Complex Phenomena and Conceptual Constructs	45
3.6	Key Issues in Methodology and Analysis of Science Indicators	52
4.1	Steps in the Construction of S&T Metrics	71
4.2	A Generalized Model of Metric Selection	76
4.3	Pool of Available Metrics	80
4.4	Criteria for Selecting Metrics for Science and Technology	88
5.1	Summary of Key Reasons for Using Input Measures	104

5.2	Illustrative Measures and Ratios of Expenditures or Inputs to R&D	104
6.1	A Generic List of Outputs from Science and Technology	116
6.2	Illustrative Outputs from S&T by Degree of Quantification	119
6.3	Illustrative Outputs from S&T by Direct or Indirect Impacts	120
6.4	Illustrative Outputs from Science and from Technology	121
6.5	Key Categories of Outputs from S&T	122
7.1	Plausible Explanations for the Productivity Paradox	134
7.2	R&D Productivity and R&D Spillovers	138
7.3	R&D Productivity, R&D Outputs, Impacts, and Spillovers	139
7.4	Strengths of the Economic/Financial Metrics	140
7.5	Weaknesses and Problems of the Economic/Financial Metrics	141
7.6	Factors That Seem to Influence the Successful Application of Economic/Financial Metrics to Evaluate S&T	144
8.1	Key Criteria in Selecting Scientific Journal for Bibliometric Analysis	157
8.2	Bibliometrics and Levels of Evaluation	158
8.3	Communities of Science and Highly Productive Core of Authors	161
8.4	Strength of Bibliometrics in the Evaluation of S&T	163
8.5	Weaknesses and Problems with Bibliometrics	164
9.1	A Simplified Model of Exploitation of Data Mining by Business Enterprises	185
9.2	Illustrative Capabilities and Tasks DM Can Perform with Large Data Sets in Health Care	186
9.3	Some Weaknesses and Problems with Data Mining	187
9.4	Some Weaknesses and Problems with Technology Roadmaps	192
10.1	Patents as Link Between R&D and Economic Outcomes	204
10.2	Some Factors Explaining Impacts of Patents on Performance	206
10.3	Strengths and Benefits of Patents	207
10.4	Weaknesses and Problems of Patents	208
11.1	Purposes/Objectives for Conducting Peer Review	218
11.2	Characteristics/Attributes of the Process of Peer Review	220
11.3	Features of the Process of Peer Review	221
11.4	Peer-Review Criteria Used by NSF	224
11.5	Peer-Review Criteria Used by NIH	225
11.6	Peer-Review Criteria Used by Industry	227
11.7	A Generalized Schematic View of the Peer-Review Process by Scientific Journals	229
11.8	Illustrative Strengths and Benefits from Peer Review	232
11.9	Illustrative Weaknesses and Problems with Peer Review	234

12.1	The Process-Outcomes Model of the Linkages Between the S&T Process and Social and Economic Systems	247
12.2	Illustrative Core Indicators and Measures of the Outputs from S&T	254
12.3	Illustrative Organization-Specific Indicators and Measures of the Outputs from S&T	256
12.4	Illustrative Strengths and Capabilities of the Metric of Process Outcomes	261
13.1	Illustrative S&T Performance Measures	269
13.2	Typology of S&T Performance Organizations: Partial Measures	273
13.3	Typology of S&T Performance Organizations: Comprehensive Measures	274
14.1	Illustrative Metrics Used to Evaluate Academic Institutions	289
14.2	Illustrative Measures of Performance of University Spin-Offs and Cooperative Programs with Industry	291
15.1	Illustrative Uses of Key Metrics of S&T in the Evaluation of the Contributions of Industrial S&T	301
15.2	Illustrative Uses of Key Metrics of S&T in the Evaluation of Efficiency and Management of Corporate S&T Operations	303
16.1	Reasons for Integration of Technology and Strategy	319
16.2	Illustrative Approaches to Technology-Strategy Alignment or Integration	320
16.3	Key S&T Metrics and the Technology-Strategy Connection	322
17.1	A Generalized Scheme of the Stakeholders of Federal S&T Laboratories	331
17.2	Metrics in Self-Evaluation of Federal Laboratories	336
17.3	Metrics in Evaluation of Federal Laboratories by Parent Agency	338
17.4	Metrics in Evaluation of Federal Laboratories by Others	339
19.1	An Illustrative Matrix of S&T Innovations and the Queries of Our Life	361

PREFACE

William Thomson, Lord Kelvin (1824-1907), is often quoted as saying that if something cannot be measured, then it does not really matter. Measuring the objects and the events in the world around us is not only a scientific necessity, but also the means to make sense of the complexity of natural phenomena. We continually live by measures of our surroundings. We measure the passage of time, the temperatures in our climate, our economic situations, and everything else with which we make contact.

In the organizational and managerial sciences, the measurement of phenomena and events becomes a crucial tool for understanding and for the study of such phenomena. Unlike the physical sciences, these branches of human knowledge are relatively less exact, and their quantities less measurable. Technology, its outcomes, the organizations that produce it, and those that are impacted by it fall into this category.

PURPOSE OF THE BOOK

This book is about the metrics in the evaluation and measurement of science and technology and their outcomes. Rather than simply listing the currently used measures and techniques, the book outlines the measurement of science and technology within the broader framework of the concepts of measurement, and the approaches used to evaluate the spectrum of activities we generally combine under the rubric of science and technology.   By combining the background of what constitutes technological achievements and progress, with the extant efforts to measure them, the book offers a comprehensive view of our past and present attempts to capture these accomplishments by means of measurement of both their qualitative and quantitative attributes.

But methods and measures alone are not enough to describe the vast activity that is focused on identifying outcomes, outputs, and impacts of technology.   There is a need to place all of these into the context of how science and technology interacts with the social and economic systems. Such a need is satisfied in this book.

The book aims to help readers comprehend the intricacies of the relationship between science, technology, the economy, and society. Most important, the book offers a detailed description of the measurement tools that we possess, designed to assess and to measure this relationship.

AUDIENCES

The Metrics of Science and Technology is directed toward several audiences. First are scientists and engineers who practice their craft in all kinds of laboratories: private, industry, and government-owned or -operated. The book offers them a platform to analyze their achievements, and points to the tools available to them to evaluate their performance.

Second, the book is targeted toward managers of research, development, and technology in private industry and government agencies. Long wrestling with the task of evaluating the activities with which they are charged, technology managers will find this book an illuminating source of not only the methods and techniques for evaluation, but, even more important, the link between their area of endeavor and the larger picture of society and the economy.

Third, scholars and students of technology management and of the innovation process will find this book of extreme interest. Because of the book's comprehensive description of the state of the art and relevant literature, the book is anchored in recent developments in both theory and practice.

Another target audience are decision-makers and policy-makers in industry, universities, and government.   The realism of the interface between history, methods, and their applications provides this target audience some exciting tools that may greatly assist them in generating science and technology policy.

Finally this book is also targeted to the general public. Anyone who is interested in how we can evaluate the technological progress around us will certainly be attracted to this book. The outline of the book is friendly to the casual reader. It offers a historical background and a theoretical foundation to facilitate the reader's grasp of the language and the concepts under study. The casual reader will thus benefit from the book through insights and examples of real-life applications.

GENESIS OF THE BOOK

The Metrics of Science and Technology began early in my career, when I served in the management team of a research institution. Concepts and ideas about evaluation of the results from research and development (R&D) began to congeal in my mind. During that period I had established methods and procedures for on-going as well as periodic evaluation of technological achievements. The successes and failures associated with these attempts gave me much to consider and caused me to reassess my beliefs.

Later, in my years in academe and experience in management consulting, I worked with hundreds of companies and research/technology institutions. Evaluation, monitoring, and measurement of their technology outputs were continuous issues, pregnant with major problems, yet offering very few constructive or feasible solutions.

Thus, the fortuitous merger of my experience, my own studies and models I had tested, and the cogent state of the art all led to the preparation of this book. In compiling it I carefully considered the complexity of the topic, as well as the diverse audiences.

APPROACH OF THE BOOK

As an organization scientist who specializes in the management of technology, my interests reside in the system and organization of technology. This book is therefore designed to accommodate my inclination. The emphasis is on the architecture of technological outcomes, as they are transferred to, and are absorbed by, social and economic subsystems.

Clearly, both the literature and the extant methods and techniques for technology evaluation and measurement are amply documented in the book. But the overall approach is to place such evaluation and its tools within the larger framework of the organizations that generate technology and those that are impacted by it.

As such, the book takes on an interdisciplinary stance, in that the technical aspects of evaluation and measurement are merged with organizational and managerial dimensions. The book is directed toward the intersection of engineering and management, drawing from both areas of scholarship.

WHAT THE BOOK IS ABOUT

We live in very exciting times, where technology is leading our economic and societal progress and dramatically changing the way we exist. Perhaps the most crucial query that continually challenges us is: how does technology impact our lives? And, more precisely: how can we, or should we, measure such impacts? This book is a modest attempt to assess what we currently know, so as to answer those questions. To that effect, the book is composed of three parts.

Part I is the historical overview of the evolution of technology and its growing role, over time, as a force in the economy of nations and in their societal activities. This part is concerned with how technology evolved from ancient times to become the major force of today. Many of the concepts, terms, and notions that are prevalent in our current discourse about technology and its impacts have their roots in history. Hence, this part of the book traces the major developments in the rise of technology in human affairs.

Part II is the theoretical background of the concepts and approaches used to evaluate research, development, technology, and innovation. This part establishes the different constructs with which the book is concerned, such as the innovation continuum, technology and technological systems, and R&D activity. In addition, this part outlines and describes the theoretical background of measuring and evaluating R&D and technology. Why are certain approaches to evaluation of these activities more suitable than others? What are the theoretical foundations for conducting evaluation of complex phenomena, such as technology and its outcomes?

Part III articulates the area of evaluation of technology. Boundaries are set for what constitutes the evaluation function of technology and its outcomes. Notions, concepts, and approaches that are specific to this function are delineated and defined. The role of evaluation of technology in management disciplines is also discussed. Finally, Part III is concerned with applications. This part of the book is designed in the form of applications in selected areas of technology generation and utilization. In a format similar to that of illustrative cases, applications of metrics are discussed in such areas as industrial companies, public technology institutes, and national innovation systems. In addition, this part also explores the application of metrics in consortia and intersector cooperation in technology.

As may be the case with any complex phenomenon, this book is a pioneering attempt to condense the state of knowledge on the measures of the outcomes of technology, and to make this area more accessible to managers, scholars, and the general public. By bringing together history, theory, measures, and applications, this book has embarked on a somewhat uncharted format. It is my hope that similar books will follow and that other critical aspects of the management of technology will be made more visible to wide audiences.

ACKNOWLEDGMENTS

This book is a product of many years of study, experience, and reflection. Many people have contributed to forging my opinions, and to the knowledge peppered in the pages of the book. Although I bear full responsibility for any mistakes in this text, I owe a debt of gratitude to colleagues, friends, mentors, critics, and my family. In particular, I am grateful to the following: Al Rubenstein, Charles Thompson, Herb Cheng, and Don Frey of Northwestern University; Ron Kostoff, Office of Naval Research; Milt Glaser; Gerald Hoffman; Ed Mansfield; and Bela Gold.

I wish to thank Dean Zia Hassan and Joel Goldhar of Stuart Graduate School of Business, Illinois Institute of Technology. Also, my thanks to Bill Souder, Falguni Sen, Yair Babad, Aaron Shenhar, Samuel Bulmash, Nava Pliskin, Tom Bramorski, Dundar Kocaoglu, Ev Rogers, John Ettlie, Sul Kassicieh, Mohammed Dorgham, and Bill McKelvey.

I am particularly grateful to Eric Valentine, editor at Quorum Books for his support and insightful inputs to this book. Special thanks are also due to my editor, Katie Chase.

Jan Goranson cooperated with me in the preparation of the manuscript from its inception to conclusion. Without her effort and expertise, this book would be no more than a collection of notes. I owe her the deepest of gratitude.

Finally, to my family, and especially to Betsy my wife, who cooperated with me and who supported me during the many months of writing, I owe my sincere thanks.

PART I

HISTORICAL OVERVIEW

If men could learn from history, what lessons it might teach us! But passion and party blind our eyes, and the light which experience gives is a lantern on the stern, which shines only on the waves behind us!

Samuel Taylor Coleridge
(1772-1834)

1

A SHORT HISTORY

In the study of research and development and the evaluation of science and technology in the United States, it is customary to refer to advances in these areas that occurred after the Second World War.[1] The unprecedented growth in both private and public investment in R&D and technology makes the second half of the 20th century a true phenomenon. Perhaps the title of "the age of technology" is very befitting, as the advanced nations of the world—led by the United States—relentlessly expanded their technological stock.

Yet, as Rosenberg (1984) accurately observed, the history of technological evolution follows closely that of human history.[2] Depending on the exact definition of technology, it is possible to state that the development of human civilization was continually peppered with technological breakthroughs and path-breaking achievements. Similarly, if we construe technology as a stand-alone concept, we are able to trace its development and evolution throughout human history.

In an interesting and well researched text, Derry and Williams (1961) identified five major areas in which technological achievements may be pinpointed historically, as critical areas of human endeavors:[3] (1) production of food, (2) extraction and the working of metals, (3) modes and methods of transportation, (4) modes and methods of generating and using energy, and (5) methods of communication and record keeping. By tracing the historical development of individual inventions, innovation, and breakthroughs in each of these areas, the authors have woven an exotic mosaic of technological achievements. Their definition of technology emphasized human mastery of the natural environment.

A similar approach was utilized by Garrison (1991), who has described technological development in the Greek term of "artful methods."[4] Garrison's emphasis was on the development of architecture and the various fields of engineering sciences, such as military and mechanical engineering.

Yet, in such texts that offer a narration of historical events shaped by technological development, there is little attention given to the link between science, technology, economy, and society. The emphasis is on technology "per se." It seems that this prevalent approach is also the easier to describe and study. Individual inventions and innovations throughout history are thus well-defined and easily investigated.[5]

By concentrating on individual technologies, historians could thus describe and explain their development, but without offering ways and means to analyze and measure their relative impact on society and the economy. Nonetheless, such studies revealed a wealth of knowledge about the participants in technological development: the inventors, their sponsors, and the users of the inventions. The studies also identified relationships between certain categories of inventions in selected areas of human endeavor, and the pace at which these inventions were adopted and added to the technological pool of people and nations.[6]

This book focuses on the measurement of the impacts of science and technology (S&T) and on understanding the processes by which science and technology have been integrated with the economy and society. Therefore, it is imperative in the following historical account to explore the degree to which society has accepted science and technology, and the degree to which it has exploited the benefits from this endeavor. The following narrative traces the relationship between S&T and the social, political, and economic institutions that supported it.

TECHNOLOGY AND SOCIETY: THE BEGINNING

The partnership between society via its social and political institutions and technological endeavors has its origins in several European countries in the late Middle Ages. Such partnership is strictly defined as the formal "embrace" of technology by the rulers and institutions of the awakening states. Positive gestures toward technology and the people who were involved with it had gone beyond the support of universities and libraries.

Henry the Navigator (1394-1460) was a prince of Portugal, third son of King John I. Prince Henry established the first school for navigation and promoted the development of new technologies and new designs of ships. The carvel, later used by Columbus in his discoveries, was a product of innovations in design from Henry's school at Sagres.

What made Henry's effort extraordinary was his call for "technologists" of his time to join the school. He offered a challenge and ample support. His program was similar to the NASA moon-landing program in the 1960s, since it attracted "the best and the brightest" in Europe of his time. Cartographers, shipbuilders, astronomers, and an assortment of entrepreneurs converged on Sagres. To an extent, it was a massive program, promoted and supported by the Portuguese crown to develop maritime technologies.[7]

Around the same period, Cosimo de Medici (1389-1464) was director of the Medici family business in Florence and the actual ruler of the rich Italian city-state. Cosimo was a noted patron of the arts, but he also supported scholars and innovators in military technology, transportation, and architecture. In addition to the large library, Cosimo created financial mechanisms to support aspiring technologists, in a form similar to current government research grants.[8]

A better known and more influential and comprehensive state initiative may be attributed to Armand Jean du Plessis, Cardinal and Duke de Richelieu (1585-1642). As the de facto ruler of France, he founded the French Academy. He also encouraged the sciences and energized resources of the state in support of technology endeavors.[9]

This tradition of marshaling resources of the state in support of technological innovations and technology development in general (in addition to the traditional support for the arts) continued in Europe during the reign of Napoleon I (1769-1821).[10] Napoleon established programs in higher education that became available to every qualified candidate, regardless of ancestry, clan, or religion. Moreover, Napoleon established a fund to support prominent scientists.

During the British blockade, Napoleon offered monetary rewards for technological breakthroughs, such as extraction of sugar from beets on a commercial scale. The German chemist Andreas Sigismund discovered sugar in beets in 1747. Another celebrated and major technological breakthrough failed to capture Napoleon's attention. The American inventor Robert Fulton (1765-1815), who later introduced the first efficient steamboat, failed in the demonstration of his prototype of a submarine. In 1800 Fulton's ship, the "Nautilus," was tested in Rouen, and was able to dive to a depth of 25 feet. The French military was not impressed and refused to acquire Fulton's invention.

In the United States, the involvement of public institutions with science and technology can be traced to Benjamin Franklin (1706-1790). As a scientist himself, Franklin invented the Franklin stove, bifocal spectacles, and the lightning rod. He was instrumental in the founding of the Philadelphia Public Library (1742) and the University of Pennsylvania.[11]

Benjamin Franklin's achievements and the institutions he founded have contributed to an even more important legacy. He imbued in the newly established nation a sense of importance of the sciences in general, and technology in particular. His political clout, in combination with his intellectual standing in the colonies, had the effect of elevating the "dabbling" in inventions and technology to a higher level of respectability. Franklin also contributed to the perception that politics and technology are in essence complementary, and that public support for science and technology benefits both.

Although the aforementioned historical figures represent isolated cases of attempts to link technology and society, they are nevertheless predecessors to the strong links that exist nowadays between governments and technological activities and institutions. There are, of course, other individuals who throughout the past two hundred years have contributed to the formal support of technology. The key element in this chapter is the identification of the historical background of the state's formal embrace of science and technology as a beneficial activity, worthy of continued public support.

REASONS FOR PUBLIC SUPPORT

Why would governments provide support for scientists and technologists? Besides the influence of venerable scientists such as Benjamin Franklin, the reasons for public acceptance and support of technology are various and well-focused.

Unlike support for the "beaux arts," such as painting, sculpture, and poetry, technological activity arrived very late on the stage of activities that are worthy of the community's purse. The arts in the case of Europe are rooted first in religious fervor, later in the revival of the classics at the end of the Middle Ages. The outcomes from artistic endeavors were on display in churches, cathedrals, and public squares. By contrast, technological outcomes were highly focused, and required some understanding of scientific principles. The appreciation of an artistic piece was a natural emotion, even to the uneducated European who wandered into the emerging city. He could appreciate the beauty and magnificence of the cathedral's architecture, the statues of saints and kings, and the paintings that expressed religious feelings.

Technology was a mystery, embedded in the writings of a very exclusive and extremely small group of people. Moreover, technology was not evident in the great structures of the time, nor in the inventions and innovations that began to spread throughout Europe, such as in construction and war. Similarly, in China, Japan, and India, technology was also the exclusive domain of a small group, detached from the larger population in brilliant isolation.

When Christopher Wren (1632-1723) designed the dome of St. Paul's cathedral in London, he had learned from Isaac Newton, Galileo Galilei, and other great scientists of his time. The result was a masterpiece in the form of a dome that was structurally sound, and that escaped the structural deficiencies of the dome of St. Peter's Cathedral in Rome.[12]

Thus, although science and technology were the exclusive domain of the very few, public support started to emerge.[13] Heralded by political and military rulers, there were at least four main reasons for this development. First, specific areas of technology were selected for support because of their clear and relatively short-term benefits to the state and its government. The most illuminating examples are transportation technology and construction technology. In both cases the military imperatives of moving troops and supplies were key parameters in fostering technological knowledge in this area and in preserving it.

In medieval Europe, the legacy of the Roman roads and bridges had been the mainstay of transportation, until the indigenous development of fluvial networks, and the development of technology in the building and operation of locks. The Renaissance period also contained the emergence of commerce and industry, which together with military considerations have constituted a strong motivator for communities to acquire and to maintain such technological know-how.

For example, several Italian cities of the Lombard League jointly engaged in the building of canals. Mariano Tacola (1382-1453) was a prolific author who was also a senior public official in Siena.[14] His writings describe the state of knowledge of his time in the construction and operation of bridges, harbors, and other modes of transportation.

Public works became a magnet for aspiring engineers and technologists and, by extension, led to both the support of technological development projects and the imprint of technology as a favorable activity, in the minds of rulers and of the general populace. In France, for example, public works and military considerations were joined in the work of Sebastien de Vauban (1633-1707), who fortified the port of Dunkirk, and was the progenitor of the French Army Corps of Engineers. In 1795 Napoleon I founded the Ecole Polytechnique, the first school of engineering, supported by the state, and open to all qualified candidates.[15]

A second reason that motivated public support of science and technology was national pride and the emerging competition among the European states. Technological applications for commerce and industry were added to the large-scale public works, thus opening new areas for the creative genius of Europe's scientists and engineers. But all was contingent upon the recognition that technology was an activity of national interest, and, as such, a strong contributor to national development. Once such recognition became engraved in the political scheme of interests and outcomes, policy actions soon followed.

Therefore, in order to promote indigenous commerce and industry, as a tool in the competitive arena with other countries, governments more fully embraced technologists and their activities. An important public action was the legal acceptance of the inventor's rights, in the form of patent law. As early as 1474, the city of Venice had a patent law. In England, the Statute of Monopolies was established in 1624, as the most comprehensive patent law in Europe.[16] These laws can be seen as part of a package of "incentives" or facilitators that helped to promote technological activity and invention.

The third main reason was the historical phenomenon known as "the Industrial Revolution." Without delving into cause and effect, the Industrial Revolution began in the mid-1700s, lasting until the 1830s. Historians of technology tend to credit technological progress in that era to the work of a large number of individual and independent inventors.[17]

Although industrial developments were triggered by a surge in individual technological contributions, the resulting "revolution" was responsible for an increase in public recognition of the role and importance of technology. These events, described here as causes and effects, are not tautological. If we consider, as do most historians, that the rapid growth of industrial machines and plants (and the demographic, social, and economic changes that followed) was due to a wave of inventions and innovations, we have thus established the background that explains the Industrial Revolution.

What follows, then, is the topic of interest of this chapter, the link between public policy and technology. As industrial growth permeated the economies and societies of Western Europe toward the mid-1800s, these nations and their rulers now recognized that at the root of their rapid industrialization was science and technology. Perhaps more important, scientists and technologists also began to recognize their influence over the new economy. This led to attempts to ascertain their power through unionization and the formalization of knowledge distribution and maintenance.

The fourth and last main reason is therefore the rapid growth in the standing of technologists in the state, via the proliferation of professional organizations. In the United States, for example, the American Society of Civil Engineers was formed in 1852; the American Institute of Mining and Metallurgical Engineers in 1871; and the American Institute of Electrical Engineers in 1884.

These associations provided added clout and political leverage for their members. With such power, scientists and engineers also established a claim to a piece of the public trough, as a seemingly on-going "right," without having to repeatedly justify their claim.[18]

OUTCOMES, PROGRESS, AND THREATS

The origins of the link between public support and technology reveal a complex phenomenon, fraught with issues of evaluation, justification, and negative reactions. As science and technology evolved into an organized activity, and as its influence increased, public scrutiny also congealed, becoming more acute and better organized. This meant a more formal assessment of science and technology, and a voice given to critics of the activity.

Early on in the evolution of science and technology, there emerged a distinction between the outcomes and the content of this activity. Outcomes were imprints on the physical world, such as navigation instruments, shipbuilding technology, and devices and gadgets in agriculture, construction, and industry. The contents of science and technology comprised the theories and principles underlying the operation and the structure, as well as performance, of the actual outcomes.[19]

Among the first public voices to react negatively to specific content areas of the emerging activity of science and technology were those based on religious considerations. From Galileo to Bruno to the Scopes trials, there appeared celebrated cases of strong religious rejection of certain scientific theories. However, in Western Europe and the United States, such reaction was confined to very specific contents of theories and new approaches to physical or biological phenomena. The vast majority of technological outcomes and their substantial impacts on society were virtually exempt from harsh criticism.[20] Only in those cases when a pathbreaking theory seemed to threaten the established religious interpretations of the world were such reactionary movements intensified.

Resistance to technological changes was not confined to rejection of ideas and theories. The history of technological progress, particularly during the Industrial Revolution, is punctuated with incidents of strong resistance to specific innovations and to their introduction into the economy. In 1811-1816, the "Luddite riots" erupted in England as weavers destroyed labor-saving machines. Riots also occurred in other cities in England in 1826 and 1830. Similar resistance occurred in France, marked by workers tossing their shoes (sabots) into machines in order to paralyze them, hence the term "sabotage."[21]

Threats to employment and perceived threats to their immediate well-being had been the key motivators of resistance to selected inventions in European countries. Historians tend to agree that technological progress in Western Europe was primarily due to individual enterprise and private investments.[22] Governments in England, France, and Germany, for example, were reported primarily to be interested in military technology, leaving industrial innovation to private entrepreneurs. When resistance to technology culminated in riots and disturbance of the public order, governments repressed such violence.[23]

Then, as now, a key issue was the means to determining which component, characteristic, or effect of technology is to be assessed, so that a certain position may be established—in favor or against the technology. Workers in the early 1800s perceived the mere introduction of machines as a threat to their livelihood. Yet they could not assess, at the time, the impacts of industrialization on their demographics, social conditions, and the economics of their surroundings. Governments were overwhelmed with the changes brought about by the Industrial Revolution, so their reaction turned out to be focused on selected events triggered by periodic conflicts.[24]

Perhaps the most influential consequence of these occurrences in this period before the advent of the 20th century and the two world wars was that technology became an *issue* of political and social relevance. As inventions multiplied, and innovations continued to be adopted by industrial concerns and in public projects, the role of technology in society became increasingly recognized. Although the full impacts of technological change were yet to be assessed and measured, public display of technical progress took the form of a sequence of world expositions.

WORLD EXPOSITIONS AND PUBLIC AWARENESS

The Society of Arts of England was the first to hold an exhibition in 1756, featuring manufactured products of the nascent industry. The Franklin Institute, founded in the United States in 1824, also began yearly expositions of inventions and manufactured products. In addition to such national events, international expositions became popular in the second half of the 19th century.

The first such exposition was in London, in 1851, with the personal involvement of Prince Albert. New York followed with an exhibition in 1883, and Paris in 1855 had its first international exhibition at the Champs Elysées. Other famous expositions were held in Chicago in 1893 to commemorate the 400th anniversary of the discovery of America by Christopher Columbus.

After the turn of the 20th century, several international exhibitions followed, becoming very popular. They exhibited the latest scientific and technological inventions and provided their audiences with an optimistic view of the future. In 1933 the exhibition in Chicago featured advances in science and technology. In 1939 the New York World's Fair embraced the theme "World of Tomorrow," exhibiting a large number of futuristic inventions and innovations in agriculture, industry, urban planning, and the individual home.

With each exposition there emerged added awareness in the public of the role science and technology play not only in the past and present, but also in a dream-like future. The World Columbian Exposition of 1893 in Chicago had almost 30 million visitors. The New York World's Fair of 1939 attracted almost 60 million visitors. Consequently, as millions of ordinary citizens in Europe and the United States were exposed to the power and promise of technology, the international aspect of these expositions imprinted on them two important lessons. The first consisted of the recognition that science and technology are global in nature. Inventions and their applications are not the sole domain of any singular nation. Second, it became apparent that there are differences among nations in the degree to which they generate and apply technology. The competitive aspect of science and technology had become a notion accepted by national publics. Thus, it behooves countries who are competing in industry and commerce to also play catch-up in the competitive world of technological progress. The seeds for widespread popular support of science and technology were planted.[25]

SOME FOUNDATIONS OF POPULAR SUPPORT

Such broad acceptance of these seemingly mysterious activities of a small group of inventors was due to some particular sentiments in both Europe and the United States. In the former, there was a sense of destiny and the superiority of European nations in bringing and diffusing civilization throughout the rest of the world. This strong belief in the role of European culture and influence had flourished alongside the territorial expansion of the colonial powers of Europe: Spain, England, France, Germany, Holland, and even Russia, Denmark, Portugal, and Italy. In all, an almost evangelistic fervor followed the European explorations into the post-Second World War era.[26]

Technology thus becomes a perfect companion to the religious, social, cultural, and political factors which had composed the colonial influences outside Europe. Moreover, since technological progress was considered a global phenomenon, it was easily applicable across national boundaries, in support of the national agenda. Thus, technology was continually used as an important tool in the implementation of international policies, with a corresponding influence on the positive manner in which it was being appraised by the domestic population.

Similarly, in the United States, the sentiment of historical preponderance had crystallized in the American concept of "Manifest Destiny." The conquest of the remainder of the North American continent continued to other strategic acquisitions throughout the 19th and early 20th centuries. Technology had served as a critical tool in achieving these expansion goals, thus acquiring a warm spot in the mosaic of the American pioneering spirit.

Together with the growth of rationalism in both Western Europe and North America, the colonial ideology and the drive westward by Americans have contributed to a positive attitude toward technology on both sides of the Atlantic Ocean.[27] In this period, which culminated with the Second World War, the public mind embraced technological achievements as a necessary, highly utilitarian, and beneficial tool for economic and social progress.

In all of this trend toward acceptance and, even to an extent, the popular veneration of technology and its progress, there was little in the form of reliable measurement of technology's outcomes. Benefits from technical innovations were primarily documented and catalogued as independent cases.[28] Large-scale measurement and assessment of the outcomes from technology were essentially nonexistent in that period. Much of the focus of historians was directed toward the evolution of selected innovations, such as military technology, manufacturing, aviation, and shipbuilding.[29]

Public opinion toward technology was based more on faith than on systematic appraisals of its benefits and shortcomings. Impressed into the collective ideology on both sides of the Atlantic, technology had become, especially in the early years of the 20th century, an accepted force that drove economic development and social welfare. As such, it was beyond large-scale criticism. The beneficial aspects of technical innovations had become an integral part of the existing culture.

In summary, this short history has shown that the foundations of public acceptance and support of science and technology are rooted in the development of the Industrial Revolution and its aftermath. While the spectrum of science and invention was a relatively amateurish and entrepreneurial activity, there was no need to justify it on a large scale with measurement and evaluation procedures. However, as science and technology became institutionalized and massively funded by industry and government, it was no longer enough to justify them on the basis of faith and a popular trust in their marvels and unlimited promise.

NOTES

1. See, for example, Jain, R., and C. Triandis, *Management of Research and Development Organizations*, 2nd ed. (New York: John Wiley & Sons, 1997); also Jelinek, M., and C. Schoonhoven, *The Innovation Marathon: Lessons from High Technology Firms* (San Francisco: Jossey-Bass Publishers, 1993).

2. Rosenberg, N., *Inside the Black Box: Technology and Economies* (London: Cambridge University Press, 1984) p. 3.

3. Derry, T., and T. Williams, *A Short History of Technology: From the Earliest Times to A.D. 1900* (New York: Oxford University Press, 1961).

4. Garrison, E., *A History of Engineering and Technology: Artful Methods* (Boca Raton, FL: CRC Press, 1991).

5. See, for example, Owens, L., "The Development of Large Technical Systems," *Business History Review*, 68/4, 1991, 1002-1004. In this paper Owens reviews the work of the historian Thomas Hughes, as a scholar who "helped dispel the myth that modern technology was a black box that developed in obedience to internal laws unaffected by culture or context." Hughes had examined railroad technology, telephone networks, electrical power, and network computers.

6. See, for example, Pursell, C., *The Machine in America: A Social History of Technology* (Baltimore: John Hopkins University Press, 1995). Also see a review of the book in Lubar, S., "The Machine in America: A Social History of Technology," *Business History Review*, 70(2), 1996, 275-277. The subtitle of this book is somewhat misleading, because Pursell discusses not the social evaluation of technology, but the growth and development of selected American technologies, such as manufacturing, farming, and bridge construction—and how these allowed for urban development and the transformation of the country from an agricultural society to an urban and industrialized international power. However, similar trends can be attributed to West European economies, such as England and Germany. The key difference for America was its expansion westward, and the opportunities that awaited new technological endeavors in this portion of the North American continent. Pursell has documented this push westward.

7. See Russell, P., *Portugal, Spain, and the African Atlantic, 1343-1490: Chivalry and Crusade from John of Guant to Henry the Navigator and Beyond* (New York: Ashgate Publishers, 1995). In particular see Chapters XI, XV, and XVII.

8. For example, see Vernon, K., *Cosimo de Medici* (Philadelphia: Associated Faculty Press, 1970).

9. See, for example, Knecht, R., *Richelieu* (New York: Longman Publishing Group, 1991); and Fedem, K., *Richelieu* (Boston: MSG House, 1970). Although the vast majority of biographical accounts of the cardinal emphasize his political and administrative activities, the studies illustrated above also recount his patronage of the arts and sciences.

10. See, for example, Draper, J., *Napoleon's Thoughts on History, Politics and the Management of Man* (Boston: American Classical College Press, 1980); and Schom, A., *Napoleon Bonaparte* (New York: HarperCollins Publishers, 1998).

11. For example, Franklin, B., *Autobiography of Benjamin Franklin* (New York: Macmillan Publishing Company, reprint edition, 1997). Also see Anderson,

D., *The Radical Enlightenments of Benjamin Franklin* (Baltimore: Johns Hopkins University Press, 1997). In this book Anderson critically examined Franklin's controversial essay "Observations Concerning the Increase of Mankind," published in 1751. This essay, among others of his writings, exemplifies Franklin's views of the role of science and technology in civilized society.

12. See Sekler, E., *Wren and His Place in European Architecture* (Cambridge, MA: MIT Press, 1964).

13. At this point in the historical review, science *and* technology are used interchangeably. Later in the book a more concise definition of these terms is provided.

14. Prager, F., "A Manuscript of Taccola Quoting Brunelleschi, on Problems of Investors and Builders," *Proceedings of the American Philosophical Society*, CXII, 1968, 130-135.

15. Garrison, E., 1991, *op. cit.*, pp. 129-133. Garrison also lists other schools of engineering which were built on the model of the Ecole Polytechnique: Polytechnium of Zurich, 1855; Polytechnique of Delft, 1864; MIT, 1865; and University College in London, 1828 (p. 130).

16. See, for example, Gille, B., *Engineers of the Renaissance* (Cambridge, MA: MIT Press, 1966); also Daumas, M. (Ed.), *The Origins of Technological Civilization* (New York: Crown Publishers, 1969).

17. Mokyr, J., *The Lever of Riches* (New York: Oxford University Press, 1990); also see Ashton, T., *The Industrial Revolution, 1760-1830* (Oxford: Oxford University Press, 1948).

18. See, for example, Ridgway, R., "The Modern City and the Engineer's Relation to It," *Transactions of the American Society of Civil Engineers*, 88(2), 1925, 1239-1248.

19. See, for example, Nelson, R., *Understanding Technical Change as an Evolutionary Process* (Amsterdam: North Holland Publishers, 1987).

20. Jones, E., *The European Miracle* (Cambridge: Cambridge University Press, 1981).

21. See Bailey, B., *The Luddite Rebellion* (New York: New York University Press, 1998). Also see Harrison, M., *Crowds and History: Mass Phenomena in English Towns, 1790-1835* (Cambridge: Cambridge University Press, 1988).

22. Mokyr, J., 1990, *op. cit.*, pp. 232-235. Also see Klemm, F., *A History of Western Technology* (Cambridge: MIT Press, 1964).

23. In England, Parliament had passed several laws that protected industrial property and that carried the death penalty to whoever committed felonious sabotage of privately held plants and machines.

24. See Caldwell, D., *The Norton History of Technology* (New York: W. W. Norton & Company, 1995).

25. See Cardwell, D., *Turning Points in Western Technology: A Study of Technology, Science, and History* (New York: Neale Watson, 1972). For an

interesting theory of cycles in the technological leadership of nations, see Brezis, E., P. Krugman, and D. Tsiddon, "Leapfrogging in International Competition: A Theory of Cycles in National Technological Leadership," *American Economic Review*, 83(5), 1993, 1211-1219.

26. There is a varied literature on this and related subjects. See, for example, Adas, M., *Machines as the Measure of Man: Science, Technology, and Ideologies of Western Dominance* (Ithaca, NY: Cornell University Press, 1989). Also see Blant, J., *The Colonizer's Model of the World: Geographical Diffusionizing and Eurocentric History* (New York: Guilford Publishers, 1993); and Cain, P. and A. Hopkins, "The Political Economy of British Expansion Overseas, 1750-1914," *Economic History Review*, 2nd Ser., 33(4), 463-490.

27. See, for example, Schluchter, W., *The Rise of Western Rationalism: Max Weber's Developmental History* (Berkeley: University of California Press, 1981).

28. A reminder that this paragraph refers to the period between the mid-1800s to the end of the Second World War.

29. The Industrial Revolution and the period in the early years of the 20th century have captured the imagination of many historians in Europe and the United States. They treated technology principally as a component of industrial progress and developments in transportation and in the art of war. See, for example, Mumford, L., *Technics and Civilization* (New York: Harcourt Publishers, 1934). Also see Sennett, R., and H. Oram, *The Marine Steam Engine* (London: Longmans, 1917); and Jackman, W., *The Development of Transportation in Modern England* (Cambridge: Cambridge University Press, 1916).

2

THE EMERGENCE OF INSTITUTIONS

The 20th century heralded several major developments, whose pace was magnified by the world wars and by internal mechanisms of accelerated growth. In science and technology perhaps the most enduring development has been the emergence of formalized and large-scale institutions.[1]

Although some of these institutions, such as American research universities, started their growth earlier in the century, the dynamics of accelerated transformations of science and technology may be credited to the aftermath of the Second World War. Few occurrences in human history have so contributed to the explosion in public support for science and technology and their institutionalization as did the global conflict of 1939-1945.

THE LEGACY OF THE SECOND WORLD WAR

What the Second World War did to propagate the institutionalization of large-scale science and technology was rooted in the several factors that are listed below. Economics, technology, and social changes conjured to create an environment for science and technology that was radically different from that of the prewar era.

The first such factor was the *rapid development of inventions* and innovations during the war years. Both sides to the conflict, the Allies and the Axis countries, vastly encouraged inventions in militarily useful areas of science and technology.[2] Crash programs were established, propelled by the necessities of the conflict and the fear from competitive advantages of the enemy.

Particular areas of technology have experienced unparalleled growth. The more glamorous have been the development of radar, aviation, communication technology, and logistics and operations research.[3] Robert Buderi (1998) has written a fascinating book on the development of microwave radar during the Second World War. He has traced the process of invention and its benefits to the Allied forces in their struggle to defeat the Axis powers.[4] In addition, Buderi has also shown how the military origins of radar later led to discoveries in many civilian areas, such as radio astronomy, the transistor, magnetic resonance (with applications in health care diagnostics), and microwave cooking and heating.

Aviation and avionics were another area with accelerated developments during the Second World War. Jet propulsion and improved instrumentation on board and at airports have led to a revolution in commercial aviation and aerospace.

These areas of rapid generation and improvements in technology are symptomatic of the overall technological resurgence during the war. However, the main legacy of the Second World War in this factor of inventions is the research on materials in the basic sciences of chemistry, physics, mathematics, biology, and in the social sciences, such as psychology and sociology. In support of total war, which engulfed entire countries and in which their populations had direct exposure to military firepower, there was a dramatic surge in studies of people, groups, and societies.

The second factor in the legacy of that war was massive investments by the feuding governments in science and technology. Among the more celebrated is the Manhattan Project, which produced the first atomic weapons. Massive funding by the American government of over $2 billion was directed toward a focused development of a weapon—from its inception as a mere scientific theory, to its doubtful accomplishment.

The United States had already forged a tradition of massive public works. The Tennessee Valley Authority (TVA), for example, had been the hallmark of American support of great public projects.[5] Yet, the Manhattan Project, and similar albeit smaller endeavors during the war, represent a departure from the usual governmental funding of public work. This was a *scientific* project, with all the unknowns and uncertainties involved in modern science. In addition, it required a comprehensive cooperative effort—directed by the government—between universities, industry, and the emerging community of science. All of this was carried out under the demands of the war effort and with constraining deadlines.

A third factor had a more subtle legacy. The countries involved in the conflict recognized the value of science and technology as a major contributor to their military power. Consequently, they also recognized the need to be the first to make the discovery and to convert the innovation to their military machine. Therefore the warring countries developed sophisticated mechanisms and agencies to spy on each other and to learn the status of the other's scientific and technological development.

Thus, strong national competitive endeavors were born, directed toward assessment of other nations' scientific and technological accomplishments. This trend eventually matured into a technological race, on a national scale, which was further inflamed by the advent of the Cold War. Figure 2.1 shows some factors that facilitated the institutionalization of S&T in the United States.

IMPACTS OF THE COLD WAR

The period following the Second World War, 1945-1989, covered almost half a century, characterized by the reshaping of the world in a muted struggle between the superpowers. Marked by confrontations in the realm of both diplomacy and military muscle-flexing, the "Cold War" conjured a climate of mutual fear, in the United States, its allies, and the Soviet Union.[6] Competition for economic and technological superiority became the foundation of the national funding patterns for science and technology. Culminating in the race for space that had begun in 1961, the main impacts of this state of affairs were in the funding in the United States of a massive network of federal agencies and federal research and development in the aerospace and defense domains.[7]

Industrial companies and research universities in America became partners of the federal investment in science and technology for meeting the objectives of the Cold War. The nuclear strategy of mutual deterrence has led to conventional conflicts around the globe, such as Korea, Vietnam, Guatemala, and Afghanistan. Thus, public investments in science and technology were now directed toward both the traditional defense requirements and the high-technology challenges of nuclear deterrence.[8]

Figure 2.1
Factors That Contributed to and Facilitated the Institutionalization of American Science and Technology

> - The rise of the higher education system and the network of research universities.
> - The GI bill.
> - Wholesale application of Second World War inventions and innovations in the civilian sector.
> - Tradition of massive public projects and the existing institutions established to carry them out.
> - Rapid expansion of the network of federal R&D and technology laboratories.
> - Growth of federal mission-oriented agencies, and founding of new agencies to accomplish the federal mission and regulatory agendas.
> - Establishment of technology corridors, in the vicinity of major research universities and federal laboratories.

The Cold War created a cultural imperative, particularly in the United States, that massive defense expenditures are not only the hallmark of a superpower, but also necessary to maintain the balance of power with the Soviet Union, and to keep the mutual deterrence unchanged.

Public support for science and technology in the United States, and to a large extent also in Western Europe, has now become the product of the convergence of two beliefs. First, that S&T is crucial to sound and sustained economic progress and for maintaining a high standard of living. Second, that S&T is the key to a strong defensive posture in the nuclear age, and to maintaining a competitive edge against Soviet accomplishments.[9]

The end of the Cold War left the United States in the 1990s in the position of the sole superpower, thus encumbered with responsibilities of global leadership. This unique international role replaced the need to balance the nuclear deterrence as the motivator for continued public support of defense science and technology.[10]

In the mid-1990s, the United States also experienced a movement to commercialize its defense industry, and with it its defense science and technology. Privatization of some institutions in charge of producing military and energy S&T became the slogan for change that would be commensurate with the post-Cold War era. Defense industries were the hardest hit by this trend, dramatically cutting back their expenditures for research and development that thus far had been funded by the federal government.

INSTITUTIONAL SCIENCE AND TECHNOLOGY COMES OF AGE

The growth of institutions of science and technology in the post-Second World War era may be credited to several interrelated factors. The analysis that follows is only a historical broad-brush of the trends and events which were responsible for the rapid formation of institutions of science and technology.

In the United States, where much of this phenomenon has occurred, the first such factor was the *rise of the higher education system*. The formation of land-grant universities fostered a state-supported system of universities, thus providing a unique opportunity for a larger segment of the population to attend postsecondary institutions. In their quest for quality and excellence, both state-supported and private research universities have grown dramatically, thus creating a hitherto unequaled network of universities of high academic caliber.[11]

Due to the growth in the economy of the United States and partly because of political and military considerations of competition in the Cold War, industrial and federal support to the system of universities systematically increased.[12] Figure 2.2 shows the upward trend of federal and industrial support for colleges and universities since 1960.

In the period 1967-1991, total enrollment in American universities doubled. In the early 1960s, federal support for university research tripled, and doubled again in the period 1970-1993—all in constant dollars. Industrial support in 1993 was eight times what it had been in 1965.

A corollary factor to the rise of American universities, at least in the early years following the Second World War, was the *GI bill*. This legislation facilitated the schooling of millions of returning soldiers, thus providing a powerful incentive to academic institutions. Figure 2.3 shows enrollment in American universities in the period 1967-1991. In that period enrollment doubled to over 14 million students.

Figure 2.2
Federal and Industrial Support for R&D Performed by American Universities, 1960-1993

(In millions of constant 1987 dollars)

Year	Federal Support	Percent Increase*	Industry Support	Percent Increase*
1960	1,552		153	
1965	3,792	144%	145	-5.2%
1970	4,760	18.5%	176	21%
1975	4,807	1%	237	35%
1980	5,813	21%	334	41%
1985	6,429	10.5%	594	78%
1990	8,550	33%	1,006	69%
1993	9,268	8%	1,220	21%

In five-year increments.
Source: National Science Board, Science and Engineering Indicators –1993 (Washington, DC: U.S. Government Printing Office, 1993), p. 332.

Wholesale *civilian applications* of innovations that started as military inventions during the war, and later as part of the military buildup of the Cold War, are another factor that led to the institutionalization of science and technology. Large-scale and continuous flow of technology from defense to civilian uses had been the norm, even before the conversion movement of the 1990s. Scientists and engineers from academia and industry who were engaged in defense-related projects transferred their knowledge and the technology thus created to nonmilitary applications, such as industrial products and processes.

A fourth factor was the *continuation of the tradition of massive projects* funded by the federal government, such as the Tennessee Valley Authority in the 1930s. By creating the institutional mechanisms to carry out such large-scale projects, the federal government had at its disposal the organizational facilities to support science and technology. There was no need to create an infrastructure for such support, as it already existed and had proven its effectiveness in the past.[13]

Figure 2.3
Enrollment in U.S. Higher Education: 1967-1991

Year	Total Enrollment	Enrollment in Doctorate-Granting Institutions
1967	6,963,687	896,135
1968	7,571,636	932,321
1969	8,066,233	997,737
1970	8,649,368	1,055,415
1971	9,025,031	1,071,652
1972	9,297,787	1,078,994
1973	9,694,297	1,087,540
1974	10,321,539	1,124,452
1975	11,290,719	1,171,754
1976	11,121,426	1,160,983
1977	11,418,631	1,180,232
1978	11,393,015	1,181,724
1979	11,707,126	1,208,221
1980	12,234,644	1,220,579
1981	12,517,753	1,245,981
1982	12,588,520	1,242,492
1983	12,633,530	1,250,051
1984	12,400,392	1,242,047
1985	12,411,945	1,237,579
1986	12,670,121	1,251,445
1987	12,925,116	1,274,001
1988	13,205,540	1,298,658
1989	13,621,203	1,333,041
1990	13,871,725	1,356,414
1991	14,527,881	1,374,101

Source: National Science Board, Science and Engineering Indicators-1993 (Washington, DC: U.S. Government Printing Office, 1993) (NSB-93-1), Appendix Table 2-4, p. 254.

Federal Laboratories and Mission-Oriented Agencies

Another important factor in the development of institutional science and technology was the rapid *expansion of the network of federal R&D laboratories,* and the establishment of new laboratories in various scientific and technical disciplines.[14] In 1997 the network of federal laboratories was composed of over 700 laboratories, employing some 150,000 scientists and engineers, with about 1 million employees overall. Actual expenditures are circa $40 billion with a set of 25 "superlabs" consuming about 50% of all federal R&D dollars. These superlabs are concentrated in the areas of energy, defense, and space.[15]

The federal network of laboratories has been instrumental in meeting the challenges and objectives of the many federal agencies which were created or had been expanded in the postwar period. The *federal agencies* are another factor in the institutionalization of science and technology in the United States. Many of these agencies had specific charters which were anchored in technology.

Illustrative organizations are the Environmental Protection Agency (EPA), the Atomic Energy Commission, the Nuclear Regulatory Commission, and the National Oceanic and Atmospheric Administration. The S&T component of these agencies was geared toward two purposes: (1) to generate scientific and technological knowledge in support of the regulatory mandate of the agency (e.g., the EPA), and (2) in support of the mission of the agency (e.g., defense laboratories such as the Naval Research Laboratory and Ames Research Center for the space agency).

Although the missions of some of these agencies and their laboratories may have changed since the end of the Cold War, and even with the movement to convert defense R&D and to privatize the federal network, the laboratories continue to be a major force in American science and technology. In addition to the wealth of their budgets and the immense concentration of scientific and technical talent in them, the laboratories also cooperate with industry and universities. Moveover, their presence in some states is an economic, educational, and cultural bonus, turned into necessity with the passage of time.[16]

Perhaps the most salient of the post-Second World War institutions was the establishment in 1950 of the National Science Foundation (NSF). Formed initially with the purpose of supporting basic scientific research, the agency has grown and its mission enlarged to include the support of engineering, and the fostering of cooperative R&D between universities and industry.[17]

In the absence of a national department or ministry of science and technology policy, the National Science Foundation has assumed many such functions. In addition to the funding of fundamental research and basic engineering projects, the foundation also collects data on expenditures and outputs of R&D and publishes the biennial *Science Indicators* compendium of R&D statistics. In essence, the foundation sets the tone for directions in basic science, provides definitions of what constitutes research and development, and altogether embodies the nation's fundamental interest in science.

Technology Corridors

The concentration in a relatively small geographical area of several leading research universities, a vibrant urban sprawl, an industrial base, and in some cases also the presence of federal laboratories, has resulted in the formation of "technology corridors." Originally, the corridor known as Route 128 came into existence on the outskirts of Boston, Massachusetts. The presence of a host of universities and scientific centers, combined with the availability of venture capital in New England, have contributed to the formation of a large number of entrepreneurial firms in pathbreaking areas of science and technology.

Another celebrated technology corridor followed Route 128 in California. Again, the concentration of leading research universities and government laboratories in the Bay Area around San Francisco, together with the emerging aerospace industry and massive federal investments in it, have led to the formation of "Silicon Valley." The hub of the computer industry in the United States was then at the heart of the technology corridor of Northern California.[18]

In the 1980s the state government of Illinois supported the creation of a third technology corridor, northwest of the Chicago metropolitan area. Based on the premise that the right ingredients were present, a basket of incentives were offered to high-technology companies who would relocate to the corridor. The idea was that there is in the area a geographical concentration of leading universities, strong financial institutions, at least two main federal R&D laboratories (Fermi and Argonne), and a strong base of large technology-manufacturing companies (such as Motorola).

The emergence of these various technology corridors helped to launch a nascent high-technology industry. By sponsoring and fermenting start-up entrepreneurial companies, the technology corridors offered a major incentive for innovators, in a kind of a sprawling geographical incubator for emerging companies and their innovative technologies.[19]

Technology corridors represented another component of the rapid institutionalization of science and technology in the period following the Second World War. They also helped to bring about the "high-technology" industry, characterized by a flow of innovative and entrepreneurial companies, particularly in the emerging technology areas such as computers and telecommunications. But, as described later in this chapter, the impact of the technology corridors and of the institution-alization of science and technology was also in other areas, such as manufacturing and services.

SUMMARY

It is important to gain insight into the historical development of science and technology, if one is interested in measuring the impacts and benefits of this activity. The historical perspective puts the measurement effort within a context of time and a set of dimensions that have shaped science and technology and the institutions that have generated S&T and those that have supported this effort.

The phenomenal rise in national and industrial science and technology worldwide, and especially in the United States, has occurred with a corresponding large-scale support from the public. Such a fortuitous merger of circumstances occurred when: (1) central and state/local governments worked in unison; (2) universities became popularized due to the GI bill, and to the growth in state universities and community colleges; and (3) massive investments by the federal govern-ment (albeit with emphasis on defense-related areas of investigation).

As institutions were constructed and existing ones were expanded, science and technology became more formalized as to its origins, develop-ment, and ultimate usage. Once the trend of institution-building had reached a comfortable level of growth, the questions being asked of it underwent a radical change.

With popular support firmly established, and with a powerful economic and social influence, science and technology is now faced not with the question, "Is it good or necessary for us to have it?" but with a different set of questions. There are no longer doubts about its existence, but about its performance. Seminal questions are now: "How can we improve its performance?" and "What exactly do we get from it?" Concerns about cost effectiveness have become the key assessment parameters.

Such a new breed of questions leads to metrics that measure different aspects of the phenomenon of science and technology. Whereas issues that explore the rasion d'être of scientific and technological endeavors require metrics about motivation and generation—issues of cost-effectiveness are geared toward outcomes. Hence, their metrics will measure evaluation of impacts and cost-effectiveness. This link determines, to a large extent, the kind of metrics this book will address in later chapters.

In summary, the second half of the 20th century thus produced a unique encounter. Technical entrepreneurs have flourished in a fortuitous menagerie of favorable conditions, among them availability of university and industrial S&T base, federal funding, and public support. This encounter has finally led to the technology-rich age of our times.

The quest for answers to the question "What do we get out of S&T?" led to the need to establish and to apply adequate evaluation tools and measurement instruments that would assess the benefits that society and the economy accrue from S&T activities.

Part II starts with a discussion of measurement and its principles. It continues with a description of how metrics are selected, and continues to describe and analyze individual metrics of S&T: their strengths and weaknesses, and cases of best usages.

NOTES

1. In this chapter I again use the terms "science" and "technology" interchangeably.
2. There is a vast literature on the emergence of science and technology during the period of the war. See, for example, Fuller, J., *The Second World War, 1939-1945: A Strategical and Tactical History* (London: Da Capo Press, 1993). Also see Avery, D., *Science of War: Canadian Scientists and Allied Military Technology During the Second World War* (Toronto: University of Toronto Press, 1998) and Lilley, S., *Men, Machines, and History* (London: Cobbett Press, 1948).
3. See, for example, Hooton, E., and P. Jarrett (Eds.), *Aircraft of the Second World War: Development of the Warplanes, 1939-45* (Washington, DC: Naval Institute, 1997). Also see Forman, P., and J. Sanchez-Ron (Eds.), *National*

Military Establishments and the Advancements of Science and Technology: Studies in 20ᵗʰ Century History (Boston: Kluwer Academic Publishers, 1996).

4. Buderi, R., *The Invention That Changed the World: How a Small Group of Radar Pioneers Won The Second World War and Launched a Technological Revolution* (New York: Simon & Schuster Trade, 1998).

5. See, for example, McCaw, T., *TVA and The Power Fight, 1933-1939* (Philadelphia: University of Pennsylvania Press, 1971).

6. Whitcomb, R., *Cold War in Retrospect: The Formative Years* (Westport, CT: Greenwood Publishing Group, 1998); and Isaacs, J., and T. Downing, *Cold War: An Illustrated History, 1945-1989* (Boston: Little Brown and Company, 1998).

7. The discussion in this chapter of the impacts of the Second World War and the Cold War concentrates on the United States, although European nations had also developed similar patterns of behavior, albeit on a modest scale.

8. See Figure 2.2.

9. See, for example, Brands, H., *The Devil We Knew: Americans and The Cold War* (New York: Oxford University Press, 1994). Also see Cronin, J., *The World the Cold War Made* (London: Routledge Publishers, 1996). Cronin also discusses, at the end of his book, the spillovers to the post-Cold War era.

10. See, for example, Buzan, B., *People, States, & Fear: An Agenda for International Security Studies in the Post-Cold War Era* (New York: Lynne Rienner, 1991). Also see Allin, D., *Cold War Illusions: America, Europe, and Soviet Power, 1969-1989* (New York: Saint Martin's Press, 1998). In this book, Allin offers a unique perspective, in that he describes the culture created in the United States by, in his words, the conservative movement. Allin argues that by exaggerating Soviet power and by constantly decrying the weaknesses of the Western alliance, conservatives were thus able to instill in the American psyche a culture of fear.

11. For example, see Geiger, R., *To Advance Knowledge: The Growth of American Research Universities, 1900-1940* (Oxford: Oxford University Press, 1986); and Rosensweig, R., and B. Turlington, *The Research Universities and Their Patrons* (Berkeley: University of California Press, 1982).

12. See Carnegie Commission on Higher Education, *The Federal Role in Postsecondary Education* (Washington, DC, 1975). The commission recommended focused federal support in critical areas of science and technology.

13. Notwithstanding the political and social impacts of projects such as TVA, which had generated some criticisms regarding the role of the federal government in the economic development of the country, a similar situation arose when the Eisenhower administration established the interstate system of highways as a massive public works project, jointly funded by the states and the federal government. See, for example, Hubbard, P., *Origins of the TVA: The Muscle Shoals Controversy* (New York: W. W. Norton & Company, 1968). Also see

Conklin, E., and P. Hargrove (Eds.), *TVA: Fifty Years of Grass-Roots Bureaucracy* (Urbana: University of Illinois Press, 1984); and St. Clair, D., *The Motorization of American Cities* (New York: Praeger Publishers, 1986). This book describes the political and economic interests of the giant automakers and others, as they supported the construction of the highway system.

14. There is a vast literature on the origins and historical development of the network of federal laboratories, as well as the unique histories by agency and for selected laboratories. See, for example, Wilde, D., and N. Cooper, "Federal Laboratories and American Industry: Fueling Innovation," *The Journal of Technology Transfer*, 15(1), 1990, 47-52. Also see Schroyer, J. A., *The Secret Mesa: Inside Los Alamos National Laboratory* (New York: John Wiley & Sons, 1997).

15. Source: Federal Laboratory Consortium, e-mail: <www.federallabs.org>.

16. For example, the case of Los Alamos in New Mexico, in Schroyer, 1997, *op. cit.* Also see Nash, G., *The American West Transformed: The Impact of the Second World War* (Lincoln: University of Nebraska Press, 1990).

17. See Belanger, D., *Enabling American Innovation: Engineering and the National Science Foundation* (West Lafayette: Purdue University Press, 1997). Also see Larsen, O., *Milestones and Millstones: Social Science at the National Science Foundation, 1945-1991* (New York: Transactions Publishers, 1992). Larsen was director of the division of social and economic research at NSF in the 1990s. His book describes the struggle of social and economic sciences for recognition as well as funding within the foundation.

18. See, for example, Saxenian, A., *Regional Advantage: Culture and Competition in Silicon Valley and Route 128* (Cambridge, MA: Harvard University Press, 1996). Also see Moschella, D., *Waves of Power: Dynamics of Global Technology Leadership 1964-2010* (New York: Amacom, 1997); and Evans, P., *Embedded Autonomy: States and Industrial Transformation* (Princeton, NJ: Princeton University Press, 1995).

19. See Sherwin, E., *The Silicon Valley Way: Discover the Secret of America's Fastest Growing Companies* (San Francisco: Prima Publishing, 1998). In his work, Sherwin composes 21 fictional companies, based on attributes of successful Silicon Valley small firms. He traces their development and growth, by focusing on 44 techniques that were used by the key executives of such companies. Also see Kaplan, J., *Startup: A Silicon Valley Adventure* (New York: Penguin Books, 1996); and Cusumano, M., and D. Yoffie, *Competing on Internet Time: Lessons from Netscape and Its Battle with Microsoft* (New York: The Free Press, 1998). This book describes the rise and the subsequent conflict of two such high-technology companies that emerged from the technology corridor of the West Coast of the United States.

PART II

METRICS: APPROACHES, METHODS, TECHNIQUES

Est modus in rebus, sunt certi denique fines, quos ultra citraque nequit consistere rectum.

Things have their due measure; there are ultimately fixed limits, beyond which something must be wrong.

Horatius 65-8 B.C.

3

MEASUREMENT:
CONCEPTS AND ISSUES

We have metrics for every facet of our life. We measure time, we measure temperature, we measure distance, and we measure work. In fact, we have metrics for virtually every aspect of our surroundings, and for every aspect of what we and others do. Measurement is a routine component of being human, and of interacting with nature. Measurement is also a fundamental aspect of our curiosity. As we observe nature and its phenomena, we are curious to know: How high is the mountain? How tall are the trees? How deep is the lake?

Measurement is critical to life, as it permits us to better gather, hunt, and even live in a social group. To some extent one may argue that science and technology have evolved in direct relation to the nature and characteristics of humankind's ability to measure. To extend this analysis further back in time, as humans initiated their organized form of life, with the move to agriculture and shelter-building (albeit primitive), their ability to exercise measurements of their surroundings became crucial to their survival.

Later on, as civilization began to produce in excess of its consumption, and as trade followed specialization, there emerged the need to determine the value of things. Agricultural practice led to the establishment of calendars, as did cycles of life and death. Other activities such as work and war-making have also required a higher degree of measurement sophistication. All of this was conditioned on the existence of adequate metrics and workable instruments.[1]

Metrics may be used generically to describe a system of measurement that includes: (1) the item or object that is being measured; (2) units to be measured, also referred to as "standard units", and (3) value of a unit as compared to other units of reference. A workable *instrument* may be composed of a physical object that provides information about the item or object being measured by showing a unit or standard relative to the characteristic of the object being measured. In other, more complex instances, a workable instrument may be a *system* that delivers the necessary information by a more complicated process.

Measurement instruments may be used simply to assess physical (natural) and other quantities, such as area, force, volume, energy, viscosity, and time. They may also be used as monitoring devices, by which standards are established in a meaningful form, so that action may be taken as soon as measurement occurs. For example, the two-minute warning in a football game and the rate of inflation in the national economy are monitoring outputs that alert the players and their coaches, and the federal reserve executives in the latter case, that some action may be necessary, in light of the "reading." Another example are vital signs used in medical care. Blood pressure, temperature, and heartbeats are measures that monitor a person's condition and alert the medical care provider. Similarly, measurement instruments may be used as control mechanisms. Thermostats in heating and cooling systems spring into automatic action as soon as a given reading is established. The entire system of measurement, information flow, and automatic feedback is predetermined ("closed-loop") and contains an agreed-upon value of the unit being measured that would trigger a built-in response.

This chapter starts with a short description of the principles of measurement and the effectiveness of metrics and instruments. The discussion then progresses to the application of metrics and instrument to the area of science and technology.[2]

PRINCIPLES OF MEASUREMENT

What to Measure

In the physical environment, hence in the physical sciences, measurement is a relatively straightforward activity. Quantities such as length, temperature, and mass may be adequately measured with the use of perhaps a single standard unit. Adequacy depends on the qualities of the instrument, but the standard unit is a well-defined and widely accepted basis for measurement of the phenomenon. Thus, time is measured in the standard unit, *second*, and electric current is measured in *ampere*. A composite unit would be ampere/second, which is an electric charge, defined as the standard unit *coulomb*. However these fundamental units are manipulated, the phenomenon they measure is relatively well-defined.

In the social, managerial, and behavioral environments and sciences, the phenomenon under consideration is much less precise. In most instances the phenomenon of interest is in the form of a process, or at least as a set of events. What we don't know about such phenomena—and sometimes what we find so difficult to measure—is precisely that which we wish to measure.

What to measure is thus the first principle of measurement. This is also the first item required for a metric, as listed in the previous section. In order to proceed to the measurement of an object or an event, one must determine with some precision: What to measure? Physical phenomena, and in particular behavioral and social phenomena, appear as complex happenings. Human senses, and even their alternative senses in the form of instruments, capture a variety of happenings, events, and changes in an object. It then becomes crucial to filter these and to arrive at a particular object or event (or portion of these) that will merit the measurement effort.

For example, a weather storm consists of a cover of dark clouds, changes in temperature, plus rain, plus lightening, plus thunder—all appearing closely in time to form the phenomenon of a storm. Which of the events above merits measurement as qualities of a storm?

Similarly, a social phenomenon is also multifaceted and usually contains several interlinked activities or events. Due to limitations of resources and time and the relative difficulty to measure, we may opt to measure a different facet of the phenomenon than the facet we actually wished to measure. The use of surrogates is an acceptable procedure, as long as we can show a causal or even a logical link between the surrogate event and the desired event. Statistical sampling in polling of large populations is a form of surrogate measurement. Another example is the selection of bibliometric outputs as a measure of scientific activity.

A decision on what to measure will determine not only the metrics and instruments that will be used, but also the value of the measurement outcome. Although in many instances decision-makers who decide on which phenomena to measure are different from those who actually select the metrics, there should be an understanding between these two parties. Lack of coordination may lead to pitfalls in the selection of the appropriate metrics.[3] Thus, agreement on "what to measure" and a lucid understanding of the impact of such decision on the metrics to be selected lead to a better chance to have a successful measurement effort.

Selecting the Appropriate Measurement

Measurement instruments are the tools used to gather the quantities or readings of the phenomena chosen to be measured. Instruments may be classified as passive or active, intrusive or unobtrusive. A matrix of the four categories of instruments is shown in Figure 3.1. Moving counterclockwise in Figure 3.1, the first class of measurement instruments is passive-unobtrusive, or *adherent*. In the social, behavioral, and managerial sciences, this may be, for example, the count of outcomes after the fact. The instrument is passive because it is influenced by the change in the outcomes and does not need an external "source" to make it work. In the physical sciences, a passive instrument

Figure 3.1
Classification Scheme for Measurement Instruments

	Unobtrusive	Intrusive
Passive	a. ADHERENT Advantages: (1) relative objectivity (2) ease of use	c. OBSERVER Advantages: (1) variety of viewpoints (2) knowledge about the phenomenon
Active	b. FOLLOWER Advantages: (1) versatility of design (2) ability to compare	d. CONFEDERATE Advantages: (1) direct measurement of on-going items (2) ability to measure processes

may be a simple thermometer or a pressure gauge. The instrument is also unobtrusive in that it does not directly (or indirectly) intervene or interfere with the phenomenon being measured.

In the case of science and technology, an adherent instrument would be the count of bibliometric outcomes. Counting the number of publications and citations is done after the fact, hence in an unobtrusive manner. The counting of the number of patents is also an example of an adherent instrument.

Some of the advantages of this type of instrument are: (1) relative objectivity because the instrument is not associated with the event it measures, and (2) ease of application. Conversely, a disadvantage is the reliance on archival data that may suffer from a variety of problems such as biases and other limitations of record-keeping.[4]

The active-unobtrusive class of instruments is a *follower* type of measurement instrument. It is active because it derives its "power" from a source external to the phenomenon being measured. In physical phenomena, an example of an active instrument is the electric cardiogram machine, where the power source is external to the phenomenon, and the value measured is the effect of the outcome from the phenomenon on an output of the instrument itself (such as changes in the electrical current of the external power source).

An example of a follower instrument in the social sciences is the questionnaire or interview conducted after the fact ("exit interview"). Such instruments are nonreactive, in that they are not intrusive to the phenomenon being measured. But they are active because they possess an external source in which the values measured are changes in this external source (the questions and the scales used in a questionnaire).

In the case of science and technology a follower type instrument is a questionnaire administered to researchers and to corporate managers that addresses issues of the impacts of R&D on the business side of the company.[5]

Some of the advantages of this class of instruments are: (1) versatility in the design of items to be measured, and (2) ability to offer comparisons within and across organizations. Yet, this type of instrument also has the following disadvantages: (1) reliance on judgment and perceptions of informants, and (2) errors and biases in the design and application of the instruments.

Intrusive Instruments

The passive-intrusive type of instrument is the *observer*. This instrument in the social sciences is the count of values and outcomes of activities by a participating member of the organization, or by a researcher—all during the event or process itself. While the activity is happening, a count is made of values in the archives or those predicted by members of the organization. The instrument is intrusive because the act of measurement and the results from the act may influence the activity and may interfere with its normal flow and outcomes.

The measuring of the performance of medical expert systems is an example of observer-type instruments. Such measuring occurs while the patient is still under treatment, thus allowing for changes in diagnosis and therapeutics, if such is deemed necessary based on the results from the measurement.[6]

Peer review is an example of an observer instrument in measuring science and technology. This instrument is passive insofar as it is built on judgmental assessment of the reviewers, as they are affected by the phenomenon itself (scientific or technical outcomes). The instrument is also intrusive as it affects the publishability, funding, or otherwise acceptance of the phenomenon being measured.

Some advantages of this type of instrument are: (1) variety of viewpoints, and (2) knowledge about the phenomenon. A major disadvantage is reliance on subjective data collection and analysis. For example, in the case of S&T, a bias may emerge in scientific outcomes that challenge an existing paradigm, or are socially distasteful to the particular group of reviewers.

Finally, the active-intrusive type of instrument is the *confederate* instrument. This type involves a questionnaire, test, or similar tool that is an integral part of the phenomenon, but also serves to measure the phenomenon. Tests that are used to hire or promote employees are such instruments. Their main advantages are: (1) ability to directly measure changes in the on-going aspects of the phenomenon under study, and (2) ability to measure the dynamics of processes and multi-events activities. Major disadvantages are (1) the difficulty in distinguishing between values obtained during and in behalf of the process itself, and (2) values for measurement purposes.

In science and technology, an example of confederate instruments is self-assessment questionnaires administered to researchers during the lifetime of their projects. When these tools are used to determine the direction of the project—thus becoming an integral part of its engine of progression—they are of the confederate type.

Effectiveness of the Instruments

Measurement instruments have a variety of characteristics that impact upon their effectiveness. Figure 3.2 lists some key characteristics. Interestingly, the majority of these characteristics apply to instruments that measure both physical and social phenomena. For some characteristics, such as validity, reliability, and amplitude, there are unique implications when the measurement is applied to social phenomena.

Accuracy is the degree to which the instrument measures the phenomenon correctly. The higher the accuracy, the lower the error (although errors may occur irrespective of the accuracy). Similarly, precision is a characteristic of an instrument in which when applied a large number of times to the same phenomenon, will yield very similar measurement values. Repeatability is similar to precision, in that it describes the ability of an instrument to yield very similar values when applied repeatedly to measure one phenomenon, and when all conditions of measurement are unchanged. Tolerance is the degree to which the instrument's readings will be different from the mean or the established or

Figure 3.2
Characteristics of Measurement Instruments

CHARACTERISTICS/ATTRIBUTES OF INSTRUMENTS
• Accuracy
• Precision
• Repeatability
• Tolerance
• Level (qualitative vs. quantitative)
• Bias
• Sensitivity
• Error
• Validity
• Reliability
• Amplitude

expected standard. This is also a measure of deviation from what would be considered the expected performance of the instrument.

Level of measurement refers to the use of qualitative or quantitative measures. Bias refers to the systemic error inherent in the instrument. Another characteristic is sensitivity that may be defined in terms of the differences in measurement that would occur for a given change in the values of the phenomenon being measured. For example, if there have been changes in the quality of research in a given organization, will the instrument be able to yield readings that would convey and indicate such a change.

Errors may be systematic or random. Systematic errors are due to problems with the instrument, and are correctable. Random errors are usually hard to detect and to ascribe their source.

Validity, Reliability, and Amplitude

Validity is an important characteristic of a measurement instrument because it links it with the phenomenon. In concise terms, validity is a term that describes the degree to which the values yielded by the instrument indeed measure what they purport to measure. For instance, does an IQ instrument indeed measure intelligence? Similarly, does the count of patents indeed measure innovative achievements? The instrument will therefore be valid if it measures what it was designed to measure.[7]

Reliability is a term that refers to the degree to which the readings of an instrument are within an acceptable range from a desired quantity when the instrument is applied over time, or in different conditions and with different objects of measurement. For example, a test of cognitive skills will be reliable when there is little variance in readings across different groups of subjects or to the same group of subjects in different time periods.

In the case of S&T, the count of patents will be reliable if its readings across industries or countries show acceptable variability, hence allowing for interorganizational comparisons.[8]

The concept of amplitude[9] is defined as the degree to which the values measured represent a higher order construct. For example, instruments that measure the satisfaction of patients with medical care may indeed be valid (designed to measure satisfaction), but may or may not be *ample*, to the extent that what they had measured (satisfaction) represents a higher order construct such as "patient value." Similarly, an instrument measuring numbers and distribution of publications will be ample if the values thus generated represent a higher order construct such as "innovativeness."

So, in light of the characteristics in Figure 3.2, an effective measurement instrument should have an acceptable score in some, if not most, of these characteristics. However, particularly in the social sciences, measurement instruments tend to be more susceptible to problems in these characteristics. This is compounded by the fact that different metrics will have different attributes of the instruments that use them.

In the case of S&T, the main categories of metrics relate to the characteristics of measurement instruments in the matrix shown in Figure 3.3. Although the figure reflects my personal assessment of S&T metrics and the effectiveness profiles of the instruments used in their application, such assessment is based on cases in the literature and many discussions with colleagues and with researchers and managers in government and industry.[10]

Measurement instruments in the evaluation of S&T phenomena are generally accurate and precise, but tend to exhibit high bias and low sensitivity, particularly when they are predominantly qualitative. As I discuss each category of metrics starting with Chapter 5, the picture that emerges is of instruments that measure well the phenomenon they are meant to measure, but that are biased and for the most part nonrepeatable. Hence the value of their measurement to the evaluation effort may raise many difficult questions. These and other constraints will lead us to regard the value of these measures merely as "crude" indices of the phenomena they measure. So, the inevitable result is the reliance of an evaluation effort of S&T on covariation of the measure with the view on the phenomenon. For example, the decline in the United States of the number of patents in the 1970s, in almost all industries and product areas, is viewed as a crude indication that the country has undergone a period of decline in industrial invention and innovativeness.[11]

MEASUREMENT OF INDICATORS

Science and technology are complex and unstructured phenomena as we address them within the social, managerial, and organizational sciences. Evaluation of S&T requires the measurement of these phenomena and the constructs that we develop to define them. Developing conceptual constructs and modeling such unstructured phenomena are tasks that call

Figure 3.3
Categories of S&T Metrics and Characteristics of Measurement

CATEGORY OF METRICS[**]	EFFECTIVENESS CHARACTERISTICS OF INSTRUMENTS[*]						
	Accuracy	Precision	Repeatability	Tolerance	Bias	Sensitivity	Level
BIBLIOMETRIC COUNTS OF PUBLICATIONS & CITATIONS	High	High	High	High	High	High	Quantitative
COUNT OF PATENTS	High	High	High	High	High	High	Quantitative
CO-WORD ANALYSIS	Low	High	Low	Low	High	Low	Mostly Qualitative
ECONOMIC IMPACTS	Low	High	Low	High	High	Low	Mostly Quantitative
PEER REVIEW	High	High	Low	Low	High	Low	Qualitative
DOWNSTREAM STAGE ANALY-SIS OF IMPACTS	High	High	High	Low	High	High	Qualitative and Quantitative

[*]*From Figure 3.2 above.*   [**]*This list is illustrative. For a more comprehensive list, see Chapters 5ff.*

Figure 3.4
The Abstraction Ladder in Capturing Critical Aspects of Complex Phenomena

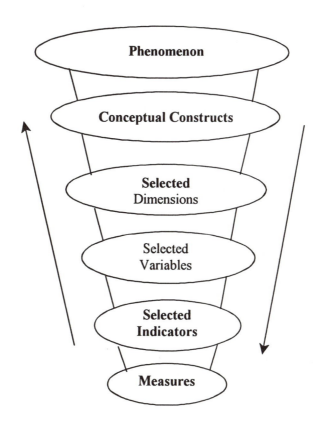

for adequate measurement of what may be defined as "unquantifiable" dimensions and variables.[12]

For complex and unstructured phenomena, conceptual constructs describe only a limited number of their dimensions or facets.[13] By descending the ladder of abstraction, from the general to the particular, we are able to decompose the phenomenon into specific facets. Figure 3.4 shows the abstraction ladder.

Conceptual constructs are composed by researchers and evaluators, with the intent of capturing critical aspects of the phenomenon. For each construct, selected dimensions are composed, again with the purpose of capturing critical aspects of the construct. This is followed down the ladder with variables, and finally indicators and measures. The latter are quantities or values as actual readings on the measurement instrument.[14]

Indicators are therefore used to capture certain aspects of the phenomenon. Thus the degree to which they actually measure the constructs is largely dependent upon the methodological issue of validity, as well as the issue of conventions about how to use measurement by indicators.[15]

Issues in Measuring by Indicators

The use of indicators to measure conceptual constructs and complex phenomena is fraught with several issues, most of which are barriers and difficulties to adequate measurement. These issues may be shown as queries that arise in any attempt at such measurement.[16] Figure 3.5 summarizes the issues and shows a brief definition for each query.

Definition of Constructs

As constructs are defined by convention, definitions may vary. The result is a situation whereby different indicators will be used to measure the construct, and convergence or interchangeability is very difficult to achieve. Similarly, the indicators selected may cover only a portion of the phenomenon, raising concerns that we may have missed the critical aspects. These concerns have contributed to the emergence of techniques such as multitrait-multimethod.[17] The objective is to utilize all available methods and indicators, so as to capture as much as possible of the phenomenon.

Consider the case of the evaluation and measurement of scientific activity or technology. We are compelled to use indicators that would capture some (but not all) of the facets of scientific processes or technology, and their outputs. We rely on the assumption that an adequate link exists between the indicators selected and the phenomenon. If we select count of publications and count of patents, we are still in doubt whether they indeed capture the critical or essential dimensions of S&T outcomes, and in an adequate manner.[18]

How Many Are Adequate?

If we opt for the use of multiple indicators to measure constructs and phenomena, how many indicators would suffice to attain adequacy for both the conceptual and statistical requirements? Adding indicators that are very similar to those we already have may not be recommended, because they would be only marginally effective and would add to our transaction costs, such as costs of obtaining the data for these indicators.

Figure 3.5
Issues in the Use of Indicators to Measure Complex Phenomena and Conceptual Constructs

QUERY	DEFINITION OF ISSUES
♦ **How well is the construct defined?**	• Using convention to assign indicators to ill-defined constructs • In such ill-defined constructs, do the indicators assigned adequately measure?
♦ **How many are adequate?**	• By using multiple indicators, under which criteria and conditions is a given number enough to adequately measure the constructs?
♦ **Can the indicators converge and be indexed or aggregated?**	• Do indicators converge by the dimensions they purport to measure? • Can indicators be aggregated into "Mono-Indicators?" • How to deal with indicators that measure surrogate variables, aspects, or dimensions of the concept? Can they be aggregated with "direct" indicators?
♦ **Are there biases and distortions in measurements?**	• Choice of indicators is a function of value judgments and social, political, and other agenda. • Some indicators have more power than other indicators in a given set, thus distorting the measurement in their favor. • Indicators may be poorly correlated in a given set, hindering convergence and adding to biases. • The mere choice of indicators may affect the behavior of the phenomena we are measuring. • Errors and biases in statistical computations.

By the same token, if we add different indicators that measure other slices of the phenomenon, we encounter such difficulties as lack of convergence, and added variability to data manipulation techniques. The answer is perhaps tied to the theoretical link between the indicators and the phenomenon. When marginal benefits of adding indicators achieve a level deemed sufficient to cover the phenomenon, this would be an adequate number.[19]

For example, if we use count of articles and other bibliometric indicators to measure the outcomes from science, then add peer review, we are adding indicators that may not converge and may be measuring different aspects of the construct of scientific output.

Convergence and Aggregation

Multiple indicators make it difficult to interpret the outcome of the measurement effort, since we may be confronted with separate sets of different indicators measuring unrelated dimensions. We may thus wish to aggregate the indicators to form an index or a "macro" indicator.

Combining bibliometric measures such as counts of publications and counts of citations and co-word analyses may yield an index of bibliometric performance. This procedure will generally require the use of weights and utilities of the indicators that will converge to form a composite framework. However, several problems are associated with the creation of these aggregate indicators. First, indicators may be poorly correlated and nonconvergent. Second, the weights and utilities are influenced by value judgments and may differ among sets of indicators, so that biases may emerge in favor of a given set of indicators in the index, or in favor of a weight-system applied to a given set, or both.

In the case of R&D productivity, researchers have criticized the use of multiple indicators and their aggregation by arguing that the indicators selected and their weights are a function of managers' prior definition of what R&D productivity means to them. This yielded inherent biases that distorted the process of index development.

Biases and Distortions

There are two kinds of biases: Those arising from values and judgments, and those that may affect the behavior of the construct or phenomenon we are attempting to measure. Biases and distortions due to the power of values and judgments lead to a choice of indicators and their weights (for indexes) that mirrors the agenda of the decision-makers or the evaluator. Social constructs and phenomena are a good example. The concept of *poverty* and how it is measured have led to criticisms about the choice of indicators.[20] Critics have argued that econometric indicators such as rate of consumption or simply income capture only a portion of the phenomenon and are insensitive to the length of its effects. Thus, social policy-makers may have selected economic or financial indicators because they are easier to measure, but more important, are easier to manipulate.[21] Hence results may be achieved and measured, but these results have not significantly influenced the core problems of the construct of poverty. The poor may have higher incomes, but they are still poor nonetheless.[22]

Biases due to impacts on behavior are inherent in the application of evaluation methodologies. Selecting a given set of indicators as an evaluation tool may influence the behavior of those being evaluated to conform to the indicator. This issue is also known as "corruption of the indicators." If bibliometric indicators are chosen to evaluate the performance of research scientists—and this is known to them—there is a good possibility that they may alter their behavior and produce higher quantities of publications to meet the expectations built into the indicators.[23] Only through understanding such biases and with careful planning and selection of indicators can we address these problems.

The Indicators Imperative

So the reality of measurement in the realm of social, managerial, and organizational phenomena is that only with the use of indicators can we achieve adequate capturing of the phenomena and their conceptual constructs. In physical phenomena a single indicator will suffice. Measurements of pressures or temperature need only one indicator. However, even for biological concepts, multiple indicators are the norm. For example, vital signs are indicators of the health status of a patient. They include temperature, blood pressure, and a variety of indicators of the blood picture. Eventually the health care provider aggregates these indicators into a combined notion of health status. Hence we are bound by the fact that social and similar phenomena must be measured by multiple indicators.[24]

For science and technology evaluation there is only one viable method: measurement by indicators. Multiple indicators are needed to provide adequate coverage of the dimensions and aspects of the complex processes, activities, and outcomes. Thus, the *indicator's imperative* is at full force as we employ different indicators for the many facets of S&T—with all the issues and problems that accompany their application.

SCIENCE INDICATORS

Science indicators is a generic term that applies to a broad range of quantitative measures of selected activities, inputs, and outcomes from research, development, and innovation. This broad set is utilized across countries as well as across organizations and research and technology institutes. It includes a variety of measures such as statistical distributions, time series, counts of different variables, results from surveys, and correlations among variables.

In the years following the Second World War there were several attempts to create a standardized form of accounting and measurement of scientific and technological activity within and across countries. Among these there are three endeavors that had relative success in establishing an acceptable and relatively standardized framework of science indicators: OECD and UNESCO, the U.S. National Science Board, and Japan's National Institute of Science and Technology Policy (NISTEP).

OECD and UNESCO

The first attempt to construct a standardized set of science indicators was initiated by the Organization for Economic Cooperation and Development (OECD) in 1963[25] and by the United Nations Educational, Scientific, and Cultural Organization (UNESCO) in 1968.[26] The OECD framework is also known as the *Frascati Manual*. It contains indicators of national funding and some outputs of specific scientific activities. For example, the manual offers measures of the commitment and use of resources in research and development (inputs) and bibliometric and patent statistics as outputs. Data are collected for industrial companies and government institutions, and the totals are tabulated as national figures. Thus, comparisons can be made among different countries. The UNESCO framework is similar. Both models also consider such statistics over time for the same country, thus generating patterns which may allow for predictions and other policy determinations.

Input indicators include the number and the expenditures on scientists and engineers by category and type of employment. They also include other expenditures for services, materials, and information by disciplinary area and by categories of basic research, applied research, and development. The output side of the framework encompasses data on publications, citations, and patents.

U.S. National Science Board

Starting in 1972, the U.S. National Science Board of the National Science Foundation has been publishing a biennial issue of its *Science Indicators*.[27] In the 1980s the title changed to *Science and Engineering Indicators*. In 1982, for example, the NSB publications contained statistical data, some as far back as 1960, of expenditures for R&D in the United States and several other developed countries. Data on these inputs included support for basic research, applied research, and development for industry, academic institutions, and government laboratories.

Federal and industrial obligations were classified by scientific fields, such as life sciences, physical sciences, engineering, and mathematics and computer sciences. Industrial support for R&D was classified by the Standard Industrial Classification (SIC) of industries.

Outputs were academic degrees (undergraduate and graduate) given by American universities by field of study, publications, citations, and patents. Ancillary statistics included scores of Scholastic Aptitude Tests of college-bound high-school seniors, and statistics of the characteristics of the scientific and engineering human resources pool by employment and scientific discipline.

In addition to such statistics and their manipulations (for example, cost of research per scientist and engineer: S&E), the NSB publications also provide commentaries and discussion of the trends and their significance within the national S&T and economic situation. The combination of raw data and analysis in effect constitutes an authoritative, data-based description of the state of American science, engineering, and technology for that period. In later publications, the NSB reports included results of surveys of public attitudes toward science and technology and additional details and analyses, including data on cooperative efforts and international consortia.[28]

Japan's System of Science Indicators

The Japanese Science Indicators System (JSIS) was a late arrival, formally established by the country's Science and Technology Agency in 1984.[29] Selection of indicators was a process guided by four criteria. First, indicators should not only measure selected inputs and outputs of R&D activities, but also measure the impact of R&D and S&T on the country's economy and society. Second, the framework of indicators should be classified by the goals and objectives that guide S&T. Third, classification by the role that S&T plays in the country's infrastructures and, finally, subjective indicators should be added to the set of quantitative indicators. Thus, the system devised in 1984 contained 103 indicators of expenditures and outcomes, selected from an original pool of 200 indicators.

Another feature of the Japanese system is its "cascading" structure, in which the indicators are divided into six interrelated categories. The top of this pyramid includes indicators of *societal infrastructure*. These are similar to the social indicators described below. Following downstream are *R&D infrastructure* that includes indicators of people and funding (inputs). Next is *R&D results*, a category that includes such outputs as publications, patents, and standards. The Japanese system also addresses indicators of the contributions of S&T to industry, society, and international relations, and the acceptance of S&T by society.[30]

Rationale for Indicator Selection

Compilations of science indicators such as the *Frascati Manual* have supplied a framework for the analysis of scientific and technological progress for national innovation systems. The guiding rationale for the structure of the OECD, UNESCO, and NSB efforts has been categorization by activities, and by inputs and outputs.

Activities included the stages of research and development, within academic disciplines and by performer. In this manner, basic or exploratory research could be measured as it was practiced by industry, universities, and government laboratories, in disciplines such as physics, engineering, and social sciences. For each activity, indicators of inputs (expenditures) and outputs (counts of publications, citations, and patents) were assembled, tabulated, and analyzed. The bulk of the effort was concentrated on the inputs side, as outputs are less representative of actual level of effort than expenditures and numbers of resources engaged in the S&T activities.

Almost by definition this rationale for the structure of the database of science indicators has been a natural choice because of the relative facility of collecting the relevant data. But it has also confined the system to a snapshot (albeit in the form of time-series and trends of multiyear measurements) of the *structural* dimensions of the S&T national and industrial scence. The resulting statistics describe who is doing what and how much it costs. At the other side of the equation, we have statistics about what are the immediate outputs from this framework. Manipulations and statistical correlations among these variables do *not* offer a more profound analysis of the state of S&T. For example, knowing how much we spend per scientist and engineer in a given discipline or activity (such as basic research) provides little new information than the individual indicators of expenditures for basic research and number of S&E engaged in this activity. Nevertheless, there have been many studies and interpretations of such data and their manipulations, particularly in terms of inputs/outputs relationships.[31]

The Japanese system of science indicators has a broader rationale that also encompasses the social dimensions of the scientific activity. The "cascading" structure allows for social objectives and social and economic implications from S&T to be counted as part of the overall system of indicators. However, the Japanese system channels the selected indicators to reflect the existing policies for S&T, so they become *de facto* measures of the accomplishment of these policies, rather than objective measures of the state of science.[32] This fact limits the generalization feature of the Japanese data.

Perhaps the more viable rationale for selection of indicators would be a mix of the two models. The resultant system should allow for relative ease in collection of available data, yet also relate to the impacts that science and technology create in the economy and society. One of the key issues is the attempt to maintain a balance between the objectivity of the system and the subjective selection and interpretation of the indicators.[33]

Conceptual and Measurement Issues

The issues involved with science indicators can be classified into two main categories: issues in the methodology of indicators' selection and data collection, and issues in the interpretation and analysis of the data. Figure 3.5 listed the general issues in measurement by indicators. Figure

3.6 portrays those issues that are specific to the methodology and analysis of science indicators.

In toto, these issues may be converged to form a nagging problem of a set of indicators that has been somewhat arbitrarily collected, but serves to arrive at far-reaching policy conclusions. Moreover, as trends are compiled, indexes formed, and correlations obtained, these indicators may lead to conclusions and recommendations about allocation of resources for R&D and S&T, at both the national and the firm's levels. Some of such conclusions may be erroneous, overly optimistic, or overly pessimistic.[34]

An interesting example concerns a technical innovation audit designed to evaluate the firm's innovative performance.[35] The authors constructed a model in which the building blocks were the stages or key

Figure 3.6
Key Issues in Methodology and Analysis of Science Indicators

CATEGORY	KEY ISSUES
Methodology: Selection and Structure of Indicators	• Lack of a unifying theory or conceptual scheme. • Influence of goals, motives, and biases of evaluators. • Problem inherent in output indicators. • Preference for available data. • Difficulties with convergence and macro indicators.
Analysis and Interpretation	• Do these indicators really represent the state and progress of science? If so, to what extent? • "Leap of faith" from the indicators to policy conclusions. • Manipulations, correlations, and indices may lead to erroneous trends and conclusions. • Indicators selected that are based on distinct theories (e.g., economic theories) may lead to conclusions biased by these theories.

processes of the innovation process in the company. Based on this framework, the model included a *process* audit and a *performance* audit. The authors then searched the literature and identified circa 40 indicators (measures) of what they had defined as core and enabling processes. For example, process innovation was measured by effectiveness (number of new processes and significant enhancements per year); speed (installation lead times); also continuous improvement (number of improvement suggestions per employee and percentage implemented); and finally, the cost of development. The authors have also suggested that the audit allows them to compare trends against company goals and to measure the internal evolution of the innovation processes within the firm.

In the absence of a unifying conceptual framework, the system in this audit is a combination of sets of indicators that represent different phenomena within the innovation process. For instance, the dimensions "concept generation," "product development," and "leadership" are distinct phenomena with unique characteristics. Some are interrelated, others strictly differentiated. Hence they may be "forced" into correlations and patterns that may produce comparisons between "apples and oranges."

As early as 1978, Robert McGinnis had criticized the American Science Indicators project.[36] He contended (as I have argued in this chapter) that "Mere data become indicators only as a result of a complex interaction between theory and measurement" (p. 15). He also argued that the Science Indicator model generated by the U.S. National Science Board is a poor model of science, among other factors because they omit what he called "the entire cognitive and social structure of science" (p. 20).

McGinnis was also concerned with the disaggregation of the data into such activities as research and development and the rationale for linking the two distinct phenomena and social systems. Finally, he was also criticizing the treatment of all input indicators as homogeneous indications of resources allocated to the process. I see one of his statements to embody the essence of the core of problems with science indicators. McGinnis wrote: "But unless one is willing to take the position that time itself is a causal variable, one must recognize that such series are only *descriptive* of recent history while the implicit model on which they bear is analytical, involving logical as well as temporal priorities, concerned with cause and effect" (p. 21).

In the final analysis the model that underlies science indicators and such frameworks as the innovation audit tend to ignore the logical, conceptual, and temporal links among the various stages, activities, and phenomena of S&T.[37] In the stage model outlined in Chapter 12 of this book, I attempt to include such linkages and their rationale into the composite of distinct sets of indicators of the various stages and phenomenon.

Some Potential Solutions

In addition to the fact that the assumptions underlying the science indicators models are not explicitly stated (except to some degree in the Japanese model), the science indicators effort has consistently presented a mere congregation of distinct sets of indicators. This model has not utilized the potential application of aggregation into macroindicators or composite indexes, as economists do with the Consumer Price Index. This macroindicator contains a set of several indicators that are different and may describe different phenomena, but that are linked through a conceptual and logical framework.[38]

Conversely, the science indicators model has also failed to identify and to elevate specialized indicators to the level of descriptors of more complex phenomena. Economists, for instance, do so with the indicator of employment or unemployment as a predictor of the growth and expansion of the national economy. Similarly, sociologists use the indicator of level of income to describe the complex phenomenon of poverty.[39]

A more consistent and useful system should be based on overall conceptual bases that provide the rationale for selection of indicators and for linking them. Linkage should also result in macroindexes as well as individual indicators with generalized appeal for more solid interpretations. Effects of behavioral variables, such as tenure for university professors and incentives and motivation to publish, share results, and cooperate with others along the innovation process, should also be added to the system and seriously considered in any attempt to construct a framework of organizational, industrial, or national indicators of science.

Such an attempt to create more indexes and to link them in a coherent manner was the development of an integrated figure of merit for research evaluation. This method, described in detail in Chapter 12 of this book, includes the design and empirical testing of leading output indicators—as indices of the impact of research organizations.[40]

SOCIAL INDICATORS

Some Definitions

"Social indicators" is a generic term for a variety of selected quantitative clues to the state of aspects of society and social interactions. More specifically, the term "social indicators" has had several definitions in various publications. The United States Department of Health, Education, and Welfare defined the term in 1969 as:

a statistic of direct normative interest, which facilitates concise comprehensive and balanced judgment about the condition of major aspects of a society. It is in all cases a direct measure of welfare and is subject to the interpretation that, if it changes in the "right" direction, while other things remain equal, things have gotten better, or people are "better off." Thus statistics on the number of doctors or policemen could not be social indicators, whereas figures on health or crime rates could be.[41]

Kenneth Land (1971) offered a somewhat different definition. He suggested that social indicators are "social statistics that (1) are components in a social system model (including sociopsychological, economic, demographic, and ecological) or of some particular segment or process thereof, (2) can be collected and analyzed at various times and accumulated into a time-series, and (3) can be aggregated and disaggregated top levels appropriate to the specifications of the model" (p. 323).[42]

Land's elaborate definition includes several methodological attributes of what a system of social indicators should contain, but stops short of defining how these attributes would interact. Similarly, Bernard Cazes (1972) defined a social indicator to be: "A measurement of social phenomena which are trans-economic. It is normative (or finalized), and is integrated in a self-consistent information system" (p. 14).[43]

The notion of social indicators is also known as "social reporting," "social accounting," "social bookkeeping," "social intelligence," and "monitoring social change." Recently it has also served as background for the U.S. government in developing the Government Performance Results Act (GPRA). This act calls for measuring the impacts and contributions of government agencies on social goals and social phenomena—which are in turn measured by social indicators.[44]

In all, these definitions are anchored in the political background and genesis of the effort to measure aspects of society. Social indicators have originated as statistical means to "show" progress in social phenomena and to ascertain the performance of social programs and policy interventions in social phenomena.[45] Concerns over social ills in the 1960s, coupled with the promise of vibrant plans for social engineering, have been conducive in the establishment of these statistical "tools" for the measurement of government initiatives and their effects on social dimensions such as poverty, health care, and welfare.[46]

Criticisms: Flaws in Concepts and Methodology

Embedded in the notion of social indicators is a strong component of political and sociological objectives and claims: what the system should do, hence how it should be structured. At the outset of the initial publications of social indicators as social accounting, many scholars have criticized both the conceptual constructs and the methodology of this system of measurement. I am primarily relying here on the early critics of the system, because they were closer in time to the genesis of social indicators and acutely aware of the political and social climate of "social engineering" within which the system was created. These early critics lived through and directly evaluated the public debate on these challenging topics.

Among these early critics, Sheldon and Freeman were perhaps the more incisive critics of social indicators in the early 1970s.[47] Their main argument was that social indicators cannot serve as a system of social accounting—that permits inputs into decision and policy-making—so that changes in the social reality and in social programs can be thus rationally achieved. They argued that there is a lack of a social theory that provides the necessary framework for relating social indicators to each other, and that offers the background for reasoned decisions based on the data.

Sheldon and Freeman therefore criticized the lack of an acceptable link between the data assembled in the social indicators system and the social phenomena it purports to measure.[48] Instead, they emphasized other less ambitious contributions of the social indicators system, such as a more precise reporting of changes in social programs and in social phenomena.

Elaine Carlisle (1972) argued that in order for a system of indicators to describe societal phenomena, there should be structural as well as performance statistics.[49] She also concluded that "social indicators are neither panaceas nor red herrings" (p. 23). Carlisle defined social indicators as "the operational definition or part of the operational definition of any one of the concepts central to the generation of an information system descriptive of the social system" (p. 25). The central concepts are: components of the fabric of society, system goals of society, social problem areas, and policy goals for actionable decisions. Hence she argued for four categories of indicators: informative, productive, problem-oriented, and program-evaluation. However, even when these types of indicators are adequately collected and used as inputs to policies, they should be viewed in a modest fashion only as information, and should not serve as surrogates for reasoned decision-making processes on social priorities and social interventions.[50]

Another perspective was advanced by Sheldon and Parke (1975) who also lamented the lack of social theory.[51] They argued that the main contribution of the system of social indicators is in stimulating "a revival of interest in quantitative, comparative, social analysis" (p. 698). They also called for additional work on defining more precisely the social phenomena to be measured and to "incorporate experimental designs into the testing of government programs" (p. 695).

Illustrative Indicators

Social indicators reflect specific social phenomena. They are measures of such social areas or activities as education, health, transportation, welfare, psychological sentiments, the environment, and economic accomplishments. For example, health indicators may include statistics on fertility per women, teenage pregnancy, life expectancy, morbidity, leading cause of death in men and women, and indicators of health care delivery such as number of hospital beds per population, hospital performance measures, and accessibility measures.

Another example is the set of indicators of the construct of environmental "sustainability." This construct is loosely defined as the area concerned with "improving the quality of human life while living within the carrying capabilities of supporting ecosystems."[52] Illustrative indicators include energy use/emissions of greenhouse gases per capita; percent of harvested forest successfully replanted; hours of work (at average wage) required to satisfy basic needs; income disparity between top and bottom segments of the population; and number of college graduates able to find appropriate employment.

Demographic measures are also incorporated into the social indicators database (births, deaths, marriages, divorces, mobility, immigration, and emigration). Psychological measures of satisfaction, happiness, and life-fulfillment indices are obtained via periodic surveys. Similarly, measures are collected in transportation (number of passengers and volume of goods transported per period) in each mode: air, fluvial and ground transportation; cost per distance traveled, and measures of urban transportation systems, their effectiveness, their accessibility, and their distribution (public versus private means of transport).

Summary

The development of a system of quantitative social indicators has helped to generate interest among academics and policy-makers. Early on there were scholarly critics who challenged the overly optimistic view of such a system, and the faults in its structure and methodology.

A shared argument seemed to have been the overextension of sets of related data, into the more complex and abstract goals, objectives, and policies regarding social phenomena. As simply a set of quantitative measures, most critics argued, social indicators have an important role in stimulating debate and in supporting policies by providing relevant and timely data. When too much credence, importance, and value are placed on this system of measures as surrogates for policy-making, the critics then called for caution and retrenchment.

Perhaps the most ardent criticism was offered by Snapper, O'Connor, and Einhorn (1974).[53] They concluded that solely quantitative measures, particularly when they are aggregated to form indexes that purport to measure complex phenomena, are inadequate for this task. Indexes, they argued, are the result of a group's policy, thus overshadowing the *quantitative* aspects, hence the advantages of quantitative measures. If so, they also concluded, the only acceptable way to use social indicators is in combination with judgmental methods.

Nevertheless, social indicators are a cohesive database that, in the very least, allows us to obtain a glance or snapshot, including trends, of key social events and social phenomena. Notwithstanding the problems, issues, and weaknesses of the lack of theory, partial definitions, and inconclusive statistical linkages, there is an important role for social indicators in giving us a more precise picture of social reality, and of social ills as well as social progress.[54]

In recent years, the emphasis in academic research of social indicators has shifted to address the methodological and construct pitfalls that had been the mainstay of earlier critics. In particular the current research has concentrated on such issues as validity, reliability, and generalizability of the indicators database and the constructs thus purported to measure.[55] These are refinements of the statistical tools and conceptual construction of variables and their analysis. Although such research has greatly contributed to the clarification of major methodological problems, the early critiques of lack of a unifying theory and specific linkages among indicators remain as valid today as they were a generation ago.

SCIENCE INDICATORS AND SOCIAL INDICATORS: ESTABLISHING THE LINK

The main reason for the above discussion of the social indicators system is that it allows researchers and analysts to *measure* the impacts of science (by means of science indicators) on the economy (by means of economic indicators) and society (social indicators). Since social indicators are primarily measures of the national phenomena of social conditions, a strong link between the outcomes of science and social indicators would opportunistically be at this macro level. As I have repeatedly argued earlier in this book, science and technology have a marked impact on educational, economic, social, and intellectual progress of nations. Individual cases of targeted impacts have generally been more amenable to measurement.

For example, the case of agriculture in the United States is an incisive illustration. Earlier in the 20th century about half the American population was engaged in farming. Nowadays, about 3% of the working population is sufficient to feed the entire country and to export massive quantities of food to many foreign countries.[56] Agricultural science and technology have provided the means to dramatically increase the productivity of the land, seeds, and crops. Technological achievements in water management have also greatly contributed to improvements in agricultural yields.[57] From 1910 to 1980, the composite index of crop yields in the United States climbed from 50 to 120.[58] Toward the end of the century science and technology have continued to impact agricultural efficiency through genetic improvements in basic crops, pest and insect control, and soil conservation and enrichment.[59]

Not surprisingly, some pioneering studies of the economic and social impacts of S&T have focused on the agricultural sector and its dramatic achievements. Seminal studies by Zvi Griliches, for example, addressed the link between science and economic benefits in agriculture.[60] Other economists studied the link between specific innovations and selected accomplishments in agriculture production and efficiency.[61] These cases form an impressive cumulative set of instances that tend to reinforce the generalized connection between S&T and agricultural performance.

Despite the proliferation in the relevant literature of cases of specific linkages between S&T indicators and social-economic benefits, the link between large-scale science and social indicators remains elusive. Statistical correlations were mostly confined to sectors and within them to well-defined innovations and their social-economic impacts.

Much of the effort to statistically manipulate data on these indicators was carried out *within* the indicator's databases. For example, at the national state of S&T, bibliometric indicators (number of publications and citations) were used for cross-comparisons among countries.[62] Yet comparisons of *generalized* effects of S&T on social and economic phenomena of nations—in the form of correlations among large sets of indicators—have not been successfully accomplished.

Part of the reason may be the internal problems inherent in each indicator's database. Chiefly among these are the lack of a theory, difficulties in creating indices, biases in formulation of the indicators, and statistical weaknesses. Thus, if we simply compare the databases of science indicators and social indicators, without anchoring the comparison in a specific innovation and corresponding impact, inherent problems will be severely compounded, resulting in meaningless or spurious relationships.

Therefore, current effort is confined to specific cases, in target sectors, and for selected industries and disciplinary cases. Some success has been attained in correlating indicator's data for evaluation of social and economic programs and policies. But, overall, the methodology is still mired in weaknesses, thus enhancing the importance of subjective and expert interpretation of any linkages that use such indicators.[63]

NOTES

1. There is a vast literature on measurement and principles of measurement. See, for example, Trout, J., *Measuring the Intentional World: Realism,*

Naturalism and Quantitative Methods in the Behavioral Sciences (New York: Oxford University Press, 1998). Also see Brown, M., *Keeping Score: Using the Right Metrics to Drive World-Class Performance* (New York: Amacom, 1996); and Freeman, C. (Ed.), *Output Measurement in Science & Technology* (Amsterdam: North-Holland, 1987).

2. This chapter is not a comprehensive treatise on measurement and measurement instruments. Its objective is to merely introduce the reader to the unique characteristics of the metrics of S&T, and to do so, introduce the reader to the more fundamental components of measurement.

3. See Hauser, J., and G. Katz, "Metrics: You Are What You Measure!" *European Management Journal*, 16(5), 1998, 517-528. This issue is further explored in Chapter 15.

4. See, for example, Webb, E., D. Campbell, R. Schwartz, and L. Seechrest, *Unobtrusive Measures: Nonreactive Research in the Social Sciences* (Chicago: Rand McNally, 1966).

5. As shown in Chapter 12 of this book, this type of instrument is widely used in project and program evaluations, as postfactum analyses.

6. For example, see Indurkhya, N. and S. Weiss, "Models for Measuring Performance of Medical Expert Systems," *Artificial Intelligence in Medicine*, 1(2), 1989, 61-70.

7. See, for example, Cook, T., and T. Campbell, "The Design and Conduct of Quasi-Experiments and True Experiments in Field Settings," in M. Dunnette (Ed.), *Handbook of Industrial and Organizational Research* (Chicago: Rand McNally, 1978), Chapter 7.

8. There is a vast literature on these attributes within the framework of research methods. See, for example, Hughes, M., L. Price, and D. Marrs, "Linking Theory Construction and Theory Testing: Models with Multiple Indicators and Latent Variables," *Academy of Management Review*, 11(1), 1986, 128-144.

9. This notion was introduced and operationally defined in Geisler, E., *Methodology, Theory, and Knowledge in the Organizational and Managerial Sciences* (Westport, CT: Greenwood Press, 1999).

10. For a review of the extant literature, see Chapters 5-8.

11. See, for example, Mansfield, E., A. Romeo, M. Schwartz, D. Teece, S. Wagner, and P. Brach., *Technology Transfer, Productivity, and Economic Policy* (New York: W. W. Norton, 1982), 132-153. Also see Chakrabarti, A., "Trends in Innovation and Productivity: The Case of Chemical and Textile Industries in the U.S.," *R&D Management*, 18(2), 1988, 131-140. For a more generic discussion, see Bailey, K., *Methods of Social Research*, 4th ed., (New York: Free Press, 1994), 61-77.

12. See Geisler, E., "Measuring the Unquantifiable: Issues in the Use of Indicators in Unstructured Phenomena,"*International Journal of Operations and*

Quantitative Management, 1(2), 1995, 145-161. The discussion in this section is based on this article (used with permission from the journal).

13. See, for example, Campbell, D., and D. Fiske, "Convergent and Discriminate Validation by the Multitrait-Multimethod Matrix," *Psychological Bulletin*, 56(2), 1959, 81-105. Also see Anderson, J., D. Gerbing, J. Hunter, A. Kumar, and W. Dillon, "On the Assessment of Unidimensional Measurement: Internal and External Consistency and Overall Consistency Criteria/Some Further Remarks on Measurement-Structure Interaction and the Unidimensionality of Constructs," *Journal of Marketing Research*, 24(4), 1987, 432-444.

14. For additional readings see, for example, Blalock, H., "The Measurement Problem: A Gap Between the Languages of Theory and Research," in H. Blalock and A. Blalock (Eds.), *Methodology in Social Research* (New York: McGraw-Hill, 1968), 5-27. Also see Bacquelaine, M., "The Measurement of Multi-dimensional Development: Comments on Commonly Accepted Indicators," *International Journal of Social Economics*, 20(11), 1993, 4-14.

15. See, for example, Pedhazur, E., and L. Pedhazur, *Measurement, Design, and Analysis* (Hillsdale, NJ: L. Erlbaum, 1991). Also see issues in measuring team performance in Brannick, M., E. Salas, and C. Prince, *Assessment and Measurement of Team Performance: Theory, Research, and Applications* (Hillsdale, NJ: L. Erlbaum, 1997). In particular see Chapters 3-5, pp. 45-110.

16. See Geisler, 1995, *op. cit.*, pp. 148-183, for a comprehensive discussion of such issues.

17. See in particular the seminal work by Campbell, D., and D. Fiske, "Convergent and Discriminate Validation by the Multitrait-Multimethod Matrix," *Psychological Bulletin*, 56(2), 1959, 81-105. Also see Edwards, W., and J. Newman, *Multiattribute Evaluation* (Beverly-Hills, CA: Sage Publications, 1982). Also see Harris, M., and A. Bladen, "Wording Effects in the Measurement of Role Conflicts and Role Ambiguity: A Multitrait-Multimethod Analysis," *Journal of Management*, 20(4), 1994, 887-902.

18. For example, Francis Narin has proposed the indicator of technology cycle time to assess corporate technology. He defined the indicator as median age of the patents cited in any of the company's patent applications. Clearly, the validity of this indicator and its ability to cover an adequate part of the phenomenon of "corporate technological progress" depends on the theoretical link between the indicators and the construct. See Narin, F., "Technology Indicators and Corporate Strategy," *Review of Business*, 14(3), 1993, 19-25.

19. See Bacquelaine, 1995, *op. cit.* Also see the seminal pages by Althauser, R., and T. Heberlein, "Validity and the Multitrait-Multimethod Matrix," in E. Borgatta and G. Bohrnstedt (Eds.), *Sociological Methodology* (San Francisco: Jossey-Bass, 1970), 151-169; and Costner, H., and R. Schoenberg, "Diagnosing Indicator Ills in Multiple Indicator Models," in D. Goldberger, *Structural Equation Models in the Social Sciences* (New York: Seminar Press, 1973), 167-199.

20. See, for example, some of these criticisms in Brown, W., and D. Gobeli, "Observations on the Measurement of R&D Productivity: A Case Study," *IEEE Transactions on Engineering Management*, 39(4), 1992, 325-331. Also see Chakrabarti, A., "Technology Indicators: Conceptual Issues and Measurement Problems," *Journal of Engineering and Technology Management*, 6(2), 1989, 99-116.

21. See, for example, Haveman, R., "Who Are the Nation's Truly Poor?: Problems and Pitfalls in (Re)Defining and Measuring Poverty," *Brookings Review*, 11(1), 1993, 24-27.

22. This example also illustrates the theoretical link of indicators to the overall phenomenon. Income measures only one facet of poverty, perhaps not even the more critical of its facets, such as level of education and psychological factors.

23. See Gonzalez, R., "A Unified Metric of Software Complexity: Measuring Productivity, Quality, and Value," *Journal of Systems and Software*, 29(1), 1995, 17-37. Also see Chen, S., *Measurement & Analysis in Psychological Research: The Failing & Saving of Theory* (New York: Ashgate Publishing, 1997), and Payne, J., *Principles of Social Science Measurement* (New York: Lytton Publishing, 1975).

24. There is a considerable literature on this and related topics. See, for example, Preston, L., *Corporation and Society Research: Studies in Theory and Measurement* (Greenwich, CT: JAI Press, 1990). Also see Kanis, H. (Ed.), *Measurement & Design: Measuring in an Interdisciplinary Research Environment* (New York: Coronet Books, 1994); Woolf, H. (Ed.), *Quantification: A History of the Meaning of Measurement in the Natural and Social Sciences* (London: Irvington Publishers, 1961); and Griliches, Z., *Output Measurement in the Service Sectors* (Chicago: University of Chicago Press, 1992).

25. OECD, *The Measurement of Outputs of Scientific and Technical Activities* (Paris: OECD, 1963, revised 1976).

26. UNESCO, Provisional Guide to the Collection of Science Statistics (Paris: UNESCO, 1968).

27. National Science Board, *Science Indicators* (Washington, DC: National Science Foundation, 1972). Further volumes are 1974 to 1998.

28. See, for example, National Science Board, *Science & Engineering Indicators* (Washington, DC: National Science Foundation, 1993).

29. See, for example, Niwa, F., "The Japanese S&T Indicator System and Industrial R&D Resource Diversification," paper presented at the International Conference on Science and Technology Policy Research, Shimoda, Japan, February 2-4, 1990. The author was director of a task group within the National Institute of Science and Technology Policy of Japan.

30. See, for example, Kodama, F., "Technological Diversification of Japanese Industry," *Science*, 233, 1986, 291-296. Also see Kodama, F., and F. Niwa,

"Structure Analysis of the Japanese Science Indicator System and Its Evaluation," *Journal of Science Policy and Research Management*, 2(2), 1986, 173-183.

31. There is a substantial literature on assessment analyses of these data sets, and policy implications that are drawn from them. See, for example, Holbrook, J., "Basic Indicators of Scientific and Technological Performance," *Science and Public Policy*, 19(5), 1992, 267-273. Also see Leyesdorff, L., and P. Van der Scharr, "The Use of Scientometric Methods for Evaluating National Research Programs," *Science & Technology Studies*, 5(1), 1987, 22-31; and Sbragia, R., and I. Kruglianskas, "R&D in Brazilian Industry: Recent Indicators," *Research-Technology Management*, 39(3), 1996, 30-35. Also, Jacobsson, S., C. Oskarsson, and J. Phillipson, "Indicators of Technological Activities: Comparing Educational, Patent, and R&D Statistics in the Case of Sweden," *Research Policy*, 25(4), 1996, 573-586.

32. See Niwa, 1990, *op. cit.*, who listed among the limitations of the Japanese system the fact that "available data are gathered according to the specific needs and purposes of the collecting body" (p. 15).

33. See, for example, Arnow, K., "A Proposed Conceptual Framework for Indicators of R&D Inputs, Outputs, and Industrial Innovation," paper published at the Science & Technology Indicators Conference, OECD, Paris, September 15-19, 1980.

34. Among many such examples of the use of science indicators in predictions and allocation of resources, see Frame, D., "Quantitative Indicators for Evaluation of Basic Research Programs/Projects," *IEEE Transactions on Engineering Management*, 30(3), 1983, 106-112. Also see Garfield, E., "Citation Analysis as a Tool in Journal Evaluation," *Science*, 178, 1972, 472-479; and Rigter, H., "Evaluation of Performance of Health Research in the Netherlands," *Research Policy*, 15(1), 1986, 33-49. Also see Terleckyj, N., "What Do R&D Numbers Tell Us About Technological Change?" *American Economic Review*, 70(2), 1980, 51-55.

35. Chiesa, V., P. Coughlan, and C. Voss, "Development of a Technical Innovation Audit," *Journal of Product Innovation Management*, 13(2), 1996, 105-136.

36. McGinnis, R., "Science Indicators—1976: A Critique," *Society for Social Studies of Science*, 3(4), 1978, 14-29. Professor McGinnis of Cornell University provided the most incisive and straightforward critique of science indicators in his time. These criticisms are as valid today as then.

37. See, for example, some early work such as: Elkana, Y., J. Lederberg, R. Merton, A. Thackray, and H. Zuckerman (Eds.), *Toward a Metric of Science: The Advent of Science Indicators* (New York: John Wiley & Sons, 1978). This seminal collection of sociological analysis of science indicators influenced the direction of academic discourse in this topic for years afterward. Also see James MacAullay of The Science Council of Canada who had forcefully argued that the

U.S. science indicators of 1976 "is not yet a system of indicators nor indicators of a system...has not yet given us the policy intelligence tool which it has always promised. But it is an achievement, and it will encourage and influence policy debate in many quarters." MacAulay, J, "The Ghost in the Big Machine Science Indicators/ 1976," *Society for Social Studies of Science*, 3(4), 1978, 34.

38. This discussion has benefitted from Holmfeld, J., "Science Indicators: Some User Observations," *Society for Social Studies of Science*, 3(4), 1978, 36-43; and Whitley, R., *The Intellectual and Social Organization of the Sciences* (Oxford: Oxford University Press, 1984); and also Leyesdorf, L., "The Development of Frames of Reference," *Scientometrics*, 9(2), 1986, 103-125.

39. See, for example, a basic philosophical paper: Fletcher, J., "Four Indicators of Humanhood: The Enquiry Natures," *Hastings Center Report*, December 1974, 4-7.

40. See Geisler, E., "Integrated Figure of Merit of Public Sector Research Evaluation," *Scientometrics*, 36(3), 1996, 379-395.

41. United States Department of Health, Education and Welfare, *Toward a Social Report* (Washington, DC: U.S. Government Printing Office, 1965) 97.

42. Land, K., "On the Definition of Social Indicators," *The American Sociologist*, 6(4), 1971, 322-325.

43. Cazes, B., "The Development of Social Indicators: A Survey," in A. Schonfield, and S. Shaw (Eds.), *Social Indicators and Social Policy* (London: Heinemann, 1972), 9-22.

44. See, for example, Bush, L., "Metrics and Benchmarking for NASA Technology Transfer," *Proceedings of the Technology Transfer Metrics Summit: How Do We Know What Works?*" Santa Fe, New Mexico, April 28-May 2, 1996, pp. 236-240.

45. See, for example, one of the seminal books on this topic, Bauer, R. (Ed.), *Social Indicators* (Cambridge, MA: MIT Press, 1966). Also see Cohen, W., "Social Indicators: Statistics for Public Policy," *American Statistician*, 22(4), 1968, 14-16; and Sheldon, L., and W. Moore (Eds.), *Indicators of Social Change* (New York: Russell Sage, 1968).

46. See, for example, Duncan, O., *Toward Social Reporting: Next Steps* (New York: Russell Sage, 1969). Also see Wilcox, L., R. Brooks, G. Beal, and G. Klonglan, *Social Indicators and Societal Monitoring: An Annotated Bibliography* (San Francisco, CA: Jossey-Bass, 1972).

47. Sheldon, E., and H. Freeman, "Notes on Social Indicators: Promises and Potential," *Policy Sciences*, 1(1), 1970, 97-111.

48. See a similar argument for the social, organizational, and managerial sciences in Geisler, 1999, *op. cit.*

49. Carlisle, E., "The Conceptual Structure of Social Indicators," in Schonfield and Shaw, *Social Indicators and Social Policy*, 1972, *op. cit.*, pp. 23-32.

50. See similar views in Sullivan, D., *Conceptual Problems in Developing an Index of Health* (Washington, DC: Office of Health Statistics Analysis, U.S. Department of HEW, 1965). Also see Moser, C., "Some General Developments in Social Statistics," *Social Trends*, 1(1), 1970, 7-11; and Gross, B. (Ed.), *Societal Intelligence for American Future: Explorations in Societal Problems* (Boston: Allyn and Bacon, 1969); and, in particular, see the seminal work: Gross, B., *The State of the Nation: Social Systems Accounting* (London: Tavistock, 1966).

51. Sheldon, E., and R. Parke, "Social Indicators," *Science*, 188 (16 May 1975), 693-699.

52. Farnel, A., and M. Hart, "What Does Sustainability Really Mean": The Search for Useful Indicators," *Environment*, 40(9), 1998, 4-16. Also see Pychyl, T., and B. Little, "Dimensional Specificity in the Prediction of Subjective Well-Being," *Social Indicators Research*, 45(1-3), 1998, 423-474; and Warren, J., J. Sherman, and R. Hauser, "Choosing a Measure of Occupational Standing: How Useful are Composite Measures in Analyses of Gender Inequality in Occupational Attainment?" *Sociological Methods & Research*, 27(1), 1998, 3-76. Also see McDowell, I., and C. Newell, *Measuring Health: A Guide to Rating Scales and Questionnaires* (New York: Oxford University Press, 1996); and Hauser, R., B. Brown, and W. Prosser (Eds.), *Indicators of Children's Well-Being* (Thousand Oaks, CA: Sage Publications 1997).

53. Snapper, K., M. O'Connor, and H. Einhorn, "Social Indicators: A New Method for Indexing Quality," Technical Report 74-4, The Social Research Group, The George Washington University, October 9, 1974.

54. For additional readings see M. Moss (Ed.), *The Measurement of Economic and Social Performance* (New York: National Bureau of Economic Research, 1973); and Francis, W., "What Social Indicators Don't Indicate," *Evaluation*, 2(1), 1973, 79-83. For more recent publications, see Land, K., "Social Indicators," *Annual Review of Sociology*, 9(1), 1983, 1-26. Also see Marcus, K., "Science, Measurement, and Validity: Is Completion of Samuel Messick's Synthesis Possible?" *Social Indicators Research*, 45(1-3), 1998, 7-35.

55. See, for example, Saris, W., and T. Van Wijk, "Validity and Reliability of Subjective Social Indicators," *Social Indicators Research*, 45(1-3), 1998, 173-200. Also see Rabinowitz, S., and D. Rule, "Some New Regression Methods for Predictive and Construct Validation," *Social Indicators Research*, 45(1-3), 1998, 201-232; and Tauber, C., and R. Lambert (Eds.), *America in the Seventies: Some Social Indicators* (New York: American Academy of Political and Social Science, 1978); and Hauser, R., and. J. Warren, "Socioeconomic Index of Occupational Status: A Review, Update, and Critique," in A. Raferty (Ed.), *Sociological Methodology* (Cambridge: Blackwell, 1997) 177-298.

56. See, for example, Wittier, S., "U.S. Agriculture in the Context of the World Food Situation," in A. Teach and R. Thornton (Eds.), *Science, Technology, and the Eighties: Policy Outlook* (Boulder, CO: Westview Press, 1982) 191-214.

57. See, for example, Anderson, J., "Selected Policy Issues in International Agriculture Research: On Striving for International Public Goods in an Era of Donor Fatigue," *World Development*, 26(6), 1998, 1149-1162. Also see Evenson, R., P. Wagoner, and U. Ruttan, "Economic Benefits from Research: An Example from Agriculture," *Science*, 205(4411), 19 September, 1979, 1101-1107; and Doorman, F., "A Framework for the Rapid Appraisal of Factors that Influence the Adoption and Impact of New Agricultural Technology," *Human Organization*, 50(3), 1991, 235-343.

58. Wittier, 1982, *op. cit.*, p. 193.

59. See Jagannath, D., "Green Thumb: From the Laboratory to the Cornfields: DeKalb Genetics is Flourishing," *Financial World*, 159(9), May 1, 1990, 93-106.

60. Griliches, Z., "Research Costs and Social Returns: Hybrid Corn and Related Innovations," *Journal of Political Economics*, 66(8), 1958, 419-431.

61. See, for instance, Ruttan, U., "Toward a Global Agricultural Research System: A Personal View," *Research Policy*, 15(6), 1986, 307-327; and Doyce, C., and M. Ridout, "The Impact of Scientific Research on UK Agricultural Productivity," *Research Policy*, 14(2), 1985, 109-116.

62. For example, see Braun, T., W. Glamzel, and A. Schubert, *Scientometric Indicators* (Singapore: World Scientific, 1985). Some economists have carefully computed the impacts of selected indicators such as publications or patents on the economy. See Mansfield, E., "R&D's Contribution to the Economic Growth of the Nation," *Research Management*, 15(3), 1972, 30-46; and Moller, K. "Technology and Growth-Measures and Concepts: A Case Study of Denmark," *Technovation*, 11(8), 1991, 475-481.

63. See Martin, B., J. Irvine, F. Marin, C. Sterritt, and K. Stevens, "Recent Trends in the Output and Impacts of British Science," *Science and Public Policy*, 17(1), 1990, 14-26.

4

SELECTING A METRIC

WHAT IS A METRIC?

Werner and Souder (1997) have conducted a comprehensive review of the literature from 1956 to 1998, and have concluded that "the choice of an appropriate R&D measurement metric depends on the user's needs for comprehensiveness of measurement, the type of R&D being measured, the available data, and the amount of effort the user can afford to allocate to it"[1] (p. 34).

Although these authors have recognized the difficulties in constructing a systematic classification of such metrics, they nevertheless categorized them into quantitative-subjective, qualitative metrics, and integrated metrics. This classification may also be adequate for the metrics of science and technology.

But what exactly is a metric? In Chapter 3 I defined this notion as a description of a system of measurement that includes the *item* being measured, the *unit* of measurement, and the *value* of the unit. If we combine this definition with Werner and Souder's classification scheme, metrics can be in the form of a single measure, a ratio, an index, or an integrated measure that combines several metrics, even with different attributes, such as objective and subjective. With such a broad range of possible modes, is there a "basic" metric that allows for combinations and manipulation to create more complex metrics? Such a "building-block" metric would be amenable to transformation by combining measures of diverse phenomena, such as peer review (subjective) and count of patents (objective).

The literature provides very few clues to the existence or the definition of this basic metric.[2] There seem to be overlapping usages and even divergent definitions that conjure to serve the unique needs and objectives of those who select and compose the metric. Standardization and coherence in rules of construction of intricate metrics are yet to be achieved.

So, in the broad area of evaluation of R&D and S&T, the practice of creating and using metrics is in the form of a "menu." Evaluators avail themselves of a selection of metrics, measures, and instruments from which they pick and choose the combination that will address their objectives and their needs.

The six steps in Figure 4.1 portray a generic view of how metrics are constructed. There seem to be two critical components to this process. The first is the conceptual guidance to the creation of the metrics, shown in steps 1 and 2. Without this framework, the metrics are simply data. The second is the available pool of measures and corresponding data. Kostoff concisely discussed the problem of data collected into metrics without a guiding framework.[3] He argued that "every S&T metric, and associated data ...should have a decision focus; it should contribute to the answer of a question which in turn would be the basis of a recommendation for future action" (p. 12). Hence, when the data become more available and the means to assemble and manipulate them become more sophisticated, there is a tendency among evaluators to concentrate on the data (steps 3-5) rather than on the constructs.

Metrics and a Single Parameter

In some instances the need for a uniquely defined and fundamental metric may be partially satisfied by manipulations of a single parameter or measure. Such a manipulation may occur even in the case of a complex phenomenon. For example, the construct of "continuity of care" in medicine has been measured in the relevant literature by four metrics that rely on a single measure of distribution of patient visits with health care providers. Citro, Ghosh, and Churgin (1997) have shown that the various continuity indexes in the literature are manipulations of the measure of distribution of visits.[4] In contrast, they argued that additional boundary

Figure 4.1
Steps in the Construction of S&T Metrics

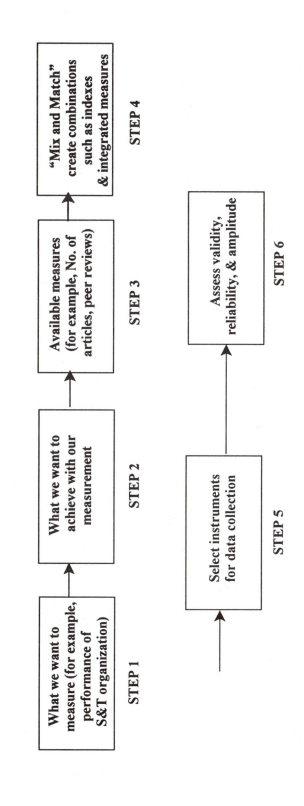

parameters should be included, such as the duration of the visits and distribution of referrals from one care provider to another.

The use of the single parameter of distribution of patient units—even when supplemented by referrals, waiting time, duration of provider-patient interaction, and referrals—creates a coherent metric. This metric purports to measure continuity of care, which in turn measures such attributes of medical care as access to care, uninterrupted care, and coordination of care among providers for the same patient. Taken together, these represent a measure of provision of medical care.

In this case such a hierarchical transition (from continuity to medical care in general) is sensible because there is an established link between provider-patient interaction and the provision of medical care. Theoretical relations are in place, so that characteristics of medical care (including quality) are conceptually influenced by provider-patient interaction and continuity of care.[5]

This is not the case, however, in the construction of metrics for S&T if we opt for a single parameter. An example would be the distribution of articles, as a measure of scientific performance. The conceptual transition in this case will be much more troublesome, regardless of the degree to which we are able to manipulate, index, and integrate the measure. The reason is that, unlike medical care which is the ultimate objective in the health care delivery system, scientific articles are but one step in the continuum of S&T. We lack not only the appropriate theory that relates them to an ultimate objective, but we also lack agreement as to what this objective is. So, although "continuity of care" is an acceptable measure of medical care, the distribution of scientific articles is a measure that is a long way from being a measure of S&T performance.[6]

Metrics and Fundamentals

Are there fundamental measures of S&T that can be used as building blocks for S&T metrics? Apparently the answer is no, since basic counts of scientific articles or patents are in themselves insufficiently descriptive of the notions that S&T metrics should provide. In the absence of such basic elements from which more intricate metrics may be constructed, the reality for measuring S&T is an opportunistic selection of metrics from an existing menu of measures.

But, even as this process encapsulates selection of measures and metrics to suit the needs and objectives of the evaluator, there are several "preferred" measures and their more complex metrics. Such preferred measures include measures of processes and outcomes.[7] This creates a reduced universe of available measures, so that their repeated use in research and practice allows for comparisons over time and among organizations. There is seldom a need to "reinvent the wheel." Perhaps the "best" metrics are not always constructed, but they are consistently utilized, thus creating a "track record" that permits the identification of strengths and weaknesses of these metrics.[8]

THE TECHNOLOGY-VALUE-PYRAMID

In a comprehensive two-year survey of members of the Industrial Research Institute (IRI), Tipping and Zeffren (1995) have suggested a menu of 33 metrics for R&D.[9] Their list of metrics is based on the Technology-Value-Pyramid (TVP) which is a hierarchy of five managerial factors: (1) value creation, (2) portfolio assessment, (3) integration of R&D with business, (4) asset value of the technology, and (5) practice of R&D processes to support innovation. The thesis underlying these factors is that they represent the link of R&D and technology to the strategic and financial position of the corporation. This is done in such a way as to allow for measurement of the means by which R&D contributes to value creation in the industrial company.

The menu of 33 metrics has been selected by the authors to correspond to the five factors in the pyramid, hence they measure the company's strategies in the longer term perspective, organizational development, and protection of the firm's core competencies. Altogether the 33 metrics are a menu from which companies may pick and choose, depending on their strategy and industry characteristics.

This extensive array of metrics includes different metrics that measure events along the entire innovation continuum. Illustrative metrics include: (1) R&D yield (gross profit contribution from sales of new and improved products), (2) R&D return (R&D yield/annual expenditures on R&D), (3) goal coverage (fraction of corporate goals that require technology development that are provided by the firm's R&D), (4) technology transfer to manufacturing, (5) use of cross-functional teams, (6) published work, (7) customer ratings, (8) peer evaluation, (9) management support, and (10) economic evaluation (price differences obtained from technology minus cost of the technology effort, multiplied by the volume of sales for these products).

Although the 33 metrics include almost all the salient metrics in the innovation literature, this comprehensive menu falls short of being the measurement core of a cohesive model of S&T contributions to the industrial company. The five managerial factors do not, in themselves, constitute a conceptual framework that links R&D to the company's business side of the house, in terms of its strategy and competitive position in the marketplace.[10] Therefore, even though some metrics offer a measure of a managerial factor, the combination of factors and metrics fails to coalesce into a coherent framework.

We are thus left with a set of factors and metrics that may exhibit some *internal* linkages, but that is insufficient to emerge beyond a pool of metrics from which we simply "pick and choose"—without a guiding conceptualization. The TVP is therefore an excellent example of an attempt to arrange a set of metrics (simple as well as complex) in a logical form, still without a strong theoretical background.

Revisiting the Definition

In light of the effort to construct sets of metrics, as illustrated above, the notion of a metric needs revisiting. First, since a metric may be composed of a single quantity, as well as a more intricate and complex set of measures (such as indexes and "macro" metrics), a definition of a metric extends beyond simply a "measure."

Second, metrics of S&T are extracted from across the entire innovation continuum. They are designed to measure a variety of activities, events, and phenomena—some simple and short-lived, others highly complex and durable along an extended time frame. Third, the absence of a unique and single building block increases the role of subjective reasons for the construction and selection of metrics.

Hence, a metric of S&T is more than a simple measure, or a quantity, or an indication of some value. A refinement of the definition of a metric in Chapter 14 extends it to include: (a) the item measured (*what* we are measuring), (b) units of measurement (*how* we measure), and (c) the inherent value associated with the metric (*why* we measure, or what we intend to achieve by this measurement). So, for instance, the metric *peer review* includes the item measured (scientific outcomes), the unit of measurement (subjective assessment), and inherent value (performance and productivity of scientists, engineers, and S&T units).

To qualify as a metric, the construct or notion must contain all three characteristics described above.[11] So, what is the difference between a metric and an indicator, and between an indicator and a measure.[12] For the purpose of the analysis of metrics of S&T, a *measure* is simply a given quantity or an item on a subjective scale or instrument. In this sense it assumes a generic form, and can be used for any purpose desired by those who conduct the measurement.

Conversely, an *indicator* is a measure earmarked for the description or representation of a given event or phenomenon. It is a measure that had been "compromised" to a given phenomenon, even though numerically it maybe equal to a generic measure. Finally, a *metric* may contain one or more indicators, but is more intricate because in addition to the indicators, it contains a notion of the slice of the phenomenon being measured. To an extent, there is a hierarchy of three levels, from measure to metrics.

MODELS OF METRIC SELECTION

Because loosely assembled sets of metrics and the pick-and-choose option are the norm in the literature and practice of S&T evaluation, the modeling of the selection of metrics is crucial to our understanding of how S&T should be assessed. A generalized model of the components of metric selection is shown in Figure 4.2.

The selection process is influenced by three sets of variables: (1) the culture in the organization (including managerial preferences and perception); (2) the available pool of metrics and the type of activity being measured; and (3) influences of others, such as customers and other stakeholders (scientific community and business or government interests).

The outcome of the selection process may be categorized into two major impacts. First are impacts on the firm or government agency or laboratory. In the industrial company the choice of metric may ultimately affect the strategy and culture of the organization. At first, the culture of the company is a factor in determining the choice of metrics. But, after the metrics is applied and experience with it is gained, the strategy and the culture may change.

Figure 4.2
A Generalized Model of Metric Selection

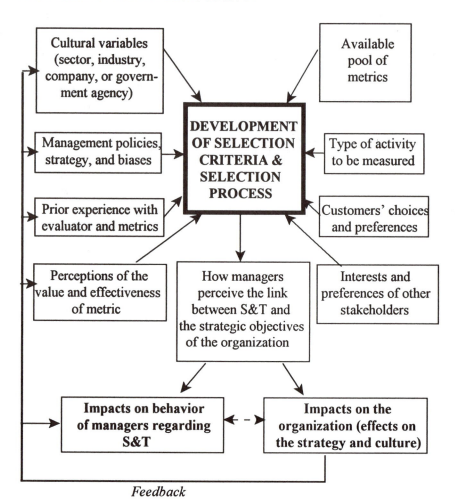

Feedback

In this respect Hauser and Katz (1998) have cited the case of Not-Invented-Here (NIH) as a cultural impediment to the selection of appropriate metrics.[13] They have also considered the example of the use of the R&D Effectiveness Index (EI) as a single or principal metric of R&D evaluation. This choice may ultimately lead to costly distortions in the firm's resource allocation process for S&T.[14]

A second possible impact is on the behavior of managers regarding S&T. Metrics that encourage certain behaviors that are risk-averse or that promote risk and offer selected rewards for certain modes of behavior may create a chain reaction in the organization. Managers may opt to abandon longer-term projects, hence suffer from the classical effects of "contamination" of the metrics, so that their behavior is now geared toward satisfying the metric rather than toward an effective discharge of their tasks in S&T.[15]

These possible impacts are mitigated by the way managers perceive the role of S&T in influencing the strategic position of their organization. The more they perceive S&T to be critical to strategic success, the more the metrics they select will tend to influence their behavior and strategic decisions.[16]

Levels of Evaluation

A different perspective of metric selection rests on the role that the level of the evaluation of S&T plays in the assessment effort. As we move up the ladder, from the individual researcher to group, project, institution, and country, different motives and objectives will dominate the selection process.

Individual researchers will opt for metrics that provide them with incentives to pursue their preferred areas of investigation, while also providing justification of the relevancy of the work and its beneficial impacts on the group and the organization. Similarly, groups or teams of researchers will prefer metrics that satisfy their goals, subject of course to cultural and managerial biases that are depicted in Figure 4.2.

As the level of evaluation becomes more complex, moving into a higher level of area thrusts, programs, and institutions, the role of culture, of other stakeholders, and prior experience increase dramatically, and may overshadow the preferences of individuals and their teams. This divergence may lead to reduction in the effectiveness of the metrics selected, making them hard to control.[17] In addition, strategic considerations and external influences tend to increase in importance. This phenomenon is akin to the notion of similarity that has been recognized by strategic and organizational researchers.[18] The growing effect of external factors may result in a higher degree of similarity in metric selection among organizations, and to a decline in the importance of individual characteristics and uniqueness of the organization.[19]

Stages in the Innovation Process

Metric selection may also be viewed within a model of research, technology, and innovation. The various stages of basic research, applied research, development, and downstream to commercialization influence the selection of metrics for assessment of S&T.

In general, certain metrics will be more appropriate in a given stage (such as exploratory research or development). This matching is discussed later in this chapter. However, the important issue is the unique situation created in each of the stages, thus amenable to adequate evaluation by means of a specific metric. For example, any metric that incorporates sales figures, as a parameter in an index or ratio, and used in the stage of exploratory research, will be wholly inadequate. Because of the conceptual and temporal distances between basic research and sales of products from R&D, such a metric fails to measure the phenomenon. Therefore, any selection of assessment metrics needs to take into account the stage of the innovation process at which the metric will be applied.[20]

Model of Evaluation Criteria

The model in Figure 4.2 identified primarily the key conditions and interested parties who tend to influence the choice of metrics. Within this model we now add the criteria, metrics, and parameters that guide the actions of these interested parties.

The criteria for evaluation are: why evaluate, source of evaluation criteria, and who benefits from the evaluation. These criteria may be incorporated into the selection processes of the parties involved. For example, managerial perceptions, preferences, and culture are all influenced by why they wish to evaluate S&T, which criteria they espouse, and what benefits they hope to derive from the evaluation.

Similarly, customers and other stakeholders also shape their selection of metrics by the criteria they had embraced for the evaluation effort. Clearly, there will be differences in why each party wishes to evaluate and what it hopes to gain from this effort, thus yielding differences in sets of metrics selected.

For example, customer-selected metrics would differ from those selected by unit managers, even though they are chosen to assess the same phenomenon at the same level of analysis and stage of the process.

Customers have different goals and motivation, and a distinct perspective of what the organization can and should do with their S&T effort.[21]

Social and Technological Attributes

Finally, the model of metric selection may be refined by adding the embedded social and technology attributes.[22] If the *technology* is the focus of evaluation, then the metrics to be selected would be influenced by such social attributes embedded in the technology as safety, health, and cost. For example, selection of metrics designed to measure the effect of a given technology on new products would be mitigated by the need to include the parameters of safety, health, and cost. Is the technology contributing to safety or health hazards that are built into the new product?

Similar arguments can be made for the technology attributes embedded in the technology and hence in the new product or process. For example, is the new product more efficient and with improved functionality to the extent that it becomes far superior to existing products, and if so, are these attributes reflected in the evaluation metrics of the S&T that generated the technology?

Consequently, in this model of metric selection the attributes embedded in the technology are added as key parameters to the factors in the generalized model in Figure 4.2. There is also a strong influence of the embedded attributes on the way managers and scientists perceive the link between S&T and the commercial side of the organization. For example, in cases where the technology that emerges from the S&T function in a company has far-reaching attributes (such as strong safety and health implications), this situation will help to reinforce the perception that S&T has considerable impacts on the strategic and commercial areas of the company.[23]

Summary

The picture that emerges from the discussion of the different models of metric selection is abundantly clear that this is a complex phenomenon, influenced by a variety of factors, processes, and actors. However one chooses to explore the selection phenomenon, it is conceivable that for each attempt there will be a different set of metrics that will thus be selected. None of the perspectives discussed above is superior to the other. Each perspective represents a different outlook that incorporates a specific core of factors. Thus, the metric selection process depends on the model embraced by the evaluators, hence on their preferred set of metrics they will pick from the available pool.

POOL OF METRICS

Based on the review of the relevant literature, there emerges a comprehensive set or pool of metrics for science and technology. These metrics are generic, as they will be applicable to different stages and dimensions of the innovation process. The key metrics are shown in Figure 4.3, classified by eight major categories.

Figure 4.3
Pool of Available Metrics

Each category contains illustrative measures. The lists are not exhaustive, nor a complete listing of all measures found in the relevant literatures. Measures are listed not necessarily in order of importance nor any other ranking or ordering criteria.

A.   INPUT/INVESTMENTS IN S&T

- Expenditures for each stage of R&D/I.
- Expenditures per time-frame, for one time period or over several time periods.
- Distribution by categories of expenditures: personnel, equipment, etc.
- Source of funding (business unit or central lab in the industrial company).
- Comparison of expenditures, per item category: by competitors, industry averages, and sector averages.
- Expenditures by discipline, technology, and scientist & engineer.
- Expenditures related to a product line or other commercial unit of reference (such as customer or market).

B.   ECONOMIC/FINANCIAL METRICS

- Cost savings (including ratio of savings in cost of goods sold).
- Return on investment.
- Return on assets.
- Payback of investment.
- Economic measures (such as price differential per unit quality characteristics that can be attributed to science and technology, computed

as differential minus cost per unit to which quality characteristics are attributable multiplied by sales volume of this given unit).
- "Dollarization": Profit/Cost of R&D employees.

C.   COMMERCIAL AND BUSINESS METRICS[24]

- New sales ratio (sales revenue from products and product or process enhancements that can be attributed to commercialization of S&T outcomes in a given year).
- Projected sales and income (from S&T projects in progress or in the innovation pipeline, by project or by categories of products and processes).
- Profit ratio (profits as percentage of sales that can be attributed to S&T outcomes that had been commercialized and integrated into new and existing products and processes that had generated the profits).
- Market share ratio (relative market share per product category or unit that can be appropriated to the contribution of S&T outcomes to product sales that have generated the market share).
- Customer satisfaction (overall ratings of the company and its products, and specific ratings of the competitive features of products or services that can be attributed to S&T outcomes incorporated in them. This measure may also be in the form of ratios of expenditures for S&T, and specific S&T outcomes, such as patents).
- Interactions with customers (*internal* contacts of scientists and engineers with their corporate customers, such as marketing and production, and *external* contacts by these S&Es with the corporate customers, such as S&Es of the client organization, as well as managers—technical and commercial—of the client organization).
- Regulatory compliance (contribution of the outcomes of S&T to the compliance of products and services with regulations, that can be attributed to the outcomes from S&T that are incorporated into products and services—including issues of safety, health, and ethics).
- Quality and reliability (contributions of the outcomes of S&T to the level of quality and reliability of the products and services sold by the organization that are considered acceptable by customers and regulators).
- Time-to-market (response time) differential to match or to surpass competitors' new products and processes. (This measures the improvement [reduction] in the time needed by the organization to introduce new products or services, as competitive weapons, that can be attributed to S&T outcomes. This measure can also be in the form of ratios of the reduction in time-to-market, for the cost and investments in S&T, or per specific S&T outcomes.)

- Proprietary sales and revenues ratio (the portion of sales of products and services, as well as revenues from licenses and similar income categories that are protected by patents and other instruments of trade secrets, that can be attributed to those patents that offer specific protection of product characteristics that provide exclusive features for the organization over its competitors).

D.   BIBLIOMETRIC METRICS[25]

- Publications (includes scientific papers, technical reports, articles in scientific journals, book chapters, and proceedings of conferences and symposia). (These measures can only be in the form of ratios to the investments in S&T that have generated these measures, or selected expenditures by category of type of industry and academic discipline—all in a given time period.)[26]
- Citation analysis (includes counts of citations of scientific and technical articles, as one measure of impacts on scientific community and quality of the scientific effort that has generated the publications cited). (This increase may also be in the form of ratios to investments in S&T, or by academic discipline and type of industry or sector in which the scientific effort has been conducted.)[27]
- Co-word Analysis and Database Tomography (DT). (These are measures of analyses performed on large databases of S&T bibliographical outcomes, in a form of data mining. DT, for example, provides a roadmap to topical areas found in relevant literatures. Key word analysis also assist in obtaining a measure of topical coherence, as well as topical lineage, which offers a measure of thematic history, thus helping in identifying the path of development of a field of S&T and a specific thematic area. Such measure is also helpful in a more accurate attribution of the origins and path of evolution of scientific breakthroughs, for both individuals and organizations.)[28]
- Special presentations and honors (including keynote presentations of scientific conferences and symposia and other *ad hoc* contributions to the literature).

E.   PATENTS

- Count of patents (produced by S&T unit and per S&E in the unit and in the organization). (This measure may also be in the form of ratio of number of patents in a given time frame per expenditures for S&T—namely, a measure of the cost per patent by type of industry so as to account for different patenting practices.)

- Relevant or current patents (the percent of patents that are current and provide the organization with competitive proprietary advantages; also in the form of ratio of these current patents per the total number of patents produced over a time period classified by industry, to account for different patenting practices).
- Comparative patent standards (ratios of the unit and organization pool of relevant and useful patents, per the benchmarks in the industry, for the key technological areas in which the organization is competing).
- Cost of patents (considering the time lag from the application of investments in S&T, to the point of registering a patent, this is a measure of the cost of a patent; also to be considered are the issues invoked by identifying the link between investments and the patents that emerge, and differences in quality and competitive impacts of the various patents).[29]

F.   PEER REVIEW METRICS

- Internal evaluation (subjective rating of the S&T unit, its activities and its outcomes, by other people and units in the organization, such as marketing and production). (This type of measure may be in the form of written evaluations and some ranking scale on an instrument that measures judgment of respondents, *ad hoc* or in a periodical manner.)
- External evaluation (subjective evaluation of the S&T unit, its activities, its outcomes, and its *overall* quality—by a panel of experts). (This measure may be in the form of an invited effort requested by the S&T unit or its organization or external S&T experts, consultants, and other knowledgeable people in the community, or in the form of routine evaluation, as part of an on-going assessment of S&T.)
- Targeted reviews (including specific panel evaluations of any outcome from S&T, such as a specific scientific paper, project, or program; also includes specific judgmental assessment of a product, a patent, and individual scientist and engineer). (This measure may be considered a measure of quality, as viewed by expert reviewers.)[30]

G.   ORGANIZATIONAL, STRATEGIC, AND MANAGERIAL METRICS[31]

- Project management: internal/cycle time. (This is a measure of the period between starting a given S&T project to the point of transforming an outcome to the downstream unit within the organization. It may serve as a measure of internal efficiency in the company.)
- Project management: external or commercial cycle time (includes a measure of the time period between the starting of the S&T project, until the ultimate sale of a product or service to an external customer).

- Existence of project champion (includes a measure of the number or portion of current S&T projects which have an identifiable "champion" in the form of a manager from *outside* the S&T/R&D unit).
- Projects with interfunctional teams. (Includes measures of the number of projects that employ teams composed of people from units across the organization and outside the S&T/R&D unit. Such "hybrid" teams may, for example, have representatives from marketing, production, and finance. Another measure here may be the point in the project lifetime in which such teams are formed. It is widely assumed that the earlier such a team is established, the greater the probability of the *commercial* success of the project.)[32]
- Evaluation of the scientific and technical capabilities of the S&T unit (and by extension of the total organization). (This is a measure of external evaluation primarily by the various customers of how the firm and its S&T unit are capable of meeting the scientific and technological challenges of their changing markets. The measure may also be used to evaluate publicly funded laboratories and agencies, such as NASA, CDC, EDA, and even academic institutions.)
- Project progress and success (includes measures of the progress of S&T projects in terms of the objectives and milestones that were established, over a given period of time; also includes measures of the number or percent of projects that exhibited *technical* success and have done so on-time and on-budget).[33]
- Evaluation of projects and programs. (This is a financial measure of the degree to which S&T projects and clusters of projects-programs have had technical *and* commercial success. Measures include the cost per *technically* successful projects, and cost of *commercially* successful projects. Differences between these measures usually indicate problems in the downstream flow of S&T outcomes. Another type of measure includes averages of cost per project, by type of project. Similar measures may be applied to programs and to the entire S&T portfolio of projects and programs.)
- Ownership, support, and funding of projects and programs. (These measures include percent of projects supported and funded by other units in the organization and that are directly related to a product line or similar commercial entity in the organization. These measures also provide the distribution of projects and programs by source of organization. They may indicate over- or underreliance or relation to given units and functions that support S&T.)
- Human relations measures of S&T personnel (including such measures as morale of S&T personnel and satisfaction with their work).

- Relation of S&T to strategic objectives. (These are measures of the degree to which S&T objectives are related to the strategic objectives of the organization, and are current with any changes in the organization's strategy. Differences or discrepancies between the two sets of objectives may lead to problems in S&T performance and its relevance to where the organization is heading.)[34]
- Benchmarking project and program performance. (These are measures that relate financial, economic, and project management metrics to benchmarks that are standards or averages in the industry, as well as benchmarks that are established in view of the performance of the "best practices" in the industry and sector. Additional measures in this set are the extent to which these benchmarks influence the strategic direction of both S&T and the total organization.)

H. STAGES OF OUTCOMES[35]

- Immediate outputs (includes measures of the proximal or direct outputs from the S&T/R&D activity, such as bibliometric measures).
- Intermediate outputs (includes outputs of the organizations and entities that have received the immediate outputs, transformed them, and are providing the transformed outputs to other entities in society and the economy).
- Pre-ultimate outputs (includes measures of the products and services that are generated by those social and economic entities that had received and transformed the intermediate outputs).
- Ultimate outputs (measures of the things of value to the economy and society that were impacted by the pre-ultimate outputs).
- Index of leading indicators (manipulation of *core* and *organization-specific* measures, in a weighted procedure). (For each stage of outputs—immediate to ultimate—the index of leading indicators is constructed. The index offers a quantitative appraisal of the value of S&T at each of the stages of its flow downstream the innovation process.)[36]
- Value indices for leading indicators (includes measures of the value of each index, at each stage in the flow downstream of the innovation continuum). (Value indices are computed by subtracting the value of each leading index from the index that succeeded it. For example, the value index for an organization in the pre-ultimate stage minus the value in the intermediate stage would measure the added value to the continuum from S&T.[37] Net value is computed by comparison with costs of S&T and transformation at each stage.)
- Portion of S&T at each stage. (These are measures of the role that S&T has in each of the stages, for each of the recipient/transforming

organization. The outputs from these organizations—products, services, processes, methods, etc.—are possible, in part, because of S&T absorbed and adopted by the organization. These measures offer a look at the size and value of the S&T contribution, for each output, as well as *in toto*.)

Organizations in private and public sectors employ various combinations of these metrics, with a variety of measures, quantitative as well as qualitative. Individual metrics are further discussed in Chapters 5-12.

CRITERIA FOR SELECTION

What is a good metric and what are the criteria that guide our selection of the "right" or "appropriate" metric for the evaluation of science and technology? These are important questions, in view of the fact that there is a pool of different metrics and measures available for use.[38]

Ronald Kostoff (1998), for example, suggested ten principles of R&D evaluation that is based on metrics.[39] In addition to such principles as senior management commitment and competency of the technical evaluator, Kostoff also included the relevance of the metric selected to future action by the evaluators; and the integration or connectivity of the metrics selected to the operations, processes, and strategy of the organization. This latter criterion is crucial to the consequent use of the metrics-based evaluation by the organization's decision-makers.

Kostoff also proposed that the cost of using certain metrics should be a criterion in their selection. Finally, he listed availability and quality of the data, complementarity of other metrics, and accuracy and quality of the metrics. Thus, his criteria include the predominant factors found in the literature.

Span, Adams, and Souder (1995) have suggested linking the choice of metrics in federally funded S&T to the role of participants as sponsors, developers, or adopters.[40] In the evaluation of the Energy-Related Inventions Program (ERIP) sponsored by the U.S. government, Marilyn Brown identified four issues, which may also be viewed as criteria for metric selection: (1) need to track progress over long periods, (2) how to account for spin-off technologies, (3) validity of evaluation, and (4) the overwhelming bias of a very small number of successes.[41]

Similarly, in the health care area, Gill and Feinstein (1994) have criticized the measurement of quality of life in the medical literature.[42] They have argued that most measurements were directed at the wrong concept, hence the need to develop criteria aimed at the investigators and how they defined quality of life, as well as at the instrument these investigators used. Thus, they concluded, metrics of quality of life should depend on who is measuring and how the data are collected.

To a large extent many criteria found in the relevant literature refer to the evaluation and its components, then specifically to selection of metrics. Yet these same criteria may also be applied to selection and usage of metrics. For example, the need to track the progress of projects over long periods of time may also be a criterion for selecting the metrics for this evaluation effort. We would select those metrics that allow for measurements across different stages of the project's time line, at the expense of metrics that are restricted to measuring only one phase in the project's life. Another criterion that emerges from this issue is the selection of metrics that, although different, would nevertheless be comparable and allow for integration and convergence across the various stages of the project's life.

A more comprehensive attempt to classify such criteria consists of three categories: methodological, ontological, and managerial and organizational. Underlying these categories are the following objectives in selecting metrics for S&T. First, the metrics selected should be able to do the job. Second, they should be available, accessible, and affordable. Third, they should allow for manipulation, analysis, interpretation, and comparison with other metrics. Hence, we now have the necessary background to create a set of criteria, as shown in Figure 4.4.

Do The Job!

Metrics selected should be able to measure what the evaluators wish to be measured. They should be intimately linked to the objectives and motives of the evaluators. Simply measuring specific attributes of S&T is not an effective way of assessment, unless the measures indeed describe relevant aspects of the phenomenon and are useful to managers. If this criterion is not met, the metrics become a set of irrelevant and useless quantities.

The criterion and the forthcoming additional criteria are similar to the criteria used in selecting indicators and to those of the Japanese government in selecting its science indicators.[43] In the final analysis, the indicators and metrics in general are the actual means we utilize to assess the S&T phenomena.

Figure 4.4
Criteria for Selecting Metrics for Science and Technology

CATEGORY	CRITERIA
Methodology (criteria related to measurement and analysis of metrics: What they should do and how)	• Quality of underlying data. • Provide data that allow for meaningful analysis and interpretation. • Allow for standardization, generalizability, or normalization across fields and disciplines. • Comprehensiveness of set to measure a substantial portion of phenomenon. • Relative ease of data collection, manipulation, and interpretation.
Ontology (criteria related to the construction of metrics: What they should be like)	• Comprehensiveness, covering critical aspects of the phenomenon. • Integration and convergence with other related metrics. • Validity: measures what it purports to measure. • Includes measures of different aspects of the phenomenon.
Organization and Management (criteria related to the use of metrics by managers and organizations: What they should accomplish)	• Relevance to organizational and managerial objectives. • Relevance to potential action by managers/decision-makers. • Credibility of metrics. • Capability of evaluation to deal with the metrics, to gather and to analyze them. • Cost and cost-effectiveness. • Relation and relevance to other metrics used in different evaluations.

This list is illustrative and not an exhaustive list of all criteria. Criteria are not in any order of importance or relevancy.

Availability, Accessibility, and Affordability

This second objective in selecting metrics for S&T is similar to the attributes of instruments described in Figure 3.3 and the issues regarding science indicators in Figure 3.6. It simply calls for the data used by these metrics to be available, accessible, and affordable. If these factors are not satisfied, the quality of the data will suffer, and in certain instances the metric will be useless since it will not contain the necessary and adequate data items.

When desired data are not available, are inaccessible, or too costly, the tendency is to explore alternatives, some of which may be in the form of surrogate data items, which in many cases are inadequate or even misleading. The urge to measure and to apply metrics to the evaluation is usually strong enough as to accept compromises that are harmful to a thorough assessment of S&T.

Manipulation and Interpretation

Finally, the S&T metrics should allow for manipulation of the data thus collected, for adequate interpretation, and for comparison with other metrics. Being able to statistically manipulate data in these metrics is not enough, unless the statistical analyses can also provide an interpretation of what these metrics mean for the assessment of S&T. For example, the number of patents generated by an industrial sector and its manipulations (by cost, employees, assets, or over time) is meaningless unless we also understand the process of patenting in the firm. Thus, by simply arriving at some numbers about patents, we lack the ability to interpret them, unless we also possess additional knowledge into which this metric can be integrated, hence interpreted.

BENEFITS FROM APPROPRIATE SELECTION

An appropriate or "right" selection of metrics will generate certain benefits to the evaluator and to management. These benefits are related to whoever defines the metrics and applies them in the assessment of S&T. Appropriate metrics allow for a meaningful measurement and evaluation of the phenomenon. For example, bibliometric measures of an R&D unit in the company may be an adequate metric for the scientists and engineers within the unit, but provide little, if any, input into the evaluation of the R&D unit by senior management. To the senior executives, the selection of metrics that tie the R&D with their own objectives and view of the world are much more desirable. To the senior executives, the selection As with any evaluation, it is therefore preferable—from both sides: evaluator and its target for assessment—to have metrics that are meaningful, and that may justify the activity or the unit's performance and mere existence.

In the case of S&T, there may be a need for two types of metrics: one that measures the activity or the outputs from the perspective of the activity and its operators, and another type of metrics that appeals to external entities. Therefore, the adjectives "appropriate" and "right" apply to the metric from the viewpoint of its ultimate user. By the same token, the benefits from a given type of metric are to be identified with the ultimate user, hence recipient of the benefits.

Another illustration in this regard is the case of the U.S. federal laboratories and their use of counts of CRADAs (Cooperative Research and Development Agreements), which are measures of a very small portion of technology transfer from these laboratories to industry. Yet this metric allows the laboratories and their parent agencies a measure of flexibility in depicting their performance and in meeting some legal obligations.

State S&T programs have been evaluated with a mix of metrics that include number of projects funded, jobs created, patents, spin-off firms, and publications. The variety of metrics provides a workable cushion for the different demands and perspectives of the many constituents in state-supported S&T.[44] Thus, each stakeholder may identify with a given metric, and extract its own benefits from its "metric of choice."

Benefits to the user are relative to the metric used, as well as to the objectives and the expectations of the user. There are no absolutely "right" or "wrong" metrics, but a need to match potential metrics with the ultimate user of these metrics and the evaluation they serve. When such a match occurs, the benefits that a user may derive from even one metric may be enough to cover "the price of admission" and to satisfy the ultimate user. A pedantic researcher may not be satisfied with such a single metric, but users are generally more willing to accept a metric of S&T that is in line with what they wish to measure, and with their strategy and perspective of S&T.

SUMMARY

Is there a "true" match between metrics and aspects or stages of the S&T phenomenon? Is there a process of metric selection that could assure an appropriate choice of metrics for given requirements of S&T evaluation? In this chapter I listed potential metrics and discussed the issues related to their selection. Perhaps, in view of the above, the answers to these two questions may be marvelously obfuscated by the academic practice of "maybe" and constraints such as insufficient research findings and the complexity of the phenomenon that defies a clear and unambiguous reply.

But the reality is that we have a pool of potential metrics that could be applicable to a variety of aspects and dimensions of S&T, and we also have a variety of stakeholders, each attracted to a different metric or combination thereof. The effort to match these two in an adequate and effective mode is rarely totally successful. By and large, this effort is successful some of the time, for some of the stakeholders. When criteria for selection are restrictive, the outcome is a weak match, biased toward a few opportunistic rather than appropriate metrics. When criteria for selection are liberal, the outcome is a weak match, biased toward a barrage of metrics, offered in a "mix-and-match" trial of multiple measures—with little connection to the evaluation effort or to other managerial concerns.

So the answer seems to be embedded in the *systemic* approach to selection criteria. Metrics that are candidates for selection should be assessed in terms of their relation to the set of stakeholders of the S&T activity, and to their potential interaction with other metrics in other evaluations conducted by the stakeholders.

S&T evaluation and its measurement is therefore not an isolated effort. As I repeatedly assert in this book, S&T is evaluated and measured as an integral component of a larger system of social and economic entities, with all their objectives, interests, biases, and accomplishments. Hence, S&T metrics are selected within these parameters, and their relation to the larger system within which S&T exist also provides the rationale for the criteria used in their selection.[45]

NOTES

1. Werner, B., and W. Souder, "Measuring R&D Performance: State of the Art," *Research-Technology Management*, 40(2), 1997, 34-42.

2. See, for example, Geisler, E., "Key Output Indicators in Performance Evaluation of Research and Development Organizations," *Technological Forecasting and Social Change*, 47(2), 1994, 189-204. Also see Schainblatt, A., "How Companies Measure the Productivity of Engineers and Scientists," *Research Management*, 25(3), 1982, 10-18; and Cordero, R., "The Measurement of Indicators in Performance Evaluation of the Firm: An Overview," *Research Policy*, 19(2), 1990, 185-192.

3. Kostoff, R., "Metrics for Strategic Planning and S&T Evaluation," *R&D Enterprise—Asia Pacific*, 1(2-3), 1998, 30-33. Also see this author's other publications on this topic at his website: <http://www.dtic.mil/dtic/kostoff/index.html>.

4. Citro, R., S. Ghosh, and P. Churgin, "A Fundamental Metric for Continuity of Care: Modeling and Performance Evaluation," *IEEE Transactions on Information Technology in Biomedicine*, 1(3), 1997, 189-204.

5. See, for example, Eriksson, E., "Continuity-of-Care Measures," *Medical Care*, 28(2), 1990, 180-190.

6. For example, Pierce, S., "On the Origin and Meaning of Bibliometric Indicators: Journals in the Social Sciences, 1886-1985," *Journal of the American Society for Information Science*, 43(7), 1992, 477-488. The author concluded that there is a correlation between presentational standards and cognitive consensus in papers produced in core journals of the social sciences.

7. For example, see Luce, D., D. Kranz, P. Suppes, and A. Tversky, *Foundations of Measurement: Representation, Axiomatization, and Invariance* (New York: Academic Press, 1990). In this comprehensive review, the authors discuss measurement in psychology and the relative implications from selection of different measures and instruments. Their arguments in this regard are similar to those I have discussed in this chapter.

8. An example of this issue may be the metrics of software complexity. Although relatively less intricate than the process and outcomes of S&T, software complexity may be addressed from several perspectives, hence the choices of different metrics. See, for example, Gonzalez, R., "A Unified Metric of Software Complexity: Measuring Productivity, Quality, and Value," *The Journal of Systems and Software*, 29(1), 1995, 17-38.

9. Tipping, J., and E. Zeffren, "Assessing the Value of Your Technology," *Research-Technology Management*, 38(5), 1995, 22-40.

10. See, for example, Welch, L., and W. Farr, "Challenges in Metrics and Measurement for Computer-Based Systems," *Computer*, 30(1), 1997, 88-91. Also see a discussion of limitations of these metrics developed by the IRI in Jacobs, M., "Measure for R&D Measure," *Chemical & Engineering News*, 75(39), September 29, 1997, 3-5; and Chidamber, S., and D. Darcy, "Managerial Use of Metrics for Object-Oriented Software: An Exploratory Analysis," *IEEE Transactions on Software Engineering*, 24(8), 1998, 629-640. In addition, there are other issues with this set of metrics, particularly methodological and statistical, such as orthogonality, duplication, and overlapping.

11. In an early discussion of measuring conceptual constructs, anthropologists have attempted to explain the move from simple measures of distance, to more complex and refined measures of conceptual notions and ideas. See Hough, W., "The Origin and Development of Metrics," *American Anthropologist*, 35(4), 1933, 443-450.

12. Metrics are therefore slated for evaluation purposes, whereas indicators merely represent a slice of a phenomenon without necessarily having *a priori* assignment in the process of assessment of the phenomenon. See, for example, the design and deployment of metrics in ergonomics where different indicators of a metric yield distinct results. Liu, Y., and C. Wickens, "Mental Workload and Cognitive Task Automaticity: An Evaluation of Subjective and Time Evaluation Metrics," *Ergonomics*, 37(11), 1994, 1843-1854. The authors refer to the indicators by the term "metrics."

13. Hauser, J., and G. Katz, "Metrics: You Are What You Measure!" *European Management Journal*, 16(5), 1998, 517-528.

14. *Ibid.*, pp. 518-519.

15. See, for example, Miller, R., "The Influence of Primary Task on R&D Laboratory Evaluation," *R&D Management*, 22(1), 1992, 3-21. Also see Havemann, F., "Changing Publication Behavior of East and Central European Scientists and the Impact of Their Papers," *Information Processing & Management*, 32(4), 1996, 489-497. In this article the author has concluded that with the lifting of political and administration constraints, East European scientists have redirected their efforts toward projects based on curiosity rather than applications. Hence, their influence in their respective disciplines is starting to rise.

16. See, for example, Mitchell, G., and W. Hamilton, "Managing R&D as a Strategic Option," *Research-Technology Management*, 31(3), 1988, 15-22. Also see McGrath, M., and M. Romeri, "The R&D Effectiveness Index: A Metric for Product Development Performance," *Journal of Product Innovation Management*, 11(2), 1994, 213-220.

17. See Hauser and Katz, 1998, *op. cit.*, p. 519.

18. See, for example, Harrison, J., M. Hitt, E. Hoskisson, and R. Ireland, "Synergies and Post-Acquisition Performance: Differences vs. Similarities in Resource Allocation," *Journal of Management*, 17(1), 1991, 173-190. Also see Ilinitch, A., "Institutional Similarity: A New Theoretical and Empirical Approach to the Related Diversification and Performance Puzzle," unpublished doctoral dissertation, University of North Carolina, Chapel Hill, 1991.

19. See, for example, the Georgia Tech project on the mapping of research. Among their publications, see, Bozeman, B., J. Rogers, D. Roessner, H. Klein, and J. Park, *The R&D Value Mapping Project: Final Report*, Report to the Department of Energy, Office of Basic Energy Sciences, Atlanta, Georgia Institute of Technology, 1998.

20. See, for example, Chung, K., H. Pak, and R. Cox, "Patterns of Research Output in the Accounting Literature: A Study of the Bibliometric Distributions," *Abacus*, 28(2), 1992, 168-185. Also see Seltzeh, M., K. Frank, and A. Bryk, "The Metric Matters: The Sensitivity of Conclusions About Growth in Student Achievement to Choice of Metric," *Educational Evaluation & Policy Analysis*, 16(1), 1994, 41-49; and Ritchie, P., and Rowcroft, J., "Choice of Metric in the

Measurement of Relative Productive Efficiency," *International Journal of Production Economics*, 46(4), 1996, 433-439.

21. See, for example, Morgan, M., "Measuring Performance with Customer-Defined Metrics," *Quality Progress*, 29(12), 1996, 31-35. Also see the insightful paper by Spann, M., M. Adams, and W. Souder, "Measures of Technology Transfer Effectiveness: Key Dimensions and Differences in Their Use by Sponsors, Developers, and Adopters," *IEEE Transactions on Engineering Management*, 42(1), 1995, 19-29. The authors employ a version of the classification scheme of Myers and Marquis of how organizations deal with innovation.

22. See, for example, Callons, M., "Is Science a Public Good?" *Science, Technology, and Human Values*, 19(4), 1994, 395-424.

23. For example, see Brown, M., "Performance Metrics for a Technology Commercialization Program," *International Journal of Technology Management*, 13(3), 1997, 229-248. Also see Freeman, S., "Infrastructure: The Key to Capturing Technology's Benefits," *Journal of Business Strategy*, 15(1), 1994, 56-61.

24. This category of metrics includes the many combinations of ratios and manipulations of economic and financial measures—with *commercial* measures of the business performance of the organization.

25. This category includes measures of the outcomes from scientific activity that takes the form of written technical reports, scientific papers, citations, co-word analyses, and other types of bibliographic outcomes.

26. This measure will be further discussed in detail in Chapter 7.

27. This measure will be further discussed in Chapter 8.

28. These measures are further discussed in Chapter 9. See the seminal work in this area by Ronald Kostoff in his website: <http://www.dtic.mil/dtic/kostoff/index.html>.

29. This measure is further elaborated in Chapter 10, including a review of the extensive literature on this measure, its advantages, and its shortcomings.

30 Chapter 11 includes a more comprehensive discussion of peer-review metrics.

31. This category includes metrics relating to project and program management, performance of the S&T unit and processes, and strategic variables that guide the S&T and the business aspects of the organization. Although these are different subcategories, they are assembled here under one rubric because they all belong to a set of metrics that measure phenomena that are under management control and subject to managerial decision making. A detailed discussion is provided in Chapter 12.

32. See, for example, Spain, D., "To Improve Quality in R&D, Improve the Team Work Processes," *Research-Technology Management*, 39(4), 1996, 42-47. Also see Wolff, M., "Teams Speed Commercialization of R&D Projects," *Research-Technology Management*, 31(5), 1988, 8-10.

33. See, for example, Graves, S., "Why Costs Increase When Projects Accelerate?" *Research-Technology Management*, 32(2), 1989, 16-18. Also see Crane, A.,and S. Ginsburg, "Evaluation in the Health Resources and Services Administration: Improving Program Performance," *Evaluation & The Health Professions*, 19(3), 1996, 325-341.

34. See, for example, Chester, A., "Aligning Technology with Business Strategy," *Research-Technology Management*, 37(1), 1994, 25-32. Also see Coleman, K., M. Perel, and J. Piniella, "Making Growth Strategies Work: The Changing Role of R&D and New Ventures," *Research Management*, 27(4), 1984, 21-25.

35. This category of metrics includes measures of the flow of S&T outputs through the innovation continuum, by moving across the various social and economic entities that adopt and transform them, toward the ultimate outputs in the form of ultimate societal and economic goals.

36. See, Geisler, E., "Key Output Indicators in Performance Evaluation of Research and Development Organizations," *Technology Forecasting and Social Change*, 47(1), 1994, 189-204.

37. This procedure is similar to the computation of the value added tax at each of the stages of product manufacturing and sale.

38. In a related topic, see, for example, Griffin, A., and A. Page, "PDMA Success Measurement Project: Recommended Measures for Product Development Success and Failure," *The Journal of Product Innovation Management*, 13(6), 1996, 478-496. The authors have concluded that "most appropriate measures of project-level and program-level success depend on the firm's project strategy and business strategy, respectively."

39. Kostoff, 1998, *op. cit.*

40. Span, Adams, and Souder, 1995, *op. cit.*

41. Brown, 1997, *op. cit.*

42. Gill, T., and A. Feinstein, "A Central Appraisal of the Quality of Quality-of-Life Measurement," *Journal of the American Medical Association*, 272(8), 1994, 619-625.

43. See Figure 3.5 and the discussion of Japan's science indicators.

44. Melkers, J., and S. Cozzens, "A Review of Performance Measurement in State Science and Technology-Based Economic Development Programs," *Proceedings of the Technology Transfer Metrics Summit*, Santa Fe, NM, April 28-May 2, 1996, pp. 109-117.

45. See, for example, Kitchenham, B., *Software Metrics: Measurement for Software Process Improvement* (London: Blackwell, 1996). In her book Barbara Kitchenham discusses software metrics and their use in the evaluation of the process that generates software. She links the metrics to the objectives of software processes, and to the type and quality of data to be used in these metrics. Also see Johnson, J., "Things We Can Measure Through Technology That We Could Not

Measure Before," in R. Ekstrom (Ed.), *Measurement, Technology, and Individuals in Education: New Directions for Testing and Measurement* (San Francisco: Jossey-Bass, 1983) 13-18. Also see Mansfield, E., "Social Returns from R&D: Findings, Methods, and Limitations," *Research Management*, 34(6), 1991, 24-27.

5

INPUTS TO
SCIENCE AND TECHNOLOGY

Inputs to science and technology are perhaps the most utilized, manipulated, and analyzed data sets in the evaluation of science, technology, and innovation. There are three reasons for this wide utilization. First, these are tangible quantities that describe, with relative precision, the financial inputs to the process. Such financial resources (expenditures or investments) can also be allocated, again with relative precision, to the various components of the process. Hence, expenditures for research, development, engineering, testing, and product development can be determined, throughout the innovation continuum.[1]

Second, as tangible quantities expressed in financial terms, these input data are easily manipulable. They lend themselves to such computations as nominal or constant figures (deflated to account for inflation), or in the creation of standards, benchmarks, trends, and complex indexes.

The third reason is the ability of analyzers to benefit from the previous two reasons and to *interpret* the inputs and their manipulations in comparative studies across organizations and even countries. Moreover, they are also able to compare these data with financial and other quantitative data from related phenomena such as sales, profits, and growth.[2]

A fundamental premise underlying the importance and ample use of input data is the accepted practice that these expenditures are surrogate indicators of S&T (and R&D). These data are believed to offer a relatively accurate indication of how powerful or potentially consequential S&T may be, so that trends in financial resources to these activities may be viewed as means to assess their potential and their impacts.

In the biennial publication *Science & Engineering Indicators*, the U.S. National Science Board devotes a significant portion of the effort in data collection and analysis to inputs, expenditures, and their trends. One such publication had the following comment:

The United States spent an estimated $161 billion on research and development (R&D) activity in 1993. This investment in the discovery of new knowledge—and in the application of knowledge to the development of new and improved products, processes, and services—was equivalent to 2.6 per cent of the total U.S. domestic products (GDP). The absolute magnitude of the effort and the manifold tasks to which it is directed *are indicative of the critical role that R&D plays in addressing such concerns* as national defense, industrial competitiveness, public health, environmental quality, and social well being. Indeed, *the long term importance of R&D expenditures to technological preeminence, military security, and knowledge growth is axiomatic.*[3] (Italics added.)

These sentences clearly establish the assumed connection between levels and trends of R&D expenditures—and economic and social impacts and ramifications—at both industrial and national frameworks. However, two hidden assumptions are embedded in this link. First, it is assumed by compilers and analysts of these input data that there are certain basic or minimum levels for funding S&T, so that meaningful impacts can be achieved. Not only does this assumption allow for comparison over longer periods of time among institutions and countries, but also for establishing workable benchmarks such as those in the *Frascati Manual.*[4]

The second assumption considers the link between expenditures and social-economic outcomes to be strong enough and valid enough to allow for covariation methods of assessment. Hence, variations in levels and trends of inputs to S&T are a sufficient measure to account for variations in social-economic outcomes. For example, sharp increases in funding of specific S&T (e.g., aeronautics or environmental S&T) will be a sufficient indicator to predict and later assess benefits to these areas.[5]

INPUTS/EXPENDITURES AS METRIC

One of the key aspects of S&T inputs as a metric in the evaluation of S&T is the manipulation of input data to form complex indices such as

"R&D intensity." These indices are designed to measure the degree to which an organization, industry, or a country invest in R&D and S&T—per selected economic quantity (such as sales, or gross national product).[6]

R&D Intensity

This index measures the commitment of resources for R&D as a ratio of investments in R&D to the gross national product (for a country) and to sales (for an industrial company). In the case of countries, international comparisons are possible. In 1993, for example, the U.S. R&D intensity was 2.6%, whereas Japan's figure was 3.0% and the United Kingdom was 2.1%.[7] Generally, scholars agree that a developed country with a strong manufacturing base should have a ratio of R&D intensity above 2%.

In the case of industry, R&D intensity measures the degree to which selected industries invest in R&D. This index is also used to indicate the "high tech" states of selected industries, and presumably also their technological competitiveness. For example, the OECD routinely assesses the R&D intensities of industries according to their standard industrial classification. The intensity measure is computed as R&D spending or percentage of production. In 1986, for example, the aerospace industry had an intensity of 22.7, followed by office and computing equipment (17.5), and communications equipment (10.4).[8]

Individual companies may also arrive at such measures of intensity and compare their performance over long periods of time. American companies in the electronics sector, such as Hewlett-Packard, have consistently performed above 20% of R&D intensity during the 1990s.[9]

Strengths and Weaknesses

Inputs to S&T and their indexing as ratios of other economic measures do provide an indication of the level of commitment of resources to the country, industry, or individual company. However, even if we stipulate that the data collected are a "true" measure of resources expended for R&D, we are still confronted with two major obstacles. First, the gap between expenditures and the performance of R&D presents a major challenge. The underlying assumption that "the more resources are allocated to R&D, the higher the possibility for meaningful outcomes" remains just an assumption. Second, inputs to R&D represent only a portion of the cost of science and technology, when computed along the innovation continuum.

What Do We Measure?

Inputs/expenditures for R&D measure only the resources committed for this activity. There remains the issues of how well these resources are actually utilized, and what the integrations of these inputs are with other inputs and assets of the organization. This means that the gap between what we invest in R&D and how such investments are utilized must be explored. Intensity measures inputs to an activity (or a set of activities), but not the manner in which these activities are conducted, nor their performance.[10]

Moreover, in addition to trends and intensity, we may also measure the cost per scientist and engineer, as well as costs per type of activity: basic research, applied research, and development. Yet, however we decide to manipulate the data and generate ratios and indexes, the reality is more prosaic and much less glamorous. All of these composite measures are relatively weak reflections of what R&D (and also S&T) actually are and perform. These measure do allow for comparisons based on size or volume of resources allocated. But they do not measure the innovative capability of the entity under consideration, nor the effectiveness or efficiency of its usage of these resources.[11]

Clearly, the more an organization or a country invests in R&D, the higher the probability that some outputs will emerge. But we are still powerless in our endeavor to measure with satisfactory precision the level of inputs or expenditures that may be considered "minimum" or benchmarks for a given level of outputs. Although an intensity level of at least 2.0 for a developed country is considered necessary for a national innovation system to operate adequately, such a standard is the result of empirical findings, not of a theoretical consideration. Similarly, although levels of R&D intensity of 15-20% are considered essential for high-tech companies—so as to assure competitiveness in a dynamic marketplace—such benchmarks are *not* the result of a social theory of corporate or industrial R&D performance.[12]

Post-R&D Expenditures

The second obstacle listed above is the fact that the investments/ expenditures for R&D—as reported by industry and even government laboratories—measure only a portion of the funding of the innovation process. Scholars such as Horesh and Kamin (1983) have suggested that about 50% of the cost of technological innovation can be attributed to the R&D phase of the process, and the remainder to post-R&D activities: tooling, manufacturing, and marketing.[13]

Much of the nature of allocation of resources to the various stages of the innovation process is a function of the mode and the accuracy of data collection, and the definition of the borders of each phase in this process. As such *organizational* boundaries are not clearly established, and exchanges and feedbacks are the usual flow among these activities, so data on expenditures are best collected when based on identifiable activities such as projects and programs.[14]

These challenges notwithstanding, expenditures/inputs to R&D, and to S&T in general, are widely applied as a measure of the strength, volume, and intensity of resources allocated to the innovation process. The distribution of these inputs among the phases of the innovation process depend on (1) the industrial sector, (2) project complexity, (3) firm size, and (4) culture and processes of product and process innovation within the individual firm.

Industry differences are a function of the need by companies in the industrial sector to engage in R&D and product or process development. Thus, companies in the electronics, computer, and pharmaceuticals industries expend much larger amounts (relative to similar companies in other industries such as food, apparel, and machinery). They also expend a larger portion of their total inputs to innovation on the upstream portion of the process: R&D and the precommercial stages of the new products and processes they generate.[15] These companies operate in a highly dynamic and competitive business environment, hence their role of innovation is much higher, and much of their technology that feeds their innovation has to be proprietary, hence originated from the company's own S&T effort. Inputs to R&D are thus much higher (as a percentage of sales, for instance) than for similar companies in other, more stable industries.

Project *complexity* also serves as a differentiating factor. The more difficult the project and the more complex the scientific and technical problems that the project addresses, the higher the proportion of resources that would be expended for R&D (of the total expended on the innovation).

Similarly, firm *size* may also serve as a differentiating factor. Larger firms will sponsor large-scale R&D laboratories in which the effort is diversified, interdisciplinary, and better equipped to generate a more comprehensive upstream effort.[16]

Finally, the *culture* within the organization may also act as a differentiating factor on the manner in which expenditures are allocated to the upstream S&T effort versus those allocated to the downstream activities. Culture is defined as the goals, procedures, and modes of conducting and managing the innovation process within the firm. Companies that consider innovation and R&D to be of strategic necessity will also develop a culture that is highly favorable to internal R&D. Thus, there will be adequate justification within the firm for the funding of upstream R&D, including consideration for the risks involved with such activities.[17]

Methodological Issues of Disaggregation

The U.S. National Science Foundation provides researchers and industry decision-makers with perhaps the most accurate and disaggregated data sets of expenditures for science and technology. As already noted, the biennial report *Science & Engineering Indicators* is based on extensive surveys of industrial companies and government agencies and their laboratories.

Disaggregation of the data by phase of the R&D process is based on the definitions offered by NSF to "basic" research, "applied" research, and "development." Moreover, these biennial reports also include a detailed account of the source of the funding for each of the phases, and details of who the performers are: universities, industry, and government. Other data include international comparison, bibliometric outputs, and data on patents.

Criteria for disaggregation and the subsequent reliability of such breakdowns are only as trustworthy as the definitions of the phases, and the methodological reliability of the surveys and data collection procedures. Moreover, the classification of the data by industries (SIC codes) is also merely an indication of a differentiating factor—if and when comparisons are conducted among the various industries and their R&D intensities. The main problem with such measures is their use in more complex analyses, such as the impact of "intensity" measures on economic criteria and performance of the organization. This issue is further discussed in the section below.[18]

Challenges to the Intensity Metric

In addition to the weaknesses of the ratio of expenditures for R&D and other economic measures, there are also some basic challenges to this metric on the basis of the use of specific denominators. Soete (1987) succinctly exposed the shortcomings in the definition of "technology-intensity," as it has been commonly used in studies of international trade patterns.[19] He argued that the use of R&D/sales ratio as a measure of technology intensity has been a metric that allowed for the classification of countries and industries as leading or lagging in their technology. Moreover, he argued that technology "input proxies" do not provide an adequate measurement to an extent that permits reliable comparisons among countries and industries. Instead, he proposed a measure of R&D/value added, as an output proxy for measuring technology intensity. The output proxy is based on the number of patent applications and patents granted for each country.

Studies such as these clearly show that when the input/expenditure ratios are compared with output ratios, the empirical findings differ. Also, output-based measures seem to portray a more accurate picture of economic activities, as supported by studies that use other, non-technological measures.[20]

BEST USES

Although input measures to R&D and S&T have severe limitations, they are nevertheless widely used as metrics of the size or volume of inventive activity, as well as metric of its intensity. The main reasons for such use are summarized in Figure 5.1. There are different ratios of expenditures/inputs to R&D and downstream economic measures. Figure 5.2 summarizes these ratios and the studies in which they were utilized.

Inputs to R&D and S&T—as R&D expenditures—are therefore utilized as proxy for measuring the R&D/S&T activity. This is done in two basic modes: (1) as new data or gross expenditures, and (2) in the construction of indexes, such as ratios.

Figure 5.1
Summary of Key Reasons for Using Input Measures

• Expenditures/inputs to R&D and S&T (upstream and downstream) are easily quantifiable and amenable to statistical manipulations. • Expenditures/inputs are easily and reliably defined in monetary terms, thus easily converted to ratios with other economic and financial measures. • Expenditures/inputs can be used as proxies for more complex and less measurable phenomena, with such proxy relatively easily justifiable. • As financial measures, expenditures/inputs can easily be computed over time to allow for inflationary effects to be reliably attenuated. • Expenditures/inputs can be justified, with relative ease, as reliable measures in theoretical linkages of R&D or S&T effort with value created and outcomes generated from this effort.

Figure 5.2
Illustrative Measures and Ratios of Expenditures or Inputs to R&D

Ratio of Expenditures or Inputs to R&D and –	Illustrative Studies
Expenditures/Sales	•Liao & Greenfield (1998)[21] •Franko (1989)[22]
Expenditures/Patents	•Henderson and Cockburn (1994)[23] •Penner-Hahn (1998)[24]
Expenditures: Internal R&D	•Nagarajan and Mitchell (1998)[25]
Effectiveness Index (% of revenue that is profit/% of revenue spent on R&D)	•Hauser (1998)[26]
Indexes: Cost Per Scientist & Engineer	•Geisler (1998)[27] •Lederman (1984)[28]
Expenditures for R&D/Assets	•Helfart (1997)[29]
Expenditures for R&D/Exports	•Ito and Pucik (1993)[30]

The use of gross expenditures is found, for example, in the definition of high versus low technology, applied to industries and countries. Data on gross expenditures may be compared with ratios of R&D intensity, but they do provide a unique attribute of the *size* and *magnitude* of the inputs or investments in R&D, hence in the technological base of the industry or country.

Some economists have considered the problems in using gross expenditures as proxy to inventive (or technological) activity, but nevertheless accepted its usefulness as a measure of magnitude.[31] Similarly, indexes of expenditures with other factors have also been widely used.

Indexes and Mixing Inputs and Outputs

There are two categories of indexes that utilize input data to R&D and S&T. The first are indexes that are composed of ratios of inputs to downstream factors, as described above. These are intensity and other measures, such as expenditures per sales, per gross domestic product, per R&D personnel, and per profits and economic turnover.[32]

The second category includes mixing input and output measures of R&D and S&T. Examples are indexes that combine input data (expenditures) with bibliometric measures,[33] and those that mix expenditures with patents.[34]

When these "mixed" measures are used, there emerges a complicated picture in which outputs are considered proxy and benchmarks to inventive activity—in comparison with input data. So a company, an industry, or a country is *expected* to produce a certain level of outputs, in response to the level of inputs in R&D it has experienced (taking into consideration the time lag between investments and outputs). The conventional wisdom among economists and researchers in the area of technology management rests on the belief that mixing inputs and outputs will reduce the negative methodological impacts of cross-comparisons of inventive capacity among S&T organizations and among countries.[35]

National Innovation Systems

In addition to the use of input data by industrial companies and scholars who study their relation to economic activity such as trade, exports, and growth, these data (in the various modes in which they appear) contribute to our analysis of national innovation systems. At the national level the magnitude of expenditures for R&D/S&T provides a strong indication of the strength of the nation's technological position.

In this regard, Mowery and Rosenberg (1993) have analyzed R&D expenditures in the United States.[36] They have considered expenditure data by industry, by source of funding, and by who performs the research. Thus, they have argued that these data indicate the type and magnitude of the country's innovation system.

Similarly, Edquist and Lundvall (1993) used R&D expenditures as an indicator that allowed them to compare between the strength of technological innovation of Sweden and Denmark.[37] These authors extended their analysis beyond simple comparisons of levels of funding. They argued, for example, that "the much more modest efforts in R&D in Denmark reflect...the fact that small manufacturing firms tend to invest proportionally less in R&D than larger companies" (p. 279). They also derive conclusions on the different science policies in the two countries and the diffusion processes of new products and their impact on the countries' economic strength and international competitiveness.

The "Synergy Effect"

Implicit in the work by economists and other scholars who used expenditures for R&D as indicators of innovation at the industrial and national levels is the "synergy effect" of such inputs. Large-scale expenditures on R&D/S&T have an additional benefit that is not fully captured by indexes such as expenditures/GDP. When expenditures for R&D are directed toward a variety of industries and scientific/technical fields, there emerges a phenomenon of cross-fertilization. Such a "synergy effect" has been studied from the viewpoint of R&D networks, particularly in the framework of the cross-impacts of public and private sectors.[38]

The more a national system spends on its R&D, and the more diversified these expenditures (public, private, and universities), the higher the ability of the system to benefit from cross-fertilization and from outputs that are enhanced by joint work as well as by cross-influences of similar explorations by different organizations.

CONCLUSIONS

By themselves, expenditures/inputs to R&D and S&T are not a sufficient indicator of inventive activity and its outcomes. Academics and practitioners have therefore resorted to "mixing" these data sets with other indicators of resources (e.g., scientists and engineers), and indicators of outputs. Combined with these indicators, expenditures thus offer a better view of a proxy to the inventive activity.

Results from studies to date do not offer a clear conclusion that the more a company or a nation spends on R&D, the more it will be technologically advanced and the more technologically competitive it will become. There are perhaps some benchmarks that depend on many other factors such as indicators of economic activity, strategic and policy determination, and industrial practices. Most of the benchmarks listed in the literature (for example, expenditures for R&D/GDP) are based on empirical findings and averages rather than on acceptable theoretical foundations. Grupp (1995),[39] for example, classified products as "high technology" based on "cut-off rules [that] were derived from frequency analysis: all products with R&D intensities above the industry average of about 35% of turnover were included" (p. 212).

Hence, classifications and categorization efforts described in the literature are *descriptive* rather than normative. They merely reflect the existing distribution of R&D/S&T expenditures by product line, companies, industries, and countries. By and large these descriptions are sufficiently powerful to indicate "best practices" of institutions and countries that spend resources on their innovation activities. After all, they compete with each other rather than against an "ideal" system of innovation.

Researchers and analysts of S&T and industry have routinely extended the *evaluation* potential of expenditures data well beyond their ability to portray the reality of invention and innovation. As these data and their indexes are proxies to the innovation effort, they merely provide a rough indication of how innovation systems behave.

Yet, as described in this chapter, researchers draw extensive and far-reaching conclusions on the economic and political/social implications and ramifications from the expenditures data. As tools of evaluation of R&D and S&T, expenditures are only one indicator of the strength and the direction of S&T. Even in their disaggregated form, expenditures data provide only a rough indication of how much and for what the entity under study spends resources in R&D/S&T. Any conclusions beyond these facts will certainly be imbued with a set of assumptions that may bias the results and lead to less than realistic evaluation.[40]

NOTES

1. There is an extensive literature on S&T and R&D expenditures that will be cited in these notes. For the tangibility factor, see, for example, Horesh, R., and J. Kamin, "How The Cost of Technological Innovation Are Distributed Over Time," *Research Management*, 26(2), 1983, 21-24. Also see Von Hippel, E., *The Sources of Innovation* (New York: Oxford University Press, 1988).

2. This factor allows for the economic assessments of R&D and S&T that are discussed in Chapter 7. See, for example, Grupp, H., "Science, High Technology, and the Competitiveness of EU Countries," *Cambridge Journal of Economics*, 19(1), 1995, 209-224. Also see Price, D., *Little Science, Big Science, and Beyond* (New York: Columbia University Press, 1986), and Holemans, B., and L. Sleuwaegen, "Innovation Expenditures and the Role of Government in Belgium," *Research Policy*, 17(6), 1988, 375-380.

3. National Science Board, *Science & Engineering Indicators—1993* (Washington, DC: U.S. Government Printing Office, 1993) (NSB 93-1), p. 89.

4. OECD, *Frascati Manual 1993—Proposed Standard Practice for Surveys of Research and Experimental Development* (Paris, 1994). Also see OECD, *Industry and Technology—Scoreboard of Indicators 1995* (Paris, 1996). And see the *Oslo Manual* in OECD, *Proposed Guidelines for Collecting and Interpreting Technological Innovation Data—The Oslo Manual* (Paris, 1993).

5. Once the gaps and other statistical validity issues are resolved. See the example of the pulp and paper industry in Laestadius, S., "The Relevance of Science and Technology Indicators: The Case of Pulp and Paper," *Research Policy*, 27(4), 1998, 385-395. Laestadius has concluded in the case of this industry that "the dominant aggregated S&T indicators are of little, if any, relevance for understanding the process of innovativeness, knowledge formation, and technical change in industry. They are thus also of little use for ranking and comparing countries and/or industries" (p. 393). This type of criticism is further explored in this chapter.

6. See, for example, Martin, B., and J. Irvine, "Trends in Government Spending on Academic and Related Research: An International Comparison," *Science and Public Policy*, 19(5), 1992, 311-319. Also see Lach, S., and M. Schankerman, "Dynamics of R&D and Investment in the Scientific Sector," *Journal of Political Economy*, 97(2), 1989, 880-904.

7. OECD, *Main Science and Technology Indicators* (Paris, May 1993).

8. International Trade Administration, *Industry Reviews and Forecasts* (Washington, DC, 1993).

9. See, for example, Sciberras, E., "Indicators of Technical Intensity and International Competitiveness: A Case for Supplementing Quantitative Data with Qualitative Studies," *R&D Management*, 16(1), 1986, 3-14. Also see Ducharme, L., and F. Gault, "Surveys of Advanced Manufacturing Technology," *Science and*

Public Policy, 19(6), 1992, 393-399; and Leyesdorff, L., "Problems with the "Measurement" of National Scientific Performance," *Science and Public Policy*, 15(3), 1988, 149-152.

10. See, for example, Rizzuto, R., and T. Cook, "How R&D Money is Spent," *Research-Technology Management*, 31(1), 1988, 34-38. Also see Dinar, A., "Resource Allocation for Agricultural Research," *Research Policy*, 20(2), 1991, 145-152.

11. See, for example, Mandez, A., and P. Salvador, "The Application of Scientometric Indicators to the Spanish Scientific Research Council," *Scientometrics*, 24(1), 1992, 61-78. Also see Office of Technology Assessment, *Research Funding as an Investment: Can We Measure the Returns?* Report #OTA-TM-SET-36 (Washington, DC, OTA, April 1984).

12. For example, see Cordero, R., "The Measurement of Innovation Performance in the Firm: An Overview," *Research Policy*, 19(2), 1990, 185-192. Also see, Ball, R., R. Thomas, and J. McGrath, "Influence of R&D Accounting Conventions on Internal Decision-Making of Companies," *R&D Management*, 21(4), 1991, 261-269; and Chan, S., J. Martin, and J. Kensinger, "Corporate Research and Development Expenditures and Share Value," *Journal of Financial Economics*, 26(2), 1990, 255-276. In this paper the authors performed a co-variation analysis to show the correlation between sustained investments in R&D and the performance of the corporate stock. This methodology suffers from problems of "imputation" and the failure to establish benchmarks and theoretical links between inputs to R&D and corporate-related measures, such as sales, profits, and the value of the stock. In this regard, see Ellis, L., "Optimum Research Spending Re-examined," *Research Management*, 23(3), 1980, 22-24; Graves, S., "Optimal R&D Expenditures Streams: An Empirical View," *IEEE Transactions on Engineering Management*, 34(1), 1987, 42-48; and Gilman, J., "You Can Calculate Optimal Spending for Industrial R&D," *Industrial Research and Development*, 22(8), 1980, 87-89. Gilman's assertions are based on empirical findings of the practices of industrial companies.

13. Horesh, R., and J. Kamin, "How The Costs of Technological Innovation Are Distributed Over Time," *Research Management*, 26(2), 1983, 21-22. Also see Kamin, J., I. Bijaoui, and R. Horesh, "Some Determinants of Cost Distributions in the Process of Technological Innovation," *Research Policy*, 11(2), 1982, 83-96.

14. See, for example, Freeman, C., *The Economics of Industrial Innovation* (Cambridge, MA: MIT Press, 1982). More recently see Gerchak, Y., "On Allocating R&D Budgets Among and Within Projects," *R&D Management*, 28(4), 1988, 305-309.

15. See, for example, Iansiti, M., "Real World R&D: Jumping the Product Generation Gap," *Harvard Business Review*, 71(3), 1993, 138-149. Also see Dasgupta, P., and E. Masian, "The Simple Economics of Research Portfolios," *The Economic Journal*, 97(2), 1987, 581-595.

16. See, for example, Roberts, K., and M. Weitzman, "Funding Criteria for Research, Development, and Exploration Projects," *Econometrica*, 49(5), 1981, 1261-1288. Also see the seminal paper by Mansfield, E., "Composition of R&D Expenditures: Relationship to Size of Firm, Concentration, and Innovative Output," *The Review of Economics and Statistics*, 63(4), 1981, 610-615.

17. See, for example, the impact of corporate culture on R&D when there is a change in ownership, in Welch, J., and P. Bolster, "Corporate Raiders Don't Cut Investments in R&D," *Long Range Planning*, 25(6), 1992, 72-78. Also see Zahra, S., and M. Feseina, "Will Leveraged Buyouts Kill U.S. Corporate Research & Development?" *Academy of Management Executive*, 5(4), 1991, 7-21.

18. For some early uses of this type of metric, see, for example, Gruber, W., D. Mehta, and R. Vernon, "The R&D Factor in International Trade and International Investment of United States Industries," *The Journal of Political Economy*, 57(1), 1967, 20-37. Also see Pavitt, K. (Ed.), *Technical Innovation and British Economic Performance* (London: Macmillan, 1980).

19. Soete, L., "The Impact of Technological Innovation on International Trade Patterns: The Evidence Reconsidered," *Research Policy*, 16(3), 1987, 101-130.

20. See, for example, Diwan, R., and C. Chakrabarti, "Input Substitution and Technical Change in U.S. High Tech Industries," *Economic Letters*, 32(2), 1990, 141-145. Also see Cheng, L., "International Competition in R&D and Technological Leadership: An Examination of the Posner-Hufbauer Hypothesis," *Journal of International Economics*, 17(2), 1984, 15-40; and Beenstock, M., and C. Whitbread, "Fixed Investment and the Technological Gap in the United Kingdom," *Applied Economics*, 22(7), 1990, 905-916.

21. Liao, Z., and P. Greenfield, "Corporate R&D Strategy Portfolio in Japanese and Australian Technology-Based Firms: An Empirical Study," *IEEE Transactions on Engineering Management*, 45(4), 1998, 323-330. The authors conducted a statistical comparison between inputs to the total "portfolio" of the firm's R&D (as well as disaggregated inputs to basic precompetitive and applied research) and various levels of sales figures. They concluded that Japanese firms invest more heavily in the various modes of R&D, as a percentage of their sales.

22. Franko, L., "Global Corporate Competition: Who's Winning, Who's Losing, and the R&D Factor As One Reason Why," *Strategic Management Journal*, 10(5), 1989, 449-474. This is an excellent example of the use of R&D inputs-sales metric. The author relies on previous work by Scherer and Mansfield to argue that R&D intensity (R&D inputs/sales) may causally explain growth patterns in his sample of 83 companies in six industries. The conclusion from this study links investments in R&D to competitive advantage, via growth and company performance.

23. Henderson, R., and I. Cockburn, "Measuring Competence? Exploring Firm Effects in Pharmaceutical Research," *Strategic Management Journal*, 15(52), 1994, 63-84. The authors correlated total research spendings by ten

pharmaceutical companies with selected measures of competence, such as stock of patents and use of cross-functional teams.

24. Penner-Hahn, J., "Firm and Environmental Influences on the Mode and Sequence of Foreign Research and Development Activities," *Strategic Management Journal*, 19(2), 1998, 149-168. Modes of entry of firms into international markets are studied. Measures used are expenditures on foreign R&D, and data on patents.

25. Nagarajan, A., and W. Mitchell, "Evolutionary Diffusion: Internal and External Methods Used to Acquire Encompassing, Complementary, and Incremental Technological Changes in the Lithotripsy Industry," *Strategic Management Journal*, 19(11), 1998, 1063-1077. The authors measured internal R&D in 44 cases of technological changes in the industry, as expenditures for R&D performed by the sample companies.

26. Hauser, J., "Research, Development, and Engineering Metrics," *Management Science*, 44(12), 1998, 1670-1689. The author measures the *development* metric as an effectiveness index of percent of revenue for new products and that in profit, per percent of revenue spent on R&D.

27. Geisler, E., "The Cost of Research," *Engineering Valuation and Cost Analysis*, 2(2), 1998, 33-44. The author constructed macroindicators of inputs and outputs of R&D. Expenditures for basic research are given as ratio to number of publications in scientific journals, to form an index of cost per publication. A similar procedure is conducted for patents, to obtain indexes of cost of patent, and for scientist and engineer.

28. Lederman, L., "The Value of Fundamental Science," *Scientific American*, 251(5), 1984, 34-41.

29. Helfast, C., "Know-How and Asset Complementarity and Dynamic Capability Accumulation: The Case of R&D," *Strategic Management Journal*, 18(5), 1997, 339-360. The author measures R&D by 26 U.S. petroleum companies expended on coal conversion to show that such shift in R&D expenditures occurs in companies with large physical assets and complementary technological knowledge.

30. Ito, K., and V. Pucik, "R&D Spending, Domestic Competition, and Export Performance of Japanese Manufacturing Firms," *Strategic Management Journal*, 14(1), 1993, 61-75. The authors measured the ratio of export to R&D expenditures of Japanese manufacturers.

31. See, for example, Grupp, H., "Science, High Technology, and the Competitiveness of EU Countries," *Cambridge Journal of Economics*, 19(2), 1995, 209-223. Grupp had compared European Union countries in the period 1980-1986, by using both gross R&D expenditures, and R&D intensity by product category. Also see Grupp, H., "The Measurement of Technical Performance of Innovations by Technometrics and Its Impact on Established Technology Indicators," *Research Policy*, 23(3), 1994, 175-193.

32. See Figure 16.2. Also see some illustrative studies in van Raan, A. (Ed.), *Handbook of Quantitative Studies of Science and Technology* (Amsterdam: Elsevier Science, 1988); and Ellis, L., *Evaluation of R&D Processes: Effectiveness Through Measurements* (New York: ARTech House, 1997).

33. See Geisler, E., 1998, *op. cit.* who constructed an index of cost per article.

34. See *ibid.*, and Soete, 1987, *op. cit.*, and also Grupp, H. (Ed.), *Dynamics of Science-Based Innovations* (Berlin: Springer, 1992); and Archibugi, D., and M. Pianta, "Specialization and Size of Technological Activities in Industrial Countries: The Analysis of Patent Data," *Research Policy*, 21(1), 1992, 79-93. The authors have concluded that there is a negative correlation between the level of S&T activity and specialization of national economies.

35. See, for example, Basberg, B., "Patents and the Measurement of Technological Change: A Survey of the Literature," *Research Policy*, 16(3), 1987, 131-141. Also see Palda, K., "Technological Intensity: Concept and Measurement," *Research Policy*, 15(3), 1986, 187-198; and Mansfield, E., A. Romeo, and L. Switzer, "R&D Price Indexes and Real R&D Expenditures in the United States," *Research Policy*, 12(2), 1983, 105-112.

36. Mowery, D., and N. Rosenberg, "The U.S. National Innovation System," in R. Nelson (Ed.), *National Innovation Systems: A Comparative Analysis* (New York: Oxford University Press, 1993, pp. 29-75).

37. Edquist, C., and B. Lundvall, "Comparing the Danish and Swedish Systems of Innovation," in Nelson, *op cit.*, pp. 265-298.

38. See, for example, Tijssen, R., "Quantitative Assessment of Large Heterogeneous R&D Networks: The Case of Process Engineering in the Netherlands," *Research Policy*, 26(7-8), 1998, 791-809.

39. See Grupp, *Cambridge Journal of Economics*, 1995, *op. cit.*

40. For an illustration of some readings that address these issues are Gibbons, M., C. Limoges, H. Nowotny, S. Schwartzman, P. Scott, and M. Trow, *The New Production of Knowledge: The Dynamics of Science and Research in Contemporary Societies* (London: Sage Publications, 1994). Also see a discussion of the cumulative effects ("Synergy Effect") in Garside, W., "Industrial Policy and the Development State: British Responses to the Competitive Environment Before and After the 1970s," *Business and Economic History*, 27(1), 1998, 47-60.

6

OUTPUTS FROM SCIENCE AND TECHNOLOGY: CATEGORIES AND METRICS

In the previous chapter the issue of using inputs/investments in S&T was investigated. Inputs, as expenditures, are also used in conjunction with output measures and with measures of downstream activities. Among the more widely used methods are research expenditures/units sold, research expenditures/sales, and "dollarization": profit/cost of research employees.

The majority of key methods used by industry employ measures of outputs. Among these outputs are new products and processes, improvements in products and services, innovations, and contributions to compliance and strategic objectives.

This chapter discusses the existing outputs from S&T and the general metrics used to measure them. It starts with definitions of outputs, and proceeds to elaborate on the various categories of outputs and the metrics that accompany them. The chapter also discusses the link between outputs and strategy, S&T and innovation audits, and sets the stage for the individual review of each metric.

WHAT ARE OUTPUTS FROM S&T?

The innovation continuum, as defined in this book, extends from the research activity downstream to development, engineering, testing, and the commercialization of the technology that is thus created. Therefore, S&T has a variety of outputs that emerge from each activity and that influence other stages and activities through a variety of ways, some short-, other long-term. These outputs vary according to several criteria, such as what or who they impact, type of impact, and the means available to measure these impacts.

It would therefore seem, at the outset, that a generalized definition of outputs from S&T would intrinsically fail to capture the variability of attributes of these outputs. At best we may be able to define them in a mode that deals with their shared rather than unique characteristics.

Outputs from S&T are events or material/physical objects (such as products, processes, and reports), or organizational/social/economic phenomena (such as savings and productivity). They include nontangibles such as items of knowledge, satisfaction of people, and other benefits or harmful effects raised (directly or indirectly) by S&T.[1]

Outputs from R&D/S&T are seldom clearly and unequivocally defined in the literature. Various terms are used as descriptors of outputs, sometimes as surrogate terms, other times even as euphemisms. Terms such as "impacts," "effects," "consequences," "benefits," "value," "advantages," "spin-offs," "returns," and "payback" are some of those found in the literature on evaluation and assessment of R&D and S&T.[2]

A major reason for the difficulty in advancing a comprehensive definition of outputs is because of the complexity of the innovation continuum, there are many different outputs. They are clustered in multiple and diverse sets, all along the continuum from research to engineering to commercialization. Such a variety of outputs leads to issues in measurement, linkage across gaps, and the use of selected outputs in different schemes of evaluation.[3]

ISSUES IN MEASURING S&T OUTPUTS

Outputs from S&T have always been difficult, not only in attempts to define them but, in particular, in many attempts to *measure* them. There are at least four key issues that hinder the measurement of such outputs. The first is the fact that some outputs, in particular downstream the innovation process, are elusive. They are "masked" behind other phenomena, such as economic or social activities of companies or public institutions. One such illustration is the impacts of technology on industrial growth, masked behind the marketing and strategic aspects of growth, in the form of hard-to-measure contributions of technology to corporate success.

Another form of "elusiveness" concerns the appearance of outputs as nontangible impacts. For example, benefits such as "improved reputation" or "added client satisfaction" due to S&T are embedded in the phenomenon of the performance of the entity that purports to benefit from S&T. This requires a special effort to "dig" and to "unearth" such outputs and thus bring them to light.[4]

A second key issue is the complexity and diversity of the S&T process. It leads primarily to gaps and delays among the various stages and activities—hence among the different outputs. Thus, when outputs across the divide of such gaps are linked in an evaluation effort, they may have different modes of measurement that defy accurate comparisons, let alone causal linkages. For example, research outputs may include publications and citations, whereas downstream the innovation process, some outputs may be related to corporate objectives and performance, hence making any credible linkage difficult. In this regard several researchers have commented on the shortcomings of measuring S&T outputs. Mittermeir and Knorr (1979), for example, criticized the use of cost-effectiveness techniques in military S&T effort.[5] They argued that such techniques are useful only when both sides of the equation—inputs and outputs—are measurable. Steele (1989) argued that technical outputs are difficult to measure because of the degree to which technical people are so specialized in their own area and since technical outputs have many potential beneficiaries, judgment seems the only credible means of measurement.[6]

The third key issue is the existence of multiple potential recipients of the outputs from S&T. As the outputs propagate in many pathways, influencing a variety of potential impactees, it becomes extremely difficult to ascertain who "really" receives the output/s. This is equivalent to what Rubenstein and Geisler (1991) denoted as the issue of identifying clients or impactees.[7] Even in cases where upstream outputs are identified (such as patents), the downstream impacts are usually diffused and diluted among the many potential impactees and constituencies of the organization that produced the outputs.[8]

Finally, the fourth issue is the problem associated with actual measurement of the outputs. Few outputs lend themselves to quantification, whereas the majority allow some qualitative assessment.[9] In the case of inputs to S&T, surrogate measures such as expenditures were feasible, but in the case of many outputs, surrogate measures magnify the problems. For example, upstream measures such as patents may be correlated with downstream measures of technological impacts on competitive strength. Since the latter cannot be directly measured, patents may be used as surrogates, but they fail to satisfactorily resolve the problem of measuring the organization's competitive position in the marketplace.[10]

CATEGORIES OF S&T OUTPUTS

A survey of the literature and practices of universities, industry, and government reveals a large number of outputs from R&D and from S&T. These outputs are shown in a list of generic outputs ("laundry list") in Figure 6.1. The figure includes a mix of outputs, some in quantitative, others in qualitative form; some denoting economic factors, other bibliometric measures. Many outputs are also scattered throughout the innovation process.

Figure 6.1
A Generic List of Outputs from Science and Technology

- Science and technical ideas
- Scientific and technical publications, reports, and citations
- Intellectual challenges
- Technical assistance
- Presentations to learned societies
- Training of scientific and technical people
- New and improved products, materials, and processes
- Patents
- Transfer of technology
- Development of new testing methodologies
- Development of R&D/S&T management practices and techniques
- Start-up of new ventures, new companies, establishment of partnership
- Development of strategic technology alliances
- Development of scientific and technical benchmarks and standards
- Cost-savings in production, product design, and redesign
- Increased productivity and utilization of resources
- Improved product/process/service quality
- Reduced dependence on outside sources
- Facilitator in ability to outsource
- Savings in materials
- Contribution to maintenance/protection of lead or position in the discipline/industry/market

Figure 6.1 Continued

- Facilitation of use by client
- Contribution to adequate response to environmental and other regulatory pressures
- Contributions to potential adaptability of manufacturing to new processes and methods
- Contributions to the competitive features of a product or product line
- Contributions to creation of new market, market segments, and new customers
- Contributions to technology and business planning, and to the strategic management of the organization
- Development, manipulation, and exchange of new knowledge in S&T
- Provision of scientific and technical information to assist managers in areas such as licensing, mergers and acquisitions, and other activities imbued with content of S&T
- Contributions to institutional memory
- Contributions to the identification of opportunities and needs for S&T
- Contributions to improved project selection and resources allocation for S&T and for the innovation process
- Contributions to sales, profits, and other economic criteria of performance
- Contributions to the perception of S&T by the sponsors of this activity and by the public at large
- Increased ability to anticipate and to effectively deal with barriers to application and implementation of results from S&T
- Contribution to expending the state of the art in S&T
- Contribution to the prestige of S&T organizations and their impactees

This is a comprehensive but not an exhaustive list. Some outputs not listed here may appear embedded in the outputs that are listed, or perhaps used as independent measures. Not necessarily listed in any order of priority or other ordinal scale.

Some scholars have attempted to formulate a taxonomy of outputs from S&T. Chakrabarti (1989) suggested three approaches to research into science indicators: literature-based, expert-based, and survey-based.[11] He also explored the impacts on innovation, primarily such characteristics as the *nature* of innovations, the degree of their *novelty*, the *source* of innovations, and the *impact* and objectives of innovations. Patents (and their relation to inputs/expenditures) were the metric of choice in Chakrabarti's analysis.

Rubenstein and Geisler (1982) are among the pioneers who attempted to collect the various types of R&D/S&T outputs in a comprehensive listing, and to construct a plausible typology.[12] They suggested four key categories of S&T outputs: (1) related to sales, (2) related to savings, (3) related to effects on profits, and (4) related to time and cost of technical solutions.

Much of the empirical effort to work with outputs from R&D and S&T has concentrated on a very small number of outputs. These attempts included either the count of the output (e.g., number of patents) or the output item as a ratio or in relation to another criterion (e.g., patents per sales). But, an analysis of the generic outputs leads to various possible categories.

These taxonomies, elaborated below, provide some order and logic into the "laundry list" of potential outputs. They are based on various rationales or perspectives of how the outputs from S&T should be categorized. By joining outputs of a similar nature we are a step closer to having an underlying logic for the arrangement of these disparate outputs into indexes, macroindicators, and multiple views to measure a given phenomenon.[13]

Quantitative Versus Qualitative Outputs

This taxonomy is based on the criterion of how the output is measured: by the use of some quantities or by a qualitative method. Figure 6.2 shows the distribution of some outputs as they are clustered into these categories.

As is the case with taxonomical analysis, there is not a very definitive distinction between quantitative and qualitative outputs and their measures. For example, although peer review is a process of combining the judgmental evaluation of individuals or a committee, these subjective assessments lend themselves to scoring, hence to some manipulation of quantities. Similarly, bibliometric measures also contain an important element of judgmental impact, such as the process by which publications are selected as citations.[14]

Outputs that allow for quantification with relative ease, and whose *primary* mode of measurement is by at least one quantity, are also touted as more useful and meaningful. Users of such outputs include both the generators of S&T as well as those individuals and organizations impacted

Figure 6.2
Illustrative Outputs from S&T by Degree of Quantification

A. QUANTITATIVE OUTPUTS
- Count of publications
- Count of citations
- Count of new products and processes
- Count of improvements in products/processes
- Count of patents
- Economic/financial outputs (e.g., cost savings, ROI)
- Performance outputs (e.g., on time and on budget)

B. QUALITATIVE OUTPUTS
- Judgment evaluation
- Goal achievement
- Compliance with regulations
- Impacts on customer satisfaction
- Contributions to capabilities and skills of S&T staff
- Contributions to the pool of innovations
- Contributions to the prestige of S&T organizations

This list is not an exhaustive listing of all outputs from S&T. Classification into the categories was a subjective decision by the author.

by the S&T activity. Quantitative outputs are more easily manipulated and associated—with convenience and added precision—with other quantitative measures of economic and organizational activities. Hence, these outputs are more "popular," but not necessarily more convincing as measures of S&T outcomes and impacts.[15]

Direct Versus Indirect Impacts

Outputs from S&T may also be classified by the degree to which their impacts are directly or indirectly received by users and impactees of S&T. Figure 6.3 shows examples of outputs thus classified. This taxonomy is similar to the classification of outputs by stages of the innovation process, advanced by Geisler and Rubenstein (1983).[16] In both instances the emphasis is on the distance between the generators of S&T and the recipients/impactees.

Figure 6.3
Illustrative Outputs from S&T by Direct or Indirect Impacts

A. DIRECT IMPACTS*
    •Publications
    •Citations
    •Patents
    •S&T performance
    •Improved products and processes
    •New products and services

B. INDIRECT IMPACTS**
    •Start-up of new companies
    •Improved performance of product line
    •Cost savings and reductions in such areas as production, design, and
      maintenance
    •Compliance with regulations
    •Goal achievement

This list is not an exhaustive listing of all outputs from S&T.
*Impactees directly receive/acquire the outputs from those who generate them.
**Impactees are affected by factors that are related to S&T outputs.

IMPACTS FROM SCIENCE AND TECHNOLOGY

This taxonomy has been widely used by scholars and practitioners in an attempt to place outputs within a process that includes science (upstream) and technology (downstream) as distinct phenomena. In general, outputs from science tend to be less tangible, as they include such items as ideas, information, and knowledge. Technology, on the other hand, is generally viewed as tangible items such as new products, innovations, and new materials, as well as the techniques and methods used in fabrication and usage of products and materials.[17] Figure 6.4 provides examples of outputs that may be classified into these groupings.

As in the case of the classification by direct versus indirect inputs, this taxonomy of science versus technology is also similar to the stage approach for outputs of R&D and S&T.

KEY CATEGORIES

In addition to the taxonomies shown in Figures 6.2-6.4, we can also group the outputs from S&T in a small number of categories by virtue of similar form and attributes of the outputs we are grouping. In this way we are better equipped to use the pool of metrics, in such a way as to target a set of similar metrics to the several outputs within a category.

Such a classification allows for multiple metrics for similar outputs, so that a more precise evaluation of a given phenomenon is now possible. For example, the category of bibliographic outputs can be measured by counts of publications, reports, presentations, citations, co-word mapping, and data mining—all directed toward the evaluation of the phenomenon of the reporting of S&T results. In this manner there are four general categories of outputs. Figure 6.5 portrays these categories and the further

Figure 6.4
Illustrative Outputs from Science and from Technology

A. OUTPUTS FROM SCIENCE
- •Ideas
- •Knowledge
- •Publications
- •Citations
- •Prestige
- •Training and education
- •New methods and techniques
- •Intellectual challenges

B. OUTPUTS FROM TECHNOLOGY
- •Patents
- •New products and processes
- •New materials
- •Technical assistance
- •Technical benchmarks and standards
- •Contributions to productivity
- •Improved quality
- •Cost-savings

This list is not exhaustive. Classification of the outputs into the categories was done by the author based on the literature and personal judgment. Not necessarily listed in any order of importance or other criteria.

Figure 6.5
Key Categories of Outputs from S&T

	METRIC	
	Quantitative (e.g., count)	**Qualitative** (peer review)
A. BIBLIOGRAPHIC OUTPUTS		
•Ideas	✓	✓
•Scientific & technical publications	✓	✓
•Intellectual challenge		✓
•Presentations to societies	✓	✓
•Scientific & technical information		✓
•Prestige		✓
•Knowledge		✓
B. PATENTS		
•Solitaire, inbred, and crossbred	✓	✓
•Applied for vs. granted	✓	✓
C. PERFORMANCE OUTPUTS		
•Training and education	✓	✓
•New and improved products & processes	✓	✓
•Methods and techniques	✓	✓
•Cost savings	✓	✓
•Benchmarks & standards	✓	✓
•Improved quality	✓	✓
•Response to regulations	✓	✓
•Contribution to sales & profit	✓	✓
•Contributions to strategic competitiveness		✓

This list is not exhaustive, nor presented in any order.

classification within them of illustrative outputs from the "laundry list" of Figure 6.1.

These key categories accommodate all the possible outputs from S&T. The third category, *performance* outputs, contains the contributions and effects that S&T may have on the S&T organization itself, as well as on the impactees. In all, the outputs in this comprehensive category are outcomes that portray the performance of the S&T organization and how well it impacts its constituents.

Why is this classification scheme into three key categories preferable to other such groupings? First, because of its simplicity, this scheme allows for adaptation to the other forms of taxonomic analysis shown in Figures 6.2-6.4. For example, this classification scheme can be matched against the criterion of direct versus indirect outputs (shown in Figure 6.3), and science and technology (shown in Figure 6.4). In the first case the bibliographic and patents categories roughly correspond to direct outputs, whereas the performance category includes many of the indirect impacts. In the second instance, the bibliographic outputs roughly correspond to outcomes from science, and the performance outputs to those from technology.[18]

Second, the key categories represent definable phenomena of innovation and its impacts. They allow for the development of indices and other complex macroindices tools for evaluation of R&D and S&T.

Third, the key categories also enable us to adequately incorporate and match metrics—both quantitative and qualitative. As Figure 6.5 shows, the metrics may be quantitative as well as qualitative.

So, this seemingly simple classification of S&T outputs into three key categories is advantageous in our effort to evaluate the phenomenon of S&T and innovation. It includes the grouping of outputs that are similar in their composition, measurability, and type of impacts. Armed with this classification scheme, we can now more effectively evaluate the outcomes from S&T, and fill in the needed space in the equation that relates S&T to other events, phenomena, and activities in the economy and in society.

OUTPUTS AND METRICS

Science and technology is an effort that produces a variety of outputs which then impact other entities in many different ways. In this chapter I categorized these outputs as being bibliographic, patents, or performance. Each of these categories describes a different evaluation phenomenon: how the outputs from S&T affect the constituency entities of S&T and other entities in the economy and society; hence the importance of identifying these outputs and grouping them into meaningful categories.

From the metrics used to assess these outputs I have selected the more "popular" and more intensely discussed in the relevant literatures. These metrics range from economic/financial measures to bibliometrics, patents, and peer review. These metrics are elaborated in the following chapters. I have also established a common format that includes: (1) description, (2) strengths and benefits, (3) weaknesses and problems, (4) best uses, and (5) conclusions.

Such elaborate discussions of the selected metrics provide the reader with a comprehensive and unique "handbook" of the methods and the measures used to evaluate R&D and S&T.[19]

NOTES

1. This definition of outputs from S&T includes elements from definitions of outputs/outcomes from research, R&D, science, *and* technology. See, for example, Kostoff, R., *The Handbook of Research Impact Assessment*, 7th ed. (1997), in Dr. Kostoff's website at: <http://www.dtic. mil/dtic/kostoff/index.html>. Also see Porter, A., "Technology Assessment," *Impact Assessment*, 13(2), 1995, 135-151. Porter lists the effects of technology (Figure 1 in his paper, p. 137) as occurring in various orders, so that they are consequences from technology that are unintended, indirect, and that are delayed. See Coates, J., "Technology Assessment, The Benefits, The Costs, The Consequences," *The Futurist*, 5(4), 1971, 225-231.

2. See National Science Foundation, *A Selected Bibliography of Research and Development and Its Impacts on the Economy* (Washington, DC: Office of Special Studies, NSF-58-18, May 1958). From this list, see, for example, Hertz, D., *Theory and Practice of Industrial Research* (New York: McGraw-Hill, 1950); and McLaurin, W., "Sequence From Invention to Innovation and Its Relation to Economic Growth," *Quarterly Journal of Economics*, 47(1), 1953, 97-111.

3. See, for example, Jones, P., "Cost Benefit and Public Policy Issues," *R&D Management*, 19(2), 1989, 127-131. Jones reviews the accomplishments of the British government's R&D program analysis effort. The author criticized this public effort for failing to evaluate long-term impacts. Instead he argued that the government unit based its effort on "uncertain causal relationships among critical inputs" (p. 127). Also see Gilbert, G., and S. Woolger, "The Quantitative Study of Science: An Examination of the Literature," *Science Studies*, 4(3), 1974, 279-294; and see Peters, T., and D. Le Baron, *The Circle of Innovation: You Can't Shrink Your Way to Greatness* (New York, Knopf, 1997).

4. See, for example, Gold, B., *Research, Technological Change, and Economic Analysis* (Lexington, MA: Lexington Books, D. C. Heath & Co., 1997). Also see Galor, O., and D. Tsiddon, "Technological Breakthroughs and Development Traps," *Economic Letters*, 37(1), 1991, 11-17.

5. Mittermeir, R., and K. Knorr, "Scientific Productivity and Accumulative Advantage: A Thesis Reassessed in the Light of International Data," *R&D Management*, 9 (Special Issue), 1979, 235-239.

6. Steele, L., *Managing Technology: The Strategic View* (New York: McGraw Hill, 1989). See, in particular, pp. 243-245, and pp. 314-316.

7. Rubenstein, A., and E. Geisler, "Evaluating the Outputs and Impacts of R&D/Innovation," *International Journal of Technology Management*, Special Publication on Role of Technology in Corporate Policy, 1991, 181-204.

8. See, for example, Soete, L., "The Impact of Technological Innovation on International Trade Patterns: The Evidence Reconsidered," *Research Policy*, 16(2), 1987, 101-130.

9. See, for example, White, B., *The Technology Assessment Process* (Westport, CT: Greenwood Press, 1988). Also see Wilensky, G., "Technology As Culprit and Benefactor," *The Quarterly Review of Economics and Business*, 30(4), 1990, 45-53; and Schroeder, D., "A Dynamic Perspective on the Impact of Process Innovation Upon Competitive Strategies," *Strategic Management Journal*, 11(1), 1990, 25-41.

10. Competitive position may be measured in terms of the company's relative share of the market. However, the issue remains: how is technology contributing to *changes* in the relative share. See, for example, Goodman, R., and M. Lawless, *Technology and Strategy: Conceptual Models and Diagnostics* (New York: Oxford University Press, 1994). In particular, see Chapters 6 and 7. Also see Sapienza, A., *Creating Technology Strategies: How To Build Competitive Biomedical R&D* (New York: John Wiley & Sons, 1997).

11. Chakrabarti, A., "Technology Indicators: Conceptual Issues and Measurement Problems," *Journal of Engineering and Technology Management*, 6(2), 1989, 99-116.

12. Rubenstein, A., and E. Geisler, "Objectives and Methods of Assessing and Evaluating R&D Programs and Projects," Paper presented at the Fourth Annual Engineering Management Conference, Washington, DC, June 1982. Even earlier work by Rubenstein had initiated the listing and compilation of outputs. See, for example, Rubenstein, A., "Setting Criteria for R&D," *Harvard Business Review*, 35(5), 1957, 95-104.

13. See, for example, the early work on evaluation of R&D and S&T and the key categories of outputs in: Bright, J. (Ed.), *Research, Development, and Technological Innovation* (Homewood, IL: R. Irwin, 1964). Also see Rubenstein, A., and E. Geisler, "The Use of Indicators and Measures of the R&D Process in Evaluating Science and Technology Programs," in J. Roessner (Ed.), *Government Innovation Policy* (New York: St. Martin's Press, 1988), 185-204; and Holbrook, J., "Basic Indicators of Scientific and Technological Performance," *Science and Public Policy*, 19(5), 1992, 267-273.

14. See, for example, Nelson, R. (Ed.), *The Rate and Direction of Inventive Activity* (Princeton, NJ: Princeton University Press, 1962). Also see Griliches, Z., "Issues in Assessing the Contribution of Research and Development to Productivity Growth," *Bell Journal of Economics*, 10(1), 1979, 82-116; and

Schmied, H., "Results of Attempts to Quantify the Secondary Economic Effects Generated by Big Research Centers," *IEEE Transactions on Engineering Management*, 29(4), 1982, 156-165.

15. This issue was discussed earlier in this book. The relative importance of exploratory power of outputs is not necessarily correlated with the proneness to quantification. Qualitative outputs such as peer review are as powerful in measuring outcomes from S&T as counts of publications or patents. Nevertheless, quantification is a crucial criterion for the adoption and utilization of an output from S&T by the producers and impactees of S&T. See, for example, Pfetsch, F., "The Measurement of a Country's Scientific and Technological Potential," *Scientometrics*, 19(5/6), 1990, 495-504. Also see Lichtenberg, F., "Issues in Measuring Industrial R&D," *Research Policy*, 19(2), 1990, 157-163; and Dror, I., "Technology Innovation Indicators," *R&D Management*, 19(3), 1989, 243-249.

16. See, for example, Geisler, E., and A. Rubenstein, "Methodology Issues in Conducting Evaluation Studies of R&D/Innovation," *Proceedings of the Symposium on Management of Technological Innovation*, Worcester Polytechnic Institute, Washington, DC, May 1983. Also see Geisler, E., "An Integrated Cost-Performance Model of Research and Development Evaluation," *Omega*, 23(3), 1995, 281-294.

17. There is a considerable literature on different outputs from science and technology. Some key publications were cited earlier in this book. In addition, see Dean, B. V., and J. Goldhar (Eds.), *Management of Research and Innovation* (New York: North-Holland, 1980). Also see Gold, B., "Some Key Problems in Evaluating R&D Performance," *Journal of Engineering and Technology Management*, 6(1), 1989, 59-70; and Leifer, R., and T. Triscari, "Research Versus Development: Differences and Similarities," *IEEE Transactions on Engineering Management*, 34(2), 1987, 71-78. Also see Pavitt, K., "Science and Technology Indicators: Eight Conclusions," *Science and Public Policy*, 11(1), 1984, 21-24. Finally, see Ravenscraft, D., and F. Scherer, "The Lag Structure of Returns to Research and Development," *Applied Economics*, 14(4), 1982, 603-620.

18. The search for a definitive and multipurpose scheme for classifying outputs from R&D and S&T has been an arduous trail of much effort reported in the literature. There is somewhat of a consensus that the three categories shown here (bibliographic, patents, and performance) are the more prevalent and acceptable groups. See, for example, Brown, W., and N. Karagozoglu, "A Systems Model of Technological Innovation," *IEEE Transactions on Engineering Management*, 36(1), 1989, 11-16. Also see an earlier attempt to classify outputs within the framework of ecosystems and organizational ecology. The paper concludes with an interesting discussion by a group of experts: Morton, J., "The Innovation of Innovation," *IEEE Transactions on Engineering Management*, 15(2), 1968, 57-65; and Whitley, R., and P. Frost, "The Measurement of Performance in Research," *Human Relations*, 24(2), 1971, 161-177. More recently see Brown, W., and D.

Gobeli, "Observations on the Measurement of R&D Productivity: A Case Study," *IEEE Transactions on Engineering Management*, 39(4), 1992, 325-337. To my knowledge, the comprehensive classification scheme advanced in this chapter is the first such attempt to gather the available outputs and metrics, and to group them in coherent and meaningful categories.

19. The choice of metrics to be described in the following chapters and the analyses themselves are of course the product of my selection criteria, my interpretation of the literature, and my personal experience. Yet the following chapters are a much needed addition to the extant literature in a very critical area of the management and evaluation of S&T and innovation. In this regard, see, for example, the pioneering discussion in Rubenstein, 1957, *op. cit.*, 95-104. Also see Sahal, D., "The Generalized Distance Measures of Technology," *Technological Forecasting and Social Change*, 9(3), 1976, 289-300. Other early research on the topic of evaluation and metrics of S&T includes, for example, Cole, S., and J. Cole, "Scientific Output and Recognition," *American Sociological Review*, 32(3), 1967, 377-390. Also see Crane, D., *Invisible Colleges* (Chicago: University of Chicago Press, 1972); and the seminal paper by Griffith, B., H. Small, J. Stonehill, and S. Dey, "The Structure of Scientific Literatures II: Toward a Macro- and Microstructures for Science," *Science Studies*, 4(4), 1974, 339-365. More recently see Crawford, M., and G. Tellis, "The Technological Innovation Controversy," *Business Horizons*, 24(4), 1981, 76-86; and see Senker, J., "Evaluating the Funding of Strategic Science: Some Lessons From British Experience," *Research Policy*, 20(1), 1991, 29-43; and Rubenstein and Geisler, 1982, *op. cit.* Also see Narin, F., and E. Noma, "Is Technology Becoming Science?" *Scientometrics*, 7(3), 1985, 369-381.

7

ECONOMIC AND FINANCIAL METRICS

Perhaps the most preferred metric of science and technology, economic and financial measures of S&T evaluation have been amply used for many years. Originally within the sole realm of economic analysis, these metrics have continually advanced to the fore of other forms of usages, primarily to support policy decisions on the nature of S&T outputs and for decisions on resources allocation for S&T.[1]

This chapter starts with a description of economic and financial metrics for S&T and the theories and principles that underlie these measures. The relevant literatures are explored and major trends and topics of discussion are described. Further, the chapter analyzes the strengths and weaknesses of these measures, and proceeds to show some applications and best uses. Finally, the chapter offers some conclusions on the theoretical aspects and empirical effectiveness of these metrics.

BACKGROUND AND DESCRIPTION

Economic and financial measures of the S&T activity are a broad spectrum of measures and techniques. They range from simple financial indices of inputs to S&T, to more complex measures of cost-effectiveness and the economic impacts of S&T, such as on national and corporate productivity.

In a report from a conference on R&D management conducted in the United Kingdom, the first trend in R&D management practice was the increase in measurement of R&D effectiveness.[2] Primarily the emphasis has been on the *economic* viability of R&D and S&T. As investments for S&T in the period following the Second World War have dramatically increased, so has the need to assess their economic justification. Economists were among the early to struggle with this question. They undertook several perspectives, by considering the contributions of S&T (in both aggregated and disaggregated forms) to economic and social phenomena.

RESEARCH STREAMS IN ECONOMIC MEASURES OF S&T OUTPUTS

Marginal Productivity

This research stream includes a variety of studies that focused on the relation between S&T and economic returns. Probably the most cited work has been by three economists: Griliches, Mansfield, and Terleckyj. Zvi Griliches (1958) had conducted some early studies on the contributions of R&D to the marketplace, as in the example of the hybrid corn.[3] More recently (1998) he summarized the many years of investigation in a collection of essays on the topic of R&D and productivity.[4]

Initially economists had considered S&T, and its outcome in the form of technological change, as somewhat of an "exogenous variable." During the 1950s and 1960s, while investments in S&T had been growing dramatically, and outcomes from these activities had begun to accumulate, economists had mainly considered technological change as a "residual." Namely, the growth in productivity in the American economy was partially due to labor and capital, so that whatever else remains to be the cause of such growth can be attributed to S&T.

Griliches and Nestor Terleckyj[5] (1984) were among the early economists who applied statistical correlations between industrial expenditures for R&D and the industry's rate of productivity increase. Edwin Mansfield continued the work by these economists, and by John Kendrick (1977) who had studied two-digit manufacturing companies as early as 1948-1966.[6] Other researchers in this pioneering group included Robert Solow (1957),[7] Jacob Schmookler (1966),[8] and Ira Horowitz (1960).[9] Mansfield's research disaggregated expenditures for basic research and applied research.[10] By and large he concluded that the composition of industrial R&D, in addition to the size of investments in such R&D, has a significant impact on the rate of productivity growth. Mansfield's (1956) work also extended to academic research and its economic impacts.

More recently, Albert Link (1982) studied the effects of disaggregated investments in R&D and productivity increases, adding more findings to the body of evidence.[11] Another economist, John Gowdy (1993), studied 58 German industries in an effort to relate R&D expenditures with productivity growth for the period 1980-1986.[12] He found a strong correlation between labor productivity and direct R&D expenditures.

The link between productivity growth (primarily in manufacturing) and S&T has been tortuous and inconclusive. Economists measure productivity in two modes: neoclassical production function and a more recent approach that considers reproducibility of capital and the effects that occur between sectors. Much of the research utilized the neoclassical approach, so that R&D data were considered a specialized type of resource (capital) and included in the production function. The estimated returns were quite low.

The Productivity Paradox

However, even with the use of more recent approaches, the link between R&D and productivity growth has not been satisfactorily established. This phenomenon of a puny measurable impact of R&D and S&T on growth in productivity (however defined) has been termed by economists "The Productivity Paradox."[13]

The discussion in the literature of this paradox has developed along two main lines: (1) R&D and S&T in general and their impact on industrial productivity, and (2) information technology (hardware, software, and other office automation) and their impact on industrial productivity.

In the case of the general impacts of S&T on industrial productivity, Griliches (1998) summarized the issue in his book on the body of knowledge in the relation between R&D and industrial productivity.[14] He and other economists have suggested that inadequate measures of productivity are partly to blame for the seeming slowdown in the 1970s, 1980s, and early 1990s. The other factor seems to be the emergence and growth of the service sector, while the manufacturing sector, although still very strong, has become smaller. Thus, in such an expansion of the economy toward services, and reduction in manufacturing, the productivity effects are not captured in the productivity data.

Another explanation has focused on the process by which companies adapt technology to their operations. Increase in productivity depends on the way companies integrate the outcomes from S&T into their operations. In this sense a company's productivity growth depends on other, complementary investments for the integration of technology, as well as on the company's ability to manage its resources effectively by redesigning its work processes and by adapting to dynamic changes in its relevant environment.[15]

Nevertheless, as early as 1995, the popular press heralded the advent of "the age of productivity" in the U.S. economy.[16] By pointing to a strong gain of over 3.5% in 1995, economists predicted that, if such a growth could be maintained, the U.S. economy will create more jobs and have a sustained noninflationary growth. Indeed, such remarkable growth continued through the 1990s, but the problem persists, as the massive investments in technology have failed to pay back in corresponding increases in productivity. As early as 1995, and in subsequent years, an additional explanation for the growth in industrial productivity was the combination of massive investments in nontechnology assets, restructuring, and the cooperation of the labor force through stagnant labor costs.[17]

In summary, although it is acknowledged that other factors influence productivity, the link between investments in S&T and productivity is disappointing. Regardless of the statistical sophistication and more accurate calculations, investments in S&T have not yielded satisfactory and comparable improvements in productivity at the aggregate level. When, however, individual companies are studied, the results appear to be more optimistic, particularly in the case of information technology.[18]

Information Technology and the Productivity Paradox

Labor productivity is measured by the American Bureau of Labor Statistics as real output (gross domestic product) per worker. When multiyear investments in information technology (IT)—including computers, hardware, software, and other office equipment—are correlated with corresponding or even lagged gains in productivity, the result is disappointing or, in some calculations, even negative.[19]

Several economists have expressed their opinions on the paradox and its explanation. Paul Krugman (1995), for example, has argued that the U.S. economic policy-makers have focused more on competitiveness than on increasing productivity ("obsession with competitiveness").[20] Krugman also argued that the Asian economic miracle has been fueled not by technology but by increased inputs of capital and particularly labor.[21]

Robert Solow (1987) encapsulated the disappointing performance of information technology by saying that computers can be found everywhere, except in the statistics on productivity.[22] Paul Strassmann (1985, 1990) compared financial indicators such as general and administrative costs, and "cost of goods," with investments in information technology for the period 1987-1996.[23] He concluded that despite massive investments in IT, the cost of running these companies have continued to rise. Thus he argued that the costs of integrating IT into corporate America are rising to the point where these costs offset any gains that IT may have contributed to productivity. Hence Strassmann (1997) concluded that the "real" value of IT is in its "alignment" with business strategy rather than with productivity.[24] This alignment should be measured in IT's impacts on the net cash flow of the corporation.

The linking of IT with strategic management of industrial companies was also investigated by Geisler (1988, 1992, 1997) in a series of studies in the financial and healthcare delivery sectors.[25] Geisler found the link to be quite tenuous, as even service companies consider IT as a "back room" cost-saving activity, rather than a partner in the strategic management process.

Similarly, Michael Dertouzos (1998), director of MIT's laboratory for computer science, compared computers to electronic bulldozers.[26] In his celebrated book on the information revolution, Dertouzos (1997) argued that although in the 1980s the manufacturing sector increased its productivity by 17% and office productivity decreased by 7%, information technology will contribute to *human* productivity, albeit at a very slow pace.[27]

Explaining the Paradox

If indeed there is such a paradox, it seems that despite Moore's law for computing power, economists are divided on the real and measurable impact of IT on companies and the economy.[28] Figure 7.1 summarizes the plausible explanations offered for the largely disappointing economic

Figure 7.1
Plausible Explanations for the Productivity Paradox

- Issues in the measurement of productivity, so that some gains are not captured.[29]
- Costs of adoption and integration of IT into corporate work process may offset gains in efficiency and productivity.[30]
- Inadequate adaptation of IT to changing business needs and strategic direction, or the inability to capture such adaptation.[31]
- IT contributes to work processes through improvements in quality or customer service rather than simply increase in production quantities.[32]
- Employees tend to use IT in ways other than strictly business needs, through learning effort and "tinkering" with computers.[33]
- Increased complexity of software program and of IT systems lead to increased training and adaptation, and to a delay in payoffs, and primarily maintenance.[34]
- IT has not yet fully penetrated the "front office" activities of many companies, contributing primarily to "back room" processes that lend themselves to routinization, but not to knowledge-based work processes.[35]
- IT has yet to become a moving force in knowledge-based systems and in the knowledge-based economy.[36]

impacts of S&T in general and IT in particular on industrial and office productivity.

In summary there are three main categories or groups of explanations for the link between S&T (and especially IT) and productivity. The first is the group that deals with factors of the conceptualization of productivity on the one hand and the nature of investments in S&T and its outcomes. The second group has factors that refer to the lack of a theoretical link between investments in S&T (and IT), and productivity. In this category the arguments are that we are essentially comparing apples and oranges.[37]

The third category includes factors related to measurement problems of primarily the productivity variable. The issue here is not only the measurement of manufacturing and office productivity, but the larger issue of the returns to organizations from investments in S&T (and IT).[38]

The generalized comparison between investments in S&T and marginal productivity (along the lines of a Cobb-Douglass production function) has shown to yield unsatisfactory results. As in the case of selected industries, investments in S&T are made for other purposes as well, such as to improve the effectiveness of the organization and its relations with customers.

FINANCIAL MEASURES

At both firm and industry levels economists have been trying to assess the impacts of S&T on the firm and the industry by utilizing financial measures such as return on investment and cost-effectiveness. Although this effort has not yielded encouraging results, the attractiveness of being able to compute expected financial return (return on investment—ROI, or return on assets—ROA) has fueled many such attempts.

As early as 1971, Richard Foster had applied the method of internal rate of return from the R&D budgets of four industries and the IBM corporation.[39] He used a straightforward approach which related the cash flow to expenditures for R&D. However, the assumptions underlying his key equations were unrealistic. In particular he assumed that it would be feasible to allocate with precision R&D investments to new products, and that it is feasible to identify and to precisely compute the proportions of sales and profits that resulted from R&D.

More recently several authors have argued that such a direct approach is tenuous, insufficient, and even misleading. Mechlin and Berg (1980) listed the imprecision of measurement and problems with allocation of overhead to R&D as key factors undermining the use of ROI.[40] They also argued that ROI would be appropriate to estimate the returns from development projects that are "particularly well defined, short term" (p. 94). Finally, they also proposed the mix of financial measures with other subjective judgments of the R&D effort.

In the case of information technology, many industry managers have argued that not all of the investments in IT can be applied to a rigorous ROI technique. Some returns can be satisfactorily isolated and defined, hence can also be estimated by ROI methodology.[41] Similar concerns and limitations are also frequently cited for the applicability of the ROA method.

Some economists have considered various factors and circumstances that affect investments in R&D and S&T. Kristiansen (1998), for example, argued that network externalities may contribute to a company's decision to partake in an R&D race, thus boosting its level of investments in the generation of new products and services.[42] He also argued that regulations regarding price and entry, as well as standards imposed early on by the industry, may affect the R&D race in the opposite direction, by removing incentives for conducting massive R&D.

Jones and Williams (1998) argued that the literature that computed *social* rates of return to R&D by means of total factor productivity growth had underestimated investments in R&D.[43] They suggested that since the said literature estimated about 30% social return from R&D, and with a private ROI of 7-14%, an economy such as the United States should increase its investments in R&D two- to fourfold.[44]

So, although used to some extent by industrial companies to measure the returns from their R&D, the methods of ROI and ROA are largely limited. Constraints of measurement issues, the nature of the R&D process, and externalities—all impinge on the organization's ability to accurately assess the financial returns from R&D and S&T investments.

R&D SPILLOVERS

Among the financial and economic measures of R&D evaluation, the focus on R&D spillovers has contributed to a more precise albeit elaborate exploration of how R&D impacts the economy. R&D spillovers are roughly defined by economists as the impacts that outcomes from R&D by other firms have on the effectiveness and outputs of any given firm's own R&D effort.

Griliches (1992) summarized the literature on the R&D spillovers phenomenon.[45] He pointed out that the key question for economists is: Why are there differences among firms in the resources they choose to invest in R&D? Spillovers may help explain the existence of technological opportunities in the industry, but they do not satisfactorily explain such differences. He asked: "Does it work because a firm benefits from the efforts of others or is it just a reflection of spatially correlated technological opportunities?" (p. 281).

Adam Jaffe (1986), for example, explored the impacts of R&D spillovers on the firm's R&D productivity.[46] He concluded that "firms whose research is in areas where there is much research by other firms have, on average, more patents per dollar of R&D, and a higher return to R&D in terms of accounting profits or market value" (p. 998). He also concluded that firms that had a very low R&D effort tend to be negatively influenced by their peers in industries that have a high R&D effort. Jaffe recognized the limitations of the evidence as "circumstantial," and the various assumptions that have to be made, and other measurement problems.[47]

R&D spillovers are therefore considered to be externalities that provide inputs to the R&D activity on the firm. Jaffe defined them as being part of the "supply side of innovation" (p. 998). This aspect of R&D spillovers may be useful in attempting to explain variations in the firms' investments in R&D. But, if spillovers could also be considered in terms of the *process* by which they "transfer" value to other firms, then the door may be opened for assessment beyond the anecdoted constraints. This issue will be better addressed below in the discussion of the difference between R&D productivity and R&D impacts.

R&D Productivity and R&D Impacts

The literature on R&D spillovers and models of growth contains research dealing with two distinct phenomena, albeit related: (1) effects of R&D spillovers on the firm's *own* R&D and its productivity measured by outputs such as patents, and (2) effects of R&D spillovers on the organization and beyond. Jaffe (1986), for example, mixed patents with profits and market value. Although the patenting activity by firms represents a market distortion that influences the decision of a firm to invest in R&D, nevertheless patents are first a measure of the productivity of the inventive activity (R&D) in the firm.

In Figure 7.2 the first phenomenon is shown graphically. Spillovers from the outputs of R&D are dispersed in the industry, whereas spillovers from other firms impact the focal firm. This figure depicts the R&D productivity and its outputs.

The second phenomenon is shown in Figure 7.3, in conjunction with the first. It describes the impacts of R&D outputs on business variables of the organization, on innovation, and the interaction between these two sets of variables. However, as widely discussed earlier in this book, the impact of R&D on firm performance is also influenced, perhaps to a larger degree, by internal management practices, strategic decisions, and other externalities.

The difficulties in isolating and measuring the precise impacts on R&D productivity and R&D impacts on the organization and beyond are an additional constraint in assessing the link between R&D, productivity, and performance.[48] Some studies may have achieved relative success by

Figure 7.2
R&D Productivity and R&D Spillovers

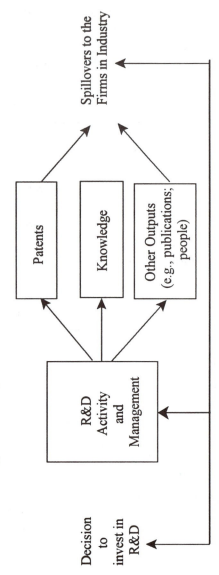

Figure 7.3
R&D Productivity, R&D Outputs, Impacts, and Spillovers

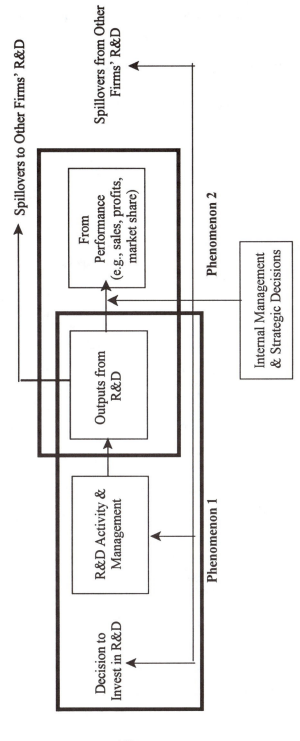

exploring aggregate figures, but at the level of the individual firm this link remains mainly anecdotal.

STRENGTHS AND BENEFITS/WEAKNESSES AND PROBLEMS

Economic and financial metrics for evaluating R&D and S&T are a highly attractive means to measure the output and impacts from R&D and S&T—within the R&D performing organization and beyond, in its industry. Figure 7.4 summarizes the strengths of this category of metrics.

However attractive to both R&D and corporate managers, economic and financial metrics nevertheless suffer from a host of weaknesses and problems. These are summarized in Figure 7.5.

BEST USES

Industrial Examples

Although economic and financial metrics are hardly the perfect means to assess R&D and S&T, they have nevertheless been used by R&D

Figure 7.4
Strengths of the Economic/Financial Metrics

• Offers quantitative measures that describe economic factors, variables, and phenomena.
• Allows for the gathering of time-series data of expenditures and other economic/financial variables, hence makes possible the statistical correlations among these data sets.
• Allows for comparisons with financial measures of other (non-R&D) activities in the firm and in the industry.
• Under certain assumptions, conclusions can be drawn on the economic viability of R&D and the allocation of economic resources to this effort.
• Allows for a link (causal or relational) between investments in R&D or S&T, their economic outputs, and accounting and managerial ratios and indices of financial activity and financial success.
• Allows for the quantification of certain externalities and their relation to the R&D function.
• Inserts an econometric input to the inventive effort.

This list is not exhaustive, nor in any order of importance.

Figure 7.5
Weaknesses and Problems of the Economic/Financial Metrics

• Difficulties in measuring the outputs and the impacts of S&T.
• Difficulties in isolating precise impacts of S&T and allocating them to inputs to S&T.
• Complexity of the innovation process makes it very difficult to apply ROI or ROA techniques, mainly because the returns cannot be attributed to specific inputs.
• Unpredictability of the innovation activity may create technical successes but commercial failures, hence making it difficult to predict outcomes, and to use present value techniques.
• Inputs to commercial success (profits and other economic returns) are varied, thus making it difficult to isolate the effects of S&T.
• Existence of a "temporal gap" between the long-term nature of S&T, and the short-term objectives and the financial tools of corporate management.
• Overall industry-wide statistical correlations provide only circumstantial link between investments in S&T and economic benefits.

This list is not exhaustive, nor in any order of importance.

performing units and by their organizations. One key element in the will of organizations to utilize these metrics is their desire to assess the risk in the R&D and S&T activities. Hence, in addition to the usual concern for the economic assessment of specific investments and the activities they support, there was also the management aspect of dealing with such risk. Clearly, companies are well positioned to assess risky investment and have developed a pool of economic and financial measures for this task—some of which are also used in assessing R&D and S&T. The special case of the inventive process is its complexity, long-term, and other limiting attributes such as multiple inputs and multiple stages in its process.[49]

The following are examples of how major industrial companies use economic and financial metrics for the assessment of their innovation effort. As seen below, in most cases companies utilize a mix of economic/financial and other metrics in their evaluation effort. The level of importance of economic measures (compared with other metrics) varies among companies. A more elaborate description of corporate uses of metrics is given in Chapter 15 of this book.

Union Carbide. The chemical company has used "project profiles" to assess its R&D at the project and program levels.[50] The method is composed of a weighted score of the project, based on several criteria.

Among them are costs, expected ROI, expected profits, and probabilities of technical and commercial success. The expected financial returns are computed in relation to the probabilities of success, which in turn are obtained by subjective evaluation performed by technical and business managers.

General Electric. Among the methods and metrics utilized by GE's R&D Center are the cost per patent and licensing income.[51] The company used such data sets at the corporate level and to assess selected products, such as in medical diagnostics. But the company also used a discounted rate of return analysis of the R&D Center. This analysis was done by an external evaluator. The questions used in determining the financial returns included: (1) what was the total cost of the "technology" generated by the R&D Center? (2) What was the economic/financial benefits to the company? and (3) What was the proportion of inputs from the R&D center that contributed to the economic payoffs from the technology?

In this example the company evaluated actual technologies that "graduated" from the R&D Center, thus making the hindsight approach relatively simpler to quantify. Yet the external consultants based their estimates primarily on *subjective* information provided by those familiar with the technology and its R&D inputs and downstream impacts.[52]

3M Corporation. The consumer products company evaluated its R&D effort by means of internal audits. These included assessment of a variety of programs, such as new product development, new processes, and technology-building programs.[53] The 3M evaluators applied three categories of factors to rate the programs: technical, business, and overall factors. In the technical factors category they included the profitability of technical success. In the business category they used the "financial potential" of the program, measured in terms of potential sales and profits. These were attenuated by the factor of "probability of marketing success."

The company evaluated its own audit.[54] On the positive side the audit helped management to predict with some accuracy the success or failure of the program. It also helped the R&D unit/laboratory to improve its effort and to better communicate with other R&D units at the 3M corporation.

Among the shortcomings of the audit, the company listed the expense of a specialized unit to continually collect data and conduct the audit, and the time and expense it takes on all parties involved in the auditing effort. Nevertheless 3M managers have generally expressed their overall satisfaction with the audits.

CONCLUSIONS

As Walter Robb of General Electric said: "If you knew in advance what the payoff would be, then it's not R&D."[55] The unpredictability of R&D (and S&T) makes any attempt to predict their economic payoff very difficult indeed. With the use of subjectively derived probabilities of both technical and commercial success, firms have tried to gain some crude estimates. Even in the case of *a posteriori* evaluation there are critical problems in first establishing the conceptual progression of R&D to product commercialization to business benefit, then attributing that part of the success to R&D. The appeal of economic/financial measures has always been that they could relate to productivity, profits, sales, and such business variables. If, therefore, problems in conceptualization and measurement hinder such a relation, perhaps the solution, albeit partial, may lie in the strategy of the business.

Managers and many scholars argue for a closer link between R&D and the business/strategic objectives and plans of the organization. Yet, even in uncommon cases where such a link is strong, the element of risk embedded in R&D and S&T, combined with the unpredictability factor, combine to hinder assessments using financial metrics. So, what are the "secrets" to the use of these metrics? An illustrative list of factors that contribute to successful application of financial measures is given in Figure 7.6.

However partially successful, the use of economic/financial metrics has largely failed to accomplish the economists' mission to gain enough knowledge that would allow us to optimize the allocation of resources to R&D and S&T. Because of the complexity of the R&D activity and other factors listed in this chapter, the economic data are circumstantial and most correlations are the result of covariation of inputs and distantly related outputs.[56]

So, as the productivity paradox has demonstrated, aggregated statistics for economic/financial measures are not viable. Alden Bean (1995) has made a succinct case for desegregated and process assessment of economic benefits.[57] He argued that "it is not just the R&D intensity that is important but how the effort is allocated across the spectrum of R&D activities" (p. 28).

Finally, there is one benefit from the use of financial measures to assess R&D and S&T. The psychological impacts of using quantitative and economic data and methods (or even attempting to do so) seem to be

Figure 7.6
Factors That Seem to Influence the Successful Application of
Economic/Financial Metrics to Evaluate S&T

• These metrics are used only as an approximation.
• These metrics are used in conjunction with other measures, such as peer-review and bibliometrics.
• Evaluation is conducted routinely, not a "one shot" activity.
• Evaluation results in reallocation of R&D resources to projects with greater potential commercial value; but *without* terminating or largely reducing basic research.
• There are active channels of communication between R&D and corporate managers on the objectives, process, and utilization of the metrics and the evaluation effort.
• Methodology and actual data collection are done by experts from outside the corporation.
• There is agreement on the use of deflators for net-present-value calculations.
• Benefits to be quantified are collected from downstream the innovation process
• Outputs (such as patents) are also used in addition to expenditures to assess the economic/financial benefits.

Not necessarily in any order of ranking. This list is illustrative. Success is defined as satisfaction of the organization (at the corporate level) with the metrics.

substantial. They raise the awareness of the R&D organization and its commercial entities to the costs of R&D and to its economic contributions.[58]

NOTES

1. There is a vast literature that centers on the *nature* and the actual *usages* of these metrics. The key publications will be cited throughout this chapter. For introductory purposes see the seminal work by economists who had concentrated on researching this issue. For example, see Griliches, Z., "Issues in Assessing the Contribution of R&D to Productivity Growth," *The Bell Journal of Economics*, 10(1), 1979, 92-116. Also see Penzkofer, H., H. Schmalholtz, and L. Scholtz, *Innovation: Wachstum und Beschäftigund* (Berlin: Walter de Gruyter, 1989); and the seminal work by Professor J. Schmookler, *Invention and Economic Growth* (Cambridge, MA: Harvard University Press, 1966). Also see Augud, D., "A Review of R&D Evaluation Methods," *IEEE Transaction on Engineering*

Management, 20(4), 1973, 114-120; and Haltmaier, J., "Measuring Technical Change," *The Economic Journal*, 94(376), 1984, 924-930. Also see the comprehensive review in Freeman, C., *The Economics of Industrial Innovation*, 2nd ed. (Cambridge, MA: MIT Press, 1986). Also see the unique approach that summarizes the trends in economic measures of R&D and S&T in Archibugi, D., "In Search of a Useful Measure of Technological Innovation (To Make Economists Happy Without Discontenting Technologists)," *Technological Forecasting and Social Change*, 34(3), 1988, 253-277. In particular, see Rubenstein, A., "Economic Evaluation of Research and Development: A Brief Review of Theory and Practice," *Journal of Industrial Engineering*, 17(11), 1966, 615-620.

2. Coombs, R., "A Reflection on the Main Themes of the 1997 R&D Management Conference," *R&D Management*, 28(3), 1998, 213-214.

3. See Griliches, Z., "Research Costs and Social Returns: Hybrid Corn and Related Innovations," *Journal of Political Economy*, 66(5), 1958, 419-431. Also see Griliches, Z., "Returns to Research and Development Expenditures in the Private Sector," in J. Kendrick and B. Vaccara (Eds.), *New Developments in Productivity Measurement and Analysis* (Chicago: University of Chicago Press, 1980).

4. Griliches, Z., *R&D and Productivity: The Econometric Evidence* (Chicago: University of Chicago Press, 1998). The book contains essays that were written between 1979 and 1994, and a revised interpretation by Griliches.

5. See, for example, Terleckyj, N., "Comment on R&D and Productivity Growth at the Industry Level," in Z. Griliches (Ed.), *R&D, Patents, and Productivity* (Chicago: University of Chicago Press, 1987) pp. 496-501.

6. Kendrick, J., *Understanding Productivity: An Introduction to the Dynamics of Productivity Change* (Baltimore: Policy Studies in Employment and Welfare, No. 31, 1977).

7. Solow, R., "Technical Change and the Aggregate Production Function," *Review of Economics and Statistics*, 34(2), 1957, 312-320.

8. Schmookler, 1966, *op. cit.*

9. Horowitz, I., "Regression Models for Company Expenditures on and Returns from Research and Development," *IRE Transactions on Engineering Management*, 7(1), 1960, 8-13.

10. See, for example, Mansfield, E., "Basic Research and Productivity Increase in Manufacturing," *The American Economic Review*, 70(5), 1980, 863-873.

11. See, Link, A., "Productivity Growth, Environmental Regulations and the Composition of R&D," *The Bell Journal of Economics*, 13(2), 1982, 548-554. Also see, Link, A., "Basic Research and Productivity Increase in Manufacturing: Additional Evidence," *The American Economic Review*, 71(5), 1981, 1111-1112;

and, Link, A., *Technological Change and Productivity Growth* (London: Harwood Academic Publishers, 1987).

12. Gowdy, J., "Innovation Spending and Productivity Growth in the German Economy 1980-1986," *Applied Economics*, 25(4), 1993, 675-680.

13. In 1960-1973 total factor productivity averaged 3.5% increase per year. In the late 1970s it dramatically slowed down to an average of 0.8%, and in the 1990s remained at this overall lower level of growth. Labor productivity declined from 4.5% per year to an annual average of about 1.5%. In 1997 there was a rise in productivity to over 3%. This surge is discussed below.

14. Griliches, Z., *R&D and Productivity*, 1998, *op. cit.* Also see the reviews of this book in: *The American Journal of Economics and Sociology*, 57(3), 1998, 305-306; and *Journal of Macroeconomics*, 21(1), 1999, 208-209; and Wakelin, K., "R&D and Productivity: The Econometric Evidence," *The World Economy*, 22(1), 1999, 148-149.

15. See the studies by Erik Brynjolfsson and Lorin Hitt. Although they and their colleagues studied the effects of computers and information technology on productivity, their assertions are nevertheless applicable to general impacts of S&T. Brynjolfsson and Hitt also introduced the role of the individual company and its strategy and operations, rather than rely solely on aggregate industrial data. See, for example, Brynjolfsson, E., and L. Hitt, "Computers as a Factor of Production: The Role of Differences Among Firms," *Economics of Innovation and New Technology*, 3(3-4), 1995, 183-195. Also see Brynjolfsson, E., and L. Hitt, "Paradox Lost? Firm Level Evidence on the Returns to Information Systems," *Management Science*, 42(4), 1996, 541-558.

16. Farrel, C., "Riding High: Corporate America Now Has an Edge Over Global Rivals," *Business Week*, October 9, 1995, pp. 134-146.

17. See *ibid.*, p. 157. Also see Urgo, M., "Computers and Productivity: Analysis of Current Literature and Some Significant Issues," *Business Information Review*, 13(3), 1996, 195-199.

18. See, for example, Lichtenberg, F., "The Output Contributions of Computer Equipment and Personnel: A Firm-Level Analysis," *Economic Innovations and New Technology*, 3(3-4), 1995, 201-217.

19. See Loveman, G., "An Assessment of the Productivity Impact of Information Technologies," *MIT Management in the 1990s*, Working Paper, 88-054, July 1988. This report revalidates Loveman's 1994 study, although some critics argue that the negative results of the marginal contribution of information technology to productivity is due to the type of deflator of the expenditures for information technology. See Barwa, A., and L. Byungtal, "The Information Technology Productivity Paradox Revisited: A Theoretical and Empirical Investigation in the Manufacturing Sector," *International Journal of Flexible Manufacturing Systems*, 9(2), 1997, 145-166.

20. See Krugman, P., *Peddling Prosperity: Economic Sense and Nonsense in an Age of Diminished Expectations* (New York: W. W. Norton, 1995). Also see a review of Krugman's book in McConville, D., "The Krugman Paradox," *Industry Week*, 243(21), 41-49. More recently Krugman tackles other issues of economic growth and risk-taking, and paints a pessimistic picture of the "drifting" of the American economy. See Krugman, P., *The Age of Diminished Expectations: U.S. Economic Policy in the 1990s* (Cambridge, MA: MIT Press, 1997).

21. Darwent, C., "The Paradox of Cheap Labor," *Chief Executive*, 116(1), 1996, p. 16. This is also the opinion of Stephen Roach, chief economist at the investment firm of Morgan Stanley Dean Witter. He argued that most of the gains in productivity had been the result of reengineering and restructuring. By reducing the workforce, the denominator in the productivity ratio is reduced, thus the same amount of production appears to be done more productively. See, for example, Roach, S., "The New Technology Cycle," *Economic Perspectives* (New York: Morgan Stanley & Co., September 11, 1985).

22. Solow, R., "We'd Better Watch Out," *New York Times*, Book Review, July 12, 1987, p. 36.

23. See Strassmann, P., *Information Payoff: The Transformation of Work in the Electronic Age* (New York: The Information Economics Press, 1985). Also see Strassmann, P., *Business Value of Computers* (New York: The Information Economics Press, 1990).

24. See, in particular, Strassmann, P., *The Squandered Computer: Evaluating the Business Alignment of Information Technologies* (New York: The Information Economics Press, 1997). See his website at: <http://www. strassmann. com>.

25. See, for example, Geisler, E., "Measures of Efficiency and Effectiveness in the Selection, Usage, and Evaluation of Information Technology in Service Industries," Paper presented at the Meeting of the Information Industry Council of Metropolitan Chicago, September 15, 1988. Also see, Geisler, E., "Managing Information Technologies in Service Companies: Strategic Versus Operational Practices," Paper presented at the International Engineering Management Conference, Eatontown, NJ, October 26-28, 1992; and, Geisler, E., A. Rubenstein, and G. Hoffman, "Planning Information Systems Strategy in the Firm," Portland Second International Conference on Management of Engineering and Technology, Portland, OR, July 27-31, 1997.

26. Dertouzos, M., "Start the E-Bulldozers," *Technology Review*, 101(6), 1998, 23-25.

27. Dertouzos, M., *What Will Be: How the New World of Information Will Change Our Lives* (New York: HarperCollins, 1997). See in particular pp. 269-272.

28. *Moore's Law* states that the number of transistors in each computer chip doubles every 18-24 months, thus doubling the performance of computers, making their advance exponential over the past three decades. Gordon Moore, Chairman Emeritus of Intel Corporation, first observed this phenomenon. Embedded in this phenomenon is the assumption that as chips become more powerful, while their price remains constant or is even reduced, their positive impacts on work and productivity should therefore be noticeable and measurable. Clearly this was not obviously so in the 1980s and 1990s. See, for example, a review of this "law" in Hunt, K., "Pixels," *The Hartford Courant*, March 5, 1998, p. 3. Also see Noor, A., "Laws That Govern Internet Growth," *The New Straits Times*, September 21, 1998, p. 6. Some economists and computer experts have argued that "Moore's Law" will perhaps continue throughout the decade 2000-2010, but will cease to exist due to physical constraints of the chip technology. See Dertouzos, *What Will Be*, 1997, *op. cit.*, p. 321.

29. See, for example, Betts, M., "Real IS Payoff Lies in Business Benefits," *Computer World*, 28(1), 1994, 10-12.

30. See, for example, Lewis, B., "IS Productivity Paradox Means We Should Be Measuring Effectiveness," *Infoworld*, 18(9), 1998, 61-62.

31. See, for example, Richman, L., "The Big Payoff from Computers," *Fortune*, 129(5), 1994, 28-30.

32. See, for example, McCune, J., "The Productivity Paradox," *Management Review*, 87(3), 1998, 38-40.

33. See, for example, Darwent, C., 1996, *op. cit.*

34. See, for example, Due, R., "The Productivity Paradox Revisited," *Information Systems Management*, 11(1), 1994, 74-75.

35. See Strassmann, P., "Computers Are Yet to Make Companies More Productive," *Computer World*, September 15, 1997, 12-18.

36. See, for example, Pinsonneault, A., and K. Kraemer, "Middle Management Downsizing: An Empirical Investigation of the Impact of Information Technology," *Management Science*, 43(5), 1997, 659-679. Also see Kelley, M., "Productivity and Information Technology: The Elusive Connection," *Management Science*, 40(11), 1994, 1406-1425.

37. See, for example, Hoos, I., "When the Computer Takes Over the Office," *Harvard Business Review*, 38(4), 1960, 102-112. Also see Markus, M., and D. Robey, "Information Technology and Organizational Change: Causal Structure in Theory and Research," *Management Science*, 34(5), 1988, 583-598.

38. See, for example, Due, R., "The New Productivity Metrics," *Information Systems Management*, 13(4), 1996, 60-63. Some progress has been achieved in selected industries where investments by companies in the industry, targeted toward IT, have yielded positive outcomes measured by benefits that include labor productivity and other impacts such as customer service. See, for example,

Goldsborough, R., "PCs and the Productivity Paradox," *Computer Dealer News*, 14(41), 1998, 25-26; Harris, C., "The Information Paradox," *Canadian Insurance*, 104(2), 1999, 5-6; and an extensive review of the topic in the hotel industry in David, J., S. Grabski, and M. Kosavana, "The Productivity Paradox of Hotel-Industry Technology," *Cornell Hotel and Restaurant Administration Quarterly*, 37(2), 1996, 64-75. This study of nine hotel chains with 4,000 properties has concluded that hotel managers invest in information technology to impact services to guests. The authors argued that although "the connection between technology and productivity in the hotel industry remains poorly understood," (p. 74), their survey revealed that managers invested in IT not always nor specifically to increase productivity, but "are also aimed at boosting customer-service levels and augmenting the number of services offered" (p. 73). A boost to the link between IT and productivity at the national level was provided by Allen Greenspan, Chairman of the Federal Reserve Board. In a speech delivered on June 14, 1999, to a technology forum, Greenspan asserted that IT indeed has contributed to new ways of conducting business and has created savings in labor costs, thus contributing to increase in productivity. He also expressed doubts in some expert opinions that such gains have not yet peaked and advised caution.

39. Foster, R., "Estimating Research Payoff by Internal Rate of Return Method," *Research Management*, 13(3), 1971, 27-43. In the Appendix Foster estimated the profits from research in terms of the sales of new products resulting from research, so that the present value of profits to R&D in Year One of the R&D project can thus be estimated. Foster's key equation was:

$$PT = S_o RP = \sum_{t=t_R+t_D+1}^{t=t_R+t_D+t_L} X+t$$

where:

R	=	corporate profits as a percent of sales
P	=	fraction of total profits that results from sales of new products
S_o	=	sales in the base years
t	=	length of the research project
t_D	=	length of project stays in development
t_L	=	product market life
X	=	$\left[\dfrac{1+r}{1+D}\right]$
D	=	internal rate of return
r	=	rate of growth of sales

40. Mechlin, G., and D. Berg, "Evaluating Research—ROI is Not Enough," *Harvard Business Review*, 58(5), 1980, 93-100.

41. See, for example, Mueller, B., "Measuring ROI: Can It Be Done?" *AS/400 Systems Management*, 25(11), 1997, 8-10. Some consulting companies offer specific software programs that contain ROI methods useful in assessing IT projects. See, for example, the website for The Meta Group: <http://www.metagroup.com>.

42. Kristiansen, E., "R&D in the Presence of Network Externalities: Timing and Compatibility," *Rand Journal of Economics*, 29(3), 1998, 531-547.

43. Jones, C., and J. Williams, "Measuring the Social Return to R&D," *The Quarterly Journal of Economics*, 113(4), 1998, 1119-1135. They defined social rate of return as the gain in consumption from reallocation of a "unit of output from consumption to R&D today" (p. 1121).

44. See, for example, Jones, C., "R&D-Based Models of Economic Growth," *Journal of Political Economy*, 103(2), 1995, 263-293.

45. For a review of the relevant literature, see Griliches, Z., "The Search for R&D Spillovers," *Scandinavian Journal of Economics*, 94 (Supplement), 1992, 29-47.

46. Jaffe, A., "Technological Opportunities and Spillovers of R&D: Evidence from Firms' Patents, Profits, and Market Value," *The American Economic Review*, 76(5), 1986, 984-1001.

47. See also Bernstein, J., and Nadiri, I., "Research and Development and Intra-Industry Spillovers: An Empirical Application of Dynamic Duality," *Review of Economic Studies*, 54(3), 1989, 249-269. Also see Griliches, Z., and F. Lichtenberg, "Interindustry Technology Flows and Productivity Growth: A Reexamination," *Review of Economics and Statistics*, 66(4), 1984, 324-329.

48. For example, in the area of international markets several authors have attempted to estimate the spillovers of technology on countries and industries. Illustrative studies are: Frantzen, D., "R&D Efforts, International Technology Spillovers and the Evolution of Productivity in Industrial Countries," *Applied Economics*, 30(11), 1998, 1459-1469. This study concluded that international R&D spillovers influence total factor productivity even more than domestic R&D spillovers. Also see Keller, W., "Are International R&D Spillovers Trade-Related? Analyzing Spillovers Among Randomly Matched Trade Partners," *European Economic Review*, 42(8), 1998, 1469-1481; and, Bayoumi, T., D. Coe, and E. Helpman, "R&D Spillovers and Global Growth," *Journal of International Economics*, 47(2), 1999, 399-428. The authors suggested that in addition to investments in domestic R&D, countries can improve their total factor productivity by creating trade relations with countries that have accumulated knowledge spillovers from their past R&D. Also see Engelbrecht, H., "International R&D

Spillovers, Human Capital, and Productivity in OECD Economies: An Empirical Investigation," *European Economic Review*, 41(8),m 1997, 1479-1488.

49. See, for example, Grabowski, H., and J. Vernon, "A New Look at the Returns and Risks to Pharmaceutical R&D," *Management Science*, 36(7), 1990, 804-821. In this study the authors concluded that the returns for a new drug is on average equal to the cost of capital in the industry.

50. Whelan, J., "Project Profile Reports Measure R&D Effectiveness," *Research Management*, 14(5), 1976, 14-16.

51. Robb, W., "How Good Is Our Research?" *Research-Technology Management*, 29(2), 1991, 16-21.

52. The consulting firm of Arthur D. Little Inc., for example, used the following formula to compute the cost-benefits of corporate R&D programs:

$$N = \frac{\log\left(\dfrac{B}{C}\right) + \log\left(-\log P_F\right)}{\left(-\log P_F\right)}$$

where: N = number of projects to maximize net benefits;
         C = cost;
         B = benefit.

53. Krogh, L., J. Prager, D. Sorensen, and J. Tomlinson, "How 3M Evaluates Its R&D Programs," *Research-Technology Management*, 26(6), 1988, 10-14.

54. See *ibid.*, pp. 13-14. See Arthur D. Little in *The National Benefits' Costs of Enhanced or Recovery Research*, Report to the U.S. Energy R&D Administration, August 1976 (Springfield, VA, NTIS document FE-2021-4).

55. Robb, W., 1991, *op. cit.*, p. 20.

56. This issue is described more fully in Geisler E., *Methodology, Theory, and Knowledge in the Managerial and Organizational Sciences: Actions and Consequences* (Westport, CT: Quorum Books, 1999).

57. Bean, A., "Why Some R&D Organizations Are More Productive Than Others," *Research-Technology Management*, 33(1), 1995, 25-29.

58. See, for example, the case of Procter & Gamble, in Tecklenburg, H., "A Dogged Dedication to Learning," *Research-Technology Management*, 28(4), 1990, 12-15.

8

BIBLIOMETRIC MEASURES: PUBLICATIONS AND CITATIONS

In this era of heightened importance of knowledge creation and management, and the heralding of the knowledge economy, bibliographic outcomes from S&T are a key measure of inventive activity. Even before the recent wave of models and books about knowledge by Tom Davenport and Ikujiko Nonaka, who brought this topic to the forefront of management practice, scientists and engineers produced knowledge as the main outcome of their work. Such knowledge was in the form of written and oral reports, publication in scientific and technical outlets, proceedings from conferences, and similar modes of propagation of their outputs. This knowledge may lead to new or improved products and processes, and other commercial applications.

But, first of all this knowledge appears in the form of documentation that specifies it and helps to distribute, transfer, store, and propagate its contents. In addition to the oral transfer of knowledge—by means of conferences and personal contacts among scientists—documentation is the most prolific and successful method of knowledge transfer. It is not surprising, therefore, that the literature on bibliographic outcomes is abundant, covering almost every aspect of scientific and technical knowledge.[1]

WHAT IS BIBLIOMETRICS?

Bibliometrics is a general term that refers to measures of scientific and technical *published* outputs from science and its disciplines. The measures are simply the count of publications in scientific and technical journals, and the indexing of citations of these publications by other scientists in these journals. The first measures *quantity* of these outputs, the second *quality*.

But bibliometricians, those who professionally count and analyze these outputs, have argued that there is more to these measures than just counts. They see in the data from these measures strong indices of the progress and the dynamics of academic disciplines, and the generation and evolution of new disciplines.

Perhaps the most celebrated pioneer in this area was Derek de Solla Price (1963, 1978) who proposed bibliometrics as the means to study the progress of scientific disciplines and their evolution.[2] Thus, when scientists (researchers in academia, industry, and government laboratories worldwide) publish their theories and findings in archival journals, a massive data base for S&T is created. This becomes the state of the art (SOA) of a given discipline.

The measures of count of publications and citations by peers of these publications are used in two complementary ways. First, as described above, scientometricians (or any interested scholar) use these data to analyze and to track science. Second, academics and scholars in general use these measures to assess the quality of the published outputs of their peers.[3]

CITATION ANALYSIS

Beyond the mere count of publications, citation analysis is a complex process in which scientific and technical articles cited in the literature are sorted, cataloged, and analyzed. The feasibility of even attempting to index and analyze the immense body of S&T publications was based on an interesting statistical discovery. In his work on sources of information, S. C. Bradford concluded that there was a relatively small number of scientific journals that form the core of any scientific discipline.[4] He also discovered that the scientific literature deals with a small number of topics, and that the importance of the published work of scientists depends on the relevancy of such work to the topic. Moreover, the more relevant the work, the more likely it is to be published in those journals that are strongly related to the given topic. Thus, the important scientific work of any great significance and impact on the state and direction of science and of the individual discipline is published in a concentrated manner in a few journals. These findings are generally called *Bradford's Law*.

Numerically, studies to validate this law have shown that of over 8,000 scientific journals, about 2,000 publish 85% of all articles and 95% of cited articles. Moreover, some 200 journals publish 25% of relevant articles and a staggering 50% of all articles cited have been initially published in this core of journals.[5]

The principle that guides the utility of citation analysis is the ability to assess the quality of scientific work and its reporting in scientific journals. It works simply as a quantitative measure of how scientific peers view the work of a colleague—by citing it in their own articles. Since science progresses incrementally, scientists report their own work as having benefitted from and influenced by the work of others (also known as "prior art"), within a given topic. Hence, the more a scientist is cited by colleagues, the higher the relevance and impact of the work (i.e., quality).

Since all accolades in science are awarded by the scientific community itself, citation analysis is a *postfactum* peer review, in a quantitative mode. Scientists thus vote with their own writing, by citing those colleagues whose work they consider crucial to their own. Comparisons between winners of the Nobel Prize, considered the most prestigious of scientific awards, and citations of their work have shown that Nobelists are also "citation superstars."[6]

Citation analysis may also be used to track developments in a given discipline and to identify new trends. As new journals emerge and the trend shifts toward new batches of citations, movements, transformations, and "revolutions" may be identified by the volume (number) of articles in a given topic and the trend in their citations.[7]

HOW BIBLIOMETRIC ANALYSIS WORKS

Bibliometrics is a procedure that counts the number of S&T publications and other means of knowledge transfer, and also performs an analysis of citations and cocitations in order to assess the quality of these publications and their trends. Bibliometric analyses are routinely conducted by every researcher who investigates the state of the art on a given topic in the researcher's disciplinary area. But a more comprehensive analysis is performed by commercial organizations dedicated to this issue, by some government agencies, and by selected universities.

As a tool for evaluation, in addition to the count of publications and citations of these articles, bibliometrics analysis also includes: (1) peer-reviewed books; (2) chapters in such books; (3) impact of citations (the citations weighted by the comparative quality of the journals in which they appear); (4) refereed conference proceedings; (5) keynote addresses at scientific meetings; (6) peer-reviewed research grants obtained, and other written communications such as personal letters, electronic mail exchanges, and personal verbal communications (although all these are difficult to quantify).

If these items appear to be headings in the curriculum vitae of a scientist, indeed they are. The above items are key indicators of scientific outcomes and productivity. They apply to individuals as well as to a discipline.

Key Bibliometric Organizations

Much of the activity in bibliometrics and citation analysis has been in European organizations. The University of Leiden in the Netherlands and the University of Sussex in the United Kingdom have specialized leading programs in this area. The Dutch Technology Foundation,[8] founded in 1981, and the Hungarian Academy of Sciences are also in the forefront of this field. The journal *Scientometrics* is published by Elsevier and edited in Hungary.[9] A more recent internet journal is *Cybermetrics*, edited in Spain.[10]

However, American organizations are leaders in the commercial utilization of bibliometrics. Two main groups conduct most of the comprehensive analyses: ISI in Philadelphia and CHI Research Inc. in New Jersey. Both companies are supported by the U.S. National Science Board, which contracts with them for analyses of its biennial *Science & Engineering Indicators*, and by other American government agencies (NIH and the Department of Commerce), as well as large industrial companies.

ISI (Institute for Scientific Information) was founded in 1958 by Eugene Garfield and Henry Small.[11] The company analyzes over 8,000 journals worldwide and an additional 8,000 books and conference proceedings from 250 disciplines in the natural and biological sciences, social sciences, and arts and humanities. ISI provides university libraries with the so-called *Web-of-Science* which includes the Science Citation Index of references and analysis. Scholars searching for publications can do so by relevance, date, first author or journal, and the number of times an article was cited.[12]

CHI was established in 1968 by Francis Narin and his colleagues. The company focuses on the technological aspects of citation analysis, with emphasis on patents and the science that has produced them.[13] CHI has databases that track the technology base of many large corporations.

Criteria for Journal Selection

Citations of articles in the core number of scientific journals are computed following a rigorous selection of journals considered to be relevant enough to be included in the disciplinary core. Figure 8.1 shows the key criteria used by bibliometricians.

BIBLIOMETRICS: AN EVALUATION TOOL

As a tool for the evaluation of S&T, bibliometric measures offer a mix of quantitative and qualitative indicators of the outcomes from this activity. Although these outcomes only cover the proximal outputs of published scientific results, they may easily be applied to various levels of aggregation—from the individual scientist to the discipline or even a country.

Figure 8.1
Key Criteria in Selecting Scientific Journal for Bibliometric Analysis

• Publishing standards as a scientific journal with an editorial board.
• Publication is continuous and additive building-up a pool of knowledge in the discipline.
• Timeliness of publication so that the journal is published at the times indicated in its editorial policy.
• Papers are accepted for publication based on a strict process of peer review.
• Acceptance rate is relatively low, reflecting a process of strict quality control.
• Structure and style follow the conventions of scientific publishing.
• Journal covers a specific area in a given discipline. Interdisciplinary journals are so stated and obey all above standards.

Compiled from several sources. This list is illustrative.

When compared with the levels of evaluation, bibliometric measures apply to all of the levels. Figure 8.2 shows a matrix of the various measures and respective levels of evaluation.[14]

In essence these measures are indicators of the *scientific performance* of individuals, groups, and institutions. The sheer volume of this output is tremendous. Scientists worldwide publish daily about 5,000 papers in refereed journals. So, if we simply limit ourselves to count of papers and their subsequent citations, this would be feasible for the levels of the individual researcher or the research group. But for macroanalysis of institutions and disciplines, as well as for comparisons among them, there is a need for computerized statistical techniques.[15]

Quantity and Quality

As an evaluation tool, the count of publications indicates the volume of scientific and technical output for each of the levels of evaluation. In

Figure 8.2
Bibliometrics and Levels of Evaluation

Level of Evaluation	Bibliometrics				
	Articles	Books	Citations	Proceedings	Grants
Individual Researcher	✓	✓	✓	✓	✓
Group or Team of Researchers	✓	✓	✓	✓	✓
Project	✓	✓	✓	✓	
Area Thrust	✓	✓	✓	✓	
Program (multiple projects)	✓	✓	✓	✓	
Institution	✓	✓	✓	✓	✓
Scientific Discipline	✓	✓	✓	✓	
Region or Country	✓	✓	✓	✓	

This list is not exhaustive nor in any order of priority or importance.

this manner, count of publications indicates levels of activity in a given discipline and for a given institution. Similarly, count of citations also offers a quantitative indication of the *scientific impacts* of the publications in a given discipline, for an institution, and for the individual scientists or the research group.

But it is the quality aspect of the count of publications and citations that ignites the imagination of scientists and those who study their performance. Analyses of citations yield conclusions that advance beyond the quantities. Movements of intellectual emphasis can be traced within an organization and a discipline. The qualitative analysis may show how a scientific topic is evolving, how it is changing, and how "paradigms" may be shifting within disciplines.[16] By linking publications and citations to journals considered "core" or "elite," citation analysis provides an indication of the quality of the scientific output. Such evaluative findings are subsequently used to rank people and organizations and are the basis for the structuring of scientific reputations of individuals and their institutions. The underlying principle is that the more a certain paper (denoting an intellectual contribution to a scientific field) is cited in the relevant and "core" journals, the higher its impact and the higher the quality and the prestige of the authors and their institution.

Measuring S&T Productivity

Counts of publications and citations analysis may be used to measure scientific *productivity* at the various levels of evaluation. When combined with other measures of the scientific activity they become components of indexes or macroindicators of productivity. The simplest method is by comparing outputs over time. This will show trends in productivity, and will also show the length of time it takes to propagate a given intellectual contribution.

For example, research on AIDS (Acquired Immunodeficiency Syndrome) began in the early 1980s and progressed along several different protocols or approaches to the detection and cure of the disease.[17] A study by researchers at Texas Woman's University explored the patterns in the AIDS literature related to women.[18] The authors scanned several databases and their findings show cross-disciplinary scattering of the studies in this specific topic. They also investigated the productivity of scientists who published on this topic but failed to find clusters of authors.

Similar studies explored the productivity of scientists and institutions by evaluating the patterns of publication of universities and large government research organizations such as the National Institutes of Health.[19] These studies have concluded that there are clusters of more productive institutions and a small group of prolific people within them, forming a small and highly influential set of very productive members of focused "community of science" within each discipline and subdisciplines.

Lotka's Law of Scientific Productivity

In 1926 A. Lotka observed a certain pattern in the distribution of scientific outputs (publications) among scientists who publish.[20] In what became known as Lotka's Law, he proposed that the number of authors who are credited with a certain number of papers published will be inversely proportional to the number of published papers for each author. In his formulation, authors who published n papers in a topical area of a discipline is about $1/n^2$ times the number of authors who have only one article to their credit. This law was further extended by Price's Law of Square Roots.[21] Price argued that about half of all the publications in a given scientific area will be published by a small number of authors equal to the square root of the total number of all the authors who published in the specific area.

Lotka's Law and Price's refinement describe the phenomenon of the focused community of science in each scientific area with a very small number of scholars who are responsible for a disproportionate volume of publications. Several researchers have since tested the validity of this law. Nicholls (1989) tested Lotka's formula with 70 author-productivity data sets and found that 90% of the cases behaved in accordance with the formula.[22] Chen (1989) used indexing to overcome problems with statistical tests of goodness-of-fit used on the data sets and also corrected his analysis by considering the productivity of new versus old journals.[23] Chen concluded that this approach helped to improve the empirical testing of the law. Similar support was given by a study of the accounting literature.[24] This study found that, based only on the *number* of publications, a very small group of scholars dominate the discipline, and a staggering two-thirds of these prolific authors are graduates of only seven top universities.

Focused Communities of Science

Counts of publications and citation analyses have shown across scientific disciplines that scientific productivity (measured by published papers and their citations) tends to be disproportionately concentrated within a very small group of authors. Figure 8.3 shows this phenomenon in two levels: the topical area in the discipline and the core of authors.

Scientific outputs are therefore concentrated with a small, self-selected group of scholars who form an elite within the discipline and who set the tone for the development and progress of the topical area. They form what Crane (1972) had named the "invisible college" within the given disciplinary area,[25] with the exception that the results from bibliometric analyses identify these "colleges" and bring them out into the light.

The importance of Lotka's Law and of the phenomenon of focused communities transcends the mere curiosity of scholars in the information and library areas. They are of great value to managers of S&T and R&D, and to senior managers of corporations and government agencies. The proven reality in scientific publishing that shows a concentration of relevant effort in small sets of performers makes it easier to manage this effort. By managing I mean appropriate actions taken to reward these performers and to consider them to be crucial resources in the progress and outputs of S&T.[26] This phenomenon is thus too valuable to be merely considered an issue of information diffusion.

Figure 8.3
Communities of Science and Highly Productive Core of Authors

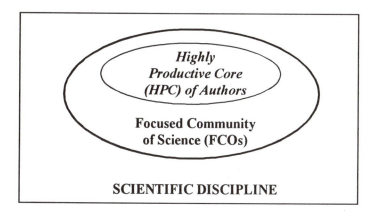

BIBLIOMETRICS AND FINANCIAL MEASURES

Counts of publications and citation analyses are a favored metric of scientific outputs. Several attempts have been made to link these output measures to financial measures discussed in Chapter 7. Two studies will illustrate such attempts to link the measures.

Fruman (1992) studied six major business areas in 30 publicly held American electronics companies.[27] He used number of articles published by the R&D units of the companies, considered with number of patents, to measure the S&T outputs. Fruman found a strong correlation between these metrics and R&D expenditures. He also found that there is a strong correlation between the volume of publications and business activity measured by deliveries to customers. Therefore he concluded that inputs to R&D (expenditures), R&D publications, and business deliveries are all highly correlated. He computed the "cost of a publication" of at least $1.5 million, whereas in order to maintain the level of the given business activity over time, companies need to spend at least 4% of sales for R&D (in some areas as high as 18%).

Geisler (1998) also computed the cost per article, but used macroindicators for the United States and Japan.[28] But Geisler used only the cost of *basic research* to arrive at his cost figures, and the number of articles published by American and Japanese scientists in the world S&T literature. For 1990 data he arrived at a cost of $120,194 for an American article compared with $221,563 for a Japanese article.[29] Because Fruman used total R&D expenditures, he could not arrive at a cost per publication for each business area. He concluded that each area has a different mix of research modes ranging from theoretical (basic research) to product development. Hence in some areas the research that generates articles may be much smaller than in other areas.

These and similar studies have established a strong relation (albeit not causal) between financial measures (such as expenditures on the input side and sales/deliveries on the output side) and bibliometric measures. Such findings help to validate the metric as a good measure of inventive activity.

STRENGTHS AND BENEFITS

Bibliometrics has a variety of strengths and a set of benefits it offers the evaluator of S&T. These strengths may be divided into three categories:

structure, measurement, and representation. Figure 8.4 shows the strength clustered under each of the categories.

The structure category includes those strengths that allow for multiple levels of analysis, and a relatively adequate cost for the analyses. In the measurement category the strengths suggest that the data are available and the analysis is straightforward, making it a relatively simple procedure to plan and to undertake. Finally, bibliometrics is considered by the S&T community to be a valid representation of the phenomenon of outcomes from inventive activity.[30]

Figure 8.4
Strength of Bibliometrics in the Evaluation of S&T

A. STRUCTURE
• Bibliometrics can be applied to various levels of generators of intellectual outputs, such as individuals, groups, institutions, and countries.
• The cost of collecting the data and conducting meaningful analysis is relatively adequate.
• The measures are already built into the metric, thus there is no need to establish them and to test them for validity.
B. MEASUREMENT
• Bibliometrics allows for quantitative assessment of S&T outputs by counts of papers and citations, and for qualitative assessment by analysis of core journals and their relative impacts.
• Bibliometrics and its analysis is a relatively straightforward approach, relying on a few assumptions.
C. REPRESENTATION
• Bibliometrics can be applied to the entire spectrum of S&T where outcomes take the form of reports, papers, and citations.
• Bibliometrics, through citation analysis, helps to determine the role that individuals and institutions have in the evolution of a scientific discipline.
• Bibliometrics analysis allows for the identification of trends and developments in science and technology and in scientific disciplines.
• By convention, bibliometrics has been accepted by the S&T community as valid representation of the outputs from intellectual and inventive activities.

This list is not exhaustive nor in any specific order.

So, in summary, it appears that bibliometrics is a relatively simple, inexpensive, and valid metric of the intellectual outcomes from science. Moreover, citation analysis can yield insights well beyond the mere numbers, to identify and describe trends in the evaluation of scientific disciplines and specific areas or topics within them.[31]

WEAKNESSES AND PROBLEMS

Four groupings of weaknesses and problems with bibliometrics are shown in Figure 8.5, and they include the often-cited shortcomings of the S&T metric.

Figure 8.5
Weaknesses and Problems with Bibliometrics

A. COVERAGE
  • Published articles are only one measure of outputs from scientific activity, hence the metric does not cover reports, other written communications such as electronic mail, letters, and personal communiques.
  • Articles published in peer-reviewed journals and their citations analysis disregard the outputs and intellectual contributions in articles published in technical outlets, as well as work-in-progress.

B. MEASUREMENT
  • The "Pied-Piper Effect": bibliometrics, particularly citation analysis, measures influence, not quality. Citations are selective and refer to those papers that "toe the line" and do not "rock the boat."
  • Published articles measure output in a given subdiscipline or discipline, hence cross-disciplinary analysis may be difficult to validate, because of the different structure and procedures of the scientific investigation in each discipline; particularly ease and rate of publishing, and the nature of the peer selection processes (the "Apples and Oranges Effect").
  • Counts of publications and citations analysis tend to disregard the influence of the stage in the life of the discipline or area, such as "mature" area versus an "evolving" new area (the "Gulliver Effect").

C.   GENERALIZABILITY
   • Counts of publications and citations lack a standard for their validation as a measure of quality. When compared with inputs (investments in R&D), the resulting analysis relies on covariation of two distinct phenomena and disregards the complexities of the R&D process.
   • The only standard for validation of bibliometrics is convention of a small and elite group of influential scientists.
   • As in the "Hindsight" project, the problem is: "How far in time should citations go?" Should articles in quantum mechanics cite Einstein's work *and* that of the Greek philosophers and mathematicians? Citations are thus highly selective and refer to a relatively short timeframe, preferably within a few years of the focal paper in which they are cited.

D.   BIASES
   • Because of the almost incestuous nature of the small group of prolific publishers, there is an inordinate amount of self-citations and citations of "friends" and other members of this elite group. Thus, authors who publish in areas that are near the boundaries of their discipline or in cross-disciplinary topics are much less likely to be published in top journals or to be cited in them.
   • Criteria for the selection of articles for publication in juried journals are built into the process and will bias the resultant counts of papers and citations in favor of those authors preferred by the reviewers.
   • Selection and analyses of key journals and the interpretation of the counts of papers and citations are based on assumptions of validity of these metrics as measures of quality and internal dynamics of the discipline. Such assumptions are the product of opinions and judgment, hence biased.
   • The selection and analysis process of key journals and papers to be included in this process is biased in that analysts who are generally outside the discipline or the area impose their own views and criteria in making determinations and drawing conclusions that transcend the data.

This list is not exhaustive nor in any specific order.

The picture that emerges from Figure 8.5 is a critique of bibliometrics as a *biased* evaluative metric. Problems arise in the interpretation of the crude numbers, and in creating scenarios of quality assessment and patterns within a scientific field.[32] Due to the high degree of specialization within scientific disciplines, analyses of publications and citation at the disciplinary level are weakened due to the "Apples and Oranges Effect," combined with other weaknesses of the metric. Hence, cross-disciplinary conclusions from this metric are even more biased and fraught with shortcomings, such as the "Gulliver Effect," where large or mature disciplines are compared with nascent or small ones.

For the specific field of economics, John Davis (1998), for example, has criticized the use of the Social Sciences Citation Index.[33] He argued that the SSCI metric (in the case of economics) is a poor measure of the performance of individual scientists and their academic departments. He concluded that the value of the index "does not lie in providing a means of evaluating scholarly productivity, but rather in providing a broad-brush picture of the overall development of the discipline" (p. 63).

Such criticisms of bibliometrics encapsulate the various shortcomings of this metric. The consensus among the critics is that the metric has some merit, but its value as a "stand-alone" metric is doubtful.[34]

BEST USES

The strengths of bibliometrics make it a widely used measure of scientific outputs, when in combination with other metrics (such as peer review), and when applied with consideration of the shortcomings discussed above. Illustrative uses are given below and they include evaluations in academic institutions, industry, and federal S&T laboratories.

Academic Institutions

Bibliometrics is used extensively by academic institutions to assess the productivity of individual scientists and university departments. Bibliometrics is also used to evaluate the productivity and volume of activity of scientific disciplines and their specialties.[35]

Although these practices are subject to the problems and weaknesses identified in Figure 8.5, they are nevertheless the centerpiece of academic assessment of colleagues and programs. Academic institutions use bibliometrics because of the following reasons. First, academic communities have invested much effort into developing a field of science and are thus protective of their interests by solidifying and encouraging the status quo. Bibliometrics concentrates on the evaluation of productivity within the limits of the status quo. Second, bibliometrics is biased toward *incremental* progress of scientific knowledge, hence giving more value to papers and citations that are mere additions to the field rather than new ideas.[36] This also helps in maintaining the existing order of the community of science so that the "boat is not rocked."

Another reason is the impact that editors of scientific journals have over the process of selection and approval of articles. These editors are "gatekeepers," at once policing the discipline and channeling the traffic of publications, largely in favor of the status quo and in strengthening the integrity of the community of science. Last, by using bibliometrics to evaluate colleagues (with all the ramifications in people's mobility and decisions on allocation of scarce resources), the core group within the community of science thus safeguards the "keys to the club." Bibliometrics provides the *quantitative* measures that support and to a large extent also justify these personnel decisions.[37]

In summary, although there are some *technical* shortcomings of bibliometrics that are recognized by academics, the *social* and *organizational* utilities of this metric make it nevertheless a very useful tool in evaluating academic performance.

Use of Bibliometrics by Industrial Companies

Industrial companies utilize bibliometrics in two basic modes: evaluation of their scientific personnel within the R&D unit, and evaluation of the R&D function in the firm. The scientific and technical personnel are evaluated in several different ways, discussed at length in Chapter 15. Bibliometrics is used to evaluate one aspect of the scientific workforce: scientific and technical productivity as perceived by the community of science.

Companies hold the general belief that, in addition to any benefits accrued to them from an outstanding R&D group, the publication record of the group generates a much-cherished reputation among peers in the scientific community. Other elements of this belief include the prestige that such a group possesses would permeate onto customers, firm's constituencies, and the public in general. Companies such as AT&T used their laboratories (such as Bell Laboratories before the breakup of the giant company in the 1980s) as showcases of pride, prestige, and scientific achievements.[38]

As in academic institutions, companies use bibliometrics as part of their system that evaluates scientific employees, although they are cognizant of its shortcomings. Corporate management tends to defer in this matter to their R&D managers and to standards established by the scientific community. So bibliometrics is thus incorporated into the firm's personnel evaluation to reflect the perceived stature of its R&D group in the external academic community.

Evaluation of the R&D function of the firm by bibliometrics is also equivalent to the evaluation of the firm itself—within its industry—relating to its scientific prominence. In the case of the pharmaceutical industry, Koenig (1983) found a strong correlation between clinical articles produced by companies in this industry and their drug outputs.[39] IBM publishes its own academic journals, and other companies such as Xerox are proud of the publication output of their laboratories, heralding such outputs as desired indicators of the *corporate* success. In firms that depend on innovations for survival, the stature of their R&D unit is paramount in establishing their reputation and in advancing their strategies and product lines. The record of publications thus becomes a strategic factor in these firms' sustained competitiveness.[40]

To summarize, industrial companies have adopted bibliometrics for two reasons. The first was reliance on the judgment of the scientific community and its rankings. The second was the recognition that by supporting a climate of publishing, the firm contributes to the intellectual enrichment of its personnel, to the fostering of interactions with other organizations, and ultimately to the economic bottom line through innovations and sustained scientific and technical competitiveness.

Evidently, not every company can afford a top-notch scientific team led by "stars" (defined by citations count). The strength of a successful R&D function is also a product of the development of interrelated skills, experience, and a supportive environment within the corporation. The use of bibliometrics portrays only the volume of outputs but fails to assess other strength factors of the scientific group.[41] However, by using bibliometrics as a tool for evaluation of research quality, the corporation becomes part of an assessment environment that idealizes S&T employees who are prolific publishers, well-cited, hence respected by their colleagues in the scientific community.

Public S&T Laboratories

Publicly supported S&T laboratories utilize bibliometrics in two distinct manners, each according to the type of laboratory. The first is use of these measures as academic institutions. Publicly supported laboratories in the United States vary by the degree to which they encourage fundamental science, as a prerequisite for supporting the mission of their parent agency.[42] These laboratories utilize bibliometrics to assess the quality of their scientists as do universities—within the range and limitations of the federal guidelines and policies for promotion, tenure, and employee compensation.

The second type of laboratories are oriented toward specific programs of the parent agency, in a way similar to industrial laboratories and their link to business product lines. Bibliometrics is a metric used by these organizations to assess the quality and reputation of *some* of its leading scientists, while also giving high consideration to other S&T employees who are not publishing but contribute different outputs. Such outputs include patenting discoveries, transferring technology to the parent agency and to industry, and involvement with professional associations. In many cases the distinction between two federal laboratories in these categories are as marked as those between a research university and a corporate or divisional laboratory.[43]

BIBLIOMETRICS, SCIENCE, AND TECHNOLOGY

Bibliometrics is used to evaluate the volume and quality of scientific activity. Although Narin and his colleagues lumped publications, citations, *and* patents in this metric, and found significant correlations between them, I have chosen to discuss them separately. Counts of publications and citations assess a phenomenon that differs from that of patents and patenting. In general terms it may be stated that counts of publications and citation analysis describe and assess outputs from *science*, whereas patents are one indicator of a given technology and its development.[44]

Although there may be a relatively seamless process by which science and technology are continually intertwined, this is also a serial and stage process. Scientific activity leads to the generation of new technology, thus preceding it both temporally and conceptually. Bibliometrics should be viewed as an indicator of written or reported outputs from the scientific activity. Patents usually describe a method, a product, or an artifact which may or may not have been the outcome of scientific activity or of scientific discovery. Thus, the incorporation of count of patents into the term "bibliometrics" is misleading.[45]

Count of scientific articles and the analysis of their citations are uniquely well-defined metrics, geared toward the assessment of bibliographical outcomes from scientific activities. This type of outcome is also present at all stages of the innovation continuum. Reports, papers, and proceedings of conferences may describe advanced stages such as testing, prototyping, and other manipulations of a technology. Yet, only in the case of citations of previous patents in patent applications do we find any useful inclusion of counts of an item for evaluative purposes. This view that distinguishes between bibliometrics and count of patents and limits bibliometrics to scientific outputs need not assume a linear or purely hierarchical structure in which science ultimately leads to the development of new technology. I agree with Derek de Solla Price that science and technology are intertwined in a wavelike fashion.[46] Albert Rubenstein and his colleagues (1969) have studied the diffusion of R&D through "coupling relations" and the role that liaison functions play in maintaining the flow between research to technology commercialization.[47]

So, even though bibliometric indicators can be used in the evaluation of technology-oriented scientific activity, they are best employed to evaluate science in the academic definition of knowledge creation. The key reason is that in this mode, such a metric is sufficient since it describes much of the phenomenon of scientific discovery, whereas when applied downstream the innovation process, it will describe only one, perhaps quite small, attribute of the phenomenon of technological development and utilization. The need to limit bibliometrics to science is based on practical considerations of methodological effectiveness, so that the science portion of the S&T process might be better described and evaluated.

CONCLUSIONS

Bibliometrics is widely used in the evaluation of scientific activity. But how well does this metric describe the phenomenon it purports to measure, and how well does it serve the S&T community and other interested parties? The well-deserved popularity of this metric is evidenced in the scholarly literature and such commercial applications as ISI and CHI.[48]

Despite the various methodological shortcomings, bibliometrics serves the *social*, *organizational*, and *psychological* needs of the scientific community and S&T policy-makers.[49] The metric offers a combination of quantitative figures of merit and judgmental inputs that are built into the analysis of the raw numbers. The use of this metric also has contributed to the progress of science. Because it measures the transfer of scientific knowledge, its use in evaluation of S&T thus encourages diffusion of scientific outcomes and their written transfer via academic and other channels. This focus on communication helped to make science more accessible.[50]

On another front the evaluative use of bibliometrics has also turned the limelight toward quality in research and science. Regardless of the degree of accuracy or validity of citation analysis as a measure of quality, its use helped to promote the notion of quality research as judged by the scientific community, to be subsequently applied as a key variable in personnel decisions.

Does bibliometrics adequately describe how science works and how S&T evolves? Perhaps not, but its importance is less in how accurately it portrays the dynamics of scientific progress as it is in the evaluative function it performs for the academic community and for S&T and other managers and policy-makers.

NOTES

1. There are several thousand references that relate to the bibliographic outcomes from S&T. See, for example, Dr. R. Kostoff's website at <http://www.dtic.mil/dtic/kostoff/index.html>. For a basic text see Garfield, E., *Citation Indexing, Its Theory and Application in Science, Technology and Humanities* (Philadelphia: ISI Press, 1983). Dr. Garfield is founder of the Institute for Scientific Information.

2. In addition to Price , D. de Solla, *Little Science, Big Science...and Beyond* (New York: Columbia University Press, 1963), see also Price, D., *Science Since Babylon* (New Haven, CT: Yale University Press, 1978).

3. This regime is commonly described as "publish or perish" in the academic environment. See, for example, Allen, C., "Assessing Research Productivity of Academic MIS Departments," Master Thesis, Naval Postgraduate School, Monterey, CA, September 1993, NTIS ADA2749596XSP. Also see Braun, T., W. Maczelka, and H. Schubert, "World Science in the Eighties: National Performances in Publication Output and Citation Impact, 1985-1989 Versus 1980-1984 in Life Sciences, Engineering, and Mathematics," *Scientometrics*, 31(1), 1994, 3-30.

4. See a discussion of Bradford and his finding in Garfield, E., *Citation Indexing* (New York: John Wiley & Sons, 1979). Garfield's prolific publications on citation analysis and bibliometrics appeared in a variety of journals and in the newsletter *Current Contents* of his company, Institute for Scientific Information. See, for example, Garfield, E., "The Relationship Between Mechanical Indexing, Structural Linguistics, and Information Retrieval," *Journal of Information Science*, 18(5), 1992, 343-354. Also see Garfield, E., "Dispelling a Few Common Myths About Journal Citation Impacts," *Scientist*, 11(3), 1997, 11-21; and Garfield, E.,

"Validation of Citation Analysis," *Journal of the American Society for Information Science*, 48(10), 1997, 962-963. In these and other publications, Eugene Garfield has been a vocal spokesperson for the utility of citation indexing and analysis, and a strong promoter of bibliometrics.

5. Bradford's Law has been widely studied. See, for example, Braun, T., W. Glanzel, and H. Grupp, "The Scientometric Weight of 50 Nations in 27 Science Areas, 1989-1993, in the Life Sciences," *Scientometrics*, 34(2), 1995, 207-237. Also see Cozzens, S., and L. Leydesdorff, "Journal Systems as Macro-Indicators of Structural Change in the Sciences," in A. Van Raan, R. Debruin, H. Moed, A. Nederhof, and R. Tijssen (Eds.), *Science and Technology in a Policy Context* (Leiden: DSWO Press, 1993), pp. 219-233.

6. See Garfield, E., "The 1991 Nobel-Prize Winners Were All Citation Superstars," *Current Contents*, 5(2), 1992, 3-9.

7. Some of this analysis is also performed by using co-word analysis and mapping. These are discussed in Chapter 9. On the link between citation analysis and changes or transformations in science, see, for example, Diodato, V. and F. Smith, "Obsolescence of Music Literature," *Journal of the American Society for Information Science*, 44(2), 1993, 101-112. Also see Dumas, T., E. Logan, and A. Finley, "In Focus—Using Citation Analysis and Subject Classification to Identify and Monitor Trends Within a Discipline," *Proceedings of the ASIS Annual Meeting*, Volume 30, 1993, pp. 135-150.

8. The website for this organization is <http://www.stw.nl>.

9. See: <http://scienceserver.orionsci.com/elsevier/01389130/>.

10. See: <http://www.cindol.csic.es/cybermetrics/cybermetrics.html>. This journal was inaugurated in 1997. Its full name is *International Journal of Scientometrics, Informatics, and Bibliometrics*, however it usually is referred to as simply *Scientometrics*. The editor can be reached at:<isidro@cindoc.csic.es>. In 1999, of the 15 members of the editorial board, eight were European and only three American.

11. See their website at <http://www.isinet.com>.

12. ISI also publishes *Current Contents* of tables of contents from journals.

13. See their website at <http://www.chiresearch.com>.

14. See, for example, Narin, F., D. Olivastro, and K. Stevens, "Bibliometrics Theory, Practice, and Problems," *Evaluation Review*, 18(1), 1994, 65-76. These authors proposed four levels of aggregation for bibliometrics: (1) policy (at the national or regional levels), (2) strategy (at the level of companies and universities), (3) tactics (at the level of the scientific area or discipline), and (4) conventional (at the level of the individual scientist). Also see Peritz, B., "On the Heuristic Value of Scientific Publications and Their Design: A Citation Analysis of Some Clinical Trials," *Scientometrics*, 30(1), 1994, 175-186.

15. See, for example, Narin, F., and A. Breitzman, "Inventive Productivity," *Research Policy*, 24(4), 1995, 507-519. Francis Narin of CHI Research is a

prolific publisher of scientific and technical papers on bibliometrics and patents. Also see Narin, F., "Patent Bibliometrics," *Scientometrics*, 30(1), 1994, 147-155; and Narin, F., and D. Olivastro, "Status-Report: Linkage Between Technology and Science, " *Research Policy*, 21(3), 1992, 237-249.

16. See the seminal work of Kuhn, T., *The Structure of Scientific Revolutions*, 2nd ed. (Chicago: University of Chicago Press, 1972). Also see Karki, R., "Searching for Bridges Between Disciplines: An Author Co-Citation Analysis on the Research Into Scholarly Communication," *Journal of Information Science*, 22(5), 1996, 323-334; and Katz, J., and D. Hicks, " A Systemic View of British Science," *Scientometrics*, 35(1), 1996, 133-154.

17. This section is based on data from the AIDS database: <http://biblioline.nisc.com>, which is a website of the National Information Service, with support from the National Institute of Medicine and the U.S. government. The database contains publications from 1980 to the present and is a combination of Aidline, AIDS drugs, and AIDS testing.

18. Huber, J., and M. Gillaspy, "A Bibliometric Description of the Literature of AIDS Specific to Women: 1980-1993," *HIV Infected Women Conference Proceedings*, February 22-24, 1995, p. 67.

19. See, for example, Narin, F., "Bibliometric Techniques in the Evaluation of Research Programs," *Science and Public Policy*, 14(2), 1987, 99-106.

20. Lotka, A., "The Frequency Distribution of Scientific Productivity," *Journal of the Washington Academy of Sciences*, 16(3), 1926, 317-323.

21. Price, *Little Science, Big Science, op. cit.* Also see Price, D. de Solla, "Networks of Scientific Papers," *Science*, 149, 1965, 510-515; and Price, D. de Solla, "The Analysis of Square Matrices of Scientometric Transactions," *Scientometrics*, 3(1), 1981, 55-63.

22. Nicholls, P., "Bibliometric Modeling Processes and the Empirical Validity of Lotka's Law," *Journal of the American Society for Information Science*, 40(6), 1989, 379-386. Nicholls also tested Price's square-root law with 50 empirical data sets. His findings did not support Price's formula. Nicholls believes that Price's law suffers because of its reliance on Lotka's Law, which argues for an *inverse* relationship. See Nicholls, P., "Price's Square Root Law: Empirical Validity and Relation to Lotka's law," *Information Processing & Management*, 24(4), 1988, 469-478.

23. Chen, Y., "Analysis of Lotka's Law: The Simon-Yule Approach," *Information Processing & Management*, 25(5), 1989, 527-545.

24. Chung, K., H. Pak, and R. Cox, "Patterns of Research Output in the Accounting Literature," *Abacus*, 28(2), 1992, 168-186.

25. Crane, D., *Invisible Colleges: Diffusion of Knowledge in Scientific Communities* (Chicago: University of Chicago Press, 1972).

26. Regardless of the evident value to S&T managers, much of the research literature on this phenomenon is concentrated in the information and library sciences

literature. See, for example, Oromaner, M., "The Diffusion of Core Publications in American Sociology," *Journal of the American Society for Information Science*, 28(1), 1977, 34-37. Also see Pinski, G., and F. Narin, "Citation Influence for Journal Aggregates of Scientific Publications: Theory with Applications to the Literature of Physics," *Information Processing and Management*, 12(2), 1976, 297-312. More recently see Harter, S., and P. Hooten, "Factors Affecting Funding and Citation Rates in Information Science Publications," *Library and Information Science Research*, 12(3), 1990, 263-280. Similarly, there are analyses of publication trends in specific disciplines, such as economics, management, and psychology. See, for example, Bairam, E., "Communication: Institutional Affiliation of Contributors to Top Economic Journals: 1985-1990," *Journal of Economic Literature*, 32(2), 1994, 674-679. Also see Beed, C., and C. Beed, "Measuring the Quality of Academic Journals: The Case of Economics," *Journal of Post-Keynesian Economics*, 18(3), 1996, 396-412. The authors argued that citation analysis of economics journals do *not* measure quality, partly because the ranking effort in economics have failed to consider arguments on the shortcomings of citations that are found in other literatures. Also see Extejt, M., and J. Smith, "The Behavioral Sciences and Management: An Evaluation of Relevant Journals," *Journal of Management*, 16(3), 1990, 539-551; and White, M., and K. White, "Citation Analysis of Psychology Journals," *American Psychologist*, 32(5), 1977, 301-305.

27. Fruman, C., "Choices in R&D and Business Portfolio in the Electronics Industry: What the Bibliometric Data Show," *Research Policy*, 21(2), 1992, 97-124.

28. Geisler, E., "The Cost of Research," *Engineering Valuation and Cost Analysis*, 2(1), 1998, 33-44.

29. Using data from the U.S. National Science Foundation for 1990, overall national expenditures for basic research amounted to about one-ninth of total R&D. Thus, Geisler's figure of $120,194 may be converted to the total spending for R&D, arriving at $1.05 million. The figure of $1.5 million is higher perhaps because it refers only to industrial outputs, whereas Geisler's figure includes universities and government research laboratories that produce a large number of publications at relatively lower overall costs (particularly in the case of universities).

30. See, for example, Peters, H., R. Braam, and A. Van Raan, "Cognitive Resemblance and Citation Relations in Chemical Engineering Publications," *Journal of the American Society of Information Science*, 46(1), 1995, 9-22. The authors concluded that co-cited articles are also highly related in their content or subject matter.

31. See, for example, Hubbard, R., and J. Armstrong, "Replications and Extensions in Marketing: Rarely Published But Quite Contrary," *International Journal of Research in Marketing*, 11(3), 1994, 233-249. The authors studied three key journals in marketing and discovered that replications of studies, *even*

when their findings contradict other studies, receive fewer citations than the original studies they had refuted. This far-reaching finding attests to the powerful effect of selected studies in a discipline, and the difficulties in challenging them.

32. See Beed and Beed, 1996, *op. cit.* Also see MacRoberts, M., and D. MacRoberts, "Problems of Citation Analysis: A Critical Review," *Journal of the American Society for Information Science*, 40(5), 1989, 342-349; and the seminal work on the social processes in science, Cole, J., and S. Cole, *Social Stratification of Science* (Chicago: University of Chicago Press, 1973); and Folly, G., B. Hajtman, I. Nagy, and I. Ruff, "Some Methodological Problems in Ranking Scientists by Citation Analysis," *Scientometrics*, 3(2), 1981, 135-147. These authors analyzed publications by 80 Hungarian scientists and have concluded that "it is clearly indicated that all quantities based on citation counts measure *something different* from those representing the output of a scientist" (p. 146).

33. Davis, J., "Problems in Using the Social Sciences Citation Index to Rank Economics Journals," *American Economist*, 42(2), 1998, 59-64.

34. See, for example, Clark, M., "Misleading Citation Indexes," *ChemTech*, 23(1), 1993, 3-4. Also see several papers published by the Society for the Social Studies of Science, founded in 1975. See the society's website at <http://www.lsu.edu/guests/ssss/public-html>.

35. For example, see the use in university assessment in Davis, G., and P. Royle, "A Comparison of Australian University Output Using Journal Impact Factors," *Scientometrics*, 35(1), 1996, 45-58. Also see the use in assessing disciplines in Glanzel, W., "A Bibliometric Approach to Social Sciences, National Research Performances in Six Selected Social Sciences Areas, 1990-1992," *Scientometrics*, 35(3), 1996, 291-307.

36. See, for example, Grant, W., "Evaluating Researcher Performance by Citation Analysis," *South African Journal of Science*, 87(11-12), 1991, 557-560. Also see Greenwald, A., and Schuh, E., "An Ethnic Bias in Scientific Citations," *European Journal of Social Psychology*, 24(6), 1994, 623-639. Not only is there ethnic bias, but critics have long contended that bibliometrics tends to favor scientific outputs that congregate around communities in the English-speaking world, as an indicator of bias toward the leading core groups in world science and technology. See, for example, Schoepflin, U., "Problems of Representativity in the Social Sciences Citation Index," in P. Weingart (Ed.), *Representations of Science and Technology* (Leiden, Netherlands: DSWO Press, 1992), pp. 177-188. Also see Hicks, D., and J. Potter, "Sociology of Scientific Knowledge: A Reflexive Citation Analysis of Science Disciplines and Disciplining Science," *Social Studies of Science*, 21(3), 1991, 459-501.

37. Hurley, J., *Organization and Scientific Discovery* (New York: John Wiley & Sons, 1997). Also see Lindsey, D., "Using Citation Counts as a Measure of Quality in Science: Measuring What's Measurable Rather Than What's Valid," *Scientometrics*, 15(3-4), 1989, 39-58.

38. See, for example, Koenig, M., and D. Gans, "The Productivity of Research Effort in the U.S. Pharmaceutical Industry," *Research Policy*, 4(4), 1975, 331-349.

39. Koenig, M., "Bibliometric Analysis of Pharmaceutical Research," *Research Policy*, 12(1), 1983, 15-36. More recently Cockburn and Henderson studied this industry and concluded that the interaction of pharmaceutical firms with the external scientific community is significantly correlated with their success in drug discovery. See Cockburn, I., and R. Henderson, "Absorptive Capacity, Coauthoring Behavior, and the Organization of Research in Drug Discovery," *The Journal of Industrial Economics*, 46(2), 1998, 157-182. The authors also found that the success of these firms in discovery of drugs is correlated with "the number of 'star' scientists employed by the firm and the degree to which the firm uses standing in the public rank hierarchy as a criterion for promotion."

40. Illustrations of individual firms and their use of counts of publications and citations analysis are routinely published as cases in journals such as *Research-Technology Management*.

41. Cockburn and Henderson's findings notwithstanding, there is of course the ability of the R&D unit and the corporation to commercialize the scientific outcomes that are reflected in and measured by number of publications and citation analysis. More on this in Chapter 15. See, for example, Miller, R., "The Influence of Primary Task on R&D Laboratory Evaluation," *R&D Management*, 21(1), 1992, 3-21. Miller studied 53 laboratories worldwide in 17 technical areas and concluded by cluster analysis that a combination of organizational *and* bibliometric indicators is a better tool for evaluation of research quality.

42. This topic is also discussed more extensively in Chapter 17. Much of the background for the discussion here benefitted from the extraordinary work of Ronald Kostoff, director of technical assessment at the Office of Naval Research. Dr. Kostoff's prolific writings on the assessment of federal R&D are widely cited in this book.

43. For example, laboratories such as Argonne and Fermi of the Department of Energy that conduct fundamental research in high-energy physics are very similar to universities and work very closely with university scientists.

44. Partly because scientific papers may describe and discuss new ideas, new concepts, and thoughts—all of which cannot be patented—but which are the backbone of scientific progress. See, for example, Narin, F., and E. Noma, "Is Technology Becoming Science?" *Scientometrics*, 7(3-6), 1985, 369-381. Also see Price, D., "The Science/Technology Relationship, The Craft of Experimental Science, and Policy for the Improvement of High Technology Innovation," *Research Policy*, 13(1), 1984, 3-20. Also see Faulkner, W., and J. Senker, *Knowledge Frontiers* (New York: Oxford University Press, 1995); and, Watts, R., A. Porter, and N. Newman, "Innovation Forecasting Using Bibliometrics," *Competitive Intelligence Review* 9(4), 1998, 11-19. Also see Kostoff, R., H. Eberhart, and D. Toothman, "Hypersonic and Supersonic Flow Roadmaps Using Bibliometrics and

Database Tomography," *Journal of the American Society for Information Science*, 50(5), 1999, 427-447.

45. See, for example, Narin, F., "Patent Bibliometrics," *Scientometrics*, 30(1), 1994, 147-155. A more detailed discussion of this topic is in Chapter 10. Also see Price, 1984, *op. cit.*, who compared pure and applied science to a dance, where partners move ahead and back of each other in accordance with the music.

46. See, for example, Wagner-Dobler, R., "Science-Technology Coupling: The Case of Mathematical Logic and Computer Science," *Journal of the American Society for Information Science*, 48(2), 1997, 171-183.

47. Rubenstein, A., and C. Douds, "A Program of Research on Coupling Relations in Research and Development," *IEEE Transactions on Engineering Management*, 16(4), 1969, 137-143.

48. The voluminous literature on bibliometrics merits perhaps a more comprehensive discussion than offered in this chapter. However, bound by the focus of the book on the evaluative aspects of the metric, this chapter emphasized only selected elements in the literature.

49. See, for example, a reminder of the bounded power of this metric in: Garfield, E., "Scientists Should Understand the Limitations as well as the Virtues of Citation Analysis," *Scientist*, 7(14), 1993, 12-13. Also see, Glanzel, W., and U. Schoepflin, "A Bibliometric Study on Aging and Reception Processes of Scientific Literature," *Journal of Information Science*, 21(1), 1995, 37-53; and, Johnes, G., and J. Johnes, "Apples and Oranges: The Aggregation Problems in Publications Analysis," *Scientometrics*, 25(2), 1992, 353-365. Also see Sellen, M., *Bibliometrics: An Annotated Bibliography, 1970-1990* (New York: Macmillan Publishing Company, 1993). And see Cronin, B., "Do Deans Publish What They Preach?" *Journal of the American Society of Information Science*, 50(5), 1999, 471-474.

50. See some supportive commentaries in, for example, Korevaar, J., and H. Moed, "Validation of Bibliometric Indicators in the Field of Mathematics," *Scientometrics*, 37(1), 1996, 117-130. Also see Kunz, M., "About Metrics of Bibliometrics," *Journal of Chemical Information and Computer Sciences*, 33(2), 1993, 193-106; and, Pao, M., "Perusing the Literature via Citation Links," *Computers and Biomedical Research*, 26(2), 1993, 143-156. Also see McAllister, P., F. Narin, and J. Corrigan, "Programmatic Evaluation and Comparison Based on Standardized Citation Scores," *IEEE Transactions on Engineering Management*, 30(4), 1983, 205-211. The authors list the advantages of bibliometrics as (1) a true numerical description of research output, (2) allowing for cross-disciplinary comparisons, (3) the unobtrusiveness of the application of the metric, and (4) cost. They also warned that the metric "should always serve in a complementary fashion to an in-depth peer or reviewer evaluation" (p. 211). Also see, Borgman, C., and R. Rice, "The Convergence of Information Science and Communication: A Bibliometric Analysis," *Journal of the American Society for Information Science*,

43(6), 1992, 397-411. Although the authors were somewhat discouraged by their findings, they were nevertheless supportive of the use of this metric, as it allowed them to "identify fairly subtle trends with the available data" (p. 409).

9

CO-WORD ANALYSIS AND MAPPING
OF SCIENCE AND TECHNOLOGY

This chapter will describe co-word analysis and the methods by which roadmaps from research to technology are constructed, followed by the description and analysis of the mapping of science and technology. In general terms, co-word analysis is an extension of bibliometrics which was defined earlier as a metric concerned with the production and quality of textual items. Co-word analysis is the focus of its own chapter mainly because whereas count of articles and citation analysis measure the number of items, co-word analysis is concerned with the actual *content* of these outputs.

CO-WORD ANALYSIS

This term encompasses several technical descriptions of different methods of extracting knowledge from the distribution of certain keywords in S&T texts. In addition to co-word analysis there are: KDD (knowledge discovery in databases), DT (database tomography), and TDM (textual data mining), all of which are content analyses and will be discussed later.

Co-word analysis originated in linguistics and lexicography, in which texts were examined with the purpose of tracing the origins and progression of certain words.[1] As languages evolve, the written records that reflect their usage can thus be analyzed to determine not only the direction in which a language has developed, but also the influence of other languages and cultures by means of the appearance of words and terms used by these cultures.

In modern co-word analysis, this metric is used in the evaluation of S&T. An underlying assumption suggests that scientific ideas, concepts, and findings are reported in written form by using simple text and selected technical terms which are also combinations of words. These words that describe scientific findings are key or index words. They possess two crucial characteristics: (1) they represent images or concepts that the author of the report or article had when translating scientific ideas into words (*descriptors* of the status of the scientific problem or area being reported); and (2) they are the linchpin of the process of transmittal of scientific thoughts, therefore they will be repeated (co-occur) in other texts that report similar thoughts or findings.[2]

How Co-Word Analysis Works

The process by which co-word analysis works is based on quite a simple idea. As Callon and his colleagues (1979) initially demonstrated, co-occurrence of keywords can be calculated for a selected database of published articles in a given disciplinary topic.[3] This count of pairs of keywords that repeatedly appear together allowed the analyst to build a matrix, where in one axis there were the keywords extracted from the articles in the database, and on the other axis the number of co-occurrences of these keywords. The resulting matrix showed the relationship among these words and provided inputs to some analytical mapping of the development of concepts within the disciplinary area or topic.[4]

In essence this was a model of *frequencies* of occurrence of certain joint keywords that portrayed the evolution of ideas and concepts. With the development of such methods as conjoint and cluster analyses, these models of frequencies of occurrence were extended to business applications, but in that instance could not rely on preestablished index or keywords. So, although the use of co-word analysis (with keywords) in the evaluation of S&T was successful in selected topics, inherent weaknesses of this method began to emerge.[5]

Weaknesses and Problems

Co-word analysis with keywords had three major flaws. First, by relying on keywords it relegated much of the validity of the search and analysis to the criteria used in selecting these keywords. Even if the assumption holds that these key terms represent ideas and concepts, they were nevertheless carefully selected by interested parties (authors, editors, and reviewers) so that their credibility and cross-disciplinary usefulness are tainted.

Second, because of the uneven, perhaps biased inclusion of some keywords in a topical area, such keywords were artificially repeated, thus inflating the frequencies to the extent that a concept they purportedly represent had gained unwarranted importance in the interpretation of frequency data.[6]

Perhaps the most crucial weakness was the inability of this method to make use of the free text, or full text of scientific documents. Scientists report findings and present arguments with free text, which contains a rich blend of their thoughts *and* the development of their rationale in the text itself.

Benefits from Co-Word Analysis Using Index Words

Although co-word analysis originally employed keywords with the limitations associated with this method, its practice in evaluating the dynamics of scientific disciplines produced several benefits. The most important benefit was the introduction of such techniques into the realm of S&T evaluation. This method supplemented the count of citations and allowed for a more incisive and in-depth analysis of patterns, relationships among concepts, and a better idea of the structures within a scientific discipline.

Some scholars have argued that citation analysis has been misused. Instead of the original purpose to retrieve information from scientific databases of journal articles by discipline, the metric has been applied primarily to evaluate individual researchers' productivity and in determining the impacts of scientific journals.[7] Therefore co-word analysis has become a preferred measure of the dynamics of scientific disciplines and of patterns of scientific thought.

Another benefit from modern co-word analysis with keywords has been the initial effort that was aimed at dynamic comparisons across disciplines. While tracing the movement of keywords within and between disciplines, analysts were thus able to establish the comparative impacts and the sharing of concepts and methods among different scientific disciplines. So, when combined with comparative counts of citations across disciplines, a structure of networking seemed to emerge.[8]

DATA MINING

With the development since the 1970s of new techniques to scan, search, and extract valuable information from large databases, the concept and practice of "data mining" has rapidly evolved. In general terms data mining includes a variety of methods and techniques to extract value from warehouses of data. These techniques are a combination of statistical tools and analytical thinking that helps to interpret the information thus extracted.[9]

Data mining (DM) has long been a tool in scientific research in those areas where massive data are collected on a given problem. Illustrative disciplinary areas include astronomy, biotechnology (biosequencing), and geosciences.[10] By increasing the sophistication of their computational techniques, scientists were better equipped to reduce these large data sets to a manageable size, and to extract meaningful patterns, correlations, and information that can be useful inputs to analysis and decisions based on the data set.[11]

Techniques Used in Data Mining

Scanning large databases and making sense of patterns and relationships has become a complex task that requires a basket of techniques. As data mining became popular in recent years among business companies, the following techniques have gained in popularity: (1) decision trees, (2) link analysis and nearest-neighbor analysis, (3) artificial neural networks, (4) automatic cluster detection, (5) memory-based reasoning, (6) market-basket analysis, and (7) genetic algorithms.[12]

In essence the application of data-mining techniques involves the joint work of rule-induction, artificial intelligence, and relational databases that go beyond the statistical methods used to uncover associations and correlations. We therefore relegate to the computerized algorithms the task of discovering valuable patterns in particular databases and data warehouses. These techniques go beyond the initial artificial intelligence systems that were known as *expert systems*. Instead of relying on codified opinions of experts, new techniques such as fuzzy logic and artificial neural networks discover patterns in data without preestablished rules or models to guide them. The neural network identifies patterns, then by induction also identifies the rules that govern these patterns. These "search and discover" systems in effect have learned while identifying patterns and relationships. They have learned the rules that emerge, they create emerging models, and they are now able to predict—based on these induced rules and models—how similar data sets will behave. The commercial applications of such techniques are clearly forthcoming and highly promising.

Commercial Applications

Business companies collect, store, and use a tremendous amount of all kinds of data, about their products and services, customers, suppliers, competitors, and regulatory agencies. In the latter part of the 1990s commercial uses of data-mining techniques have emerged in such diverse industries as apparel and financial services.[13] In the former case, mining of data accumulated at point-of-sale allows apparel manufacturers and retailers to gain valuable insights into buyers' behavior and characteristics of products (such as colors, sizes, location of point-of-sale, and demographics). In the case of financial services, companies such as American Express are mining demographic data to discover patterns that illuminate potential customers, thus adding value to their market predictions.

A major potential area for commercial applications of data mining seems to be health care delivery organizations and those organizations that are part of the health care system such as insurance companies, state and federal governments, and manufacturers of medical technology and pharmaceuticals.[14] The volume of data these organizations collect and store on patients, illnesses, and medical experience is staggering and quite diversified. Potential areas are patterns in resources utilization and patient behavior and preferences.

Data Mining and Knowledge Discovery and Management

Not surprisingly, the late 1990s also witnessed the rapid emergence of the area of knowledge management (KM) and the dramatic rise in importance that business executives have begun to assign to "knowledge" and its manipulations for corporate decisions.[15] The advent of sophisticated information retrieval and mining techniques seems to have coincided with this movement of conceptual emergence of knowledge management. The two phenomena had converged in the application of data mining to the task of "knowledge discovery" (KD).[16]

The value of such convergence to business is clear and has started to be exploited by corporations. Simultaneously this has led to the design of knowledge-management systems and to a more intensive exploration of warehouses of data that companies collect and store. The phenomenon may thus be graphically shown as massive movement from data, to information, to knowledge (see Figure 9.1). In addition to obvious logistic and economic issues, the value of data mining to corporations is in the meaningful interpretation of the knowledge discovered (patterns and relationships) and its integration within the KM system.[17]

But a tangential yet important impact of the congruence of data mining and KM is on corporate R&D. As knowledge about markets, marketing, products, and other behaviors emerges from KM and data mining, the role that corporate S&T plays in successful commercialization of innovations may become more amenable to quantitative assessment. For example, relationships between product characteristics and market behavior which hitherto had been hidden in the maze of data, may now be discovered and uncover the contribution of R&D to product design as well as to its market strengths.[18]

What Data Mining Can Do

The tremendous awakening of KM applications that followed the fusion of DM technologies and KM was partially driven by the ability of DM to correlate both quantities and text. The resultant analysis yields results that are richer in content than the traditional co-word analyses.

Consider the case of DM in health care organizations. As patterns and relationships are uncovered, the health care professional is now free to analyze these patterns so that decisions may be made, without the effort previously expended to scan the data and to identify meaningful patterns.[19] Figure 9.2 lists illustrative tasks that DM can perform with databases in health care.

Figure 9.1
A Simplified Model of Exploitation of Data Mining by Business Enterprises

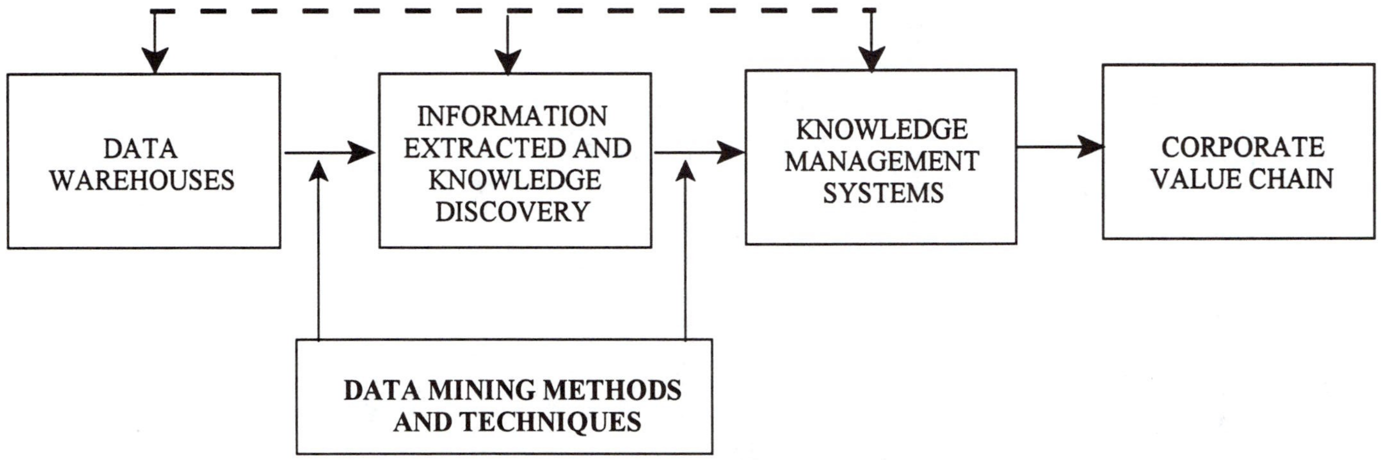

Figure 9.2
**Illustrative Capabilities and Tasks DM Can Perform with Large
Data Sets in Health Care**

- Identify factors that influence or control the allocation and use of financial and human resources.
- Correlate patient-encounter data (demographics, diagnoses, treatments, insurance) with patterns of resources expended.
- Develop models of continuity-of-care, and of relative effectiveness of providers.
- Develop models that compare effectiveness among types of providers (e.g., PPOs, HMOs).
- Develop models that compare among categories of treatment and resources expended on them, across time, regions, demographics, and approaches (e.g., by-pass surgery versus noninvasive approaches for heart disease).
- Develop models that predict behaviors from the aforementioned patterns.
- Develop models that predict the diffusion of medical technologies (e.g., telemedicine).

Weaknesses and Problems of Data Mining

As a mix of techniques, data mining has already yielded some tangible benefit to industry. But some weaknesses are present and they are summarized in Figure 9.3.

The overreliance on computerized methods of patterns and knowledge discovery is illustrated in an interesting discussion of the growing role of machine intelligence. George Dyson (1998) had argued—to the delight of anyone who feels overwhelmed by the information revolution and by techniques such as DM—that we are on the brink of a new evolutionary era.[20] Dyson believes that machines are evolving in a nonbiological type of evolution, so that nature will favor machines, not humans.[21]

DATA MINING AND S&T EVALUATION

What is the value of DM in the evaluation of science and technology? In the preceding sections I outlined the use of DM in business corporations and the strengths and weaknesses of this set of methods. If co-word analysis considers key or index words, DM extracts information from both

Figure 9.3
Some Weaknesses and Problems with Data Mining (DM)

- With all its ability to generate models, *interpretation* of the implications of patterns uncovered *is still the key element.*
- In essence, DM *mainly saves time and effort* of manually going through large databases.
- Effectiveness of DM *depends on the quality of the data* and data sources.
- DM is *difficult to implement, costly*, and requires experienced workers.
- *Patterns* and relationships identified by DM may be *largely of little value.*
- Mix of techniques used may not be complementary but yield *conflicting scenarios.*
- "Hype" with DM may have led to *overpromising.*
- Overreliance on computerized discovery of patterns may *diminish* the *role of human reasoning.*

This list is illustrative and not in any particular order or ranking.

structured and unstructured databases by considering the entire stock of words, quantities, and images.

In the evaluation of scientific outcomes, such as bibliographic outputs, textual data mining seems an appropriate metric since it focuses on unstructured or "free" text, searching for words, sentences, and constructs that appear in such documents. Kostoff (1999) has conducted extensive research on the nature and implementation of textual data mining.[22]

Kostoff and his colleagues (1994) at the U.S. Office of Naval Research developed in the early 1990s the method of database tomography. This method identified the frequency of sentences in technical and scientific documents, so that high frequencies were indicative of the main "themes" of the document. In essence, DT identified scientific themes (or constructs), the relationships among these themes, and their development and evolution in the document database. This allowed the analyst to create a model of the evolution of a scientific theme, or topic, or theory. Kostoff also argued that DT should be used to supplement the work of technical experts, not to replace them. Once themes are identified via DT and their dynamics is established, human expertise provides the analysis of the value and the significance of these findings.[23]

DT is a step forward in the traditional co-word analysis. It provides a much richer analysis of technical documents by focusing on themes or constructs rather than index words. The strengths and weaknesses of DT are similar to those of DM exhibited in Figures 9.2 and 9.3.

Use of DM and DT in Evaluating Technology

Even though data mining and database tomography are primarily methods designed to explore bibliographic outcomes from research and science, they can also be used to evaluate technology. As was mentioned earlier, analyses of bibliographic outcomes provide a measure of prolific authors, themes of research, productive institutions and countries, and the dynamics of scientific topics. A similar set of results may be obtained in the evaluation of technology.

DM and DT are useful in the analysis of bibliographic components of technologies, such as documents that describe or delineate technical, economic, social, and legal aspects of the technology. For example, documents related to patents may shed light on the development that led to the patent and to the said technology. In effect, *any* database that contains technical (quantitative) as well as textual material can be explored by DM and DT to uncover patterns, relationships, themes, and frequencies. Since there is always a "data or paper trail" to each technological innovation, the use of DM and DT becomes an operational possibility.[24]

In this context, patent data are the initial focus of attempts to use DM and DT as tools in technology evaluation. Assuming, of course, that patents provide a good description of the technology, their data can thus be extended to measure technological innovation. Once this is accomplished, a natural extension would be to link such technology databases with business-related databases to obtain a more comprehensive analysis of the impacts of technological innovation on corporate commercial activities.[25]

In summary, although DM and DT are used primarily for scientific bibliographic outcomes, there is some progress in their application, albeit in a rudimentary fashion, in technology evaluation by focusing on patent databases. As theoretical considerations on the link between science, technology, and organizational performance are better framed and validated, DM and DT will be optimal candidates for extracting patterns and relationships that measure the value of technological innovations.[26]

MAPPING OF SCIENCE AND TECHNOLOGY

This section focuses on the *mapping* and creation of *roadmaps* for science and technology. The section starts with a description of the nature of maps in science and technology, then proceeds to a discussion of roadmaps. Strengths, and weaknesses of this metric are listed, followed by some best uses and conclusions.

Mapping of Science

What is "mapping" of science and why do we need this as a metric of the value of science? Maps of science are interpretations of word co-occurrence data matrices to the effect that they seem to represent the structure and the evolution of a scientific field. Several techniques have been used to create such maps, based on co-word analyses.[27] In principle, the proponents of this method utilize the means available in co-word analyses to create the matrices for a given scientific field.

For example, Peters and Van Raan (1993) constructed a co-word-based "map" for chemical engineering.[28] They selected this field because of its size, cross-disciplinary reach, and economic impact. First, the authors built a co-word structure from publications in leading journals in the field of chemical engineering for the period 1983-1988. A second structure was built from a smaller set of publications by world-class scientists in the field, which corresponded to "leading research front."[29] Finally, they created a co-word structure from conference proceedings which, in their view, was a "special topic map." By using cluster analysis and multidimensional scaling they created a map from the three data sets, and obtained "validation" from a sample of 50 top scientists in the field of chemical engineering.

Although the authors were concerned with the traditional problems of co-word analysis (indexer effects, different terms describing same phenomenon, and redundancy) they nevertheless have argued that their maps provide a visualization of the structure and dynamics of the field of science.[30] This is the claim of the proponents of science mapping: that the methodology they use is sufficient to create validated visualizations or maps of structural changes in science.

Criticisms of Science Maps

Co-word and co-citation analyses used to establish maps of science had been criticized on the grounds of methodological faults and the lack of adequate theory. Leydesdorff (1987) exemplifies the critics.[31] He has argued that these maps "do not represent or represent only very partially the structure and the dynamics of science" (p. 296). The aggregates or clustering techniques seem to yield not only stable (rather than dynamic) structures, but also structures that are independent and tend not to configure in a meaningful fashion.

However we statistically manipulate citation and co-word data, maps of science are not an adequate representation of the mobility and progress of a scientific field. The crucial critique is the need for a *theory* of scientific evolution that would help to explain the structures generated in the maps.[32]

Mapping of Technology: Roadmaps

In the case of technology there have been attempts to construct *roadmaps*, as tools that portray the relation between technology and its subsequent outcomes. In an excellent discussion of the nature of roadmaps for science and technology, Kostoff (1997) concluded that they suffer from a clear measure of quality.[33] Kostoff argued that the quality dimension of roadmaps depends on the technical adequacy as well as the objectives of constructing such a document.

In essence, technology roadmaps portray the prospective movement along the innovation process, as technological outputs are converted into commercial products. Thus, a technology roadmap is a document and a process. The document displays the stages of such prospective conversion down the innovation continuum, and the structural transformations in the technology on the road to a commercial product.[34]

As in any road, the technology roadmap portrays stages of development and the barriers and facilitators that the technology commercializers are likely to encounter along the way.[35]

Strengths and Benefits

Technology roadmaps are potentially a powerful decision aid for both technology and business managers. The strengths are of two kinds. First, technology roadmaps describe a critical part of the innovation process, thus allowing for a "meeting of minds" of the generators of technology and those who use it in commercial products.[36] Roadmaps can be viewed from the developer of technology with a forward view ("which technologies would more likely lead to commercialized products?"), and from the perspective of the business managers looking backwards ("which technologies are needed to make these products feasible and commercially successful?").

A second type of benefit is the ability of a technology roadmap to provide the organization with a *framework* for analysis and evaluation of technology within the product generation and development process. The much-touted "strategic integration" of technology and business objectives may potentially be realized within such a framework. Technologists and managers are able to discuss critical issues of product development in a shared platform of conceptual and temporal stages of development.

Weaknesses and Problems

Figure 9.4 shows some weaknesses and problems that seem to hinder the successful application of technology roadmaps. As planning and decision tools, roadmaps suffer from problems that are common to such techniques, particularly in the areas of managerial and organizational support.

The weaknesses and problems are organized in four categories: technical, managerial, organizational, and metrics. In summary, the weaknesses of technology roadmaps are split between the inherent shortcomings in the design of such documents, and the issues of implementation in their organizations. Managers and technologists find it difficult to bridge the gap between their disciplines, ways of thinking, and strategic and operational priorities.[37]

Illustrative Uses

Two cases of successful use of technology roadmaps come to mind and are described below. The first is the technology roadmap process practiced at Motorola.[38] The second is the product-technology roadmap process practiced by Phillips Electronics.[39]

Figure 9.4
Some Weaknesses and Problems with Technology Roadmaps

A.   **TECHNICAL PROBLEMS**

  - Lack of independent tests of quality and reference standards for benchmarking.
  - Design of roadmap may be too conservative or too optimistic, reflecting difficulties in forecasting of the technology and its potential applications.
  - Chronic underestimation of time and effort required for design and implementation of roadmap.

B.   **MANAGERIAL PROBLEMS**

  - Management commitment not always secured because roadmaps are considered a mere decision aid.
  - Objectives for roadmaps are established by managers without awareness of what technology can and should do.

C.   **ORGANIZATIONAL PROBLEMS**

  - Technology roadmaps are integrative tools, so when an organization is functionally structured, there are difficulties in having a cross-functional activity charted.
  - Reengineering and restructuring activities tend to disrupt the implementation of roadmaps.

D.   **METRICS**

  - Difficulties in evaluating quality.
  - Complexity of roadmaps makes it difficult to use accurate metrics.

The Motorola Roadmap.   Motorola is a communication and electronics industrial giant. In the mid-1980s it developed and used corporate plans that focused on technological development. These plans are documented in technology roadmaps. Two kinds of roadmaps were used: (1) *Emerging Technology Roadmap,* which tracks the development and potential of the individual technology, and (2) *Product Technology Roadmap,* which tracks the technological basis of the company's product lines.

One important component of the Product Technology Roadmap is a matrix that generates the technological requirements for future products. It is obtained by the summaries of product plans and technological forecasts. This integrative viewpoint of where the company is headed and the role of technology in its future is a fundamental benefit of the roadmap.

The Phillips Roadmap. Phillips Electronics is also a worldwide company based in the Netherlands. As in the case of Motorola, the Phillips technology roadmaps are designed to provide a better link between products and the technologies that are embedded in them.

In particular, the Phillips Technology roadmaps use a model of the Innovation Matrix in which questions related to technology are being asked, such as, Is it feasible? Do we want it? How do we do it? and How is the specific technology integrated into the product?

Roadmaps allow the company to identify gaps in technology (present and future) and to provide managers with a solid perspective over time of the degree to which their technology in integrated in the company's product lines.

SUMMARY

Mapping of science and technology can be a beneficial tool for technical and business managers at all levels. With the new techniques for exploration and analysis of documents, there is a much higher probability that mapping can become a more desirable and advantageous tool. Although to date the documented benefits have not been outstanding, mapping has been useful for large technology-based companies, and for selected fields of S&T.[40]

The confluence of positive experience with applications of technology roadmaps and new exploration techniques may lead to a higher degree of use of the document and the process by business companies and government organizations.

NOTES

1. For example, see Morgenlbrod, H., and E. Serifi, "The Sound Structure of Verb Roots in Modern Hebrew," *Journal of Linguistics*, 17(1), 1981, 11-16. Also see Evers, A., "A Review of New Developments in Text Retrieval Systems," *Journal of Information Science*, 20(6), 1994, 438-445.

2. See Beach, L. (Ed.), *Image Theory: Theoretical and Empirical Foundation* (Mahwah, NJ: Lawrence Erlbaum Associates, 1988). Also see the

literature on psychological and managerial cognition, for example, Gioia, D., "Symbols, Scripts, and Sensemaking: Creating Meaning in the Organizational Experience," in Sims, H., and D. Gioia (Eds.), *The Thinking Organization* (San Francisco: Jossey-Bass, 1986) pp. 49-74. Also see James, L., and R. James, "Integrating Work Environment Perceptions: Explorations into the Measurement of Meaning," *Journal of Applied Psychology*, 74(3), 1989, 739-751.

3. Callon, M., J. Courtial, and W. Turner, "PROXAN: A Visual Display Technique for Scientific and Technical Problem Networks," Second Workshop on the Measurement of R&D Outputs, Paris, December 5-6, 1979. Also see Callon, M., J. Courtial, and F. Laville, "Co-Word Analysis as a Tool for Describing the Network of Interactions Between Basic and Technological Research: The Case of Polymer Chemistry," *Scientometrics*, 22(1), 1991, 155-205.

4. Assuming, of course, that these keywords represent ideas, concepts, and notions expressed by the authors.

5. See, for example, the analysis of *neural networks* in Van Raan, A., and R. Tijssen, "The Neural Net of Neural Network Research: An Exercise in Bibliometric Mapping," Center for Science and Technology Studies, University of Leiden, The Netherlands, 1991; and the case of *chemical engineering* in Peters, H., and A. Van Raan, "On Determinants of Citation Scores: A Case Study in Chemical Engineering," *Journal of the American Society for Information Science*, 45(1), 1994, 39-49; and Peters, H., R. Braam, and A. Van Raan, "Cognitive Resemblance and Citation Relations in Chemical Engineering Publications," *Journal of the American Society for Information Science*, 46(1), 1995, 9-21. And on the same topic, see Peters, H., and A. Van Raan, "Co-Word-Based Science Maps of Chemical Engineering, Part II: Representations by Combined Clustering and Multidimensional Scaling," *Research Policy*, 22(1), 1993, 47-72.

6. See, for example, Studt, T., "Scientific Data Miners Make Use of All the Tools Available," *Research & Development*, 39(5), 1997, 62C-62D. Conversely, see Courtial, J., P. Callon, and M. Sigogneau, "Is Indexing Trustworthy? Classification of Articles Through Co-Word Analysis," *Journal of Information Science*, 9(2), 1984, 47-58. These authors argued that variations introduced by different indexers do *not* impact the "general structure" that, in their view, generates the key words used in indexing. They illustrated this point with analysis of research on dietary fiber. But a powerful critique in the work of Leydesdorft had emphasized the weakness of the method due to reliance on keywords. See Leydesdorft, L., "Why Words and Co-Words Cannot Map the Development of the Sciences," *Journal of the American Society for Information Science*, 48(5), 1997, 418-427.

7. See, in particular, Wormell, I., "Informetrics: Exploring Databases on Analytical Tools," *Database*, 21(5), 1998, 25-30. Others have argued that co-word analysis can supplement citation analysis by extracting keywords from the text itself. See, for example, Coulter, N., and I. Monarch, "Software Engineering

As Seen Through Its Research Literature: A Study in Co-Word Analysis," *Journal of the American Society for Information Science*, 49(13), 1998, 1206-1223.

8. See, for example, Nieminen, P., and M. Isohanni, "The Use of Bibliometric Data in Evaluating Research on Therapeutic-Community for Additions and in Psychiatry," *Substance Use & Misuse*, 32(5), 1997, 555-570; and Oppenheim, C., "The Correlation Between Citation Counts and the 1992 Research Assessment Exercise Ratings for British Library and Information Science University Departments," *Journal of Documentation*, 51(1), 1995, 18-27.

9. There is a growing literature on data-mining and the various techniques it employs. See, for example, Stolorz, P., H. Nakamura, E. Mesrobian, R. Muntz, E. Shek, C. Mechoso, and J. Farrara, "Fast Spatiotemporal Data Mining of Large Geophysical Datasets," *Proceedings of the 1st International Conference on Knowledge Discovery and Data Mining*, Montreal, August 1995 (Menlo Park, CA: AAAI Press), pp. 300-305.

10. See, for example, Fayyad, U., D. Haussler, and P. Stolorz, "Mining Scientific Data," *Association for Computing Machinery-Communications of the ACM*, 39(11), 1996, 51-57. Also see Uthurusamy, R., U. Fayyad, G. Piatetsky-Shapiro, and P. Smyth (Eds.), *Advances in Knowledge Discovery and Data Mining* (Boston: MIT Press, 1996).

11. For an excellent text on data mining, see Berry, M., and G. Linoff, *Data Mining Techniques: For Marketing, Sales, and Customer Support* (New York: John Wiley & Sons, 1997).

12. There is a rapidly growing literature on these techniques. I have limited the discussion in this chapter to bring these issues to the readers' attention, while keeping in mind that the emphasis of this book remains the evaluative aspects of the metric for S&T.

13. See Hill, S., "Crystal Ball Gazing Becomes a Science," *Apparel Industry Magazine*, 59(5), 1998, 18-23. Also see Bigus, J., *Data Mining With Neural Networks: Solving Business Problems—From Application Development to Decision Support* (New York: McGraw-Hill, 1996).

14. Borok, L "Data Mining: Sophisticated Forms of Managed Care Modeling Through Artificial Intelligence," *Journal of Health Care Finance*, 73(3), 1997, 20-36. Also see the interesting and technically oriented book on data mining of biological databases: Balch, P., and S. Brunak, *Bioinformatics: The Machine Learning Approach* (Cambridge, MA: MIT Press, 1998); in particular see pages 91-142 on neural networks and pages 251-270 in which the authors provide useful Internet resources.

15. The rapidly expanding literature on "knowledge management" deals with a variety of topics. For illustrative purpose, see Silverstone, S., "Distill Human Competence," *Knowledge Management*, 2(6), 1999, 40-41. This is a new and dedicated journal in the KM area. Also see Johnson, S., and B. Davis "Smart Moves: The Pursuit of Knowledge," *Information Week*, 736, May 31, 1999, 18-

20. Also see Geisler, E., "Harnessing the Value of Experience in the Knowledge-Driven Firm," *Business Horizons*, 42(3), 1999, 18-26.

16. See, for example, Trybula, W., "Data Mining and Knowledge of Discovery," *Journal of the American Society for Information Science*, 32 (Special Issue: Annual Review of Information Science and Technology), 1997, 197-229. Also see Krzyztof, J., W. Dedrycz, and R. Swiniarski, *Data Mining Methods for Knowledge Discovery* (Boston: Kluwer Academic Publishers, 1998).

17. See, for example, Teece, D., "Research Directions for Knowledge Management," *California Management Review*, 40(3), 1998, 289-294. Also see Zytkow, J., and Quafafou, M., "Principles of Data Mining and Knowledge Discovery," *Proceedings of the Second European Symposium PKDD, '98*, Nantes, France, September 1998, Vol. 101. In particular see pp. 273-308. Also see Westphal, C., and T. Blaxton, *Data Mining Solutions: Methods and Tools for Solving Real-World Problems* (New York: John Wiley & Sons, 1998). This book focuses on visual data mining techniques. Another source is Thuraisingham, B., *Data Mining: Technologies, Techniques, Tools, and Trends* (New York: CRC Press, 1999).

18. For example, see Coombs, R., and R. Hull, "Knowledge Management Practices and Path-Dependency in Innovation," *Research Policy*, 27(3), 1998, 237-254. Also see Amidon, D., "The Evolving Community of Knowledge Practice," *International Journal of Technology Management*, 16(1-3), 1998, 45-64; and, Volney, D., "Technology Innovation and Processing Information," *Vital Speeches*, 65(7), 1999, 201-206. Volney was CEO of the Dun & Bradstreet Corporation. He argued that only when technology such as information technology yields knowledge, then knowledge yields action. He also gave the example of a manufacturer who failed to understand why a given region was underperforming. By mining this company's data, D&B was able to uncover knowledge that led them to conclude that the region was doing very well, but was evaluated in a manner that precluded the emergence of truthful information. In this regard, see a similar discussion in the area of research methodology and design in: Geisler, E., *Methodology, Theory, and Knowledge in the Managerial and Organizational Sciences: Actions and Consequences* (Westport, CT: Quorum Books, 1999).

19. For an excellent discussion of DM in health care, see Borok, 1997, *op. cit.* Also see the influential books that pioneered KM as a respectable topic in business: Davenport, T., and L. Prusak, *Working Knowledge: How Organizations Manage What They Know* (Boston: Harvard Business School Press, 1998); and Nonaka, I., and H. Takeuchi, *The Knowledge-Creating Company* (New York: Oxford University Press, 1995). Also see Davenport, T., and L. Prusak, "Blow Up The Corporate Library," *International Journal of Information Management*, 13(4), 1993, 405-412.

20. Dyson, G., *Darwin Among the Machines: The Evolution of Global Intelligence* (Reading, MA: Perseus Books, 1998).

21. In this regard also see Davenport, T., "I Was Just Thinking...," *CIO*, 11(20), 1998, 28-29. Tom Davenport commented on information technology and DM by arguing that these and similar techniques are not yet used by industry to a degree that would allow these organizations to fully exploit them. Also see Morris, R., *Artificial Worlds: Computers, Complexity, and the Riddle of Life* (New York: Plenum Press, 1999). In particular see Chapter 7, pp. 123-140, in which Morris offers a fascinating discussion of artificial life on the Internet.

22. See a list of publications for Ronald Kostoff at <http://www.dtic.mil/dtic/kostoff/index.html>.

23. See, for example, Kostoff, R., and H. Eberhart, "Database Tomography: Applications to Information, Logistics, and Personnel Management," *Proceedings of Advanced Information Systems & Technology for Acquisition, Logistics, & Personnel Applications*, Williamsburg, VA, March 28-30, 1994, pp. 186-223.

24. Although the vast majority of applications of DM and DT have been on scientific databases, some attempts have been reported on modeling and data mining of technology databases. These efforts have primarily been pioneered by economists. See, for example, Cincera, M., "Patents, R&D, and Technological Spillovers at the Firm Level: Some Evidence From Econometric Count Models for Panel Data," *Journal of Applied Econometrics*, 12(3), 1997, 265-280. In this paper the author studied 181 firms for a database of nine consecutive years. Patenting activity was estimated based on nonparametric analysis of technology-reported variables. Also see Winkelman, R., and K. Zimmerman, "Recent Developments in Count Data Modeling: Theory and Application," *Journal of Economic Surveys*, 9(1), 1995, 1-24.

25. See, for example, Trajtenberg, M., "A Penny For Your Quotes: Patent Citations and the Value of Innovations," *Rand Journal of Economics*, 21(1), 1990, 172-187. In this paper the author analyzed CTS (Computed Tomography Scanners) by citation-based patent indices, and concluded that these indices are closely associated with other measures of the social value of this innovation. Another example is: Lanjouw, J., A. Pakes, and J. Putnam, "How To Count Patents and Value Intellectual Property: The Uses of Patent Renewal and Application Data," *The Journal of Industrial Economics*, 66(4), 1998, 405-432. Here the authors have utilized patent *documentary data* to measure the extent of technological innovation.

26. For some recent publications on this topic, see, for example, Kleinknecht, A., *Determinants of Innovation: The Message From New Indicators* (New York: Macmillan, 1996); and Jaffe, A., M. Fogarty, and B. Banks, "Evidence From Patents and Patent Citations on the Impact of NASA and Other Federal Labs on Commercial Innovation," *The Journal of Industrial Economics*, 66(2), 1998, 183-205. The authors analyzed patent citations as a measure of technology diffusion and "spillovers" from government laboratories to industrial innovation effort. Also see a technical note on this topic in: Pliskin, N., M. Eben-Chaime, and D. Sosna,

"Empowering Simulation Analysis with Data-Management Tools," *IEEE Transactions on Engineering Management*, 46(2), 1999, 230-234.

27. Early description of this methodology and its implications can be seen in: Callon, M., J. Law, and A. Rip (Eds.), *Mapping the Dynamics of Science and Technology* (London: Macmillan, 1986); and Healey, P., H. Rothman, and P. Hoch, "An Experiment in Science Mapping for Research Planning," *Research Policy*, 15(4), 1986, 233-251. Also see Braam, R., H. Moed, and A. Van Raan, "Mapping of Science by Combined Co-Citation and Word Analysis: Structural Aspects," *Journal of the American Society for Information Science*, 42(4), 1991, 233-251. Also see Dasgupta, P., and P. David, "Towards a New Economics of Science," *Research Policy*, 23(3), 1994, 487-521; and Bozeman, B., and G. Kingsley, "R&D Value Mapping: A New Approach to Case Study-Based Evaluation," *Journal of Technology Transfer*, 22(2), 1997, 33-42.

28. Peters, H., and A. Van Raan, "Co-Word-Based Science Maps of Chemical Engineering. Part I: Representations by Direct Multidimensional Scaling," *Research Policy*, 22(1), 1993, 23-45. In the medical technology area, see the initiative to construct a map of the knowledge-base in: Geisler, E., "Mapping the Knowledge-Base of Management of Medical Technology," *International Journal of Healthcare Technology and Management*, 1(1/2), 1999, 2-12.

29. Peters and Van Raan, 1993, *op. cit.*, p. 26.

30. See the second part of their work in: Peters, H., and A. Van Raan, "Co-Word-Based Science Maps of Chemical Engineering. Part II: Representations by Combined Clustering and Multidimensional Scaling," *Research Policy*, 22(1), 1993, 47-71.

31. Leydesdorff, L., "Various Methods for the Mapping of Science," *Scientometrics* 11(5-6), 1987, 295-324.

32. See, for example, MacLean, M., J. Anderson, and B. Martin, "Identifying Research Priorities in Public Sector Funding Agencies: Mapping Science Outputs on to User Needs," *Technology Analysis & Strategic Management*, 10(2), 1998, 139-155. The authors describe the British study of evaluating scientific output in environmental science by needs of its potential and actual users. Also see Kopesa, A., and E. Sohliebel, "Science and Technology Mapping: A New Iteration Model for Representing Multidimensional Relationships," *Journal of the American Society of Information Science*, 49(1), 1998, 7-17.

33. Kostoff, R., "Science and Technology Roadmaps," August, 1997. This paper can be accessed on the website <http://www.dtic.mil/dtic/kostoff/index.html>.

34. See, for example, the diffusion of technology in Japan, in which the structure of such "roadmaps" is made of: (1) prime contributors (horizontal diffusion), (2) suppliers and subcontractors (vertical diffusion), and (3) military and commercial applications. Such a multidimensional diffusion process demands a complex roadmap, so as to portray all the prospective transformations. See:

Samuels, R., "Pathways of Technological Diffusion in Japan," *Sloan Management Review*, 35(3), 1994, 21-32.

35. To an extent, the basic characteristics of technology roadmaps are similar to the process-outcomes approach discussed in Chapter 12. See, for example, Geisler, E., "The Metrics of Technology Evaluation: Where We Stand and Where We Should Go From Here," *Proceedings of the 24ᵗʰ Annual Technology Transfer Society Meeting*, St. Petersburg, Florida, July 15-17, 1999.

36. See, for example, Callon, Law, and Rip (Eds.), 1986, *op. cit.*

37. These issues are also discussed in, for example, Tijssen, R., and A. Van Raan, "Mapping Changes in Science and Technology: Bibliometric Co-Occurrence Analysis of the R&D Literature," *Evaluation Review*, 18(1), 1994, 98-115. Also see Barker, D., and D. Smith, "Technology Foresight Using Roadmaps," *Long Range Planning*, 28(2), 1995, 21-29; and Engelman, E., and A. Van Raan, *Mapping of Technology: A First Exploration of Knowledge Diffusion Amongst Fields of Technology*, Research Report to the Ministry of Economic Affairs, CWTS-91-02, Center for Science and Technology Studies, Leiden, 1991.

38. Willyard, C., and C. McClees, "Motorola's Technology Roadmap Process," *Research Management*, 30(6), 1987, 13-19.

39. Groenveld, P., "Roadmapping Integrates Business and Technology," *Research-Technology Management*, 40(5), 1997, 48-55.

40. See, for example, Kostoff, R., H. Eberhart, and D. Toothman, "Database Tomography for Technical Intelligence: A Roadmap of the Near-Earth Space Science and Technology Literature," *Information Processing & Management*, 34(1), 1998, 69-85. Also see Menon, S., and R. Sharda, "Digging Deeper: Data Mining Update and New Modes to Pursue Old Objectives," *OR/MS Today*, 26(3), 1999, 26-29; and Kostoff, R., H. Eberhart, and D. Toothman, "Hypersonic and Supersonic Flow Roadmaps Using Bibliometrics and Database Tomography," *Journal of the American Society for Information Science*, 50(5), 1999, 427-447. More recently, see Kostoff, R., and E. Geisler, "Strategic Management and Implementation of Textual Data Mining in Government Organizations," *Technology Analysis & Strategic Management*, 11(4), 1999, 493-525.

10

THE METRIC OF PATENTS

The count of patents as a metric of technology progress has long been favored by economists.[1] There are several reasons for their choice. First, patents can be counted, thus can be quantitatively applied in economic models.[2] Second, patents represent a clearly defined output in the invention and innovation process, hence allow for a realistic model of technology progress and its link (via patents) to economic progress.[3] Third, patents represent a legal document describing intellectual property rights, hence serving as a strong indicator of individual and corporate assets.[4] Finally, patents serve as an indicator of both ends of the innovation process: as measures of outcomes from R&D activity, and as economic instruments by which companies compete in the marketplace.[5]

This chapter briefly summarizes the state of knowledge on patents and their use in evaluating S&T. The chapter concentrates on the strengths, weaknesses, and best uses of patents.

WHAT ARE PATENTS AND
HOW DO THEY MEASURE S&T OUTPUTS?

Patents are basically an inventor's registration with the appropriate government agency of the technical description and potential applications of the inventor's novelty, not previously so registered. Inventors may be individual or corporations, and such registration protects them for a determined period of time so they can exploit the economic benefits that may accrue from the invention.

As a measure of S&T, patents are considered by many economists to be indicators not only of inventive activity but also of technological progress and change at the industrial and national levels. CHI Research, Inc., discussed earlier in Chapter 8, uses count of patents and their analysis to measure the technological weaknesses and strengths of a company's portfolio of S&T. Patents are considered to be "tangible evidence of technological innovation,"[6] therefore CHI and others believe that they are a reliable measure of technological capability and achievement.

Economists are also interested in how well patents measure the value of innovations and intellectual property. To be of value to the patenting organization, patents must be able to provide protection of intellectual property, thus to enhance the organization's competitive strength that technology offers its owners.

Traditionally, patents were studied in connection with the link between incentives for R&D and monopolistic advantages from patenting activities.[7] More recently patents have also been explored as an instrument that promotes sequential innovations, so that a stream of inventive activities can stimulate economic progress.

For instance, O'Donoghue (1998)[8] has argued that, in order to increase rewards to innovation, "patents must provide protection against future innovators" (p. 654). He also proposed a "minimum innovation size required for patents" so that such a requirement will stimulate investments in S&T, hence contribute to improved social welfare (p. 668).

Schankerman (1998) studied the role of patents in providing companies with economic returns.[9] By using a model of patent renewal in four technology areas (pharmaceuticals, chemicals, machinery, and electronics) he concluded that, although important, the value of patent protection varies by technology and by the topic of legal and regulatory constraints on the industry.

The cumulative impact of S&T outputs and patenting levels has also been investigated. Kortum (1997),[10] for example, argued that "technological breakthroughs, resulting in patents, become increasingly hard to find as the technological frontier advances. This explains why patenting has been roughly constant as research employment has risen" (p. 1389). The level of patenting thus becomes a victim of its own success.

Similarly, Lim (1998)[11] has proposed a model of multistage R&D competition, in which investments vary by stage, hence patent policies dictate levels of investments in these stages. Firms that are leaders in their industry will invest more heavily as the patent disclosure data approaches.[12]

Patents as Measures of S&T Inputs

What are the attributes of patents that make them acceptable surrogate measures of S&T inputs? First, economists have found a correlation between R&D expenditures and levels of patenting.[13] Such covariation suggested that patent activity may serve to indicate the level of R&D, in particular since the time lag between R&D and patenting was not a variable in the relationship.[14]

Second, patents are a measure applied across industries and companies within them, so that a comparison can be drawn among different disciplines and organizations. The format of this measure is uniform on an international basis, hence comparisons can be made across countries.

Finally, patents contain information on the invention to an extent that allows for a possible gross reconstruction of the R&D effort that was expended into the invention. So, not withstanding different patenting strategies among companies and industries, the more companies invest in S&T, the higher their overall patent activity.[15]

Patents as Measures of S&T Outputs

A different perspective and other characteristics are attributed to count of patents as a measure of S&T outputs and as an indicator of the outcomes from the innovation process. In general, patents are viewed as indicators of the potential market applications of the invention.[16] Hence there may be economic impacts from patented inventions that appear in the form of new products, technological improvements, and shifts in markets.[17]

Perhaps one of the more important factors inherent in a patent that makes it an acceptable measure of S&T outputs is the content of its documentation. In addition to the *count* of patents, the patent application submitted to the granting authorities contains a particularly revealing source of information.[18]

Patent databases have been in existence (at least in Europe) since the late Middle Ages. Patent applications contain information on the invention itself, and on some "prior art" in the area of the invention.

Taken as a set of converging items, patent applications from a company (or even a country) offer an incisive look at the areas in which the company has been working, and its successes and accomplishments, reflected in its desire to gain protection from competitors via patents.

Furthermore, trained analysts are able to extract from a patent data set some indications of a company's level of S&T effort required to arrive at this level of patenting.[19] Analysis of patent data may also indicate subsequent economic activity (e.g., sales and profits), which may then be attributed to patenting and to the S&T effort that had generated them.

For example, Ernst (1995) studied German machine-tool (mechanical engineering) firms.[20] His analysis showed that, when considering a two- to three-year lag, there was a positive correlation between patent applications and increased sales of these companies.

Such a link illustrates the role that patents play as measures of S&T outputs. Figure 10.1 shows that patent data and their analyses act as intermediaries that describe or even explain inputs and outputs of the S&T activity.

Figure 10.1
Patents as Link Between R&D and Economic Outcomes

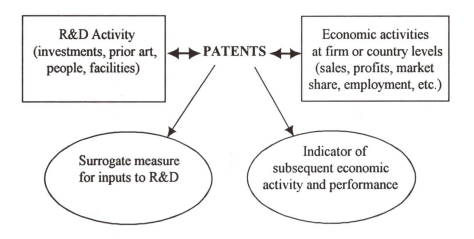

By using a method equivalent to "knowledge production function," Crepon and Duguet (1997) have advanced the notion of the *Patent Equation*.[21] They studied the relationship between R&D investments and patent applications by a sample of 698 French manufacturing companies in the period 1984-1989. Patents were considered a measure of incremental knowledge for the firm, hence improving the stock of knowledge which leads to improved innovation.[22] They concluded that "past successes in the production of innovation (patents) increases the efficiency of the R&D-innovation relationship" (p. 262). But they also concluded that: "the past number of patents has a nonlinear effect: small but positive numbers of past innovations affect positively the production of innovation but the effect slowly vanishes as the number of innovation increases" (p. 262).

Patents, Quality, and Their Impacts

How do patents affect the economic outcomes of the firm? As seen in the previous section, patents are viewed as measures of investments in the knowledge stock, so they contribute to improved innovation. But the link between patents and such variables as sales and market share is credited to several other factors.

One such factor is *quality*, which is usually indicated by (1) counts of patents granted, (2) patent applications in major foreign markets, and (3) patent citations as background for other patents. Since several studies have found a positive relationship between patenting and corporate performance, it would be logical to assume that the higher the quality of these patents, the higher the technological base of the firm and the more advanced its pool of skills—hence a better starting position to create innovations and to impact the marketplace.[23]

Figure 10.1 summarizes the main arguments in the literature that link the impacts of patent activities with performance of the firm. Griliches (1990) has provided a survey of the literature on statistics of patents.[24] The impacts of patents are not only in terms of their quality, but are also reflected in the organization's ability to protect its most successful (or potentially successful) products.[25]

Figure 10.2
Some Factors Explaining Impacts of Patents on Performance

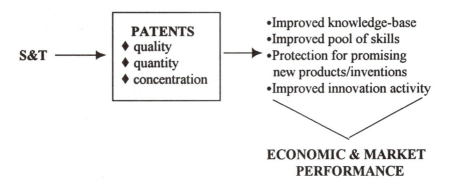

STRENGTHS AND BENEFITS FROM PATENTS

The count, citation analysis, and examination of the content of patent applications (and valid patents) all may lead toward several benefits, some of which are shown in Figure 10.2. As a metric of science and technology, patents offer a variety of additional benefits. Figure 10.3 summarizes the strengths of patents (as a metric of S&T) and their benefits.

From a methodology perspective, patents are an attractive database, easily manipulable, and allowing for time-series and cross-industries comparative analyses.[26] Structurally, patent data include relevant information whose content offers a wealth of knowledge about the patent.

But above all, patents are viewed as a link between S&T and the economic performance of the organization. As such they are elevated to the level of concrete measures of the innovation phenomenon, perhaps (as seen below) undeservedly.

Yet economists have long emphasized the role that patents play in establishing a strong competitive position for a firm in its industry. Cardon and Sasaki (1991),[27] for example, have argued that "a patent grants the winner monopoly power" (p. 324) and "if firms search on the same R&D path, as soon as the first firm completes development and patents the new technology, other firms must switch to another technology and start development afresh" (p. 325). This phenomenon, the authors claim, helps to prolong the patenting firm's monopoly, so patent protection "becomes a contributor to preemptive strategy."[28]

Figure 10.3
Strengths and Benefits of Patents

A.   METHODOLOGY
- Patent data are quantitative measures.
- Patent databases have been in existence for many years.
- Patent data are relatively easy to manipulate.
- Patent data can be related to other economic/financial measures.
- Patent citations allow for co-citation analyses.

B.   STRUCTURE
- Patent data have a similar structure as a legal document.
- Contain revealing information.
- Indicate levels of S&T effort.
- Similar items of information facilitates cross-industries and even cross-national comparison.

C.   IMPACTS AND CONTRIBUTIONS
- Considered as a link between S&T and firm performance, patents offer an elegant way of establishing such a link.
- Patents are viewed as indication of technological achievements.
- Patents are viewed as measures of the knowledge-base.
- Patents are viewed as measures of the quality of S&T.

So patents effectively provide the firm with a legal instrument that compels the competition to accept temporary monopolistic domain of the patenting company in a given technology. This circumvents the spirit of the Sherman Act and similar antimonopoly legislation. The patenting firm that integrates such possibilities into its strategic planning may find itself in a comparatively advantageous position.[29]

WEAKNESSES AND PROBLEMS

There are three major weaknesses in the use of patents as a metric of S&T: (1) organizations have different propensities in their patenting decisions, (2) there are distortions in the marketplace, and (3) the link between S&T and corporate performance (that patents presumably measure) is not supported by theory. These and other weaknesses are shown in Figure 10.4.

Figure 10.4
Weaknesses and Problems of Patents

A.   FIRM-INDUSTRY STRATEGY
- There are marked differences among firms and industries in the propensity to patent inventions.
- Industrial firms only spend less than 1/3 of their R&D effort to develop new products that would result in patents.[30]
- Firm-specific information in patent data impacts decisions to invest in S&T.
- Past performance of patenting activity impacts the propensity to patent.

B.   MARKET CONSIDERATIONS
- Distortions in market due to monopolistic behavior.
- Market factors may impact patenting behavior.
- Patents do not always lead to commercial applications.

C.   STRUCTURE AND METHODOLOGY
- Patents represent only a small portion of the actual R&D and S&T effort.
- Patents reveal only selected information about S&T.
- Patentable inventions have become increasingly harder to discover.
- The link S&T-Patents-Performance is based on covariation methodology and lacks a description of the process and factors that impact this presumed link.
- There is a lack of a theory to explain how patents contribute to performance and to strategic advantages (except for the link to possibly monopolistic manifestations of the power from patent protection).

Although these shortcomings are, in the aggregate, powerful enough to cast doubt on the validity of patent counts and analysis as a viable metric, universities, industrial companies, and government laboratories nevertheless use this metric for a variety of evaluations.[31]

PATENTS AND OTHER METRICS

As a metric, patents are positively correlated with bibliometrics and peer review. In the first case, patents and the production of publications are associated as they describe different perspectives of the outcomes from S&T.[32] For example, a statistical analysis of outcomes in textile research compared counts of scientific papers and patents, respectively, as measures of more basic and more applied research.[33] In the international scene, Amsden and Mourshed (1997) found a strong correlation between growth in patents and growth in publication in late-industrializing countries such as Korea, Turkey, Brazil, Malaysia, China, Indonesia, and Argentina.[34] They found a correlation coefficient of 0.85 between the two metrics.[35] The authors have suggested that this high degree of association is perhaps because the two metrics describe outputs from the same investments in research and technology.[36]

The evaluation of university research at Chalmers University in Sweden has shown a correlation coefficient of 0.60 between citations of scientific publications and patents by departments.[37] The authors therefore concluded that " those departments which have high academic visibility as reflected by citations are also active in commercializing their results, as indicated by their patent activity" (p. 179).

So, although there are differences in the propensity of organizations and countries to publish and patent, as a general rule, the more intensive the S&T activity, the higher the outputs, manifested in the form of publications, citations, and patents. These metrics measure the outcomes from S&T, albeit different aspects of them, that are subjected to different processes of decisions on when and how to publish or to patent.

Patents and Peer Review

The issue of *quality* is paramount in the link between patents and other metrics. The fact that a patent is issued for an invention is not necessarily a certification of quality nor of scientific merit. A case in point is the patenting of medical processes. The American Medical Association (AMA) issued in 1994 its unfavorable opinion opposing the patenting of medical processes, such as surgical techniques.[38] The AMA was concerned with the possible confusion between the approval—by means of peer review—of medical procedures, and the patenting of such procedures without the quality control that is embedded in the peer-review process.

In evaluating the performance of S&T units such as university departments or industrial R&D, the statistical evidence on the correlation between patents and peer review is inconclusive. Research teams that are highly respected by their peers may not be prone to patenting their findings. Similarly, breakthroughs in science that receive high peer acclaim may be far from ready to be patented.[39]

Patents and peer review measure different dimensions of the innovation phenomenon. But in a bizarre twist they come together in view of their information content. Consider the case of Cistron Biotechnology.[40] A peer review of an article that a Cistron scientist submitted to the journal *Nature* was carried out by the director of research for Cistron's competitor, Immunex Corporation. Cistron contended that the scientist, Steven Gillis, inappropriately used the chemical sequence for a gene critical in making interleukin (a key protein in the immune system with several therapeutic applications) to patent the gene for his company. Such possible occurrences would influence company policy on releasing proprietary information even in the context of scientific papers—before a patent is filed.[41]

BEST USES

The most prevalent use of patents, particularly by industrial firms, is in affording protection to intellectual property. Following a decision by the U.S. Supreme Court in 1996 that gave judges added latitude in deciding patent cases, there has developed a climate whereby companies are more inclined to litigate issues of intellectual property.[42]

An illustrative case is the invention of the magnetic resonance imaging (MRI). Fonar Corporation, whose Dr. Damradian had a patent of the scanning technology that forms the basis of the MRI, sued for patent infringement. The company filed suits against General Electric, Siemens, Phillips, Johnson & Johnson, and Hitachi. All of Fonar's opponents, except General Electric, settled out of court. In June 1997 a U.S. Federal Court ruled in favor of Fonar.[43]

A different use of patents allows companies to chart their strategic growth in directions otherwise deemed unreasonable and risky. Consider the case of Monsanto and its herbicide, Glyphosate, sold under the brand name of "Roundup." As the most successful herbicide, Roundup's original patent was to expire in the year 2000. However, due to the protection the patent afforded Monsanto, the company has developed new crops (such as soy beans) that are genetically engineered to tolerate Roundup. The company has obtained a patent on these crops, so it continues to maintain its market superiority. Instead of the exclusive hold on the herbicide, it now has the exclusive rights to the plants themselves.[44]

A third use of patents and their data is for mapping out competitors' strategy. Patent data are analyzed to obtain a picture of a competing company's technological competencies. In this fashion patent data are used for protection of intellectual property, but they also help to disclose the strengths and weaknesses of the patenting company.[45]

SUMMARY

Are patents a credible metric of the S&T effort and outcomes? Although of extensive use because of their legal and economic characteristics, in my view patent counts and analyses provide only a limited measure of the S&T activity. Patents contain valuable information about the inventions and the effort that has led to them, but they are not sufficient to be used as a sole metric of S&T.

When used in combination with other metrics, patents offer a manageable piece of data on the level of S&T effort by individuals and organizations. But one should not confuse the relative ease in obtaining such data and their manipulation with the amount of knowledge that such data provide on the S&T phenomenon. Such knowledge is limited, bounded by the weaknesses and problems displayed in Figure 10.4. In particular, patents—as a metric—are of limited value as a metric of S&T because of different patenting behaviors, and the fact that they are designed to be a legal instrument offering some measure of protection of intellectual property. They were not designed as a metric of S&T activity nor outcomes.

A study of the evaluation of technology in U.S. corporations provides an illustration of the shortcomings of the metric of patents. Geisler (1999) compared the covariation and process-outcomes methods in evaluating R&D in 23 large companies.[46] The count of patents positively correlated with investments in R&D and the bibliometric outputs of the scientists in the sample companies. However, a process-outcomes approach, which included detailed interviews with researchers and business managers, revealed that over 80% of patents have not led to any commercial applications. Another finding showed multiple patents filed for a given area of investigation, whereas another area had a total "blackout" of patenting, due to threats from competitors and the fear of revealing confidential and proprietary information on the R&D effort being conducted in this area.

So, when count of patents are extensively used as a surrogate measure of inputs to S&T, and as a measure of S&T outputs, such use must be tempered with caution. Although count of patents seems to positively correlate with other metrics (e.g., count of publications and peer review), the limitations of patent counts as a metric for S&T should be carefully considered, and its use viewed in concert with other S&T metrics.

NOTES

1. See, for example, Griliches, Z. (Ed.), *R&D, Patents, and Productivity* (Chicago: University of Chicago Press, 1984); and the classical book: Machlup, F., *The Production and Distribution of Knowledge in the United States* (Princeton, NJ: Princeton University Press, 1962). More recently, see Scherer, F., "Firm Size, Market Structure, Opportunity, and the Output of Patented Inventions," *American Economic Review*, 55(3), 1995, 1097-1125.

2. See, O'Donoghue, T., S. Schotchmer, and J. Thisse, "Patent Breadth, Patent Life, and the Pace of Technological Progress," *Journal of Economics and Management Strategy*, 7(1), 1998, 1-32. Also see Schotchmer, S., "Standing on the Shoulders of Giants: Cumulative Research and the Patent Law," *Journal of Economic Perspectives*, 5(2), 1991, 29-41.

3. See, for example, Wright, B., "The Economics of Invention Incentives: Patents, Prizes, and Research Contracts," *American Economic Review*, 73(4), 1983, 691-707.

4. See, for example, Gilbert, R., and D. Newberry, "Preemptive Patenting and the Persistence of Monopoly," *American Economic Review*, 72(4), 1982, 514-526. Also see Kitch, E., "The Nature and Function of the Patent System," *Journal of Law and Economics*, 20(3), 1977, 265-290.

5. The vast literature on patent counts and their usage in economic analysis of S&T is illustrated in the notes to this chapter. Several important and comprehensive books have been published on the topic of patents. In addition to the seminal work by Zvi Griliches, see, for example, Nordhaus, W., *Invention, Growth and Welfare: A Theoretical Treatment of Technological Change* (Cambridge, MA: MIT Press, 1969); and Taylor, C., and Z. Silberston, *The Economic Impact of the Patent System: A Study of the British Experience* (Cambridge: Cambridge University Press, 1973).

6. See CHI's website at <http://www.CHIResearch.com>.

7. See, for example, Van Dijk, T., "Patent Height and Competition in Product Developments," *Journal of Industrial Economics* 44(3), 1996, 151-167.

8. O'Donoghue, T., "A Patentability Requirement for Sequential Innovation," *Rand Journal of Economics*, 29(4), 1998, 654-679.

9. Schankerman, M., "How Valuable Is Patent Protection? Estimates by Technology Field," *Rand Journal of Economics*, 29(1), 1998, 77-107.

10. Kortum, S., "Research, Patenting, and Technological Change," *Econometrica*, 65(6), 1997, 1389-1419.

11. Lim, W., "Multistage R&D Competition and Patent Policy," *Journal of Economics*, 68(2), 1998, 153-173.

12. Some economists have argued that increasing patent protection may *not* necessarily stimulate economic growth. See, for example, Mazzoleni, R., and R. Nelson, "The Benefits and Costs of Strong Patent Protection: A Contribution to the Current Debate," *Research Policy*, 27(3), 1998, 273-284.

13. See, for example, Griliches, Z., "Patent Statistics as Economic Indicators: A Survey," *Journal of Economic Literature*, 18(4), 1990, 1661-1707.

14. See Hall, B., Z. Griliches, and J. Hausman, "Patents and R&D: Is There a Lag?" *International Economic Review*, 27(2), 1986, 265-283.

15. See, for example, Wang, P., I. Cockburn, and M. Puterman, "Analysis of Patent Data: Mixed-Poisson-Regression-Mode Approach," *Journal of Business & Economic Statistics*, 16(1), 1998, 27-41. The authors analyzed the correlation between patents and R&D spending by U.S. Pharmaceutical companies. They found "a significant effect of log (R&D) on patent counts" (p. 39).

16. There is a diverse and extensive literature on patents as measures of S&T outputs. Illustrative studies include Grupp, H., and U. Schmoch, "Patent Statistics in the Age of Globalization: New Legal Procedures, New Analytical Methods, New Economic Interpretation," *Research Policy*, 28(4), 1999, 377-396. Also see Kortum, S., "Equilibrium R&D and the Decline in the Patent-R&D Ratio: U. S. Evidence," *American Economic Review*, 83(2), 1993, 450-457; and Mansfield, E., "Patents and Innovation: An Empirical Study," *Management Science*, 32(2), 1986, 173-181.

17. See, for example, Smith, G., and R. Parr, *Valuation of Intellectual Property and Intangible Assets,* 2nd ed. (New York: John Wiley & Sons, 1994). Also see, Dematteis, R., *From Patent to Profit: Secrets and Strategies for Success* 2nd ed. (New York: Inventions, Patents and Trademarks Co., 1998). In this book Bob Dematteis provides a detailed guide on how to commercialize inventions, thereby giving the reader an insight into the complexity of the patenting system.

18. See Campbell, R., "Patent Trends as a Technological Forecasting Tool," *World Patent Information*, 5(3), 1983, 137-143. Also see Narin, F., E. Noma, and R. Perry, "Patents as Indicators of Corporate Technological Strength," *Research Policy*, 16(3), 1987, 143-155.

19. See, for example, Tijssen, R., and J. Korevaar, "Unraveling the Cognitive and Interorganizational Structure of Public/Private R&D Networks: A Case Study of Catalysis Research in the Netherlands," *Research Policy*, 25(8), 1997, 1277-1293. Also see Cincera, M., "Patents, R&D, and Technological Spillovers at the Firm Level: Some Evidence from Econometric Count Models for Panel Data," *Journal of Applied Econometrics*, 12(3), 1997, 265-280. This paper explained the level of company patenting (applications) by "current and lagged levels of R&D expenditures and technological spillovers" (p. 265).

20. Ernst, H., "Patenting Strategies in the German Mechanical Engineering Industry and their Relationship to Company Performance," *Technovation*, 15(4), 1995, 225-240. Also see, Ernst, H., "Patent Portfolios for Strategic R&D Planning," *Journal of Engineering and Technology Management*, 15(3), 1998, 279-308.

21. Crepon, B., and E. Duguet, "Estimating the Innovation Function from Patent Numbers: GMM on Count Panel Data," *Journal of Applied Econometrics*, 12(2), 1997, 243-263.

22. For example, see Narin, F., and A. Breitzman, "Inventive Productivity," *Research Policy*, 24(4), 1995, 507-519. Also see Narin, F., "Patents as Indicators for the Evaluation of Industrial-Research Output," *Scientometrics*, 34(3), 1995, 489-496.

23. This assumption appears in many studies in the literature, under different formats. See, for example, Amsden, A., and M. Mourshed, "Scientific Publications, Patents and Technological Capabilities in Late-Industrializing Countries," *Technology Analysis & Strategic Management*, 9(3), 1997, 343-359. Also see Segestrom, P., "Endogenous Growth Without Scale Effects," *The American Economic Review*, 88(5), 1998, 1290-1310; and Baily, M., and A. Chakrabarti, "Innovation and Productivity in U. S. Industry," *Brookings Papers on Economic Activity*, 2(1), 1985, 609-632.

24. Griliches, 1990, *op. cit.*, 1661-1707.

25. See, for example, Hausman, J., B. Hall, and Z. Griliches, "Econometric Models for Count Data with an Application to the Patent-R&D Relationship," *Econometrica*, 52(4), 1984, 909-938.

26. See, for example, Narin, F., M. Carpenter, and P. Wolf, "Technological Performance Assessments Based on Patents and Patent Citations," *IEEE Transactions on Engineering Management*, 31(4), 1984, 172-183. Also see Loury, G. "Market Structure and Innovation," *Quarterly Journal of Economics*, 93(3), 1979, 395-410.

27. Cardon, J., and D. Sasaki, "Preemptive Search and R&D Clustering," *Rand Journal of Economics*, 29(2), 1998, 324-338.

28. See also Gilbert, R., and D. Newberry, "Preemptive Patenting and the Persistence of Monopoly," *American Economic Review*, 72(2), 1982, 514-526. See some earlier discussion of this issue in Nelson, R. (Ed.), *The Rate and Direction of Inventive Activity* (Princeton, NJ: Princeton University Press, 1962).

29. See, for example, Miller, A., and M. Davis, *Intellectual Property: Patents, Trademarks and Copyright in a Nutshell*, 2nd ed. (St. Paul: West Publishing, 1990); and Gallini, N., "Patent Policy and Costly Imitation," *Rand Journal of Economics*, 23(1), 1992, 52-63.

30. Scherer, F., *Industrial Market Structure and Economic Performance* (Chicago: Rand McNally, 1980). Other researchers have also concluded that, vertical and horizontal structures notwithstanding, firms spend only a portion of

their R&D on new products. See also, Grossman, G., and E. Helpman, "Quality Ladders in the Theory of Growth," *Review of Economic Studies*, 58(1), 1991, 43-61.

31. Evidently, the popularity of the use of patents as S&T metric overshadows the weaknesses and problems in Figure 10.4. See, for example, Wright, D., "Optimal Patent Breadth and Length with Costly Imitation," *International Journal of Industrial Organization*, 17(3), 1999, 419-436. Also see Shulman, S., *Owning the Future* (Boston: Houghton-Mifflin, 1998). In this book the author describes the shortcomings of the U.S. patent system and questions the appropriateness of the privatization of scientific knowledge via the process of patenting of inventions, as it currently exists in the American economy. In particular see Shulman's discussion of medical inventions in Chapters 4 and 8 of his book.

32. See, for example, Narin, F., "Patent Bibliometrics," *Scientometrics*, 30(1), 1994, 147-155. Also see Narin, F., "Globalization of Research, Scholarly Information, and Patents—10-Year Trends," *Serials Librarian*, 21(2-3), 1991, 33-44; and Haitun, S., "The Problem of Indicator-Latent Relationship in Metric Models. 1: Statement and General Solutions," *Scientometrics*, 23(2), 1992, 335-351. Also see Albert, M., D. Avery, F. Narin, and P. McAllister, "Direct Validation of Citation Counts as Indicators of Industrially Important Patents," *Research Policy*, 20(3), 1991, 207-260. The authors studied 20 researchers and managers at Eastman Kodak and concluded that highly cited patents were also considerably higher rated by peer review of the company's researchers.

33. David, H., L. Piip, and A. Haly, "The Examination of Research Trends by Analysis of Publication Numbers," *Journal of Information Science*, 3(6), 1981, 283-290. In this study of a low- R&D-intensity industry the authors could not reach definite conclusions about the overall trend in textile research. Also see Reiss, A., "Investment in Innovations and Competition: An Option Pricing Approach," *Quarterly Review of Economics and Finance*, 38(Supp. 1), 1998, 635-650.

34. Amsden, A., and Mourshed, M., "Scientific Publications, Patents, and Technological Capabilities in Late-Industrializing Countries," *Technology Analysis & Strategic Management*, 9(3), 1997, 343-359.

35. When omitting China from their sample, because of China's unusual growth in patenting activity.

36. See, for example, Archibugi, D., and M. Pianta, *The Technological Specialization of Advanced Countries* (Boston: Kluwer Academic Publications, 1992). Also see Patel, P., and K. Pavitt, "Uneven and Different Technological Accumulation Among Advanced Countries: Evidence and a Framework of Explanation," *Industrial and Corporate Change*, 3(1), 1994, 59-87.

37. Wallmark, J., D. McQueen, and K. Sedig, "Measurement of Output from University Research: A Case Study," *IEEE Transactions on Engineering Management*, 35(3), 1988, 175-180.

38. Lewis, J., "Medical Patents: How Far Can They Go?" *Health Systems Review*, 28(5), 1995, 22-25.

39. See, for example, Pappas, R., and D. Remer, "Measuring R&D Productivity," *Research Management*, 28(3), 1985, 15-22. Also see McQueen, D., and J. Wallmark, "Innovation Output and Academic Performance at Chalmers University of Technology," *Omega*, 12(3), 1984, 457-464. Also see Nichols, K., *Inventing Software: The Rise of Computer-Related Patents* (Westport, CT: Greenwood Publishing Group, 1998). See in particular Chapter 8, pp. 151-156, for a discussion of patent paradigm.

40. Day, K., "Patents and Peer Pressures: Two Firms' Legal Fight May Shake a Mainstay of Scientific Research," *The Washington Post*, April 19, 1996, p. D1. In 1998, Rhone-Poulenc acquired 1.3 million Cistron shares and received an exclusive license to market the interleukin-1 beta vaccine adjuvant (a compound that enhances the performance of other vaccines).

41. In the economic literature, see, for example, Somma, E., "The Effect of Incomplete Information about Future Technological Opportunities on Pre-emption," *International Journal of Industrial Organization*, 17(6), 1999, 765-799.

42. For example, see Myers, R., "Fighting Words: Growing Ranks of Litigants Are Putting Price Tags on Ideas," *CEO*, 14(3), 1998, 49-56.

43. General Electric paid to Funar a judgment of $128.7 million. See Deutch, C., "Patent Fights Aplenty for M.R.I. Pioneer," *New York Times*, July 12, 1997, Section 1, p. 33.

44. See, Monbiot, G., "Watch These Beans," *The Guardian*, September 17, 1997, pp. 1, 17:2.

45. See, for example, Wilkinson, S., "Competitors Reveal Own Strengths, Weaknesses," *Chemical & Engineering News*, 76(15), 1998, 27-30. This article describes the method used by International Technology Information, by which the company counts the frequency of the codes assigned to patent documents.

46. Geisler, E., "Generating Knowledge in Strategy Research: Co-Variation Versus Process-Outcomes Methods in the Evaluation of Corporate Technology," Working Paper, Stuart Graduate School of Business, Illinois Institute of Technology, Chicago, 1999.

11

THE METRIC OF PEER REVIEW

There is a saying that the American Constitution is what a simple majority of Supreme Court justices find it to be. Perhaps by the same token one may presume that science is what scientists find it to be. Peer review is the formal manifestation of the subjective, yet learned, appreciation of what constitutes science and its qualitative valuation.

WHAT IS PEER REVIEW?

Peer review generally means a process by which a selective jury of experts in a given scientific field is asked to evaluate the undertaking of scientific activity or its outcomes (e.g., research, projects, or scientific publications).[1] Such a group of experts may be consulted as a group or individually, without the need for personal contacts among the evaluators.[2]

Perhaps historically, peer review is the oldest metric used to evaluate the work of scholars and their scholarship. Ever since the Greek philosophers and the work of religious juries (such as the Jewish "Sanhedrin"), scholarship tended to be assessed by people whose work also focused on the same area. With the advent of universities and as scientific inquiry became formalized, peer review also evolved into a better structured method of evaluation.

Peer review is primarily designed to ensure the quality of the scientific endeavor. This is achieved by emphasizing two complementary tasks: (1) the research effort is (or will be) conducted according to the scientific method, and (2) the research is valid and generalizable.[3] Peer review is used for assessing planned as well as completed scientific effort: projects, programs, and their specific outcomes (such as papers and reports). Thus, peer review is a method that provides quality control for the allocation of resources for S&T, and for the postevaluation of the S&T activity and its performers, at any level of aggregation (from the individual to institutions and countries).

Attributes and Dimensions of Peer Review

In this section I describe the peer-review metric by considering: (1) for what purpose do we conduct the review? (2) what are the general attributes or characteristics that peer review should have to achieve the purpose? and (3) what are the features of a potentially successful review? The various purposes for conducting peer review of S&T are shown in Figure 11.1.

Peer review is designed to be a unique and self-contained process of evaluation. By using the judgment and opinions of peers and members of

Figure 11.1
Purposes/Objectives for Conducting Peer Review

PURPOSES/OBJECTIVES
• To determine the level of quality of the S&T endeavor.
• To promote accountability for S&T and its performers.
• To contribute criteria and metrics for allocation of resources for S&T.
• To contribute criteria and metrics for the evaluation of S&T performance of individuals and organizations.
• To contribute criteria and metrics for the establishment and assessment of S&T policy-making.
• To provide judgmental assessment of the validity and reliability of S&T projects and programs.
• To contribute criteria and metrics for the comparative evaluation of S&T performers.

Not necessarily in any order or importance. Judgmental assessments via peer review are conducted for scientific endeavors as well as for technology projects, programs, and outcomes.

the "community of science," the process of peer review is aimed at keeping the review "in the family." In principle this means that science (and to an extent also technology) can only be evaluated by scientists. This process represents the ultimate power exercised by experts who police themselves and who evaluate each other.[4]

There are three main reasons for such an inherent claim of peer review. First, science has reached a point in its development where the levels of *complexity* and *specialization* make it nearly impossible for any individual (or organization)—who is not intimately familiar with the activity—to effectively and credibly evaluate it and its outcomes.[5] Second, when called upon to render judgment on the work of colleagues, reviewers are highly professional individuals who are able to provide objective opinions, motivated by the desire to advance the state of science, and to weed out "bad" or "poor" science.

The third reason is the widespread belief that the scientific method is highly conducive to testing, replication, and, if necessary, to refutation. Hence, scientists-as-reviewers possess the tools to verify the validity of scientific studies and to pronounce judgment on any of the assumptions, methods, and conclusions from such studies.[6]

Desirable Attributes of Peer Review. Figure 11.2 shows seven key desirable attributes or characteristics of successful or high-quality peer review.[7] The process should be rational, timely, cost-effective, and clearly understood by the participants. In effect, these desirable attributes describe a process that is objective, fair, and open, insofar as the objectives and criteria are defined and publicized. Yet the process should also promote the anonymity of the reviewers and those being reviewed. The idea here is to ensure objectivity as well as to eliminate any possible actions (following the review process) to the detriment of the reviewers and the reviewed.[8]

Features and Underlying Conditions of Peer Review. What are the underlying conditions and features that contribute to the successful implementation of peer review of S&T? The seven key conditions are shown in Figure 11.3.

These conditions include the support from management, the relative independence of the review process, and the credibility of the reviewers. These underlying conditions are essential for having a peer review of high quality, reliability, fairness, and objectivity.[9] Yet, in many instances some of the conditions/features in Figure 11.3 are not present, resulting in peer

Figure 11.2
Characteristics/Attributes of the Process of Peer Review

CHARACTERISTICS/ATTRIBUTES

- The process should be formal, with all the steps clearly defined and known to all participants, including the purpose of the review.
- The process should be rational and easily understood. The criteria should be preestablished and acceptable to all participants.
- The process should have a high degree of "fairness" built into its criteria and stages.
- The process should be timely (the longer the process takes, the less likely are the findings to be useful for the researchers and the scientific community).
- The process should be cost-effective (costly reviews will likely not be repeated).
- The process should provide timely, complete, and accurate feedback to the individuals or organizations under review.
- Anonymity of reviewers and reviewed should be maintained.

These are attributes of the peer-review process that are valid, acceptable, and potentially beneficial. Not necessarily in any order of importance.

review that is flawed. Some studies have shown that low-quality peer review may generate evaluations that are biased and of little reliability.[10]

The Process: Evaluating Potential Performance

Peer review is used to evaluate both the prospects and potential success (and contributions) of proposed research, and the outcomes from completed research. In the first task, peer review serves as a predictor of future accomplishments. Reviewers are asked to determine—to the best of their judgment—not only how a given project may fare in the future, but also how it may succeed *in comparison* with other projects. Thus, peer review is generally the metric of choice in the allocation of resources for research by funding agencies and by industrial companies.[11]

The process involves the assembling of a panel of experts and an evaluation based on preestablished criteria. But how credible are such prospective assessments? Despite the popularity of this metric as a prediction of scientific performance, there is very little empirical evidence that the metric is highly reliable.[12] A seminal study by Cole and Cole (1978

Figure 11.3
Features of the Process of Peer Review

FEATURES

- The process should have, as a feature or underlying condition, the support of higher levels of management (e.g., in the corporation or the publisher or the scientific/technical association in the case of scientific journals).
- The process should have relative independence in the conduct of the review and in arriving at its conclusions.
- The reviewers selected should be credible.
- The reviewers selected should be willing to provide their impartial expertise as objectively as possible.
- The process should allow for comparison with other metrics of S&T evaluation.
- There should be a number of specialties represented by the reviewers selected, to allow for in-depth evaluation of a specific topic, as well as potential ramifications of other outcomes and impacts.
- Any composite index of value of S&T reviewed or a figure of merit should be methodologically sound and credible to allow its use with other efforts of evaluation.

These are the underlying conditions of peer review that contribute to its success in achieving the purposes of the review. Not necessarily in any order of importance.

and 1981) of the peer review practiced by the U.S. National Science Foundation concluded that about half of the evaluation was due to the attributes of the proposed research and the reputation of the principal investigator, and the remainder was due to other (perhaps random) factors.[13]

Consensus among reviewers seems to be occurring more frequently when the resultant opinion is in the extreme: prospective research that is very poor or highly promising. There seems to be much less agreement in cases that are mid-road. Some scholars suggested that this is a positive attribute of peer review, since it leads to consensual elimination of potential "losers" and the promotion of potential "winners."[14]

Peer review is also used as an *a posteriori* metric to evaluate scientific projects and programs during and after their completion. In the task of assessing potential performance, peer review acts primarily as a contribution to the allocation of scarce resources among proposals, so that those with the highest probability of success would be funded.[15] In the case of assessment after the fact, peer review contributes to a judgment on how well the research was conducted and its scientific contributions. Hence, as I argue below, there are different criteria used in the evaluation of these two tasks, and there are also differences in some of the cognitive processes by which such assessment is conducted.

CRITERIA FOR SELECTION AND REVIEW

In any formalized process when peers are asked to review S&T, they are provided with a set of preestablished criteria. In addition to the "free" expression of their opinion, peers are asked to abide by these criteria. The motive behind the use of criteria is primarily to achieve some form of standardization or at least similarities in the underlying dimensions of the review—for purposes of comparisons and cross-disciplinary analyses. Another reason for applying criteria is the desire to channel the reviewers' thoughts toward a more organized form of expression of their opinions.[16]

However detailed and specific, criteria in peer review are used with caution, to avoid imposing undue pressure on reviewers. Hence, the part of the review that emerged in response to the criteria is used in conjunction with the portion of the review that includes "free text" of the uninfluenced thoughts and opinions of the reviewers, expressed in their own words and in their chosen format.

Different Criteria for Proposals and Publications

Peer review of proposals for the conduct of S&T studies are principally an evaluation of the *potential* of such studies to accomplish their promised goals. Such reviews are prognostications of future possibilities.

The case for the peer review of scientific and technical publications is different in that publications report *outcomes* and *results* from S&T studies that have already been completed (or are in process, but in any event some work has been accomplished). Therefore the criteria used for these evaluations will differ, as they would be prospective or retrospective. In both cases, however, the criteria are designed to assess the quality of the work, its contributions (potential or actual), and its relative scientific standing in the state of the art.[17]

Criteria Used by Public Sector Agencies

In the U.S. federal S&T system, the National Science Foundation (NSF) and the National Institutes of Health (NIH) are the key civilian agencies that fund research and development. Their use of peer review and the criteria they apply to assess the potential of proposals have become benchmarks for other agencies and sponsors of S&T.[18]

The Case of NSF. In 1981 the National Science Foundation established four comprehensive criteria for peer review of research proposals. They are summarized in Figure 11.4. As of October 1997, the NSF had collapsed these criteria into two basic criteria, also shown in Figure 11.4

The main reasons for this change was the desire to add relevancy and fairness to the research funded by the Foundation. So the questions that accompanied each of the broad new criteria have provided clues to the issues that had arisen in the 1990s, such as underrepresentation of selected groups in U.S. society.[19]

In addition to the written responses to the questions in the criteria, reviewers are also asked to assign a summary rating, ranging from "poor" to "excellent." My own experience (as a reviewer and proposer for NSF) has been that proposals that are funded usually have the majority of reviewers rating it "excellent." Due to the scarcity of funding and the immense volume of proposals, program managers at NSF feel compelled to accept only those proposals that score the highest (by most or all of the respective reviewers). In practice, therefore, the written comments serve the purpose of providing feedback to the proposer, rather than be the background factors for a learned decision by the NSF program managers.[20]

The Case of NIH. The U.S. National Institutes of Health have a two-tier review process. Proposals undergo a preliminary peer review by an external group of academics. These Initial Review Groups (IRGs) number over a hundred sections in the many specialties within the general fields of medical and biological research. The agency processed over 25,000 grant applications in 1999 and funded over $5 billion in research, 40% of which was clinical research.[21]

In addition to the external peer review, the agency also evaluates proposals for their relevance to the NIH objectives. This evaluation is conducted by an advisory council which is staffed by a mix of researchers and nonscientists.[22]

Figure 11.4
Peer-Review Criteria Used by NSF

1981-1997
  • Research Performance—competence.
  • Intrinsic merit of proposed research.
  • Utility or relevance of proposed research.
  • Effect of proposed research on the infrastructure of science and engineering.
  ◊ Rank: "poor" to "excellent."

As of October 1, 1997
  ♦ **Intellectual Merit of Proposed Research**
    • Importance to advancing knowledge within own field and across fields.
    • Qualifications of the proposer.
    • Creativity and originality of proposed work.
    • Access to sufficient resources.
  ♦ **Broader Impacts of Proposed Research**
    • Advancing discovery while promoting teaching, training, and learning.
    • Broadening the participation of underrepresented groups (e.g., gender, ethnicity).
    • Enhancing the infrastructure of research and education (e.g., facilities, networks, and partnerships).
    • Broad dissemination of results.
  ◊ Rank: "poor" to "excellent."

The criteria need not be weighted equally.

The two-tier approach at NIH was designed to make the peer-review process more accountable to the overall program requirements of the agency, and to add a measure of fairness, so that biases embedded in peer review could be attenuated. The approach was also aimed at a larger role for public inputs to the grants process in the medical and biological sciences.

Critics of the NIH model of peer review explored both aspects of the process. Scientists criticized the process for the undue influence of the members of the public and the NIH staff—at the expense of the purely scientific judgment. On the other side the process has been criticized by scientists and nonscientists alike for its overly restricted view of the disciplines, fueled by the "inner sanctum" of a small number of scientists

Figure 11.5
Peer-Review Criteria Used by NIH

REVIEW CRITERIA*

◆   SIGNIFICANCE
  • Importance of the problem.
  • Advancement of scientific knowledge.
  • Effect on concepts and methods that drive the field.
◆   APPROACH
  • Are conceptual framework, design, methodology, and analysis adequate and well-integrated?
  • Are potential problems and alternatives considered?
◆   INNOVATION
  • Are the objectives original and innovative?
  • Are the concepts, approaches, and methods novel and innovative, and does the proposed research challenge existing paradigms?
◆   PRINCIPAL INVESTIGATOR
  • Attributes, skills, and experience of the Principal Investigator and other proposed researchers.
◆   ENVIRONMENT
  • Is the scientific environment supportive and is there institutional support.

*Overall score, weighted approximately by above criteria.

---

who dominate the disciplines, thus perpetuating their preferred areas of research and their paradigms.[23] This debate has been going on for many years and undoubtedly will continue.

Other Examples. In the emerging economies, for example, peer review is also applied in public-sector agencies that fund S&T research. An illustrative case is the Kuwait Institute for Scientific Research (KISR), which used a two-tier process similar to the NIH.[24] The first peer-review stage was composed of the review by a scientific panel. Proposals were judged by their scientific excellence and contribution to the state of the art. The second stage was a managerial review, using the following criteria: (1) management of the proposed research, (2) national and socioeconomic considerations of its impacts, (3) relation to the Institute's strategy and objectives, and (4) the preparation and presentation of the proposal.

The Case of DARPA. The U.S. Agency for Advanced Research Projects (formally the Defense Advanced Projects Agency–DARPA) employs a variant of peer review in deciding on proposals to be funded. The review is conducted by an *internal* staff of experts, without the benefit of a formal review by external peers.

The "DARPA model" illustrates the bias toward the overall criterion of relevancy to the agency's strategy and program need—at the expense of scientific merit. Although proponents of this model have argued that internal review boards may possess as much scientific credibility as external peers, the issue remains in dispute. The key problem is not any differences in scientific skills, rather in a skewed preference for strategic and managerial criteria, and the downplaying of scientific merit.[25]

Criteria Used by Industry

Industrial companies utilize a set of various techniques and metrics to evaluate their potential R&D projects, and the outputs and impacts from those projects funded and completed. An important component in this set is the metric of peer review.

Peer review in U.S. industrial companies is a process that employs a blend of evaluation teams composed of members from the scientific and technical units, and from the managerial/executive side of the firm. The role of these "committees" is to assess two dimensions of proposed S&T/R&D projects: (1) probability or potential for *scientific/technical success,* and (2) probability or potential for *commercial success.*

Project Selection and Resources Allocation. The early studies that empirically investigated the ways in which industrial companies assess their R&D were conducted by Albert Rubenstein and his colleagues.[26] They used the term "project selection and resources allocation" (PS/RA) as the descriptor of the activity in which industrial companies evaluated and selected their more promising projects—in an effort to best allocate their scarce S&T resources.

Corporate committees or ad-hoc groups of evaluators employ three categories of criteria for peer review of R&D projects. A more detailed list of illustrative criteria is shown in Figure 11.6.

The first category is the potential success of the proposed work (normally in the form of a project). Success is defined as both scientific/technical and commercial. Probabilities are computed by the committee and a rating system is established.

Figure 11.6
Peer-Review Criteria Used by Industry

ILLUSTRATIVE REVIEW CRITERIA

- Potential returns and payoff within a foreseeable time line.
- Probability of technical success within a project time-cost estimate.
- Probability of commercial success within a given time frame.
- Relevancy to corporate strategic plan.
- Relevancy to product lines and businesses.
- Amount and sufficiency of resources available.
- Prior experience with the project team and with similar research.
- Level of senior management's support for such research.
- Relation to the overall corporate R&D portfolio.
- Relation to an established need from marketing or another unit in the corporation, such as clients, users, regulators, or vendors.

These are examples of criteria used by peer-review committees.

The second category includes criteria of economic payoff and returns, as illustrated in Figure 11.6.[27] Expenditures for R&D and the outcomes from this activity are normally assessed against traditional economic and financial indices, such as return on investment, "dollarization," payback of investments, and sales. These criteria are considered by the peer-review committees and in their procedure to assign a rating to each project. These criteria are used in prospective as well as retrospective manners. Projects are evaluated as to their potential economic payoff, and are evaluated after the fact whether their economic contribution has been of merit to the organization.[28]

The third category focuses on criteria of the degree of relevancy of the proposed projects to the company's product lines and businesses. Committees judge the projects in accordance with the knowledge they possess of the strategic direction of the company, and the needs and market potential of the product lines.

Normally, the industrial committee judges the set of proposals by these criteria, assigns a rating, and proceeds to establish a *cutoff point* below which projects are not accepted. Such points are primarily based upon the available resources for the S&T activity.[29] Similar procedures are used by technology advisory boards that companies establish to make use of the expertise of external people in the judgments of the company's S&T portfolio.

ROLE OF EDITORS, REVIEWERS, AND S&T JOURNALS

Peer review is a system or set of procedures that relies heavily on the subjective judgment of "expert" reviewers. In addition to the committees established by industry and government to assess the potential success and the scientific merit of proposals, there is an even more potent and ubiquitous form of review: the scientific and technical journals that utilize peer review and editorial determination in the acceptance or rejection of S&T publications.

Reviewers for "peer-reviewed" or "juried" journals are usually of three types: (1) Ad hoc reviewers, recruited to assess a single submission. Normally reviewers are unaware of the identity of the other reviewers in this transitory group of experts. (2) Permanent reviewers who form the editorial board of the journal and are continually called upon by the editor to review submissions. (3) A combination of the previous two types.[30]

A "peer" is defined as "one that is of equal standing with another."[31] S&T professionals have accepted the premise that scientific progress can be achieved only by a strict method of quality control, exercised by other scientists of equal standing in the scientific community. Hence the concept of "peer" and "peer review." However, due to the intricacies and shortcomings of the peer-review process, in some instances the reviewers are *not* on equal standing with the author(s). For example, reviewers selected by the editor may have some knowledge of the research area, but not enough to render an expert opinion. Reviewers may also be unduly influenced by the reputation of the author(s) (even when the process is "double-blinded"). Similarly, if editors engage the services of "true" peers, they will have a very small group of scholars evaluating each other, leading to incestual influences and shortly to ossification of the scientific progress.[32]

The Editorial Review Process

A general schematic view of the editorial review process of peer-review journals is shown in Figure 11.7. The review process may vary in some details among disciplines, but in general the figure captures the main steps taken to assure a quality review.

Criteria for review of a paper submission vary slightly across disciplines, but are usually focused on two principal dimensions: (1) the scientific contribution of the paper to the state of the art in the discipline

Figure 11.7
A Generalized Schematic View
of the Peer-Review Process by Scientific Journals

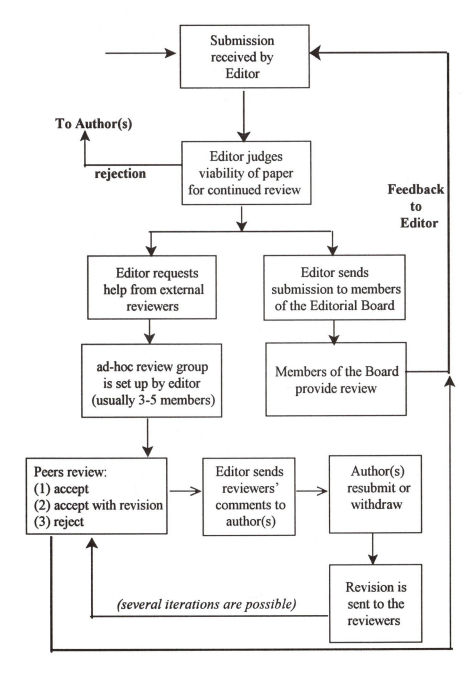

and in the area of research, and (2) characteristics of the paper itself: logic, adequacy of methodology, writing style, and readability. An overall recommendation is elicited and a rating is given in comparison to similar papers the reviewer haed seen published orhad previously reviewed.[33]

The Role of Reviewers. When summoned to serve as reviewers for scientific journals and in the service of foundations, industry, and government agencies, scientists-turned-reviewers wield a strong influence over the course of science and technology. In most instances, particularly in review for journals, reviewers are not compensated and their effort remains anonymous. Hence, many scientists are hesitant to join review boards or serve ad-hoc as journal reviewers.[34]

Like prospective members of juries in the American justice system, many S&T reviewers are unhappy about their summons to service because (1) reviews take too much of their time and disrupt their on-going interests and (2) there is little or no remuneration. In the case of journals, the pool of qualified reviewers for each subspecialty is small, so that repeated requests are regularly sent to the same people. Moreover, reviewers for agencies such as NIH sometimes find themselves treated as pariahs in the eyes of their colleagues who did not receive funding and who know, in general, who are the reviewers for the agency.

Blind Review. Is the feature of blind review in peer review beneficial in alleviating the problems listed in the previous section? Some scholars believe that "double blind" review provides sufficient conditions for an unbiased process. "Double-blind" reviews require that the names of both the authors and reviewers be kept confidential. Other scholars have disputed the benefits of blind review.[35] Their chief argument is based on the high degree of recognition of an author's publication by the reviewers—even when the names are not revealed to reviewers. This is because in subspecialties of science there is a relatively small core of scientists researching certain topics, and they are well known to their colleagues in the subspecialty. Second, self citations are common, so that authors cite their prior work, thus revealing the background for their current research.

The Role of Editors

Editors of S&T peer-review journals wield an enormous amount of power in their academic discipline and in S&T in general. Their influence is manifested and operationalized in (1) acceptance or rejection of submissions, and (2) deciding on the direction that a discipline or a specialty would take, by publishing a concentrated number of articles in a given area.[36]

In the process of peer review, editors wield their inordinate power by (1) choice of reviewers, in that editors may direct favored papers to more "agreeable" reviewers, (2) overruling reviewers' recommendations, so that ultimately the decision to publish or to reject rests with the editors, (3) showing preference for the editors' "pet topics", and (4) making decisions based less on scientific merit and more on political considerations.[37]

Another aspect of the power of editors is the fact that peer reviews of scientific papers are cursory, and do not require replication or testing of the hypotheses or the methodology, nor empirically challenging the results. The papers are assessed almost face-value, based on the logic of the approach and the feasibility of the findings. Therefore, the recommendations by reviewers, although sometimes very specific, leave the bulk of the decisional burden to the editor. In effect, editors are peers of the authors, and may be viewed as a peer-review committee of one, with the added authority to make the ultimate and binding decision.[38]

The *JAMA* and *NEJM* Cases

The preponderant influence of scientific editors was reflected in the attention given by the popular press to the dismissal in 1999 of the long-time editors of the two major medical journals. On January 15, 1999, Dr. George Lundberg, editor-in-chief of the *Journal of the American Medical Association* (*JAMA*), was dismissed by the association. The reason for this action was provided in the association's website: "(he) has threatened the historic tradition and integrity of *JAMA* by inappropriately and inexcusably interjecting it into a major political debate that has nothing to do with science or medicine."[39]

Lundberg's dismissal was due to the publication of the findings from a survey on the definition of "oral sex" at the time when the topic was in public discussion due to the impeachment procedures against the president of the United States.[40] Dr. Lundberg had been the editor of *JAMA* for 17 years. Highly respected in the medical community, Dr. Lundberg had instituted strict peer-review procedures, making the *Journal* a key publication in American (and world) medicine.

On July 27, 1999, the Massachusetts Medical Society announced that it would not renew the contract with the editor of its *New England Journal of Medicine* (*NEJM*)—Dr. Jerome Kassirer, who would step down the following March 31, 2000. The dismissal of Dr. Kassirer, who edited *NEJM* for eight years, was due to his strong disagreement with the society over the commercial use of the journal's name and reputation.[41]

In comments on the dismissal of Dr. Kassirer, the former editor of *JAMA*, Dr. Lundberg said: "Medical editors continue to espouse professional roles while the organizations that own their publications are acting more and more like pure businesses, even if they are professional associations."[42]

STRENGTHS AND BENEFITS FROM PEER REVIEW

The metric of peer review offers several benefits and enjoys some strengths that make it a desirable means to assess the potential and the outcomes from S&T. Illustrative strengths are shown in Figure 11.8.

Figure 11.8
Illustrative Strengths and Benefits from Peer Review

ILLUSTRATIVE STRENGTHS/BENEFITS
• Provides judgmental assessment by qualified experts in the S&T discipline and subspecialty.
• Provides a measure of quality control by preventing acceptance of "bad" science.
• Provides detailed opinions, comments, and suggestions from acceptable and respected peers.
• Allows for checks and balances among diverse opinions and "schools of thought."
• The peer-review process is understood by all participants.
• Provides scientific accountability.
• Relies on the intellectual resources of the S&T community.
• The process is rational, valid, and fair.
• Although qualitative, peer-review assessments provide adequate data for decisions on allocation of resources for S&T.

Not necessarily in any order of importance or priority.

The strengths of peer review may be grouped into two categories. The first is the use of acceptable, expert, and respected members of the S&T community as judges of the S&T activity and its outcomes. This leads to a measure of quality control, scientific accountability, and to keeping alive the principles of scientific integrity.[43]

The second category contains strengths related to the process of peer review, chiefly because—by design—it allows for the interchange of ideas, comments, suggestions, and feedback from colleagues in the discipline and its subspecialty.[44] Such an interchange facilitates the progress of science, as colleagues learn from other scientists and maintain open channels of communication.

WEAKNESSES AND PROBLEMS OF PEER REVIEW

There are two major categories of weaknesses and shortcomings of the metric of peer review. First, there are problems due to the frailties and biases that are inherent in human behavior, hence are apparent in the weaknesses of the work of editors and reviewers.[45]

The second category includes attributes of the process itself. Inordinate power given to reviewers and editors and the effects of the secrecy of the process combine to generate several shortcomings. Examples from both categories are shown in Figure 11.9.

SUMMARY: THE THIN LINE OF CONTROL

Although there are problems and shortcomings with peer review, in my view it has served well the community of science. Because of the way we define the scientific method and the high degree of specialty and expertise required in S&T endeavors, self-discipline, self-policing, and self-evaluation by the S&T community are the only means available to control the S&T effort. Peer review is the operational control process, designed to differentiate between "poor" and "good" science.

Peer review is the mechanism of this "in-house" policing by the S&T community. It represents the thin line that stands between what scientists believe constitutes "science," and claims made by those who are unqualified to judge. In the absence of reliable and quantitative data on the prospects of S&T and its merit, expert judgment is the best possible tool to measure and to assess science and technology.

Figure 11.9
Illustrative Weaknesses and Problems with Peer Review

ILLUSTRATIVE WEAKNESSES/PROBLEMS
• Delphi-type surveys are constrained by time, limited response rate, and preponderance of conservative views.
• Reviewers may show bias, jealousy, revenge, and intolerance toward other authors.
• Reviewers may protect their own "turf" and subspecialty by promoting papers in these areas.
• Reviews are cursory, hence there is no guarantee that "good" science will prevail and "bad" be rejected.
• Reviewers and editors tend to stick to existing paradigms in their disciplines and reject change.
• Editors wield inordinate power and channel the discipline in their preferred direction, rather than in a "bottom up" approach from the bench scientists.
• Secrecy of the process.
• Tendency to prefer established, well-published scientists.
• Problems with rating and raters, based on judgmental data.
• Cultural bias toward English-speaking publications.
• Good, specialized reviewers are increasingly hard to recruit.

Not necessarily in any order of importance or priority.

Is peer review honest? unbiased? efficient? As the shortcomings illustrated in Figure 11.9 have shown, not entirely. There is ample room for improvements, such as reduction in the effects of cultural and human biases. Clearly, peer review is the "sacred cow" of S&T metrics—the traditional "right" of scientists to critique and review the work of their colleagues. It is also at the core of the method by which science progresses.

For two decades I have reviewed countless scientific papers for leading journals in my discipline, as well as research proposals for the NSF and other government agencies. In addition I have reviewed, analyzed, and evaluated many R&D programs and their resultant technologies for a variety of industrial companies.

I have grown to appreciate the value of peer review as a metric. In the case of technology it should certainly be used in conjunction with other quantitative and objective metrics. Overall, peer review remains an indispensable metric in the "basket" of measures of S&T we currently possess.[46]

NOTES

1. See, for example, Speck, B., *Publication Peer Review: An Annotated Bibliography* (Westport, CT: Greenwood Publishing Group, 1993). Speck provides 780 sources on the process and effectiveness of peer review. Also see Noble, J., "Peer Review: Quality Control of Applied Social Research," *Science*, 185, 1974, 916-921; and National Research Council, *Research Management and Peer Review Practices in the U.S. Environmental Protection Agency* (Washington, DC: National Academy Press, 1999).

2. This method is used extensively for predictions and forecasting of technology, and is known as the "Delphi" method. See, for example, Cuhls, K., and T. Kuwahara, *Outlook for Japanese and German Future Technology* (New York: Springer-Verlag, 1994). In particular see pages 1-4, a description of the Delphi technique and its use in technology forecasting. For a basic text, see Porter, A., A. Roper, T. Mason, F. Rossini, and J. Banks, *Forecasting and Management of Technology* (New York: John Wiley & Sons, 1991). The authors offer a toolkit of the forecasting techniques, including Delphi. For specific applications see, for example, Clayton, M., "Delphi: A Technique to Harness Expert Opinion for Critical Decision-Making Tasks in Education," *Educational Psychology*, 17(4), 1997, 373-387; and Coates, J., and M. Wolff, "UK Delphi Report Merits Study by R&D Leaders," *Research-Technology Management*, 40(1), 1997, 5-8.

3. In this context, see for example, Harnad, S. (Ed.), *Peer Commentary on Peer Review* (Cambridge: Cambridge University Press, 1982); and Nederhof, A., and A. van Raan, "Peer Review and Bibliometric Indicators of Scientific Performance: A Comparison of Cum Laude Doctorates with Ordinary Doctorates in Physics," *Scientometrics* 11(4), 1987, 333-350.

4. See, for example, Wallmark, J., D. McQueen, and K. Sedig, "Measurement of Output from University Research: A Case Study," *IEEE Transactions on Engineering Management*, 35(3), 1988, 175-180. The authors argued that "in combination with the peer-review method it can be valuable in identifying especially productive departments or individuals, or the opposite" (p. 180). Also see Islei, G., G. Lockett, B. Cox, and M. Stratford, "A Decision Support System Using Judgmental Modeling: A Case Study of R&D in the Pharmaceutical Industry," *IEEE Transactions on Engineering Management*, 38(3), 1991, 202-209; and Frankel, M., and J. Cave (Eds.), *Evaluating Science and Scientists: An East-West Dialogue on Research in Post-Communist Europe* (Prague, Czech Republic: Central European University Press, 1997). In particular see Part II on peer review and an excellent review of this compendium in Shaw, B., "Book Review," *R&D Management*, 28(4), 1998, 323-324.

5. See, for example, Stodolsky, D., "Consensus Journals: Invitational Journals Based Upon Peer Review," *The Information Society*, 11(2), 1995, 247-260; and Hanson, D., "Struggling with Scientific Evidence," *Chemical & Engineering News*, 76(50), 1998, 31-32. Also see the discussion in the United Kingdom about what constitutes "good science" and the role of peer review in Nonbiot, G., "Blinkered Science Labs are Fuel of Researchers Who Can't See Beyond the Microscope," *The Guardian*, February 25, 1999, pp. 26-28.

6. Universities are a good example of self-policing and the congruence of these three reasons. Academic degrees given by universities are the outcome of a peer review. Members of the academic faculty decide who will or will not join its ranks, based on a review of the scientific achievements of the prospective candidates, who are asked to complete a highly formal curriculum.

7. The term "high-quality peer review" was originally proposed by Ronald Kostoff. See, for example, Dr. Kostoff's website at <http://www.dtic.mil/dtic/kostoff/index.html>.

8. See, for example, McCutchen, C., "Peer Review: Treacherous Servant, Disastrous Master," *Technology Review*, 94(7), 1991, 28-37. The author discussed peer review at the NIH and argued that anonymity may lead to personal motives that drive the evaluation, such as self-interest and revenge.

9. See, for example, Berk, R., "Threats to the Validity of Peer-Reviewed Radiology Journals: Identification of the Problem and Possible Solutions," *American Journal of Roentgenology*, 150(1), 1988, 19-71. Also see Atkinson, M., "Regulation of Science by Peer Review," *Studies in History and Philosophy of Science*, 25(2), 1994, 147-158; and Marshall, E., "Peer Review: Written and Unwritten Rules," *Science*, 270 (5244), 1995, 1913-1914; and, Burnham, J., "The Evolution of Editorial Peer Review," *Journal of the American Medical Association*, 263(10), 1990, 1323-1329.

10. These issues and examples are discussed in the section on weaknesses and problems of peer review.

11. There is a vast literature on this topic. See some illustrative studies: Chubin, D., and E. Hackett, *Peerless Science: Peer Review and U.S. Science Policy* (Albany: State University of New York Press, 1990); Daniel, H., *Guardians of Science: Fairness and Reliability of Peer Review* (New York: John Wiley & Sons, 1993); and Kiesler, A., "Confusion Between Reviewer Reliability and Wise Editorial and Funding Decisions," *Behavioral and Brain Sciences*, 4(1), 1991, 151-152. Also see Lind, A., C. Bewtra, J. Healy, and K. Sims, "Prospective Peer Review in Surgical Pathology," *American Journal of Clinical Pathology*, 104(5), 1995, 560-566.

12. See, for example, studies that addressed the issue of agreement among reviewers, and the randomness in the choice of reviewers: Abrams, P., "The Predictive Ability of Peer Review of Grant Proposals: The Case of Ecology and the U.S. National Science Foundation," *Social Studies of Science*, 21(3), 1991, 111-

132. Also see Cicchetti, D., "The Reliability of Peer Review for Manuscript and Grant Submissions: A Cross-Disciplinary Investigation," *Behavioral and Brain Sciences*, 14(2), 1991, 119-186.

13.   Cole, S., and J. Cole, *Peer Review in the National Science Foundation—Phase One* (Washington, DC: National Academy Press, 1978) and Cole, J., and S. Cole, *Peer Review in the National Science Foundation—Phase Two* (Washington, DC: National Academy Press, 1981).

14. See, for example, Feinstein, A., and D. Ciccetti, "High Agreement But Low Kappa: The Problem of Two Paradoxes," *Journal of Clinical Epidemiology*, 43(6), 1990, 543-549. Also see Hargens, L., "Further Evidence on Field Differences in Consensus from the NSF Peer Review Studies," *American Sociological Review*, 53(3), 1988, 157-160; and Dancik, B., "The Importance of Peer Review," *Serials Librarian*, 19(3-4), 1991, 91-94.

15. See, for example, Zurer, P., "NIH Peer Reviewers to Watch for High-Risk, High Payoff Proposals," *Chemical & Engineering News*, 71(23), 1993, 25-27. Also see Crane, M., "Is Junk Science Finally on the Way Out?" *Medical Economics*, 73(8), 1996, 59-62; and, Ianniello, L., "DOE Peer Review," *Science*, 265 (5170), 1994, 302-303; and also Kelly, K., "The Department of Defense External Civilian Peer Review of Medical Care," *Journal of the American Medical Association*, 262(14), 1989, 1950-1951.

16. See, for example, Luukkonen, T., "Scientific Research Evaluation: A Review of Methods and Various Contexts of Their Application," *R&D Management*, 17(3), 1987, 207-222. Also see National Research Council, *Improving Research Through Peer Review* (Washington, DC: National Academy Press, 1987); and Gidez, L., "The Peer-Review Process-Strengths and Weaknesses: A Survey of Attitudes, Perceptions, and Expectations," *Serials Librarian*, 19(3-4), 1991, 75-85.

17. See, for example, Anderson, R., "Guidelines for Review of a Manuscript," *Human Pathology*, 21(4), 1990, 359-360. Also see Jefferson, T., and V. Demicheli, "Are Guidelines for Peer-Reviewing Economic Evaluations Necessary: A Survey of Current Editorial Practices," *Health Economics*, 4(5), 1995, 383-388.

18. See, for example, Lepkowski, W., "Peer Review Adds Social Relevancy," *Chemical & Engineering News*, 75(14), 1997, 9-10.

19. See Blount, H., "Peer Review of National Science Foundation Grant Proposals," *Abstracts of Papers of the American Chemical Society*, 195(6), 1988, 6-12. See the Foundation's website of <http://www.NSF.gov.index. html>. In particular see the discussion of the motives that led to the changes. For example, Goodwin, I., "Faulted by GAO on Proposal Reviews, NSF Seeks More Efficiency and Fairness," *Physics Today*, 48(9), 1995, 76-77.

20. In 1995 a Stanford University biophysicist, Oleg Jardetzky, publicly complained that his proposal, rated "excellent," had been rejected. The NSF replied that indeed many excellent proposals cannot be funded. See Macilwain, C.,

"Even Excellent Is No Longer Good Enough for the NSF," *Nature*, 375 (May 18), 1995, 173.

21. See, for example, Agnew, B., "NIH Invites Activities into the Inner Sanctum," *Science*, 283, (5410), 1999, pp. 1999-2001. Also see Wadman, M., "NIH Peer-Review Revision Panel Is Named," *Nature*, 391 (6669), 1998, p. 725; and Nathan, D., "Clinical Research: Perceptions, Reality, and Proposed Solutions," *Journal of the American Medical Association*, 280(16), 1998, 1427-31. Also, Marshall, E., "NIH Plans Peer-Review Overhaul," *Science*, 276 (May 9), 1987, 888-889.

22. See, for example, the description of the process by the director of the Division of Research Grants at NIH, Ehrenfeld, E., "Peer-Review: Priorities for the 21ˢᵗ Century," *Journal of NIH Research*, 9(8), 1997, 33-35; also see Hopkin, K., "Judging the Judges: NIH Reexamines Peer Review," *Journal of NIH Research*, 9(8), 1997, 48-50.

23. See, for example, Deegan, C., and R. Mullan, "Does NIH Need a DARPA?" *Issues in Science and Technology*, 13(2), 1997, 25-28. Also see Lock, S., *Difficult Balance: Editorial Peer Review in Medicine* (New York: ISI Press, 1986); and, Long, D., *Medical Staff Peer Review: A Strategy for Motivation and Performance* (Chicago: American Hospital Association, 1991).

24. Al-Mazidi, S., and A. Ghosn, "A Management Model for Technology and R&D Selection," *International Journal of Technology Management*, 13(5,6), 1997, 525-541.

25. See, for example, MacLean, M., J. Anderson, and B. Martin, "Identifying Research Priorities in Public Sector Funding Agencies: Mapping Science Outputs onto User Needs," *Technology Analysis & Strategic Management*, 10(2), 1998, 139-155.

26. See, for example, Rubenstein, A., "Setting Criteria for R&D," *Harvard Business Review*, 35(1), 1957, 95-104. Also see Rubenstein, A., "Field Studies of Project Selection Behavior in Industrial Laboratories," in B. V. Dean (Ed.), *Operations Research in Research and Development* (New York: John Wiley & Sons, 1963), pp. 189-206; and Lee, J., S. Lee, and Z. Bae, "R&D Project Selection: Behavior and Practice in a Newly Industrializing Country," *IEEE Transactions on Engineering Management*, 33(3), 1986, 141-147.

27. See an extensive discussion of these criteria and industrial practices of peer review in: Rubenstein, A., *Managing Technology in the Decentralized Firm* (New York: John Wiley & Sons, 1989); in particular, see Chapter 7, pp. 289-342.

28. See, for example, early studies of peer review and rank ordering of projects and units: Glass, E., "Methods of Evaluating R&D Organizations," *IEEE Transactions on Engineering Management*, 19(1), 1972, 2-12. Also see Souder, W., and T. Mandrakovic, "R&D Project Selection Models," *Research Management*, 29(4), 1986, 36-47; and the illuminating book that is still very relevant: Souder, W., *Project Selection and Economic Appraisal* (New York: Van

Norstrand Reinhold, 1983). More recently see, for example, a discussion of peer review as an instrument in the generating of arguments for modeling the future: Guice, J., "Designing the Future: the Culture of New Trends in Science and Technology," *Research Policy*, 28(1), 1999, 81-98.

29. A more detailed description of these divisional and corporate R&D committees, frequency of their use, and other factors is given in Chapter 15.

30. See, for example, Mayland, H., and R. Sojka, *Research Ethics, Manuscript Review, and Journal Quality* (Chicago: American Society of Agronomy, 1992).

31. *Webster's New Collegiate Dictionary* (Springfield, MA: G&C Merriam Company, 1977), page 845.

32. See, for example, Rossbacher, L., "What Goes Around Comes Around," *Geotimes*, 42(2), 1997, p. 44. Also see Bowen, D., D. Perloff, and J. Jacoby, "Improving Manuscript Evaluation Procedures," *American Psychologist*, 27(3), 1977, 221-225; and the illuminating review, Gans, J., and G. Shepherd, "How Are the Mighty Fallen: Rejected Classic Articles by Leading Economists," *Journal of Economic Perspectives*, 8(1), 1994, 165-179. Also see Lock, S. and J. Smith, "What Do Peer Reviewers Do?" *Journal of the American Medical Association*, 263(10), 1990, 1341-1343.

33. For example, see Moller, J., "Who Should or Can Peer Review Assess Subspecialty Programs," *Pediatrics*, 81(1), 1988, 172-173; and Nolkin, D., "Threads and Promises: Negotiating the Control of Research," *Daedalus*, 107(2), 1978, 191-210. Also see Simon, R., V. Bakanic, and C. McPhail, "Who Complains to Editors and What Happens," *Sociological Inquiry*, 56(3), 1986, 259-271.

34. Fliesler, S., "Rethinking Grant Peer Review," *Science*, 278 (March 7), 1997, 1399-1400. Also see Polak, J., "The Role of the Manuscript Reviewer in the Peer-Review Process," *American Journal of Roentgenology*, 165(3), 1995, 685-688.

35. Rosenblatt, A., and S. Kirk, "Recognition of Authors in Blind Review of Manuscripts," *Journal of Social Service Research*, 3(4), 1980, 383-394.

36. I was department editor for information technology of the *IEEE Transactions on Engineering Management* for much of the 1990s, editor of special issues in two other journals, and a member of the editorial board for three journals in the field of management. I was always acutely conscious of the power vested in my position, as ultimate arbiter of what is scientifically acceptable, as well as my power over the careers and reputation of my colleagues who submitted articles to these journals.

37. See, for example, Gupta, A., "The Peer-Review Process, Multiple Publications, and the Overcrowded By-Line: Roles of the Editor, Reviewers, and Author," *International Journal of Insect Morphology & Embryology*, 25(1-2), 1996, 19-24. Also see Altura, B., "Is Anonymous Peer Review the Best Way to

Review and Accept Manuscripts?" *Magnesium and Trace Elements*, 9(3), 1990, 117-118; and Armstrong, J., "Research on Scientific Journals: Implications for Editors and Authors," *Journal of Forecasting*, 1(2), 1982, 83-104. Also see Fiske, D., and L. Fogg, "But the Reviewers Are Making Different Criticisms of My Paper," *American Psychologist*, 45(5), 1990, 591-598.

38. See, for example, Robinson, G., "NSF Review Process Should Be Revamped, Not Taken for Granted," *Physics Today*, 50(3), 1997, 82-83. The author argues that peer reviews are harming the frontiers of science by being self-serving and shortsighted. He also argues that they also generally ignore progressive ideas. Also see Fogarty, T., "The Imagery and Reality of Peer Review in the US: Insights from Institutional Theory," *Accounting, Organizations, and Society*, 21(2-3), 1996, 243-247; and, Lock, S., "Does Editorial Peer Review Work?" *Annals of Internal Medicine*, 121(1), 1994, 60-61.

39. See the AMAS's website at: http://www.ama-assn.org. Also see the very focal and negative reaction from the British medical community in Horton, R., "The Sacking of JAMA," *The Lancet*, 353(9149), January 23, 1999, in Commentary.

40. The said article was Sanders, S., and J. Machover Reinisch, "Would You Say You 'Had Sex" If...?" *JAMA*, 281, January 20, 1999, 275-277. The article reported findings from a survey of 599 students of a midwestern university, conducted in 1991 (eight years prior to publication).

41. See the story in Jaspen, B., "New England Journal of Medicine Fires Top Editor," *Chicago Tribune*, July 27, 1999, Section 3, pp. 1,4.

42. *Ibid.*, p. 4.

43. See, for example, Grol, R., and M. Lawrence (Eds.), *Quality Improvement by Peer Review* (New York: Oxford University Press, 1995); in particular see Chapters 4 and 5, pages 26-38. Also see Cook, R., "Crime Lab Trio Out After Problems. Routine 'Peer Review' Finds Some Scientists May Have Cut Corners," *The Atlanta Journal Constitution*, February 13, 1999, p. F01.

44. See, for example, Benfield, J., "The Anatomy of Peer Review," *Journal of Thoracic and Cardiovascular Surgery*, 101(2), 1991, 190-195. Also see Kassirer, J., and E. Campion, "Peer Review: Crude and Understudied, but Indispensable," *Journal of the American Medical Association*, 272(2), 1994, 96-97; and Klein, C., "Benefits of Peer-Reviewed Publication," *American Journal of Hospital Pharmacy*, 48(7), 1991, 1424-1426.

45. See, for example, Moran, G., *Silencing Scientists and Scholars in Other Fields: Power Paradigm Controls, Peer Review, and Scholarly Communication* (San Francisco: Ablex Publishing Corporaiton, 1998). Also see Karl, K., "The Art and Science of 360 Degrees Feedback," *The Academy of Management Executive*, 11(3), 1997, 100-101; and Crane, M., "Is 'Junk Science' Finally on the Way Out?" *Medical Economics*, 73(8), 1996, p. 59.

46. Even probabilities used in quantitative methods for S&T evaluation are also the result of expert opinions. Peer review, in all of its modes and formats, presumably with some degree of objectivity, clearly brings to the process the scientific/technical expertise to judge the work of others. There have been very few cases of misconduct and gross misutilization of the peer-review process, and they ultimately were discovered in subsequent peer review. See, for example, Guston, D., and K. Keniston, "Updating the Social Contract for Science," *Technology Review*, 97(8), 1994, 60-63.

12

THE METRIC OF
PROCESS OUTCOMES

*In each action we must look beyond the action at our past,
present, and future state, and at others whom it affects, and see
the relations of all those things. And then we shall be very
cautious.*

Blaise Pascal, 1623-1662
(*Pensees*, 1670)

INTRODUCTION

The previous chapters introduced several metrics of S&T: economic and
financial, bibliometrics, co-analysis and mapping, patents, and peer review.
These metrics are the mainstay of the current arsenal of metrics used to
evaluate S&T. With the exception of peer review, all the above metrics
rely on some data on the inputs or the outputs of S&T.

Geisler (1992) proposed a classification of S&T evaluation models
and metrics that would include three categories: (1) input-related, (2)
output-related, and (3) input-output.[1] Economic/financial metrics of
investments in S&T are input-related, whereas patents and bibliometrics
are considered outputs. Metrics that relate investments and outputs are of
the input-output category. Economic metrics are in this group, in the sense
that they correlate financial measures for both investments/expenditures
and outputs. However, even this metric suffers from various problems and

shortcomings that are common to all the metrics discussed in previous chapters.

Problem of Imputation

This problem refers to the effort by which evaluators using the aforementioned metrics of S&T ascribe or attribute events—such as corporate success—to the S&T activity and its expenditures. Effects are thus imputed, without empirical evidence to account for such effects, or to show how they came about as a result of the S&T activity or its outputs.[2] Metrics that suffer from this problem are not measuring the phenomenon they purport to measure. Hence their validity may be seriously impaired.[3]

One of the reasons for the existence of imputation is the nature of the process of S&T and innovation. Its complexity is due to the action of inputs and contributions from sources other than S&T, compounded by the high rate of diffusion of S&T outputs, making them very difficult to identify and measure.

This is true even for judgmental assessment done by peer review. Scientists who assume the role of evaluators make assumptions about the potential or actual contributions of S&T to organizations, the economy, and society. Hence, these reviewers are imputing the cause-and-effect connection between S&T and its contributions.

Problem of Confounding Criteria

The metrics in the previous chapters were designed to utilize two sets of confounding criteria. The first set is criteria related to control—usually for short-term purposes. These criteria tend to be in conflict with longer term criteria designed for evaluation and for assessment of purported contributions of S&T.[4] Metrics that suffer from this problem have inner contradictions of their criteria.

For example, bibliometrics is designed to measure the proximal outputs from S&T, and is generally used as a means of control of the S&T activity and its expenditures. But this use of bibliometrics is in conflict with longer term criteria of S&T contributions to the economy and to society.

Problem of Link Between Science and Technology

Most of the metrics listed previously measure the intensity or out-comes from scientific activity. There is a tendency to confuse the impacts of science as metrics of technology, in particular when economic and financial measures are employed. Bibliometrics, patents, and the economic potential of investments in science are projected toward the evaluation of technologies that are utilized by public and private organizations.

The missing link in this projection is the conceptual and temporal connection between what scientific activity produces and what technology can and does accomplish. Simply by projecting measures of science to technological achievements, evaluators face a problem of the definition and boundaries of crucial economic and societal activities, as well as the accuracy and relevancy of the measures used in the evaluation.[5]

Problem of Reliance on Distant Covariation

Similar to the problem of imputation, evaluators of S&T tend to use metrics in a covariation approach. The concept of covariation means that researchers or evaluators measure two seemingly unrelated events (such as investments in research, and market share of the corporation), then correlate the events in a way that suggests a strong relation. Although statistically the events may be positively correlated and there is some theoretical explanation of the link, nevertheless the differences in the characteristics and time frames of the events preclude the drawing of valid or reliable conclusions from the relationship.[6]

Other Problems

Problems of imputation, link between science and technology, and covariation are powerful shortcomings of the employment of certain metrics in the evaluation of the entire innovation spectrum. The use of metrics designed for one portion of the spectrum in evaluation of a different portion or component of innovation is also mired in difficulties.

In addition to the problems listed above, there are difficulties related to impacts of human nature. In S&T organizations many actors in the S&T process are reluctant to assign quantitative values on outputs from one portion of the spectrum (such as research) when these values are to be employed elsewhere (as in technological improvements by other units).

There are also problems in claiming credit for achievements and in the precision with which credits are assigned to different actors.[7]

Consequently, there seems to be a need for a model or approach that would provide an evaluation of the S&T continuum, without the burden of such problems. Since the existing set of metrics suffers from these problems, a fresh approach and new metrics would thus be a welcome addition to the S&T tools for evaluation.

THE PROCESS OUTCOMES MODEL

Rubenstein and Geisler (1991)[8] and Geisler (1995)[9] have advanced the model of process outcomes to evaluate S&T. The approach is based on the following key components or dimensions:

1. There are identifiable stages in the innovation process.

2. These stages may serve as the building-blocks of the process and flow of S&T.

3. S&T flows through the stages, from research, development, new products, to the final stage of technology that is commercialized and used.

4. There are distinct outputs at each stage that can be measured and compared across stages.

5. The S&T process is composed of transformation and diffusion activities, in which the outputs from the various stages flow toward the downstream of the innovation continuum.

6. There are social and economic organizations that compose the various subsystems in which the transformation and diffusion activities occur.

The overall model is shown in Figure 12.1, which contains the S&T stages and the economic/social subsystems through which S&T flows in the innovation continuum.

Figure 12.1
The Process-Outcomes Model of the Linkages Between the S&T Process and Social and Economic Systems

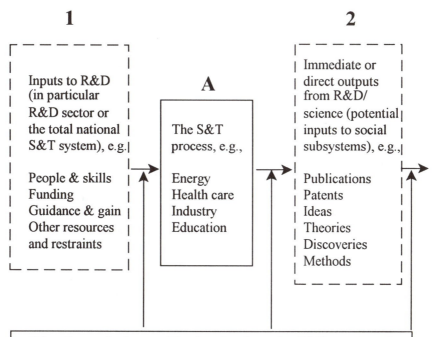

Other factors in the specific situation (e.g., the S&T sector or the social subsystem) which affect the transition, transportation, adoption, usefulness, cost or economic benefit from transfers between adjacent and more distant stages. Such factors may include economic, cultural, organizational, technical, personal, or political ones. Some are particular to a given stage (e.g., the barriers and difficulties involved in designing economical and socially acceptable energy or safety devices and systems or the diffusion problems in curing a disease); others may apply to several stages in the overall process (e.g., capital shortages or regulations); and still others are pervasive across the whole process (e.g., organizational barriers to innovation, individual risk preferences, diffuse decision-making responsibility).

Figure 12.1 Continued.

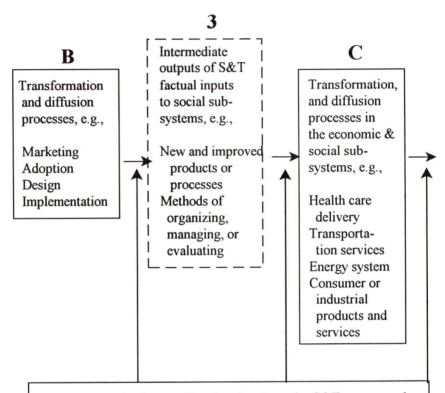

3

B

Transformation
and diffusion
processes, e.g.,

Marketing
Adoption
Design
Implementation

Intermediate
outputs of S&T
factual inputs
to social sub-
systems, e.g.,

New and improved
products or
processes
Methods of
organizing,
managing, or
evaluating

C

Transformation,
and diffusion
processes in
the economic &
social sub-
systems, e.g.,

Health care
delivery
Transporta-
tion services
Energy system
Consumer or
industrial
products and
services

Other factors in the specific situation (e.g., the S&T sector or the social subsystem) which affect the transition, transportation, adoption, usefulness, cost or economic benefit from transfers between adjacent and more distant stages. Such factors may include economic, cultural, organizational, technical, personal, or political ones. Some are particular to a given stage (e.g., the barriers and difficulties involved in designing economical and socially acceptable energy or safety devices and systems or the diffusion problems in curing a disease); others may apply to several stages in the overall process (e.g., capital shortages or regulations); and still others are pervasive across the whole process (e.g., organizational barriers to innovation, individual risk preferences, diffuse decision-making responsibility).

Figure 12.1 Continued.

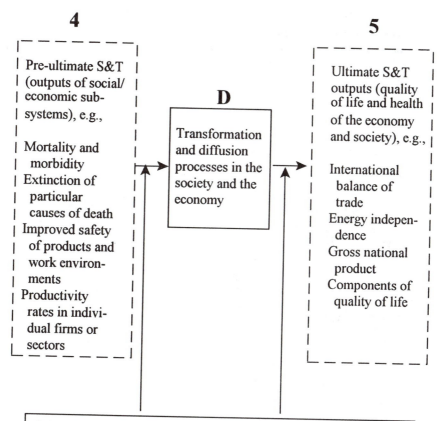

4

> Pre-ultimate S&T
> (outputs of social/
> economic sub-
> systems), e.g.,
>
> Mortality and
> morbidity
> Extinction of
> particular
> causes of death
> Improved safety
> of products and
> work environ-
> ments
> Productivity
> rates in indivi-
> dual firms or
> sectors

D

Transformation
and diffusion
processes in the
society and the
economy

5

> Ultimate S&T
> outputs (quality
> of life and health
> of the economy
> and society), e.g.,
>
> International
> balance of
> trade
> Energy indepen-
> dence
> Gross national
> product
> Components of
> quality of life

Other factors in the specific situation (e.g., the S&T sector or the social subsystem) which affect the transition, transportation, adoption, usefulness, cost or economic benefit from transfers between adjacent and more distant stages. Such factors may include economic, cultural, organizational, technical, personal, or political ones. Some are particular to a given stage (e.g., the barriers and difficulties involved in designing economical and socially acceptable energy or safety devices and systems or the diffusion problems in curing a disease); others may apply to several stages in the overall process (e.g., capital shortages or regulations); and still others are pervasive across the whole process (e.g., organizational barriers to innovation, individual risk preferences, diffuse decision-making responsibility).

Stages of the Process

The model describes the innovation process, from the inputs or investments in science, to the outputs and impacts of technology, on the economy and society. The model has four main activities along the innovation continuum. These are marked A-D in Figure 12.1. These are the formal manifestations of the transformation of inputs to S&T—to their outputs. There are also one *input* and four *output* stages. These are marked 1-5 in Figure 12.1.

1. Inputs to the S&T Process. The inputs are the resources invested in S&T and the constraints that are imposed on the S&T process and its environment. These constraints may be the nature of the discipline, the skills and experience of the people involved in S&T, and the state of the art (SOA) of the particular discipline. Inputs include all the resources that are put into S&T at all the stages of its progression. Human resources as well as capital, facilities, and such intangibles as reputation and past performance are also included.[10]

2. Immediate or Direct/Proximal Outputs. This is the stage in which the model identifies the outputs from the initial S&T activity. They are the traditional proximal outputs that have long been used as indicators of the performance or productivity of S&T. They include such measures as bibliometric outputs, count of patents, ideas, discoveries, inventions, and methods/techniques.[11]

As mentioned earlier in this book, many scholars have used these *immediate* outputs as indicators of the outcomes from activities that in this model are downstream the innovation process. An important aspect of this model of process-outcomes is the localization of certain outputs within the confines of corresponding activities.

3. Intermediate Outputs. These are the outcomes that emerge from the transformation and diffusion activities that occur within organizations that absorb the immediate outputs. For example, a new method discussed in a scientific publication may be transformed by the organization into a design module, which leads to a new way of designing a product. This new way is the intermediate output.[12]

4. Pre-Ultimate Outputs. Once the intermediate outputs are absorbed and transformed by social and economic organizations (subsystems), the outputs from these activities are the pre-ultimate outputs. They are the consequences from the S&T inputs into these organizations and the transformations that such inputs had undergone within these organizations. As shown in Figure 12.1A, they are rates of mortality or morbidity, productivity, and similar consequences.[13]

5. *Ultimate Outputs.* These outputs are all the things of value to the economy and to society, such as their well-being, quality of life, and their growth and progress. In a way these are the ultimate goals to which we all aspire. The various outputs from S&T that have been identified in the model move downstream toward their contribution to the ultimate outputs. These outputs therefore measure the final, overall benefits from our investments in S&T.[14]

Transformation and Diffusion Activities

The flow of S&T downstream the innovation process is captured in the process-outcomes model in the form of stages of outputs (described above) and four activities/towards. The latter are depicted in Figure 12.1 as A-D. These are the processes by which S&T outputs are serially transformed, until they are absorbed and transformed by society and the economy to benefit the ultimate goals of human and national existence.

A. *The S&T Process.* This activity refers to the process known as research and development, or the science portion of the S&T process. These are the operations of research organizations who transform their inputs of human, physical, and financial resources into research and development. They transform such inputs into the *immediate* outputs described above.

B. *Transformation and Diffusion Processes.* The second activity in the process-outcomes model is the set of transformation and diffusion efforts of the immediate outputs from S&T. Examples include the transfer, marketing, and adoption of immediate outputs such as patents, ideas, theories, methods, and inventions.[15] These outputs are transferred and diffused within the same organizations that conduct S&T, and in other organizations and entities to which the outputs are exported.

These transformation and diffusion processes produce the intermediate outputs. As the immediate outputs are adopted, absorbed, and transformed by the respective organizations, they become different outputs. Among these newly transformed outputs are new and improved products or processes, methods, systems, and other such outputs that characterize industrial and publicly funded innovation.[16]

C. Social and Economic Subsystems. These are transformation and diffusion activities that act on the intermediate outputs. For example, new products are incorporated into economic or social entities, such as industrial companies or health care delivery organizations. These organizations adapt the intermediate outputs and integrate them into their routine work. The results may turn into the pre-ultimate outputs, such as improvements in safety, reduced mortality and morbidity, and similar consequences.[17]

There are many mechanisms by which economic and social entities adapt, use, adopt, and process the intermediate outputs. A good portion of the literature on the management of technology and innovation traditionally focused on such mechanisms and ways to improve them.[18]

D. The Society and the Economy. These are transformation and diffusion processes that act on the pre-ultimate outputs. The results are the ultimate outputs that impinge on the quality of life of the society and on the strength of its economy.

For example, the pre-ultimate outputs such as improved safety of products and the work environment may lead to a better quality of life of the population. The way this is achieved is through the transformation of a safer work environment into a more satisfied and healthier workforce, hence a higher quality of life of the entire population. This transformation is the process embedded in Box **D** in Figure 12.1.

The flow of activities and outputs is certainly not as smooth and uninterrupted as shown in Figure 12.1. There are feedback loops among the various stages. In addition, the factors that act as barriers and facilitators in each node (link between a stage and outputs) may create delays and feedbacks among the stages. The overall picture that emerges is one of a very complex and intricate system and process by which S&T is created, transformed, and utilized.

A different note concerns the value of the outputs, particularly the pre-ultimate and ultimate outputs. All the examples in Figure 12.1 are of benefits to the respective organizations and to society and the economy. Some outputs may certainly bring about negative consequences. Pollution, stress, psychological impacts on the workforce, and similar consequences are examples of negative impacts of S&T outputs. They are also discussed in Chapter 19.

METRICS AND INDICATORS

The process-outcomes model spans across the main stages of the entire innovation continuum. It provides an approximate description of the flow of activities *and* outputs, from investments in science and research all the way to the ultimate "users," recipients, or "clients" in the social/economic organizations.

The model identifies the various stages of such a flow of S&T activities and outputs. Although some stages flow into each other in a continuous movement and almost in a mode that makes distinction and identification of a stage very difficult, nevertheless the outputs from S&T are used, absorbed, transformed, and transferred in different time frames and by different organizations. This allows us to distinguish, both conceptually and empirically, among the stages of the process.

Because each stage has different outputs and different institutional transformations, the metrics used to measure such outputs will differ among the stages.[19] In a series of publications, Geisler[20] argued for two different measures of each category of outputs: *core* indicators and *organization-specific* indicators.

Core Indicators

For each category of constructs (boxes 2-5 in Figure 12.1), the *core* indicators are measures of the outputs that are independent of any organizational characteristics. Figure 12.2 shows illustrative indicators for each of the four categories of outputs.

The difference between indicators and measures in the figure is as follows. Indicators describe identifiable slices of the output, whereas measures are the actual figure (quantitative or qualitative) that measures the indicator. Thus, each indicator may be measured by multiple measures.

Figure 12.2
Illustrative Core Indicators and Measures of the Outputs from S&T

I.   IMMEDIATE OUTPUTS
1.   Written Scientific and Technical Outputs
1.1 Number of publications in refereed journals.
1.2 Number of technical reports.
1.3 Number of patents.
1.4 Number of citations in refereed journals.
1.5 Number of patent disclosures.

2.   Other Outputs
2.1 Number of licenses signed for own patents.
2.2 Number of new products conceived
2.3 Number of key improvements suggested.
2.4 Number of new and improved test methods, models, standards, concepts, and databases.
2.5 Number of new ideas transferred downstream.
2.6 Number of problems solved for users/clients.

3.   Overall Reputation
3.1 Number of complaints by clients/users.
3.2 Judgment of quality of S&T by clients/users.
3.3 Number of awards received.
3.4 Milestones/objectives met.

II. INTERMEDIATE OUTPUTS
1.   Scientific/Technical Impacts on Direct Users of S&T
1.1 Number of improved or new products produced.
1.2 Number of improved or new processes applied.
1.3 Number of improved or new materials made.

2.   Economic/Financial Impacts on Direct Users of S&T
2.1 Income from licensing patents and inventions.
2.2 Cost reductions/savings from new and improved products/processes.
2.3 Improvements in productivity of people and materials/equipment.
2.4 Costs associated with implementation and adoption of new products/ processes (e.g., training, regulatory adjustments).

3.   Responsiveness of S&T
3.1 Judgment by direct clients/users (their satisfaction; benefits from S&T).
3.2. Judgment by other organizations (S&T and non-S&T).

III. PRE-ULTIMATE OUTPUTS
1.   Economic Benefits and Costs
1.1 Improvements in productivity levels in people and equipment by sector and industry.

    1.2 Savings, cost reductions, and income generated by improved health, productivity, safety, and mobility of the workforce at sectoral and national levels.

    1.3 Costs to the economy and to society from the absorption of S&T into social/economic subsystems (such as transportation, energy, information, telecommunications, and health care).

2. Improvements and Problems in Social Conditions

    2.1 Improvements in overall health of population.

    2.2 Improved life expectancy of population.

    2.3 Improved satisfaction and levels of optimism of the population.

    2.4 Problems in social conditions (associated with the pre-ultimate outputs and their impacts on society and the economy) such as increased alienation, decrease in feelings of security and job loyalty.

    2.5 Changes (positive and negative) in the nature of work.

IV. ULTIMATE OUTPUTS

1. Economic Benefits and Costs

    1.1 Improved gross national product.

    1.2 Improvements in the balance of trade and balance of payments.

    1.3 Improved GDP/capita.

    1.4 Costs of living in a highly technological economy.

2. Social Benefits and Costs

    2.1 Improved level of overall satisfaction and happiness of population.

    2.2 Expanded "middle" or "professional" class.

    2.3 Costs of living in a technological society.

Source for some of the indicators and measures is from Table 1 and Appendix A, in Geisler, "An Integrated Cost-Performance Model of Research and Development Evaluation," Omega, 23(3), 1995, 281-294.

Core indicators and measures provide a picture of the outputs from S&T—as they evolve through the flow of the innovation process—that represents the generic outputs from S&T. These outputs measure outcomes from S&T that occur in all sectors and disciplines.

Organization-Specific Indicators

Organization-specific indicators are measures of some specific attributes of the organizations that are involved in generating, trans-forming, or absorbing S&T outputs. These indicators describe the characteristics of these organizations that may impact the processing of S&T outputs. Some of these characteristics are included in the "other factors" in the lower box of Figure 12.1.

Illustrative organization-specific indicators and measures are shown in Figure 12.3, which depicts indicators and measures that can be applied to any organization in the innovation continuum—from the S&T producing laboratory, to social subsystems such as health care delivery organizations.

Figure 12.3
Illustrative Organization-Specific Indicators and Measures of the Outputs from S&T

I. IMMEDIATE OUTPUTS
   ### 1. Level of Technical Expertise
   1.1 Ratio of doctorate holders to scientific workforce.
   1.2 Relative experience of scientists and engineers (total years of technical work).
   ### 2. Attractiveness of the S&T Organization
   2.1 Number of candidates applying for scientific position, per position.
   2.2 Age profile of scientists and engineers.
   2.3 Judgment of quality of the organization by peers.

II. INTERMEDIATE OUTPUTS
   ### 1. Level of Investment in Exploitation of S&T
   1.1 Funds allocated to technology commercialization by the focal organization (e.g., company, government agency).
   1.2 Number of personnel from non-S&T units working with S&T units (per scientists & engineers).
   ### 2. Level of Importance of S&T Outcomes
   2.1 Role of new products/services in the organization's success and survival (as perceived by senior managers of the organization).
   2.2 Perceived success of the transfer process and implementation/absorption of S&T outputs in the organization (perceived by senior managers of the organization).
   ### 3. Climate and Leadership
   3.1 Degree of support that senior management gives to S&T generation, adoption, and transfer.
   3.2 Overall "climate" in the organization: favorable or unfavorable to S&T (perceived by workers and managers).

III. PRE-ULTIMATE OUTPUTS
   ### 1. Investments in Adoption of S&T
   1.1 Funds allocated to the total adoption, adaptation, and utilization of S&T intermediate outputs by the focal organizations (as ratio of total budgets, and over time).
   1.2 Ratio of products, services, and processes impacted by S&T outputs that are adopted, implemented, and utilized by the organization.

2. **Structure of the Industry**
   2.1 Structural variables such as size, centralization, and vertical integration.
   2.2 Traditional perception of S&T in the industry: How important is S&T to the progress and survival of the industry?
3. **Strategy and Life Cycle**
   3.1 Role of S&T in strategic management of the industry and sector.
   3.2 Impact of S&T on the industry in its stage of life cycle.

IV ULTIMATE OUTPUTS

1. **Role and Importance of S&T**
   1.1 Role of S&T in the economy, as perceived by the population.
   1.2 Role of S&T in social progress, as perceived by the population.
   1.3 Importance of S&T as a political issue.
2. **S&T Level of Population**
   2.1 Levels of S&T literacy in population.
   2.2 Acceptance of the importance of investments in S&T by the population,.

Source for some of the indicators and measures is from Table 2 and Appendix A in Geisler, "An Integrated Cost-Performance Model of Research and Development Evaluation," Omega, *23(3), 1995, 281-294.*

Clustering and Indexing

The large number of indicators and measures that are assigned to the various outputs would be excellent candidates for some form of clustering and aggregation. Ideally, we would be able to create meaningful "macro" indicators, in the form of indexes, for each of the outputs from S&T.

Such was the approach suggested by Geisler (1995).[21] An index is computed for each category of outputs, and an overall, comprehensive index for *all* outputs is derived, based on computation of normalized weights of the indicators and the indexes.[22]

If we were to construct a cost-effectiveness model of S&T, along the innovation continuum, it would have to be done piecemeal. At every stage of the innovation continuum/process, the costs and outcomes (including benefits and negative consequences) would have to be computed. Unlike the approach favored by economists, in which investments and outputs are compared across the innovation process—in covariation designs—any meaningful cost-benefit analysis must consider the various transformations and the mediating costs and benefits in the progression of S&T toward the ultimate outputs to society and the economy.[23]

The process-outcomes model inherently contains a cost-benefits possibility. Since costs are spread across the various entities in the innovation process, and benefits (outcomes) are also generated in a diversified manner among the participating entities, traditional cost-benefits analyses may be replaced by an attempt to cluster and index inputs and outputs in the process-outcomes model.

Issues in Clustering and Indexing

Building macroindicators or indexes at each stage and across stages must obey the condition of orthogonality. This means that multiple counting of indicators/measures in the construction of indices is avoided. We achieve the relative independence of such measures entered into the index by the following criteria. First, measures thus selected describe as many characteristics as possible. Second, we use a limited number of measures to form the indicators, then to construct the index with these indicators. Hence, the indicators are diverse but conceptually applicable in that a small set represents the phenomenon.[24] Third, the sets we construct contain mutually exclusive indicators and measures.

A cascading method of constructing indices is thereby employed, moving from stage to stage, with the macro index of output indicators for the entire innovation process. Similarly, an index of inputs/investments or costs may be constructed.

Clearly, the weights applied in building the indices and the macro-index are the result of our analysis of relative importance (and other factors) in each stage. In some ways this depends on the viewpoint of the evaluator. If the emphasis is on the downstream stages, then the pre-ultimate and ultimate outputs will be awarded higher levels of importance and higher weights. However, the contributions of earlier stages must never be totally excluded from the macroindex. Similar emphasis may be placed on the transformations that occur in the social subsystems and in the society and the economy. Thus, an index of costs and inputs to these systems will place higher weights on these costs than on those in the upstream stages.[25]

The overall indices and the macro- (comprehensive) index are approximations to the relations between aggregated impacts of S&T and the costs/inputs associated with these impacts all along the innovation continuum.[26]

Creation of Factors

As clusters of metrics are composed, at each stage of outputs we can identify a cluster or index which has unique attributes and managerial implications. In the cluster of immediate outputs, positive normalized weights (W_{ia}) are given to each measure of each indicators so that:

$$0 < W_{ia} < 1 \qquad a = 1,2,\cdots,n(i)$$

and

$$\sum_{a=1}^{n(i)} w_{ia} = 1$$

where i = number of the indicator, and n(i) = number of measures of the *i*th indicator. Thus, for each indicator the value is the sum of the weighted measures, so that the index value for the *i*th indicator is:

$$\text{IV (index value)} = \sum_{a=1}^{n(i)} d_{ia} w_{ia}$$

where w_{ia} = weight of the *a*th measure of indicator i; and n(i) = number of measures of the *i*th indicator; and d_{ia} = values of *a*th measure of indicator i. So, the index for each stage of output will be:

$$\text{Index}_s = \sum_{i=1}^{n} \text{IV}_i w_{is}$$

where s = stage of output; and n = number of index values. ($W_{is} = 0$ if indicator i does not bear on stage s.)

Such an overall index for stage of outputs (e.g., immediate or intermediate) may also be named "factor." For example, the index for immediate outputs may be termed the Alpha (α) Factor, so that:

index of immediate outputs	=	*Alpha Factor*
index of intermediate outputs	=	*Beta Factor*
index of pre-ultimate outputs	=	*Gamma Factor*
index of ultimate outputs	=	*Omega Factor*

The *omega factor* is computed so that

$$\text{Omega Factor} = \sum_{s=1}^{4} \text{Indexes } 1\text{--}3 \; \overline{W}_s$$

where $\overline{W}_s$ = normalized weights for each index and s = stage of output. Note that the normalized weights are designed with reference to the transformations that affect the outputs, and the conditions (barriers and facilitators) that impinge upon these transformation and diffusion processes.[27]

So the *Alpha Factor* describes the outputs and consequences from R&D and the science segment of the S&T process. This factor is itself a macroindex that provides an approximate aggregation of how science (R&D) benefits the organizations that produce it. Similarly, the *Beta Factor* describes how companies and other social/economic subsystems absorb and utilize S&T outputs and transform them further, within their own processes. The *Omega Factor* is the descriptor of the *total* impacts of S&T on the economy and on society.

Each factor can also be compared against goals and objectives of the impacted organizations. In the ultimate analysis, the *Omega Factor* can be compared with the goals and objectives that society at large poses for S&T.[28]

The value of these factors is primarily in giving managers and policy-makers a powerful tool for evaluation of S&T at different stages and time frames. More important, each factor can be measured and utilized by a different evaluator, with its own goals and priorities. Policy-makers and others at the national level may wish to concentrate on the *Omega Factor*. Nevertheless, the computation of the *Omega Factor* depends on and draws from the previous segments of the innovation process.[29]

STRENGTHS OF PROCESS OUTCOMES

The process-outcomes model for measuring the outputs and benefits from S&T has several outstanding strengths. These are summarized in Figure 12.4.

There are three key categories of strengths: (1) the process-outcomes metric covers the entire innovation continuum, and is applicable at any of its stages, (2) the metric allows for evaluation of S&T that may be tailored to unique needs of the individual evaluators, and (3) the metric helps to overcome problems of imputation and covariation.

WEAKNESSES AND PROBLEMS

Some of the weaknesses of the process-outcomes metric are primarily methodological. First, the problem of creating indexes and the clustering of indicators of the various outputs leads to difficulties in aggregation of the diverse data on outputs. Second, there may be issues related to how well the stages indeed represent the actual phenomena of the flow of outputs. Third, how well do the outputs and the transformation and diffusion processes represent the phenomena of S&T and innovation?

Finally, there are problems associated with data collection and the cost of computing the various indexes. As indices are interrelated within the flow of S&T outputs, the cost of constructing such clusters tends to rise as we move downstream toward the ultimate outputs.

Figure 12.4
Illustrative Strengths and Capabilities of the Metric of Process Outcomes

- Identifies the conceptual and temporal stages in the innovation process/continuum.
- Helps to overcome the shortcomings of covariation by providing a more realistic view of how S&T progresses and generates outcomes.
- Provides a framework for the development of indices.
- Incorporates other metrics such as bibliometrics and patents, within their corresponding institutional boundaries, and in their conceptual & temporal scheme.
- Allows for longer-term and conceptual extension of the impacts of other metrics of S&T.
- Identifies the transformations that S&T outputs go through, thus allowing for managerial interventions at appropriate time and place.
- Allows for interorganizational comparisons and comparisons among stages and outputs.
- Allows for the measurement of impacts at any given output or output category, and any organization in the innovation continuum.
- Helps resolve the problems of imputation.
- Evaluators have an important say in the emphasis placed on the weights, at each segment of the innovation process.

Not necessarily in order of importance

BEST USES

Geisler used the metric in the case of two federal laboratories.[30] The immediate and intermediate outputs were indexed by the method of Weighted Attributes Method. The overall index for laboratory A was 8.90, whereas for laboratory B it equaled 24.41. However, a further analysis showed that laboratory B had a higher level of performance due to its achievements at the stage of immediate outputs. This result may be attributed to the bias in such laboratories of assigning a higher value to scientific outcomes (immediate outputs) while giving lower value to commercialization of immediate outputs to industry (intermediate outputs).[31]

Thus, the application of the process-outcomes metric has proven not only to be feasible, but also to provide an estimation of the reasons behind the quantitative computations of the macroindexes. By understanding the nature of the process, analysts are able to identify biases in the assignment of weights to the various outputs.

CONCLUSIONS

The process-outcomes metric seems superior to the more simplistic metrics such as bibliometrics and patents. It spans the entire innovation continuum and adds a measure of structure and framework to the unique outcomes from S&T.

This metric also provides the means to approach and measure the complex arrays of institutions and metrics that compose the S&T processes. Moreover, its initial empirical applications have been successful and have yielded meaningful results in the comparative evaluation of S&T organizations. This metric shows promise and should be tested in a variety of S&T situations.

NOTES

1. Geisler, E., "Evaluation of R&D: Approaches, Methods, and Techniques," Paper presented at the TIMS/ORSA National Meeting, Orlando, FL, April 24-29, 1992.
2. This phenomenon has already been described in Chapter 10 in the discussion of the metric of patents. The dictionary defines imputation as "To lay the responsibility or blame for often falsely or unjustly."

3. See discussion of this problem in Geisler, E., and A. Rubenstein, "Methodology Issues in Conducting Evaluation Studies of R&D/Innovation," *Proceedings of the Symposium on Management of Technological Innovation*, Worcester Polytechnic Institute (Washington, D.C., 1989).

4. See, for example, Geisler, E., "Key Output Indicators in Performance Evaluation of Research and Development Organizations," *Technological Forecasting and Social Change*, 47(2), 1994, 189-204. Also see Green, S., M. Gavin, and L. Aiman-Smith, "Assessing a Multidimensional Measure of Radical Technological Innovation," *IEEE Transactions on Engineering Management*, 42(2), 1995, 203-214.

5. See a discussion of this issue in Geisler, E., "Integrated Figure of Merit of Public Sector Research Evaluation," *Scientometrics*, 36(3), 1996, 379-395. Also see Rubenstein, A., and E. Geisler, "The Use of Indicators and Measures of the R&D Process in Evaluating Science and Technology Programs," in D. Roessner (Ed.), *Government Innovation Policy* (New York: St. Martin's Press, 1988), pp. 185-204.

6. See an in-depth discussion of the phenomenon of covariation and its shortcomings in Geisler, E., *Methodology, Theory, and Knowledge in the Managerial and Organizational Sciences: Actions and Consequences* (Westport, CT: Quorum Books, 1999).

7. See, for example, Balachandra, R., and J. Friar, "Factors for Success in R&D Projects and New Product Innovation: A Contextual Framework," *IEEE Transactions on Engineering Management*, 44(3), 1997, 276-287. The authors concluded that there is a large number of factors used to measure R&D projects' successes and new product development, and that they differ in context, meaning, and direction. They also concluded that "very few studies provided any benchmarking for the ratings of the factors. It is usually assumed that the factor descriptions and the scales are self-evident" (p. 286).

8. Rubenstein, A., and E. Geisler, "Evaluating the Outputs and Impacts of R&D/Innovation," *International Journal of Technology Management*, Special publication on the Role of Technology in Corporate Policy, 1991, 181-204.

9. Geisler, E., "An Integrated Cost-Performance Model of Research and Development Evaluation," *Omega*, 23(3), 1995, 281-294.

10. See for example, Mansfield, E., "Social Returns from R&D," *Research/ Technology Management*, 34(6), 1991, 24-27.

11. See the use of immediate outputs in various S&T evaluations, in Cordero, R., "The Measurement of Innovation Performance in the Firm: An Overview," *Research Policy*, 19(3), 1990, 185-192. Also see Fernelius, W., and W. Waldo, "Role of Basic Research in Industrial Innovation," *Research Management*, 23(4), 1980, 36-40; and McGrath, M., and M. Romeri, "The R&D Effectiveness Index: A Metric for Product Development Performance," *Journal of Product Innovation Management*, 11(2), 1994, 213-220.

12. See, for example, Park, J., and J. Chong, "A Model to Assess the Value of an Intermediate R&D Result," *IEEE Transactions on Engineering Management*, 38(3), 1991,157-163.

13. See, for example, the use of such outputs in S&T evaluations in Venderwerf, P., "Explaining Downstream Innovation by Commodity Suppliers with Expected Innovation Benefit," *Research Policy*, 21(4), 1992, 315-333. Also see Petroni, G., "Strategic Planning and Research and Development: Can We Integrate Them?" *Long Range Planning*, 16(1), 1983, 15-25.

14. See, for example, Goodman, R., and J. Pavon, *Planning for National Technology Policy* (New York: Praeger, 1984). This topic is also discussed in Chapter 18.

15. See, for example, Shaw, B., "Innovation and New Product Development in the UK Medical Equipment Industry," *International Journal of Technology Management*, 15(3/4/5), 1998, 433-445.

16. The transformation and diffusion processes happen inside industrial companies, where outputs from R&D are transformed into new and improved products and processes. But such transformation and diffusion processes also occur in other R&D laboratories such as government labs, in which outputs from their R&D are transferred and diffused to their parent agencies and to other recipients (e.g., industry). Similar activities occur with regard to university research.

17. See, for example, Teece, D., "Profiting from Technological Innovation: Implications for Integration, Collaboration, Licensing, and Private Policy," *Research Policy*, 15(6), 1986, 285-306. Clearly, mechanisms such as collaboration and licensing are means to achieve transformation and diffusion of the S&T outputs, as they flow among organizations. See the classic book: Crane, D., *Invisible Colleges: Diffusion of Knowledge in Scientific Communities* (Chicago: University of Chicago Press, 1972). Also see the special case of medical technology in Gelijns, A., and H. Dawkins, *Medical Innovation at the Crossroads: Volume 4—Adopting New Medical Technology* (Washington, DC: National Academy Press, 1994).

18. See, for example, Tushman, M., and W. Moore (Eds.), *Readings in the Management of Innovation* (New York: Harper Business, 1986). Also see Kogut, B., and U. Zander, "Knowledge of the Firm, Combinative Capabilities, and the Replication of Technology," *Organization Science*, 3(3), 1992, 383-397.

19. There is an illuminating literature on the topic of measuring S&T programs and issues of metrics. See, for example, Mullins, N., "Evaluating Research Programs: Measurement and Data Sources," *Science & Public Policy*, 14(2), 1987, 56-58. Also see Callon, M., J. Law, and A. Rip (Eds.), *Mapping the Dynamics of Science and Technology* (London: Macmillan, 1986); and Utterback, J., and W. Abernathy, "A Dynamic Model of Product and Process Innovation," *Omega*, 3(4), 1975, 639-656.

20. See, in particular, Geisler, 1994, *op. cit.*, Geisler, 1995, *op. cit.*, and Geisler, 1996, *op. cit.*

21. See Geisler, *1995, op. cit.*, pp. 287-288.

22. See issues of multidimensionality in Green, S., M. Gavin, and L. Aiman-Smith, "Assessing a Multidimensional Measure of Radical Technological Innovation," *IEEE Transactions on Engineering Management*, 42(2), 1995, 203-214.

23. Some economists, such as Edwin Mansfield, have compared investments in research to benefits accrued to companies. In Geisler's terminology they compared box 1 with box 3 in Figure 12.1 (investments in R&D with intermediate outputs).

24. See the seminal work by Campbell, D., and D. Fiske, "Convergent and Discriminant Validation by the Multitract-Multimethod Matrix," *Psychological Bulletin*, 56(2), 1959, 81-105. Also see Geisler, E., and M Radnor, "Monitoring Change in Organization Design," in R. Killman and L. Pondy (Eds.), *The Management of Organization Design, Vol. II* (New York: Elsevier, 1976); and Geisler, 1999, *op.cit.*

25. See, for example, issues in building indexes and macro indexes, Blomquist, G., M. Berger, and J. Hoehn, "New Estimates of Quality of Life in Urban Areas," *The American Economic Review*, 78(1), 1988, 89-107. The authors estimated QOL rankings based on a hedonic model with wages and housing expenditures for 253 counties. They used preference-based weights, the amenity values that they extracted from the hedonic estimation. Also see Goel, R., "Innovation, Market Structure, and Welfare: A Stackelberg Model," *Quarterly Review of Economics and Finance*, 30(1), 1990, 40-54. And see Stainer, A., and W. Nixon, "Productivity and Performance, Measurement in R&D," *International Journal of Technology Management*, 13(5,6), 1997, 486-496.

26. See, for example, Hale, W., "Modeling a New Technology Transfer Algorithm," Paper presented at The Second International Congress on Intellectual Property, McMaster University, January 1998. Hale proposed an insightful approach in which he compared investment by federal laboratories and leverage factors for these laboratories. He thus identified four regions that may explain the nature and behavior of firms that receive federal technology from the laboratories.

27. In this regard see the methodology discussion in Zaidman, B., and G. Cevidalli, "The Technology Efficiency Index: A Method for Measuring Process Technologies," *Technological Forecasting and Social Change*, 35(1), 1989, 51-62. Also see Cordero, R., "The Measurement of Innovation Performance in the Firm: An Overview," *Research Policy*, 19(2), 1990, 185-193. The author proposed measuring inputs against marketable outputs.

28. See, by comparison, the Tushman-Rosenkopf model in which stages of the firm's life-cycle are identified in the evolution of technologies. Tushman, M., and L. Rosenkopf, "Organizational Determinants of Technological Change: Towards

a Sociology of Technological Evolution," *Research in Organizational Behavior*, 14(3), 1992, 311-347.

29. See, for example, Auster, E., "The Relationship of Industry Evolution to Patterns of Technological Change," *Management Science*, 38(6), 1992, 778-793. The author analyzed the attributes of each of the stages of industrial growth.

30. Geisler, 1995, *op. cit.*, Appendix A, pp. 289-293.

31. See, for example, the case of Exxon in which gatekeepers and a stage approach was tested. Yapps-Cohen, L., P. Kamienski, and R. Espino, "Gate System Focuses on Industrial Basic Research," *Research-Technology Management*, 41(4), 1998, 34-37. Also see Achilladelis, B., A. Schwarzkopf, and M. Cines, "The Dynamics of Technological Innovation: The Case of the Chemical Industry," *Research Policy*, 19(1), 1990, 1-35.

13

PERFORMANCE OF
SCIENCE AND TECHNOLOGY

In the previous chapters I described the various metrics currently in use to evaluate science and technology. In this chapter the focus is on the effort to assess the overall performance of S&T organizations, and organizations in general as they are impacted by S&T.

In general, most authors in the field of S&T management have dealt with performance of S&T in a cursory manner.[1] The reason for this oversight may be their perceived need to concentrate on key dimensions of the *management* of R&D and S&T, such as how to lead and manage R&D projects, how to lead and motivate scientists and engineers, and how to best utilize the resources invested in S&T.

Yet some attempts to measure the overall performance of S&T and S&T organizations were reported in the literature. In this chapter I focus on the *overall* performance of S&T and measures used to assess its organizational and sectoral results.

PERFORMANCE AND PRODUCTIVITY

Industrial companies use rudimentary linkages between S&T expenditures and some immediate S&T outputs and the productivity and performance of their organizations. Productivity was discussed earlier in Chapters 6 and 7. In this chapter the focus is on overall performance.

S&T is considered of value to the organization when its effect can be projected onto the usual measures of performance. There is a tendency among senior managers to explore the benefits of an activity such as S&T to the *overall* performance of the organization. This mode of thinking is not confined to corporate managers, as it also is found in managers of public and not-for-profit organizations.[2]

Measuring the impacts of S&T on organizational performance has always been problematic. Hence many S&T managers and their corporate superiors have resorted to "cases of success."[3] These cases tell the stories of innovations that contributed to one or more of the measures of organizational performance, such as sales, profits, and market share. These cases of success ignore the trail of failures and the investments in those outputs from S&T that have not borne such successful results. The negative aspects of this method are that it fails to show impacts on performance. This is due to the emphasis of the entire S&T activity on the benefits accrued from a very small number of "cases," and the persistent difficulties of translating the elements of the case into the organization's performance measures.[4]

METRICS OF S&T AND PERFORMANCE

The link between S&T and performance depends upon a solid set of measures of both S&T and performance. For any such link there is also a need to define the benefits or impacts of S&T on the overall performance of the organization.

Defining Benefits

To quality as measures of benefits, appropriate metrics must have the following attributes.[5] First, the metric must measure all relevant information about the benefits: what they are, how they manifest themselves, and what their contributions are to the organization. Second, the metric must be distinguishable from other effects that may be merged into the pool of benefits. Third, the metric must allow for quantitative assessment and, finally, be additive across units and over time.

Empirically this means that one measure will be inherently insufficient to capture all the information required of an appropriate metric. Hence, the more plausible approach would be a set of measures of performance that can be linked to the outputs from S&T.[6]

Measures Used

The widely used measures of S&T performance are shown in Figure 13.1. These measures are illustrative and reflect those used by various kinds of private and public organizations.

There are two categories of performance measures listed in Figure 13.1. The first is measures of contributions to the *internal* operations of the organizations. These are measures of S&T contributions to individual units, selected processes, and to elements of the value chain. For example, cost savings, new and improved processes, benchmarks, and improved quality are measures in this category.

The second category includes S&T performance measures of contributions to the entire organization and its position in the marketplace. This distinction between the categories becomes valuable when we attempt to define high-technology industries and companies.

Figure 13.1
Illustrative S&T Performance Measures

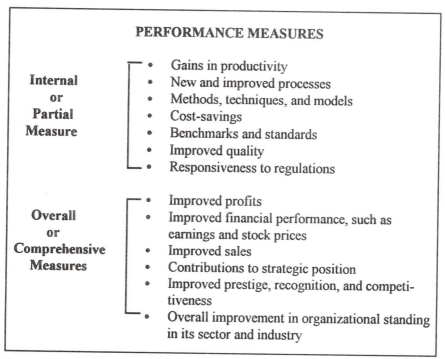

Some of these measures were first listed in Figure 6.5.

Defining High-Technology Industries and Companies

In general, high-technology industries (HTIs) are broadly defined as those industries and their companies whose performance and business success are highly dependent on innovations from science and technology. Medcaf (1999) proposed two metrics to identify and measure HTIs: research intensity and total R&D expenditures.[7] *Research intensity* was defined as the ratio of R&D expenditures to total sales. Medcaf and others who advanced these measures have argued that they are valuable metrics because they have "a clear, simple conceptual definition, can be calculated with readily available data at both the industry and firm levels, and are used by managers to make practical decisions" (Medcaf, p. 32).[8]

A different view was advanced by Francis Narin and his colleagues (1999).[9] They argued that the measure of R&D expenditures "the sole innovation-related item required to be disclosed in financial statements, is too coarse an indicator for valuation of the nature, quality, and expected benefits" (p. 2). Instead, they proposed *patent citations*, because they argued that such references that are cited in the documentation required for patenting indicate the importance of the invention. Hence, the more frequently its patents are cited, the more the company (and industry) will succeed.[10]

Research Intensity, Patent Citations, and Process Outcomes

Using the terminology of the Process-Outcomes Model in Chapter 12, research intensity seems to be a measure that links two distinct events at the extreme ends of the innovation process. Patent citations seem to be a measure that moves farther downstream, relating *immediate* outputs to *intermediate* and pre-ultimate outputs. Still, these measures fail to isolate the effects of S&T on the total performance of the firm. The relationships that they measure seem to be spurious. Medcaf argued that the advantages of the research intensity measure are the facility with which it can be calculated with data available at the firm and industry levels, and the fact that this measure is widely used.[11]

But readily available data and use by company decision-makers are not criteria that make a measure both valid and reliable. The case with which expenditures and patent citations can be related to sales figures and stock performance fails to explain the role of variables other than S&T, in the generation of sales, profits, and the value of corporate stocks.

As much as we try, we are unable to contend that "all other things remain equal." The best statistical techniques cannot assure the satisfactory accounting of plausible alternative explanations and the working of intervening variables in the relation between S&T and organizational performance.

The process-outcomes model is superior to those measures in that it allows for the innovation process to be unraveled. It also considers the impact of partial outputs along the way, from S&T activities to the overall performance of organizations, the economy, and society.[12]

Emergence of Ancillary Technologies

A coherent example of the need to evaluate S&T within the full spectrum of the innovation process is the emergence of *ancillary technologies*.[13] This is the phenomenon by which the adoption of a major innovation necessitates a process of transformation and adaptation by the adopting organization. In this process, several ancillary technologies emerge, because they are necessary to forge the successful adoption. Such ancillary technologies may also be by-products of the adoption process, as learning outcomes that translate into useful new technologies.

The introduction of ironmaking and iron tools in ancient China is an excellent illustration of this phenomenon. As iron technology was adopted in the third century BC, its use in making military and agricultural tools allowed the inhabitants of the northern provinces to conquer wooded parts of eastern and central China, beyond the basin of the Yellow River.[14] Hence, the expansion due to superior agriculture and military technology generated other technologies in administration, water management, allocation of resources, and similar achievements.

Thus, the following hypothesis may be advanced: "The more radical the innovation and technological change, the more *intense* and *varied* the ancillary technologies needed to adopt and to utilize it, and the more the ancillary technologies that emerge from this adoption process."[15]

The combined effects of the main and ancillary technologies during and after the process of adoption, and via the transformation and diffusion of these technologies, are the key to our understanding of how S&T impacts organizations, the economy, and society. Therefore, covariation of the original investments in a technology with ultimate measures of performance totally ignores the midway transformation and combined impacts of ancillary technologies.

A Typology of S&T and Performance Factors

The factors that emerge from the clustering of outputs, described in Chapter 12, may now be juxtaposed with the performance measures listed in Figure 13.1. The outcomes are two sets of categories of organizations that form a typology of S&T performance.

Internal or Partial Measures. The first set is the combination of internal or partial measures of performance, with the α and β factors. This set is shown in Figure 13.2. The resultant categories are the following. Category 1 is a type of organization in which S&T performance is focused on upstream measures (in the innovation process). This type of organization evaluates its S&T only to the extent that proximal partial measures are utilized, so that an index of immediate outputs can be constructed and applied. This type is usually the S&T organization itself, or a short-sighted parent organization concerned with immediate results.

Category 2 is a type of organization concerned with the evaluation of the impacts of S&T on its direct outcomes. Such an organization tends to focus its concern on the short-term impacts and benefits of S&T. Its evaluation methods are usually simple counting of outcomes (e.g., number of new products, revenues from patents and licensing, etc.). Consequently, this type of organization will strive to maximize these outcomes, yet will generally fail to consider the longer-term effects of S&T impacts.

Overall or Comprehensive Measures. The second set is the combination of overall or comprehensive measures of performance, with the γ and Ω factors. This set is shown in Figure 13.3. The resultant categories are labeled 3 and 4. Category 3 is a type of organization that evaluates its S&T by taking a downstream focus. The organization utilizes the γ factor, which is a clustering of the S&T process thus far in the organization. The measures applied are the usual performance measures, such as sales, earnings, and market share. Category 3 organizations have a more comprehensive understanding of how S&T impacts their operations *and* their outcomes.

The more sophisticated are Category 4 organizations. They have an overall focus, in that they apply the Ω (omega) factor. The *convergence* of the omega factor and the usual comprehensive measures of performance provide a solid ground for the longer term evaluation of S&T. This type of organization is able to adequately evaluate the successful accomplishment of its mission and goals, both for S&T and for its institutional objectives.

Figure 13.2
Typology of S&T Performance Organizations: Partial Measures

FACTOR[1]	CORRESPONDING PARTIAL MEASURES OF PERFORMANCE[2]	RESULTANT CATEGORY
α	• Methods, techniques, and models • Benchmarks and standards	**Category 1:** **"Upstream Focus"**
β	• New and improved products and processes • Cost-savings • Improved quality • Gains in productivity • Responsiveness to regulations	**Category 2:** **"Midstream or operational focus"**

(1) Source: Chapter 12.
(2) Source: Figure 13.1. These measures are illustrative.

This typology is a valuable tool in the operational and strategic evaluation of organizational performance. The categories discussed here provide a solid analytical classification that may explain differences in managerial actions and in the role that S&T plays in the perceptions of managers and in the rationale of their decision-making processes.[16]

THE TECHNOLOGY/INNOVATION AUDIT

Borrowed from the accounting terminology, the technology/innovation (T/I) audit is an approach and an instrument that, analogous to financial audits, evaluates certain attributes of technology and innovation. The term implies an examination, usually periodic, of the state of the focal unit or activity.

Figure 13.3
Typology of S&T Performance Organizations: Comprehensive Measures

FACTORS[1]	CORRESPONDING COMPREHENSIVE MEASURES OF PERFORMANCE[2]	RESULTANT CATEGORY
γ	• Improved profits • Improved earnings and stock prices • Improved sales • Improved market share	**Category 3:** **"Downstream Focus"**
Ω	• Contribution to strategic position • Improved prestige, recognition, and competitiveness • Overall improvement in organization standing	**Category 4:** **"Overall Focus"**

(1) Source: Chapter 12.
(2) Source: Figure 13.1. These measures are illustrative.

In the literature on S&T management there have been several attempts to describe T/I audits. One of the pioneers in this area was Albert Rubenstein.[17] He correctly pointed out that "Many managers are sick of audits" (p. 330), and offered a checklist of seven major elements of an audit, each to be measured by multiple indicators.[18] Among these elements (dimensions) are: capability of company's technology staff, and cost/benefits of technology projects. The first dimension may be measured by such metrics as: (1) total size of R&D staff, (2) number or percent of professionals to total size, and (3) work experience of professionals in industry and in the specific product-line.

The second dimension (cost/benefits) may be measured by such metrics as: (1) ratio of total cost of R&D to total life-cycle revenues from selected projects, and (2) contributions of projects or program to company profits.

Rubenstein compared T/I audits to medical exams, where the outcomes point to general problems rather than rims of quantitative data that detail every aspect of the operation. The key to a successful audit, Rubenstein argued, should be the insights that senior managers can draw from this evaluation effort.[19]

Another approach was offered by Chiesa, Coughlan, and Voss (1996), and illustrates the link between T/I audit and the innovation process.[20] These authors, working in the United Kingdom, considered four core processes of product development, and constructed an audit model to assess the innovative capability of the company. They also distinguished between process audit and performance audit. The first evaluates the best practices of those processes that lead to innovative products. The performance audit is an evaluation of how innovation contributes to the competitive position of the firm.

Among the performance measures used in this T/I audit are many of the traditional measures, such as number of new products, customer satisfaction, time-to-market, cost, technical performance, and number of patents.[21] Contributions to competitiveness were measured by such metrics as sales, market share, profits, and several ratios of the above for new products.

The strengths of this audit model are in its consideration of the various processes in the innovation phenomenon in the industrial company. As in the case with any audit, benchmarks are necessary to establish evaluation gaps between current and desired practices. By proposing to establish benchmarks for individual core processes, and for overall performance, these authors have added flexibility and realism for managers who utilize the audit. They also introduced the concept of "scorecards."[22] In the case of the T/I audit, the scorecard measures the difference between what are considered "best" practices and "poor" practices for each of the core processes of innovation.

SUMMARY

How well do the metrics of S&T measure the performance of respective organizations? This seems to be the perennial question of evaluation. It becomes even more important in the case of the relationship of S&T performance. Although there may be a theoretical connection between these two phenomena, the problems are with the measurement.

In a similar vein, Stephen Roach, chief economist of a major investment firm, has argued in a review of two books on productivity, that the bright picture of productivity in the United States in the 1990s was a statistical illusion.[23] He contended that there were problems with the data, particularly the denominator in the ratio of the productivity metric: hours worked in the economy. Service-sector employees worked longer hours per week, bolstered by innovations in information technology. Therefore, he concluded, sustained productivity improvement is "not about working longer—it's about adding more value per unit of work time" (p. 160). Similarly, improving performance is about adding value from S&T, not about measures of S&T achieved.

Unless we are able to reliably measure the contributions of S&T to performance—beyond just statistical correlations—the phenomenon will remain illusory. Measures such as "R&D-intensity" are simply ratios that constitute statistical artifacts. As with productivity measurement, the denominator of "total sales" may be influenced by a variety of other factors and economic or market challenges.

The solution seems to be a systematic design and understanding of the process by which S&T impacts organizational performance, in the sectors of academia, industry, and government. This requires the painstaking tracking of outputs and technologies, and the careful measurement of their relative impacts, as they progress through the innovation process.

NOTES

1.   For example, Afua, A., *Innovation Management: Strategies, Implementation, and Profits* (New York: Oxford University Press, 1998) discusses the potential for innovation, but not the performance of S&T. Bennet, L., *The Management of Engineering* (New York: John Wiley & Sons, 1996) focuses on managing engineers and engineering projects, but not on the performance of S&T and how to measure it. Similarly, Jain, R., and H. Triandis, *Management of Research and Development Organizations* (New York: John Wiley & Sons, 1997) offer some discussion of measuring the performance of R&D employees (pp. 172-195), and some discussion of R&D productivity, as measured by literature, patents, and economic activity (pp. 279-291). They also offer a list of evaluation criteria for research programs of national significance, including social benefits (Table 1.2, pp. 289-290). Finally, see, for example, Levy, N., *Managing High Technology and Innovation* (Upper Saddle River, NJ: Prentice-

Hall, 1998), and Compton, D., *Engineering Management* (Upper Saddle River, NJ: Prentice-Hall, 1997), who devoted very few pages to performance of S&T, with emphasis on employee productivity. The exception is Rubenstein, A., *Managing Technology in the Decentralized Firm* (New York: John Wiley & Sons, 1989), who described in detail the evaluation of R&D and the technology/innovation audit (pp. 330-338).

2. See, for example, an industrial case in Carayannis, E., and Stokes, R., "A Historical Analysis of Management of Technology at Badische Anilin und Soda Fabrik (BASF), AG: A Case Study," *Journal of Engineering and Technology Management*, 14(2), 1997, 175-193. Also see Leonard-Barton, D., "Core Capabilities and Core Rigidities: A Paradox in Managing New Product Development," *Strategic Management Journal*, 13(3), 1992, 111-125; and the case of public organizations in Branscomb, A., L. Brooks, H. Carter, and G. Epstein, *Beyond Spin-Off: Military and Commercial Technologies in a Changing World* (Boston: Harvard Business School Press, 1992). Also see Kogut, B. (Ed.), *Country Competitiveness: Technology and the Organizing of Work* (New York: Oxford University Press, 1993).

3. See, for example, the results from the SAPPHO Project in the United Kingdom in SPRU (Science Policy Research Unit), *Success and Failure in Industrial Innovation: Report on Project SAPPHO* (London: Center for the Study of Industrial Innovation, 1972). Also see in this regard, Pavitt, K., M. Robson, and J. Townsend, "Technological Accumulation, Diversification, and Organization in U.K. Companies, 1945-1983," *Management Science*, 35(1), 1984, 81-99.

4. See, for example, Kortum, S., "Research, Patenting, and Technological Change," *Econometrica*, 65(6), 1997, 1389-1419. Also see Kerssens-Van Drongelen, I., and J. Bilderbeek, "R&D Performance Measurement: More Than Choosing a Set of Metrics," *R&D Management*, 29(1), 1999, 35-46. Also see Alvarez, P., and A. Pulagrin, "Equating Research Production in Different Scientific Fields," *Information Processing & Management*, 34(4), 1998, 465-470.

5. This taxonomy is a modified version of Dr. David Eddy's classification. See, Eddy, D., "Cost-Effectiveness Analysis: Is It Up to the Task?" *JAMA*, 267(24), 1992, 3342-3348.

6. See, for example, Lau, R., "How Does Research and Development Intensity Affect Business Performance?" *South Dakota Business Review*, 57(1), 1998, 1-7. The author utilized two performance measures: sales and return on assets (ROA).

7. Medcaf, J., "Identifying 'Super-Technology' Industries," *Research-Technology Management*, 42(4), 1999, 31-36.

8. Also see, for example, Lee, J., and E. Shiu, "Moderating Effects of R&D on Corporate Growth in U.S. and Japanese Hi-Tech Industries: An Empirical Study," *The Journal of High Technology Management Research*, 6(2), 1995, 179-191. Also see Whitley, R., and T. Parish, "Evaluating R&D Performance Using the New Sales Ratio," *Research-Technology Management*, 41(5), 1998, 20-

22. The authors discuss the "new sales ratio (NSR)" metric. They define it as "the ratio of current annual sales of new products to total annual sales" (p. 21).

9. Deng, Z., B. Len, and F. Narin, "Science and Technology as Predictors of Stock Performance," *Financial Analysts Journal*, 55(3), 1999, 20-26.

10. See some supporting references in Notes to Chapter 15. Also see Albert, M., D. Avery, F. Narin, and P. McAllister, "Direct Validation of Citation Counts as Indicators of Industrially Important Patents," *Research Policy*, 20(3), 1991, 251-259.

11. Medcaf, 1999, *op. cit.* Also see, Baruch, Y., "High Technology Organization: What It Is, What It Isn't," *International Journal of Technology Management*, 13(2), 1997, 179-195. Also see Lev, B., and T. Sougiannis, "The Capitalization, Amortization, and Value-Relevance of R&D," *Journal of Accounting and Economics*, 21(2), 1996, 107-138.

12. Geisler, E., "Clustering of S&T Outputs: A Typology of the S&T-Performance Relationship," Working Paper, Stuart Graduate School of Business, Illinois Institute of Technology, 1999.

13. See, Geisler, E., "The Omega Hypothesis: Main and Ancillary Technologies in the Adoption of Innovations," Working Paper, Stuart Graduate School of Business, Illinois Institute of Technology, Chicago, 1999.

14. See, for example, Wagner, D., *Iron and Steel in Ancient China* (New York: Brill Academic Publishers, 1993). In particular see pages 247-260.

15. See Geisler, "The Omega Hypothesis," 1999, *op. cit.*

16. See additional details on the applications of this typology in: Geisler, "Clustering of S&T Outputs," 1999, *op. cit.*

17. Rubenstein, A., 1989, *op. cit.* See in particular section 7.6, pps. 330-342.

18. *Ibid.*, figure 7.26, p. 331.

19. Also see Griffin, A., "Metrics for Measuring Product Development Cycle-Time," *Journal of Product Innovation Management*, 10(2), 1993, 112-125.

20. Chiesa, V., D. Coughlan, and C. Voss, "Development of a Technical Innovation Audit," *Journal of Product Innovation Management*, 13(2), 1996, 105-136.

21. *Ibid.*, Table 3.

22. See, for example, the seminal work on scorecards in Kaplan, R., and D. Norton, *The Balanced Scorecard: Translating Strategy into Action* (Boston: Harvard Business School Press, 1996). See in particular Chapter 7, pages 147-166. Also see Brown, M., *Keeping Score: Using the Right Metrics to Drive World-Class Performance* (New York: Quality Resources, 1996). Brown argued that the appropriate metrics should focus on the past, present, and future, and should be measuring the needs of the organization's customers, employers, and shareholders. See especially Chapter 12: "Linking Measures to Strategy and Success Factors," and Chapter 14: "Linking Measures, Goals, and Plans."

23. Roach, S., "In Search of Productivity," *Harvard Business Review*, 76(5), 1998, 153-161. The books Roach reviewed were: (1) Davis, B., and D. Wessel, *Prosperity: The Coming 20-Year Boom and What It Means to You* (New York: Times Business, 1998) and (2) Lester, R., *The Productive Edge: How U.S. Industries are Pointing the Way to a New Era of Economic Growth* (New York: W. W. Norton & Company, 1998). Also see Krugman, P., "Unleashing the Millenium," *Fortune*, 141(5), 2000, F16-F20.

PART III

APPLICATIONS:
THE VALUE, IN PRACTICE,
OF SCIENCE AND TECHNOLOGY

It is knowledge that influences and equalizes the social condition of man; that gives to all, however different their political position, passions which are in common, and enjoyments which are universal.

Benjamin Disraeli (1804-1881)
First Earl of Beaconsfield
Speech on October 23, 1844

14

METRICS AND EVALUATION
OF ACADEMIC SCIENCE
AND TECHNOLOGY

Part III of this book will focus on applications of metrics in the evaluation of people and organizations in three different sectors: in academia, in industry and public institutions, and at the level of national innovation systems. This part also includes a chapter on strategy and science and technology. Finally, this part ends with a chapter on values, ethics, and implications from the impacts of S&T.[1]

The term "applications" in the title of Part III refers to the use of metrics and evaluation frameworks and models in selected instances. These include specific sectors of the economy and selected components of the innovation process. So an application may be the use of metrics to evaluate scientists and engineers, or the use of metrics to evaluate an industry or a government S&T laboratory. The sectoral classification is a framework that incorporates multiple S&T metrics that are utilized by similar organizations.

MEASURING THE VALUE AND PERFORMANCE
OF ACADEMIC WORKERS

The Finnish scholar T. Luukkonen-Gronow (1987) wrote an insightful paper that reviewed several metrics in the evaluation of science and technology.[2] Following Weinberg's (1984) original typology,[3] she correctly concluded that "there does not exist a standardized set of evaluation methods which can be used as a routine manner" (p. 219). She also argued that there is a need for studies to assess the effect of evaluations of S&T on the working environment of the S&T communities.[4] In this regard, the evaluation of academic workers, scientists, engineers, and university researchers is the focus of this section.

How do we measure the performance of scientists and engineers? Edwards and McCarrey (1973)[5] reviewed the literature and concluded that there was "very little agreement from one investigator to another as to what constitutes scientific output or what measures could be used to reflect the output" (p. 40). They identified such measures as peer ratings, quantity of written outputs (bibliometrics), and the quality of outputs. The latter was usually a simple ranking. Finally, count of citations was found to be a common measure used to evaluate researchers.[6]

CATEGORIES OF METRICS

Twenty-five years later, the metrics in the evaluation of scientists and engineers have remained essentially unchanged. Three categories of outputs seem to emerge.[7] The first is bibliometrics, which I have described in Chapter 8. The second category is patents and licenses obtained from patenting activity, which is discussed in Chapter 10.[8]

The third category is a hybrid set of performance metrics, which includes strategic variables such as sales and other contributions to the overall success of the organization. But the other side of this set is the manner in which these measures are incorporated in the more subjective evaluation conducted by the managers of scientists and engineers.[9]

Why has the topic of metrics not played a key role in research on S&T in the recent past? Perhaps because much of the attention was on overall performance appraisal models for scientists and engineers, and the extant metrics seemed to suffice for this purpose. Another reason may be that, although reengineering, cost-cutting, and downsizing had dominated the 1990s, the issues regarding scientists and engineers have focused on their involvement, commitment, and contributions to product and process improvements. When lumped into one group of S&T workers, the existing metrics again seem to suffice, particularly when the appraisal system more frequently utilized had been managerial assessment that relied, in large measure, on expert opinions and executive perceptions.[10]

JOB INVOLVEMENT AND ORGANIZATIONAL COMMITMENT

In his excellent study of 532 scientists and engineers, Keller (1997) investigated the factors that affect job performance of these workers.[11] His findings indicated that there are differences between *scientists* and *engineers* (or *technologists*). Keller hypothesized that scientists would respond more favorably to job involvement and the satisfaction that comes from their work, because of their loyalty to the profession and the community of science. Engineers, however, would identify with the organization in which they are employed, hence they would exhibit higher commitment to the organization. Keller found support to his hypothesis, and has also shown that such different orientations may be helpful in predicting the performance for each of these groups.[12]

The distinction between the orientation of those involved with science and those involved with technology may also lend support to the process-outcomes model in Chapter 12, and to my argument for different metrics for the various stages in the S&T/Innovation process. As engineers and technologists are responsible for the transformations of scientific outputs, *within the framework of their respective organizations*, they not only develop stronger commitment to these entities, but also produce different types of outputs than scientists. These outputs are now closely linked to organizational attributes, hence need to be thus measured.[13]

Issues of Age and Dual Ladder

In the evaluation of scientists and engineers, there recently emerged the issue of aging scientists. In parallel, the issue of the dual ladder mode of mobility for scientists and engineers in organizations has increasingly become an important topic in the evaluation of S&T workers.[14]

In the late 1990s and early 2000, the "baby boom" scientists and engineers have reached the 50-plus age group, and the generation that follows has entered the early 40s and late 30s age group. There is a persistent belief in many organizations that scientists and engineers reach their peak in their early 30s. Therefore, the remaining years of their careers are characterized by continuous decline. This invariably leads to the conclusion that these "older" workers are more of a burden to their organizations, and need to be replaced by younger people.

Some researchers have argued that the problem lies not with the scientists and engineers, but with the biased perception of many managers, and especially in the way they measure the performance of scientists and engineers.[15] Older workers seem to enjoy a stronger network of professionals, and tend to work in a more cohesive work environment. Their contributions may be better described (and measured) as supporting effective S&T by providing the anchor and the hub of communication of the S&T workplace.

A different yet related issue is the dual ladder approach to the mobility of scientists and engineers. When workers are promoted to management positions, their upward mobility is then dictated by the evaluation of different measures of performance. The emphasis shifts to *organizational* measures of success, at the expense of the more personal and *professional* metrics.[16]

However, as S&T managers move back to the S&T career path, the metrics used by the organization revert to the professional outputs (e.g., bibliometrics and patents), thus making the transition painful for those S&T managers who have not kept up their professional outputs.[17]

Strengths and Weaknesses

The *strengths* of the metrics used to evaluate academic (S&T) workers are of three types. First, the metrics are segmented by the organizational charge of the S&T worker—as is the case of the dual ladder. Second, scientists and technologists are evaluated by two different sets of metrics. Scientists are evaluated primarily by their production of knowledge (bibliometrics), whereas technologists are evaluated by the utilization and transformation of S&T outputs, and their contributions to organizations.[18] Thus, some metrics (such as patents) have dual usage for both groups.

Third, metrics that measure individual and group performance of scientists are good indicators of the effort and the talent expended. Metrics such as bibliometrics and peer review provide a good estimation of performance. When combined with organization-based metrics (such as organizational performance measures), they are also adequate estimators of the performance of engineers and technologists.

The weaknesses of these metrics are primarily in the area of combining individual and organization measures, and managerial perceptions of performance and the role that S&T professionals play in their organizations. In general, I suggest that it's not the metrics themselves that are at the core of any shortcomings in the evaluation of academic workers, but their utilization in a *managerial* system of performance evaluation.

First, the distinction between the nature of the work performed by scientists and technologists (shown as a strength above) is not clearly nor consistently applied in the interpretation of the metrics by organizational managers.

Second, managers at the higher levels of organizations have difficulties in their assessment of the entire innovation continuum, and the downstream contributions that S&T professionals make to innovation. This is also exacerbated by the difficulties that managers have in clearly linking S&T employees' contributions to the value chain—at specific stages of the process.

Third, there is also a role that the metrics themselves play in the weakness or shortcomings of the evaluation of performance for academic workers. The metrics currently used for evaluation measure a limited outcome, well-specified and defined in a mode that constrains its broader utilization. For example, bibliometrics measures published outputs and their impact on the academic community (via citations). Yet the limited definition of this metric precludes the measurement of other outputs. Among these outputs are nonpublished work, progress achieved on the learning curve, mentoring younger or newer colleagues, contributions to the work group, academic leadership, and personal development. Such outputs are seldom captured by the extant metrics.[19]

MEASURING THE VALUE AND PERFORMANCE OF ACADEMIC INSTITUTIONS

There are two types of academic institutions: teaching institutions (universities and colleges) and research institutions. Each is evaluated with a unique set of metrics.

Teaching Institutions

Universities and similar institutions of higher learning and research that engage in postsecondary teaching are evaluated with a variety of metrics. Two main categories are widely utilized: evaluation of the quality of the academic program and evaluation of the students.

The academic programs are evaluated primarily by department or discipline. The more common metrics are peer review and bibliometrics.

Faculty members are evaluated by the amount and quality of their work and publications, through counts of papers and citations, as well as peer review of their prestige and standing in their respective discipline. The sum of such evaluations in a given department or school represents the overall assessment of the academic unit.[20] Such evaluations are based on a balance of quantitative measures (counts of publications and citations), and the judgmental nature of peer review. The latter also incorporates such measures as research funding received.

But a crucial dimension in the evaluation of academic institutions are the students. They are usually considered, in addition to research, the main outcome of the institution.[21] The quality of students admitted to the institution and the success of the graduates in the marketplace are two key metrics in assessing the student body, and, by extension, the institution.

Consider the case of business schools in the major American universities. These are reviewed annually by such magazines as *Business Week* and *U.S. News & World Report*. The latter conducts a survey in which business school deans are asked to rate their peer institutions. This peer-review metric is supplemented by the survey of business leaders.

Business Week conducts a more comprehensive survey in which students are asked to rate several measures of academics and administration. For example, they are asked to rate the variety of courses offered, and the ability of the school to offer placement services. In addition, the survey also procures the opinions and ratings of recruiters in major corporations. Students are therefore considered the outputs from the university and their success means a reflection on the value and the quality of the curriculum and the school.[22]

Other measures of performance are membership in prestigious accreditation agencies, such as the American Assembly of Collegiate Schools of Business, and the overall prestige of the university. Figure 14.1 summarizes the metrics listed above.

Strengths and Weaknesses

The *strengths* of the metrics used to evaluate academic institutions are multiple measures and mix of quantitative and qualitative measures. The first strength of the metrics is in the fact that multiple measures are used, in a variety of dimensions. Education, research, and graduates' success are combined with peer review to evaluate the performance of academic units and institutions. Second, the mix of measures provides a balance of quantitative measures and peer review.

The *weaknesses* are of two types. First, although quantitative measures are used, the bulk of the metrics considered in performance evaluation is peer review. The emphasis is on a review within the community of science, particularly within the narrow disciplinary boundaries. The case of professional schools, such as business, medicine, and law, is more amenable to review by nonacademic sources, such as employers and other stakeholders.

Figure 14.1
Illustrative Metrics Used to Evaluate Academic Institutions

CATEGORY	METRICS
EDUCATION	• Admission criteria • Students' characteristics • Curriculum • Attractiveness of graduates in marketplace • Peer review
RESEARCH	• Faculty productivity (bibliometrics) • Research grants received • Faculty participation in professional association, editorships, and other aspects of visibility • Peer review
OVERALL REPUTATION	• Ranking of discipline or department by external peer review • Perception of reputation of the institution by community of science and public at large
OTHER	• Accreditation and membership in prestigious associations • Administrative services • Research endowments

This list is not exhaustive, and not in any order of importance.

Second, metrics thus used are primarily measuring the proximal or immediate outcomes from the academic institution. This is especially true in the evaluation of research and the quality of the faculty. Even in the case of measuring the attractiveness of students in the marketplace, little importance is given to the long-term success of such students.

MEASURING PERFORMANCE OF ACADEMIC SPIN-OFFS

A different and perhaps more complex dimension is the performance of spin-offs from academic institutions. As universities struggled in the 1980s and early 1990s to maintain their budgets and levels of activity, they resorted to several mechanisms for coping and for growth. Chiefly among them were incubators, research parks, and intense cooperation with industry.[23]

These outreach activities were designed to achieve two complementary objectives. Universities created mechanisms to exploit their discoveries, hence increase the flow of income from patents and licenses. In parallel, universities hoped to increase their revenues from improved interaction with industry.[24] The performance of these programs was, and continues to be, measured by a variety of metrics, as illustrated in Figure 14.2.

The U.S. federal government has been a considerable force in promoting university-industry cooperation. The National Science Foundation has been advancing this objective since 1973, when it instituted a program of Industry-University-Cooperative-Centers. In 1999 there were over 50 such centers, four of which dated back to the original program in the early 1970s.[25] This program operated with a small budget and has resulted in sustained cooperation between dozens of research universities and hundreds of companies in over a dozen disciplines.[26]

This program served as a model for the creation of Engineering Research Centers, also supported by the U.S. National Science Foundation. The latter centers received a substantial financial grant from the foundation, but were also required to attract and to maintain industrial collaborators.

The performance of these centers was evaluated by the metrics of scientific and technical accomplishment, coupled equally with the *sustained membership* of the industrial companies. Satisfaction of the corporate members was deemed critical to the operations and the success of the centers.

Figure 14.2
Illustrative Measures of Performance of
University Spin-Offs and Cooperative Programs with Industry

A. RESEARCH PARKS AND SPIN-OFFS
  • Companies that successfully graduate from incubators
  • Licenses and income from patents
  • Contributions to increased cooperation with industry

B. COOPERATIVE PROGRAMS WITH INDUSTRY
  • Funding for the university
  • Students hired by cooperating companies
  • Use of industrial facilities by faculty and students
  • Opportunities for research and consulting for faculty
  • Gateway to relations with other companies
  • In-kind donations by industry (e.g., equipment, software, executive talent)
  • Opportunities for internships for students
  • Opportunities for industrial experience for faculty
  • Improved mutual understanding of the different cultures of academia and industry

This list is illustrative and not necessarily in any order of importance or rank.

Advantages and Benefits

University spin-offs and cooperative programs have contributed to the more "practical" orientation of academic research, its increased relevancy, and closer ties with industry. The metrics used for evaluation of these outreach programs have themselves contributed to an increased acceptance of cooperative research among the faculty and university administrators.

In addition to the inflow of funds and other resources, the use of measures such as opportunities for students and faculty have in themselves created a more favorable climate for these programs in the university environment. Students who have graduated from such outreach programs have assumed managerial positions in many companies, and have continued to support this type of cooperation.[27]

Problems and Shortcomings

Detractors and critics of university outreach programs have argued against such efforts because of ethical issues and the dangers in commercializing scientific outputs, hence compromising academic integrity.[28] But the shortcomings of such programs are primarily in the metrics used for their evaluation, and the effects such metrics have on behavior of faculty and students. There is an inherent conflict between the measures that assess academic performance, and those used for cooperative programs. The former are primarily research outputs in the form of bibliometrics (publications and citations), participation in professional societies, and the conduct of sponsored research. These are the criteria used for the promotion and tenure processes for faculty in research universities.

In contrast, most of the measures used to evaluate cooperative programs are indicative of industrial concerns and the exchange of value. Thus, faculty who participate in these programs have difficulties in obtaining promotion and tenure in their universities. Many young faculty tend to shy away from cooperative programs for this very reason.[29]

Therefore, until the two sets of evaluation measures are synchronized, there will be resistance on the part of university faculty to cooperative programs. The metrics used reflect the benefits to the participants—university and company—but not to the professors. Key measures of success of these programs fail to address those measures used to advance the individual careers and academic agendas of university professors.

In summary, although American universities have cooperated with industry in an intense mode for several decades, the jury is still out on the success of these programs.[30] The dilemma many universities face resides in the metrics used by companies (and perforce by the universities themselves) to evaluate the success of these programs. These metrics reflect relevancy, operational problems of the companies, and their desire to obtain research that is "useful" and implementable. Yet universities and their faculty are evaluated by metrics that emphasize scholarship and bibliometrics.[31]

SUMMARY

Metrics used to evaluate academic science and technology reflect a mixture of conflicting objectives, inherent in organizational variables and in problems in the measures themselves. The disparate goals of academic workers and their organizations reach a state of divergent expectations when such metrics are used as tools in the evaluation of academic performance. Career objectives of academic workers tend to clash with organizational exigencies. In nonacademic institutions managers usually underestimate the conflicts inherent in their systems of performance evaluation. Even in universities there is tension that tends to appear more openly in the case of cooperative programs with industry.

I believe that improved understanding of the problems in the use of sometimes conflicting metrics to evaluate performance will result in a better convergence of the metrics. For example, academic workers who are active in cooperative efforts should benefit from such activities. Similarly, academic workers who opt for pure research would be also evaluated in their contribution to the *organizational* goals. In essence, I refer to a *seamless dual system* of metrics that would interchangeably accommodate the different strings of equally important metrics.[32]

NOTES

1. Although Part III describes applications of metrics in the various sectors and the national level, not all metrics are represented in the text. In most instances the analyses are illustrative, albeit I had explored the recent literatures for appropriate cases and for the more updated studies and opinions.

2. Luukkonen-Gronow, T., "Scientific Research Evaluation: A Review of Methods and Various Contexts of Their Application," *R&D Management*, 17(3), 1987, 207-221.

3. Weinberg, A., "Values in Science: Unity as a Criterion of Scientific Choice," *Minerva*, 22(1), 1984, 1-12.

4. See, for example, the seminal work: Rogers, E., *Diffusion of Innovations*, 4th ed. (New York: Simon & Schuster, 1996). Also see the classical paper: Churchman, C., and A. Schainblatt, "The Researcher and the Manager: A Dialectic of Implementation," *Management Science*, 11(1), 1965, 69-73.

5. Edwards, S., and M. McCarrey, "Measuring the Performance of Researchers," *Research Management*, 16(1), 1973, 34-40.

6. See, for example, the seminal and much-cited book of the same period: Pelz, D., and F. Andrews, *Scientists in Organizations* (New York: John Wiley & Sons, 1966). Also see Crane, D., "Scientists at Major and Minor Universities: A Study of Productivity and Recognition," *American Sociological Review*, 30(3), 1965, 699-714. Crane also wrote the foundational book that introduced the notion of the "invisible college." See Crane, D., *Invisible Colleges: Diffusion of*

Knowledge in Scientific Communities (Chicago: University of Chicago Press, 1972).

7. There is a vast literature that has emerged since the early 1970s, largely focused on the overall management of S&T personnel. Common topics in this literature include motivation, compensation, and leadership of researchers and research teams. Specific studies of metrics are usually embedded in this literature, yet have failed to achieve prominence in the overall agenda of these studies. For some outstanding exceptions see, for example, Wilson, D., Mueser, R., and J. Roelin, "New Look at Performance Appraisal for Scientists and Engineers," *Research-Technology Management*, 37(1), 1994, 51-55. Also see, Schainblatt, A., *Measuring the Productivity of Scientists and Engineers in R&D: A State of the Practice Review* (Washington, DC: The Urban Institute, 1981).

8. See, for example, Koenig, M., "Bibliometric Indicators Versus Expert Opinions in Assessing Research Performance," *Journal of the American Society of Information Science*, 34(2), 1983, 136-147. The author studied research performance in pharmaceutical companies and concluded that bibliometric data outperformed expert judgments in predicting the performance of drug researchers. He also found that bibliometric data could predict expert opinions, but not vice-versa.

9. See, for example, Gomez-Mejia, L., D. Balkin, and G. Milkovich, "Rethinking Rewards for Technical Employees," *Organizational Dynamics*, 18(1), 1990, 62-75.

10. This is my personal observation. However, see for example, Shapira, P. (Ed.), *The R&D Workers: Managing Innovation in Britain, Germany, Japan, and the United States* (Westport, CT: Quorum Books, 1995). In particular, see pp. 93-120 on rewarding R&D personnel, and patenting and productivity. Also see Wilson, D., R. Mueser, and J. Raelin (1994), *op. cit.* The authors have concluded that although performance appraisal models of S&T workers satisfy the organization's evaluation agenda, they are "often incompatible with the needs of the technical staff" (p. 51).

11. Keller, R., "Job Involvement and Organizational Commitment as Longitudinal Predictors of Job Performance: A Study of Scientists and Engineers," *Journal of Applied Psychology*, 82(4), 1997, 539-545.

12. See Page, D., "Predicting the Job Performance of Scientists and Engineers," *The Academy of Management Executive*, 12(2), 1998, 98-99. Diana Page reported Keller's findings and extended them to the management of knowledge workers. In this regard, see, for example, the distinction between disciplines, based on spatial visualization skills, in Humphreys, L., D. Lubinski, and G. Yao, "Utility of Predicting Group Membership and the Role of Spatial Visualization in Becoming an Engineer, Physical Scientist, or Artist," *Journal of Applied Psychology*, 78(23), 1993, 250-262. Also see the fascinating book: Price, D., *Science Since Babylon* (New Haven: Yale University Press, 1962). Derek de Solla

Price discussed the differences between the quantitative skills of ancient Babylonian astronomers who excelled in their calculations, and the ancient Greeks who excelled in logic and geometrics "but totally lacking in any depth of knowledge of calculation" (p. 13).

13. See, for example, the argument for adjusting performance measures to meet needs of S&T workers, in Despres, C., and Hiltrop, J., "Compensation for Technical Professionals in the Knowledge Age," *Research-Technology Management*, 39(5), 1996, 48-51. Also see, in particular, Daniels, P., "Research and Development, Human Capital and Trade Performance in Technology-Intensive Manufacturers: A Cross-Country Analysis," *Research Policy*, 22(3), 1993, 207-242. In this solidly designed study, Daniels argued that such measures as capital formation and actual innovative activity are more indicative of technology intensity than S&T output measures. This finding lends further support to the process-outcomes model of Chapter 12, and to the need to distinguish between different sets of metrics along the S&T/innovation continuum.

14. See, for example, Katz, R. (Ed.), *The Human Side of Managing Technological Innovation* (New York: Oxford University Press, 1997). In particular, see pages 461-486.

15. See, for example, Cassidy, R., "Are You Over the Hill at 40? And Other Issues," *Research & Development*, 37(6), 1995, 27-29.

16. There is a substantial literature on the topic. In this chapter I concentrated on issues of measurement of performance within the dual-ladder approach, hence the brevity of the discussion. See, for example, Katz, R., and T. Allen, "Managing Dual-Ladder Systems in RD&E Settings," in Katz, *The Human Side of Managing Technological Innovation*, 1997, *op. cit.*, pp. 472-486. Also see Reynes, R., "Training to Manage Across Silos," *Research-Technology Management*, 42(5), 1999, 20-24.

17. See, for example, Allen, T., and R. Katz, "Age, Education, and the Technical Ladder," *IEEE Transactions on Engineering Management*, 39(3), 1992, 237-245. Also see Allen, T., and R. Katz, "The Dual Ladder: Motivational Solution or Managerial Delusion," *R&D Management*, 16(2), 1986, 185-197. Allen and Katz distinguished between two sets of success (performance) factors: commercial/product and academic/scientific. They also described the educational system that produces S&T professionals and their innate preferences, which seem to determine their choice of a ladder (technical or managerial). I have indicated in this section that it is ultimately the performance metrics used by the organization that will influence the successful transition between ladders. See, for example, the comprehensive study that supports such assertions in Katz, R., M. Tushman, and T. Allen, *Managing the Dual-Ladder: A Longitudinal Study* (Greenwich, CT: JAI Press, 1991).

18. See, for example, Allen, T., "Distinguishing Science From Technology," in Katz, *The Human Side of Managing Technological Innovation*, 1997, *op. cit.*, pp. 307-319.

19. Although some scholars have argued that such outputs will collapse into the metrics of bibliographic outcomes, citations, and patents, such a process is speculative. These outputs are not captured by the existing pool of metrics. Perhaps experience, additional learning and mentoring may eventually contribute to improved research and higher quality publishing, but performance evaluation at periodic intervals measures periodic activities in the short run, not the *total growth and progress* of the academic worker. In this respect see, for example, Rebne, D., and N. Davidson, "Understanding Patterns of Publishing Activity in Academic Research Occupations," *Decision Sciences*, 23(4), 1992, 944-956. Also see Cetron, M., and J. Goldhar (Eds.), *The Science of Managing Organized Technology* (New York: Gordon & Breach, 1970).

20. See, for example, Crane, D., "Scientists at Major and Minor Universities: A Study of Productivity and Recognition," *American Sociological Review*, 30(5), 1965, 699-714. Also see Phillimore, A., "University Research Performance Indicators in Practice: The University Grants Committee's Evaluation of British Universities, 1985-1986," *Research Policy*, 18(5), 1989, 255-271.

21. There is a vast literature on teaching and educational outcomes that the reader may wish to consult. This literature is extraneous to the discussion in this chapter.

22. In a study of 25 leading business schools in the United States, the researcher found that the structure of the program in terms of the core courses and concentration areas was not a factor on the performance of those schools. That is, the particular mix of courses and disciplines did not determine superior performance. Among them are the quality of the faculty and the students, and ancillary services to students (such as placement and an effective socialization climate). See, Segev, E., A. Raveh, and M. Farjoun, "Conceptual Maps of the Leading MBA Programs in the United States: Core Courses, Concentration Areas, and the Ranking of the School," *Strategic Management Journal*, 20(6), 1999, 549-565.

23. See, for example, Geisler, E., A. Furino, and J. Kiresuk, "Toward a Conceptual Model of Cooperative Research: Patterns of Development and Success in University-Industry Alliances," *IEEE Transactions on Engineering Management*, 38(2), 1991, 136-145. Also see Geisler, E., "Industry-University Technology Cooperation: A Theory of Interorganizational Relations," *Technology Analysis & Strategic Management*, 7(2), 1995, 45-53; and, Geisler, E., and A. Rubenstein, "University-Industry Relations: A Review of Major Issues," in A. Link and G. Tassey (Eds.), *Cooperative Research: New Strategies for Competitiveness* (New York: St. Martin's Press, 1989), pp. 43-62.

24. See, for example, Goldhor, R., and R. Lunt, "University-to-Industry Advanced Technology Transfer," *Research Policy*, 12(3), 1983, 121-152. Also see Heatherington, K., B. Heatherington, and A. Roberson, "Commercializing Intellectual Properties at Major Research Universities: Income Distribution," *Journal of the Society of Research Administrators*, 17(4), 1986, 27-38. The trend to create and increase the interaction of American universities with industry may also be credited to the call by policy makers for "relevancy" and "commercialization" of S&T that followed in the wake of the end of the "cold war," and the dramatic reduction in military spending on S&T in the early 1990s. See Geisler E., "When Whales are Cast Ashore: The Conversion to Relevancy of U.S. Basic Research and Universities," *IEEE Transactions on Engineering Management*, 41(1), 1995, 3-8.

25. See, for example, Walters, G., and D. Gray (Eds.), *Managing the Industry/University Cooperative Research Center* (Columbus, OH: Battelle Press, 1998). Also see Gray, D., E. Johnson, and T. Gridley, "Industry-University-Projects and Centers: An Empirical Comparison of Two Federally Funded Models of Cooperative Science," *Evaluation Review*, 10(6), 1986, 776-793; and, Geisler, E., "Explaining the Generation and Performance of Intersector Technology Cooperation," Working Paper, Stuart Graduate School of Business, Illinois Institute of Technology, Chicago, 1999.

26. With the managerial consultation of the U.S. National Science Foundation, similar initiatives were established in the United Kingdom, Sweden, Ireland, and France.

27. See, for example, Colton, R., "National Science Foundation Experience with University-Industry Centers for Scientific Research and Technological Innovation (An Analysis of Issues, Characteristics, and Criteria for Their Establishment," *Technovation*, 1(2), 1987, 97-108. Also see Williams, B., "The Direct and Indirect Role of Higher Education in Industrial Innovation: What Should We Expect?" *Minerva*, 24(2/3), 1986, 145-171; and Ruscio, K., "The Changing Context of Academic Science: University-Industry Relations in Biotechnology and the Public Policy Implications," *Policy Studies Review*, 4(2), 1984, 259-275.

28. See, for example, Cichy, K., "Ethical Implications of For-Profit Corporate Sponsorship of Research," *SRA Journal*, 22(1), 1990, 23-27. Also see Fassin, Y., "Academic Ethos Versus Business Ethics," *International Journal of Technology Management*, 6(5/6), 1991, 533-546. Other criticisms involved the role of government in bringing together industry and universities. See, Lepkowski, W., "University-Industry Research Ties Still Viewed with Concern," *Chemical and Engineering News*, 62(26), 1984, 7-11. Also see Gibbons, M., and B. Wittrock (Eds.), *Science as a Commodity: Threats to the Open Community of Scholars* (London: Longman Group Limited, 1995).

29. See, Peters, L., and H. Etzkowitz, "University-Industry Connections and Academic Values," *Technology in Society*, 12(4), 1990, 427-440. Also see

Weiner, C., "Universities, Professors, and Patents: A Continuing Controversy," *Technology Review*, 89(2), 1986, 32-43.

30. For studies of similar efforts in other countries, see, for example, Waissbluth, M., G. Cadena, and J. Solleriro, "Linking University and Industry: An Organizational Experience in Mexico," *Research Policy*, 17(6), 1988, 341-347. Also see Segal, N., "Universities and Technological Entrepreneurship in Britain: Some Implications of the Cambridge Phenomenon," *Technovation*, 4(3), 1986, 189-204; and McQueen, D., and J. Hallmark, "Spin-Off Companies From Chalmers University of Technology," *Technovation*, 1(4), 1982, 305-315.

31. Geisler, E., "Intersector Technology Cooperation: Hard Myths, Soft Facts," *Technovation*, 17(6), 1997, 309-320.

32. See, for example, Molas-Gallart, J., and T. Sinclair, "From Technology Generation to Technology Transfer: The Concept and Reality of the Dual-Use Technology Centers," *Second International Conference on Technology Policy and Innovation*, Lisbon, August 3-5, 1998. Also see Etzkowitz, H., A. Webster, and P. Healey (Eds.), *Capitalizing Knowledge: New Intersections of Industry and Academia* (Albany: State University of New York Press, 1998); and Prins, A., "Behind the Scenes of Performance: Performance, Practice, and Management in Medical Research," *Research Policy*, 19(6), 1990, 517-534. Also see the interview given by James Halpin, CEO of CompUSA, in Puffer, S., "CompUSA's CEO James Halpin on Technology, Rewards, and Commitment," *The Academy of Management Executive*, 13(2), 1999, 29-36.

15

METRICS AND
EVALUATION OF INDUSTRIAL
SCIENCE AND TECHNOLOGY

Without a doubt, the topic of evaluation of industrial science and technology (IS&T) has been the most prolific in the literature on the management of S&T.[1] As I was compiling this chapter, my main concern was to filter and select those items and references that would adequately narrate the issue, yet be representative of the virtual "ocean" of studies, models, and perspectives on the evaluation of industrial S&T.

This chapter is therefore structured in a concentric manner, so that very limited discussions of selected subtopics are conducted, with emphasis on the key metrics and their usage in the evaluation of IS&T. Moreover, the chapter is structured in a way that distinguishes between the different objectives of evaluation, and the organizational levels at which evaluations are conducted.

The chapter starts with a general discussion of metrics used in the evaluation of IS&T. The next section describes metrics used in the evaluation of S&T *projects*, followed by *industries* and *sectors*. I have selected this structure because industry utilizes different mixes of metrics for different levels of the organization, and because such a structure also provides a framework for classification of metrics, as they are operationally implemented.[2] In the service of brevity, I have also limited the discussion in this chapter primarily to the metrics described in Chapters 7-12 and to the key issues, strengths, and shortcomings of their implementation in industrial S&T settings. Such a constraint is perforce a highly limiting imposition, so that the chapter is merely a very brief and illustrative (yet hopefully also illuminating) description and analysis of metrics and evaluation of industrial S&T.

METRICS AND EVALUATION OF INDUSTRIAL S&T

Industrial companies evaluate their science and technology activities for two complementary purposes: (1) to assess the contribution of the activity to their commercial objectives, and (2) to assess the efficient management of such activities as corporate operations.[3]   Although congruent, these two objectives require different metrics for their evaluation.   In addition, the complexity of industrial S&T and the professional nature of scientists and engineers make matters even more difficult, because there is also a need to evaluate these human resources at different stages of the process.

Contributions to Corporate Success

The importance of industrial S&T is not only because it has consistently comprised over half of the total U.S. investments in S&T, but also because of the impacts that its outputs have had on the economy and on society. Industrial companies generate the main body of innovations that are translated into new products and services, which then fuel economic progress and prosperity.[4]

These far-reaching impacts of industrial S&T are reflected in the evaluation conducted by corporations. One of the purposes for evaluation is to assess the contributions of the S&T activity in the firm—to the commercial/business goals and outcomes. Figure 15.1 shows the use of key metrics of S&T in the measurement of such evaluation.

Economic measures and patents are the most favored metrics used by industrial companies to assess the business contributions. In general, S&T is viewed by the firm as an investment, and patents are considered an acceptable and relatively easy to measure outcome from these investments.[5] The quantitative attributes of these metrics make them more amenable to calculations and to comparison with other quantitative measures of corporate activities and outcomes (e.g., sales, profits, other investments).[6]

Figure 15.1
Illustrative Uses of Key Metrics of S&T in the Evaluation of the Contributions of Industrial S&T

METRIC	ILLUSTRATIVE USES
• **Economic and Financial**	• Correlation with sales & profits • Measures of ROI and ROA • Ratios of new product sales • Measures of cost-effectiveness
• **Bibliometrics**	• Measure of prestige
• **Mapping of S&T**	• Relation to marketing research
• **Patents**	• Stream of revenues from licenses • Relation to competitive position and market share • Ratios of sales and profits from patented new products
• **Peer Review**	• Project selection and allocation of resources • Overall contribution of IS&T
• **Process Outcomes**	• Stepwise contributions of innovations • Project selection & resources allocation

Not necessarily in any order of priority or importance.

A different set of criteria is used by corporations to assess the performance of their S&T in terms of contributions to processes and to the value chain. For example, in the new product development (NPD) process, companies assess the "time to market" as a goal to be achieved via the outcomes from S&T.[7] This and similar corporate attributes are considered to be positive forces in the firm's struggle to sustain its competitive position in its market. Concepts such as "agility" are interpreted in the firm as enhanced ability to transform the outputs from S&T into viable new products that are ready for their markets.

But the key metrics are primarily used to evaluate the overall contributions to corporate success and performance. Expenditures for S&T and proximal outputs (such as patents) are the main form of measurement, via correlations with downstream business indicators (such as sales, profits, and market share). The process itself, and the attributes such as time to market, are usually implemented in the evaluation of the efficiency of operations.

Efficiency and Management of S&T Operations

Balachandra and Friar (1997) reviewed the literature that explored the success factors of industrial S&T projects and new product innovation.[8] They found contradictory results, with a long list of factors which they grouped into four categories: (1) market related, (2) technology related, (3) environment related, and (4) organization related. They concluded that there are very few, if any, benchmarks for rating the factors.[9]

Roy Rothwell and his colleagues in the United Kingdom studied successes and failures in industrial innovation in the British chemical processes and scientific instrument companies.[10] They identified four key factors that were present in successful (but not in failed) innovations: (1) understanding of user needs, (2) attention to marketing, (3) efficient work development, and (4) use of external advice and technology.

These and other studies have generated a host of measures and indicators. Figure 15.2 shows some illustrative uses of the key metrics discussed in Chapters 7-12, and their application with some measures of efficiency and success of S&T projects.

Efficiency of operations is generally conducive to four general areas: project selection, project management, termination of projects, and resources allocation. These are the main topics that served as foundation for over 50 years of scholarship in R&D management and MOT (management of technology) at the level of the project.[11] Knowledge accumulated in these areas allowed for more efficient management of S&T projects in industry.

Metrics, Management, and The Role of S&T in Industry

Industrial S&T is a special case of investments in innovative activity, perhaps due to its origins and to the corporate environment in which S&T is practiced. Historically, the industrial S&T laboratory is a relatively new institution, starting in the late 1800s, then steadily and dramatically expanding throughout the 20th century.[12]

Figure 15.2
Illustrative Uses of Key Metrics of S&T in the Evaluation of Efficiency and Management of Corporate S&T Operations

METRIC	ILLUSTRATIVE USES
•**Economic and Financial**	•cost savings and reduction •high contribution margin •sales/profit potential •efficient use of resources
•**Bibliometrics**	•identification of state of the art for probability of technical success
•**Mapping of S&T**	•planned portfolio of S&T work •management review and audits •termination criteria for projects
•**Patents**	•potential applications in NPD •life-cycle of products •market competitiveness
•**Peer Review**	•evaluation of technical success of projects and project selection •potential applications in business units
•**Process Outcomes**	•evaluation of learning from projects •resource allocation and project selection

Not necessarily in any order of priority or importance.

As a general rule, corporations spend a substantial portion of their investments on science and technology, in the form of generating them or by acquiring goods and services that are "technology rich" or "embedded," including the whole range of information technology. With investments in the generation of S&T approaching—in some industries—12-15% of sales, senior management has to pay close attention to this activity.

But S&T (or R&D in many companies) is usually viewed as a *cost* center, not as an entity that generates revenue. As an organizational unit, S&T is a support activity, not seen as a key element of the value chain of the corporation. S&T has no control over sales and marketing in the decentralized firm, and no direct and accountable income or profit can be computed from it.[13] The only link that exists between S&T and the future stream of revenues and profits is philosophical. The argument is that new products *are likely* to generate a flow of income, and these can perhaps be attributed to the S&T activity that originally led to new products.

The paradoxical situation that emerges is the valuation of corporate S&T on the basis of *future* flows of revenues, so that the measures assessing S&T are entirely out of its control. It is a far cry from senior managers asking the S&T managers: "What have you invented for us today?" to senior managers inquiring: "How well do the new products sell?" The former question refers to metrics of immediate outputs, where the S&T function has some leverage and the ability to improve. In the latter case S&T is virtually "out of the loop."

Who is the Customer? A different, yet central issue in the evaluation of industrial S&T is the definition of the *customer* for this corporate activity. Several questions seem to emerge. Is there a customer at all? In his address to the Industrial Research Institute in 1995, Robert Frosch argued that the customer for technology is always wrong.[14] Even when a customer is identified, it is likely that the marvelous invention that came out of the laboratory this past year will not solve the problem as framed and understood by this customer.

Often there are multiple customers to the industrial S&T function. Is the customer new product development, or is it marketing, or the entire company? Perhaps we may even consider the corporate external customers as the ultimate customer for industrial S&T. Such a complex and uncertain view of the customer is characteristic of the nature of S&T and of scientists and engineers who engage in this activity. For example, Dean Eastman, director of the Argonne National Laboratory, suggested in his 1997 address to the graduates of a business school that the scientific community has difficulties in grasping even the *concept* of a customer.[15] Although industrial scientists are well aware of their corporate processes, criteria for allocation of resources for S&T, and evaluation criteria for S&T, they nevertheless have conflicting allegiances to the generation of scientific outputs and to corporate needs and objectives.[16]

Consider the case of Westinghouse Electric Corporation. The company measures its S&T effectiveness by using a variety of measures embedded in the premise that the customers for S&T are the *business units*.[17] The company has made little use of patents and bibliometrics in the assessment of S&T because very few of these had any measurable impacts on business operations. Westinghouse relies on close relations between

S&T and business units. They establish quantifiable objectives for S&T through negotiations with the business units and subsequent consensus between the parties. S&T is then evaluated on their achievement of these objectives. An important component in this link between S&T and business units is that the units provide their business strategies and the technologies required to meet them, so that more specific objectives can now be generated for the S&T function.[18]

Some Examples. Consider the case of Caterpillar, Inc., the world's largest maker of construction and earthmoving equipment and diesel and gas and turbine engines. In order to be able to meet the needs of its S&T customers, Caterpillar has *centralized* the links between its S&T function and its business units.[19] The company has created a Technology Council as a strategy setting group, and a Technology Management Review Board that develops specific strategies and plans that interfaces customer needs with the S&T resources and strategies. Through centralization and such linkage and partnering mechanisms, Caterpillar's organization has been designed to better channel the needs and strategies of the business units into the world of its S&T function.

On the other side of the spectrum is the case of L. M. Ericsson, the Swedish maker of cellular and telecommunications equipment. Ericsson decided to entirely distribute its S&T effort in total decentralization.[20] The company established 40 S&T centers, distributed over 20 countries, so that almost half of its S&T personnel is working overseas, in direct contact and under the management of the local business unit. The aim of such an organization was to bring S&T "closer to the customer," by building current and relevant expertise via direct interface with the business units.[21]

The "Right" Metrics

So which of the metrics we listed in Chapter 7-12 and in Figures 15.1 and 15.2 are better measures of industrial S&T? The picture that emerges from the current chapter is that there are a variety of approaches by different companies. The choice of metrics depends on (1) the company's experience with S&T evaluation, (2) its mode of organization, (3) the power and influence of the business units, (4) the degree to which the customers for S&T have been clearly identified and construed within the corporate structure and processes for S&T, and (5) senior management's perception of what S&T does, how it contributes to the business of the company, and how it should be evaluated.

Is there a preferred or "best" approach and metrics to evaluate industrial S&T? The answer seems to be that all the metrics listed above are useful to some degree. Perhaps some metrics (such as bibliometrics and patents) are best in measuring one set of attributes that describe the S&T activity itself. Other metrics are better at measuring impacts of S&T on business. Through the link with business units and convergence with these units' strategies, it is thus up to the company to consider the available metrics, to weigh their usage against its needs and constraints, and to select the set that best fits its situation at the various stages of its innovation process.[22]

Industrial Scientists and Engineers

The third aspect of the complexity of industrial S&T evaluation is the cadre of scientists and engineers who compose the S&T function in the firm. The alienation of these knowledge workers and the problems inherent in the evaluation and measurement of their work have been identified early on in our study of S&T organizations. Miller (1967), for example, concluded that the conflict between the bureaucracy of corporations and the professionalism of S&T workers generates alienation from work among these employees.[23] The primary factors in this relation are the freedom of choice (to pursue individual research interests), and the nature of the professional climate (how supportive of the S&T professional). The literature on this topic also found a connection between climate and productivity of S&T workers in industrial firms—and the organizational structure and corporate policies of the firm.[24]

The main issue in evaluating industrial S&T workers seems to be the conflict between the firm's desire for relevancy and business-related outputs, and the S&T professional's need for personal recognition and satisfaction. There is a difference in this regard between *scientists* and engineers, or *technologists*. The former tend to identify with their peers (outside the company) as their reference group. Technologists are more inclined to identify with their own work organization.

Yet, even when these differences are considered, the more the company leans toward relevant S&T and closer relations with customers and the business units, the more it will shift its S&T metrics to the downstream measures of commercial and organizational performance. Hence, industrial scientists and engineers find themselves evaluated by measures of how well they *cooperate* with other units in the company, rather than measures of their scientific and technological achievements, and the impacts of these on their standing in their profession.

Companies have attempted to alleviate this problem by offering two types of incentives: awards for S&T workers, and programs for professional development. Awards are designed to recognize the scientific and technical achievements of individual researchers and research teams. Professional development includes resources expended in academic improvement, degree studies, conference attendance, and similar travel opportunities.[25]

But these incentives, albeit soothing to the collective and individual egos of S&T workers, are not solutions to the conflict of metrics between what the company desires and what the workers would prefer. The use of bibliometrics and peer review may alleviate some of the effects of this conflict. In practical terms this would entail a double evaluation: one that assesses the contribution of the S&T function, and a parallel assessment of the S&T workers. Should such a separate evaluation (with its own metrics) be an integral part of industrial S&T evaluation?

To some degree industrial companies already make such distinction, *de facto* perhaps rather than as a formal component of their evaluation procedures. Along the innovation continuum, some companies distinguish between the downstream new product development process, and the S&T function that contributed to it. The latter is evaluated as a separate activity by means of proximal measures such as bibliometrics, patents, and peer review. This practice has received support from the concept of "core competencies" in strategic management. In addition to evaluating the contributions from S&T, companies are also assessing the skills and competitiveness of their S&T functions by measuring their proximal outputs.[26]

METRICS AND EVALUATION OF PROJECTS

The project is the basic organizational unit by which the company conducts its S&T activity. Industrial S&T projects are evaluated in two distinct phases of the project's life: (1) selection of the project from a set of competing projects, and (2) termination of a project. Although both phases may share attributes of a similar phenomenon of project management, they are nevertheless evaluated by means of different metrics.[27]

Selection of S&T Projects

S&T projects are selected according to three key factors: (1) probability of technical success, (2) capabilities of the investigators and their teams, and (3) probability of commercial success. The first two factors are assessed by qualitative measures that rely primarily on peer review and past performance of the proposed team.[28]

The potential for commercial success of S&T projects is assessed by a variety of measures, such as relevance, risk, reasonableness, and possible economic returns.[29] These measures incorporate the downstream metrics of business performance (such as sales and profits), and the expected contributions of S&T to these measures. The resultant indicator of potential success is the potential "returns."

A different view in the literature opted to emphasize the generation of new projects by means of relevancy to corporate priorities and implementation potential.[30] Other factors considered important for project selection were a combination of the traditional criteria with measures of project scheduling.[31]

Termination of S&T Projects

Commonly used measures for termination decisions of S&T projects include technical and organizational factors. Some studies have identified time, technical success, and probability of technical success or factors used to monitor S&T projects as to their progress—with a possible decision to terminate.[32] Similarly, a study of the chemical industry identified six factors as "best predictors" of project termination: (1) commercial objectives, (2) authority of project members to make timely decisions, (3) volatility of the potential market for the new product expected from the project, (4) priority given the project by R&D managers, (5) existence of a business gatekeeper, and (6) efficient use of resources such as time, materials, and information.[33]

Such measures used in decisions to terminate S&T projects seem to be universal, when market and technological conditions are similar. As a general rule these measures range across technical and organizational variables, so companies have the choice of emphasizing the *technical* perspective in certain projects, or the *organizational* aspects in other projects.[34]

METRICS AND EVALUATION OF INDUSTRIAL S&T

Overall, industrial S&T impacts the economy and society by means of inventions, innovations, new products and processes, the knowledge that is introduced, and indirect effects through diffusion to other sectors of the economy. Although the United States lacks a central technology planning policy and strategy mechanism for its industrial S&T, there have been periodic assessments of the composition and effectiveness of the American industrial S&T strength. In 1992, a committee of the National Science Foundation suggested that U.S industrial S&T is suboptimal in that inadequate resources are spent on process-oriented S&T, the S&T horizon is too short, and results are not adequately nor quickly commercialized.[35]

These studies illustrate the use of two types of metrics: (1) measures of the internal structure of industrial S&T, and (2) measures of its commercial and social ramifications. They key issues are the strategic perspective of industrial S&T as a major force in economic and social progress. But the analysis is not only at the macronational level. It starts at the level of the industry and the company, where strategic considerations of what S&T to fund and how to structure it are paramount components that form the background for future impacts on the national scene. These strategic considerations are discussed in the following chapter.[36]

SUMMARY

American industry has virtually shelved the idea of corporate technology centers. The trend during the 1990s has been to distribute the firm's S&T assets to the operating divisions and business units. Fueled by the desire for closer and more intensive interface with customers, industrial S&T has become more relevant, with the justification centered around *alignment* with the strategies of the business units.

Although S&T is now pervasive in almost every aspect of corporate life, many senior managers have financial, legal, and marketing training and experience. They routinely fail to understand S&T, or worry about its potential contributions, with the exception being its constantly increasing cost.

So the metrics used by companies to evaluate their S&T reflect these executive perspectives and shortcomings. Distinctions are made between measuring the *process* of S&T and its structure—and the potential or even actual contributions to the business of the company. We thus end up with "two worlds" that seem to operate (and are hence evaluated) almost independently.

Economists may continue to utilize patent data to approximate the impacts of industrial S&T, but the more operational metrics that are commonly used by industrial firms are a varied mix of upstream and downstream measures. Such diversity allows both S&T and general managers the flexibility to tailor given metrics to their perspectives and biases. The most appropriate metrics of S&T are contingent upon the company and the targeted use for which managers employ these metrics. This state of affairs may not be optimal nor desirable, but it seems to somehow work, albeit with limited power to truly describe the strategic threats to industrial S&T and its performers.

NOTES

1. The literature is vast and diverse, including various perspectives from economics, management, social-psychology, and finance. Systematic studies were initially reported in the 1950s, and this trend mushroomed in the next four decades. See some of the early literature in Rubenstein, A., "Setting Criteria for R&D," *Harvard Business Review*, 35(1), 1957, 95-104; and Rubenstein, A. (Ed.), *Coordination, Control, and Financing of Industrial Research* (New York: King's Crown Press, 1955). Also see Gold, B., G. Rosseger, and M. Boylan, *Evaluating Technological Innovations* (Lexington, MA: Lexington Books, 1980); and Langenhagen, C., "An Evaluation of Research and Development in the Chemical Industry," M. S. Thesis, School of Industrial Management, M.I.T., June 1958. More recently see, Dodgson, M., and R. Rothwell (Eds.), *The Handbook of Industrial Innovation* (Cheltenham: Edward Elgar, 1994); and Steele, L., "Evaluating the Technical Operation," *Research-Technology Management*, 31(5), 1988, 11-19. These references are but an illustrative sample of the extant literature.

2. See, for example, Mansfield, E., "Industrial R&D: Characteristics, Costs, and Diffusion of Results," *American Economic Review*, 59(1), 1969, 65-71. Also see Augood, D., "A Review of R&D Evaluation Methods," *IEEE Transactions on Engineering Management*, 20(4), 1973, 114-120; and more recently, see Bacon, F., and T. Butler, *Achieving Planned Innovation* (New York: The Free Press, 1997); and Souder, W., *Managing New Product Innovations* (Lexington, MA: Lexington Books, 1987).

3. The terms research and development (R&D) and science and technology (S&T) will be used interchangeably in this chapter. The term industrial S&T (IS&T) also includes the process usually called new product development (NPD). I recognize that there are organizational and managerial differences between R&D,

S&T, and NPD, but such differences tend to become almost marginal where evaluation of the overall innovation process in the company is conducted. See, for example, Allen, T., *Managing the Flow of Technology* (Cambridge, MA: MIT Press, 1977); and, Roberts, E., "Managing Invention and Innovation," *Research-Technology Management*, 31(1), 1988, 11-29; and Souder, W., "Managing Relations Between R&D and Marketing in New Product Development Projects," *Journal of Product Innovation Management*, 5(1), 1988, 6-19.

4. This seems to be the prevailing view in the literature. See, for example, Hall, B., "Industrial Research During the 1980s: Did the Rate of Return Fall?" *Brookings Papers on Economic Activity*, Issue 2, Microeconomics, 1993, 289-322. Also see Reinganum, J., "Innovation and Industry Evolution," *Quarterly Journal of Economics*, 100(1), 1985, 81-99; and, Ghingold, M., and B. Johnson, "Technical Knowledge as Value Added in Business Markets," *Industrial Marketing Management*, 26(3), 1997, 271-280.

5. Much of the relevant literature was illustrated in the references to Chapter 8. Also see Gupta, A., S. Raj, and D. Wilemon, "R&D and Marketing Dialogue as High-Tech Firms," *Industrial Marketing Management*, 14(3), 1985, 289-300; and, Mansfield, E., "Patents and Innovations: An Empirical Study," *Management Science*, 32(2), 1986, 173-181. Also see Wheelwright, S., and K. Clark, *Revolutionizing Product Development: Quantum Leaps in Speed, Efficiency, and Quality* (New York: Free Press, 1992).

6. See Hauser, J., and G. Katz, "Metrics: You Are What You Measure," *European Management Journal*, 16(5), 1998, 516-528.

7. See, for example, Smith, P., and D. Reinertsen, *Developing Products in Half the Time: New Rules, New Tools* (New York: John Wiley & Sons, 1998).

8. Balachandra, R., and J. Friar, "Factors for Success in R&D Projects and New Product Innovation: A Contextual Framework," *IEEE Transactions on Engineering Management*, 44(3), 1997, 276-287.

9. See, for example, Coombs, R., A. McMeekin, and R. Pybus, "Toward the Development of Benchmarking Tools for R&D Project Management," *R&D Management*, 28(3), 1998, 175-186. The authors identified three types of "styles" of project management: (1) projects that yield or are linked to "new products or processes for major business impact" (p. 178), (2) projects that enhance "core products or technologies to defend market position" (p. 179), and (3) projects that yield new product technology platforms. The authors contended that each type requires a different mode of management, hence also different metrics to assess progress and outcomes. In this regard, also see Shenhar, A., and D. Dvir, "Towards a Typological Theory of Project Management," *Research Policy*, 25(4), 1996, 607-632.

10. Rothwell, R., C. Freeman, A. Horseley, and J. Townsend, "SAPPHO Updated—Phase II," *Research Policy*, 3(2), 1974,. 258-291; and Rothwell, R.,

"Project SAPPHO: A Comparative Study of Success and Failure in Industrial Innovation," *Information Age*, 7(4), 1985, 215-230.

11. See, for example, Balachandra, R., K. Brockhoff, and A. Pearson, "R&D Project Termination Decisions: Processes, Communication, and Personnel Changes," *Journal of Product Innovation Management*, 13(2), 1996, 245-256. Also see Basberg, B., "Patents and the Measurement of Technological Change: A Survey of the Literature," *Research Policy*, 16(2-4), 1987, 131-141.

12. See the fascinating historical review in Price, de Solla, D., *Science Since Babylon* (New Haven, CT: Yale University Press, 1961). Price discusses the origins of Liebig's laboratory in Germany (1840) and Cavendish Laboratory in England (1874).

13. In several studies my students and I conducted in the 1990s, we found weak links between R&D and strategic management in major service companies in the sectors of banking, insurance, transportation, and healthcare. R&D, and technological explorations in general, were found to be usually evaluated as contributors to cost cutting and other "efficiency" variables, and seldom to the corporate strategic management of the firm. See, Geisler, E., "How Strategic Is Your Information Technology?" *Industrial Management*, 36(1), 1994, 31-33. Also see Geisler, E., and W. Hoang, "Purchasing Information Technologies: An Empirical Study of Some Behavior Patterns in Service Companies," *International Journal of Purchasing and Materials Management*, 32(3), Summer 1992, 38-42; and, Geisler, E., and S. Kassicieh, "Information Technologies and Technology Commercialization: The Research Agenda," *IEEE Transactions on Engineering Management*, 44(4), 1997, 339-346.

14. Frosch, R., "The Customer for R&D Is Always Wrong," *Research-Technology Management*, 39(6), 1996, 22-25.

15. Eastman, D., "How Science Will Affect Business Opportunities: Perceived Science and Real Science," *Vital Speeches of the Day*, 64(4), 1997, 111-114.

16. Assuming, of course, that such needs and objectives (that incorporate S&T) are clearly established and defined by the firm—which may not be the case. This is the issue of how well is the company aware of the capabilities, potential, and role of S&T in its business endeavors, and how well is the management side of the company able to absorb such S&T results. Industrial customers also change their demands from S&T, as in the case of lubricants, where customers are buying fewer gallons but demanding higher performance from them.

17. Foster, T., "Making R&D More Effective at Westinghouse," *Research-Technology Management*, 39(1), 1996, 31-42.

18. See a similar approach in Australian companies. Liao, Z., and P. Greenfield, "Major Considerations in the Corporate Development of R&D Strategies Within Australian Technology-Based Firms," *International Journal of Technology Management*, 13(5/6), 1997, 588-600. The authors studied 112 companies and found that Australian S&T managers considered "consistency with

customer requirement" to be a crucial component of their S&T decision making. In this case the customers were defined as the *corporate* customers.

19. Zadocks, A., "Managing Technology at Caterpillar," *Research-Technology Management*, 40(1), 1997, 49-51.

20. Blau, J., "Ericsson Decentralizes for Quicker Research Payoff," *Research-Technology Management*, 41(2), 1998, 4-6.

21. The company has indeed recognized the dangers inherent in this mode of organization, such as becoming "too short-signed." To deal with the threat, Ericsson supports some fundamental research at all its S&T centers. Such a "band-aid" cure may not be sufficient for identifying emerging technologies. Robert Forsch (1996, *op. cit.*) in effect severely criticized such an approach. He argued that "the current fad of...taking short-term views and distributing R&D assets to operating divisions, is like a farm investor who is interested only in harvesting and will not invest in planting, cultivating, or irrigating; neither is likely to get much good harvest for very long" (p. 22). This is an excellent allegory and a sound argument against such extreme distributions of corporate S&T to business units. Also see Friar, J., and R. Balachandra, "Spotting the Customer for Emerging Technologies," *Research-Technology Management*, 42(4), 1999, 37-43.

22. See, for example, Dunn, D., J. Friar, and C. Thomas, "An Approach to Selling High Tech Solutions," *Industrial Marketing Management*, 20(2), 1991, 149-159. Also see Gupta, A., and E. Rogers, "Internal Marketing: Integrating R&D and Marketing Within the Organization," *Journal of Services Marketing*, 5(2), 1992, 55-68; and, Coombs, R., and M. Tomlinson, "Patterns in UK Company Innovation Styles: New Evidence from the CBI Innovation Trend Survey," *Technology Analysis & Strategic Management*, 10(3), 1998, 295-310.

23. Miller, G., "Professionals in Bureaucracy: Alienation Among Industrial Scientists and Engineers," *American Sociological Review*, 32(5), 1967, 755-768.

24. See, for example, Cheng, J., "Organizational Staffing and Productivity in Basic and Applied Research: A Comparative Study," *IEEE Transactions on Engineering Management*, 31(1), 1984, 3-6. Also see Andrews, F. (Ed.), *Scientific Productivity: The Effectiveness of Research Groups in Six Countries* (Cambridge: Cambridge University Press, 1979); and an early study that correlated structure and productivity and recommended the use of peer review to overcome structural differences, in Gordon, G., "The Problem of Assessing Scientific Accomplishment: A Potential Solution," *IEEE Transactions on Engineering Management*, 10(4), 1963, 192-196; and more recently, Kelley, R., and J. Caplan, "How Bell Labs Creates Star Performers," *Harvard Business Review*, 71(3), 1993, 128-139.

25. See, for example, Badawy, M., "Managing Human Resources," *Research-Technology Management*, 31(5), 1988, 19-35. Also see Miller, D., *Managing Professionals in Research and Development: A Guide for Improving Productivity and Organizational Effectiveness* (San Francisco: Jossey-Bass Publishers, 1986).

26. See, for example, Ghinghold, M., and B. Johnson, "Technical Knowledge as Value Added in Business Markets," *Industrial Marketing Management*, 26(2), 1997, 271-280. Also see Liberatore, M., and G. Titus, "Synthesizing R&D Planning and Business Strategy: Some Preliminary Findings," *R&D Management*, 13(4), 1983, 207-216, and Souder, W., "Autonomy, Gratification and R&D Outputs: A Small Sample Field Study," *Management Science*, 20(8), 1974, 1147-1156. In particular see the case of pharmaceutical companies in Koenig, M., "A Bibliometric Analysis of Pharmaceutical Research," *Research Policy*, 12(1), 1983, 15-36.

27. S&T project management is one of the more prolific areas in the literature. An extended review of project management is provided in Rubenstein, *Managing Technology in the Decentralized Firm* (New York, John Wiley & Sons, 1989). Also see Wheelwright and Clark, 1992, *op. cit.*, and Liberatore, M., and G. Titus, "The Practice of Management Science in R&D Project Management," *Management Science*, 29(3), 1983, 962-974.

28. See, for example, Bard, J., R. Balachandra, and P. Kaufmann, "An Interactive Approach to R&D Project Selection and Termination," *IEEE Transactions on Engineering Management*, 35(3), 1988, 139-148. Also see Hendricksen, A., and A. Traynor, "A Practical R&D Project-Selection Scoring Tool," *IEEE Transactions on Engineering Management*, 46(2), 1999, 158-170. This article includes a review of the literature on project selection in S&T. Also see Martino, J., *R&D Project Selection* (New York: John Wiley & Sons, 1995).

29. See Henricksen and Traynor, 1999, *op. cit.*

30. Bordley, R., "R&D Project Selection Versus R&D Project Generation," *IEEE Transactions on Engineering Management*, 45(4), 1998, 407-413.

31. See, for example, Coffin, M., and B. Taylor, "Multiple Criteria R&D Project Selection and Scheduling Using Fuzzy Logic," *Computers & Operations Research*, 23(3), 1996, 207-221.

32. See, for example, Balachandra, R., K. Brockhoff, and A. Pearson, "R&D Project Termination Decisions: Processes, Communication, and Personnel Changes," *Journal of Product Innovation Management*, 13(3), 1996, 245-256.

33. See, Green, S., and A. Welsh, "Red Flags at Dawn; or Predicting R&D Project Termination," *Research-Technology Management*, 36(3), 1993, 10-14.

34. See, for example, Balachandra, R., and K. Brockhoff, "Are R&D Project Termination Factors Universal?" *Research-Technology Management*, 38(4), 1995, 31-34. Also see Brockhoff, K., "R&D Project Termination Decisions by Discriminate Analysis: An International Comparison," *IEEE Transactions on Engineering Management*, 41(3), 1994, 245-254.

35. National Science Board, Committee on Industrial Support for R&D, *The Competitive Strength of U.S. Industrial Science and Technology: Strategic Issues* (Washington, DC: Government Printing Office, 1992).

36. See, for example, Klein, K., and J. Sorra, "The Challenge of Innovation Implementation," *Academy of Management Journal*, 21(4), 1996, 1055-1080; and Iosso, T., "Industry Evolution with a Sequence orf Technologies and Heterogeneous Ability; A Model of Creative Destruction," *Journal of Economic Behavior and Organization*, 21(2), 1993, 109-129.

16

SCIENCE, TECHNOLOGY, AND STRATEGY

In this chapter I approach S&T strategy from two perspectives: the *internal* alignment of S&T with the strategy of the organization, and the relation of the S&T-strategy link to the broader issue of national innovation systems.

Although the analysis in this chapter includes both private and public S&T organizations, the emphasis will be on the S&T-strategy relationship of industrial companies. The primary reason for this focus is that these companies place an inordinate importance on their strategic management as a competitive weapon, and that such emphasis dictates the direction taken by industry—with corresponding consequences to the economy and society.

Similarly, public S&T institutions also develop strategies and policies that guide their S&T effort. These strategies are dictated by the overall mission and direction of their parent agencies and by the federal government—Congress and the White House. The priorities and biases thus established contribute to determining the direction of S&T at the public institution.

This chapter starts with some definitions of the phenomenon of strategic management, continuing with alignment of technology-strategy in business organizations, public institutions, and finally a summary of the topic.[1]

SOME DEFINITIONS

The relationship between science technology and strategy is based on two key questions: (1) What is the role of S&T in the sustained success, growth, and survival of the organization? and (2) How can we measure such a role? A corollary question is: Are the existing metrics capable of adequately doing the job of such measurement?

Strategy and strategic management are complex notions, variously defined as roadmaps, processes, and as a conceptual framework for organizational performance.[2] Briefly, strategy is the process by which the mission and goals of an organization are established, followed by the establishment of the ways and means by which these goals are to be accomplished, including choice of resources, their allocation, and their disposition and architecture.

Goodman and Lawless (1994)[3] have argued that "the value of good strategy is the shield it provides against competition, ensuring a measure of certainty, and allowing an organization to create effective approaches to the needs of the marketplace" (p. 7). They have also correctly pointed out that "the organizational costs of employing technological elements within corporate strategy (technology strategy) are accompanied by the need to cope with an added measure of uncertainty and disruption" (p. 7).

There is agreement among scholars that technology is an essential ingredient in formulating and implementing organizational strategy. Much of the literature is normative, amply declaring that there is a need to integrate technology into the organization's strategy process and that there is a crucial need to bring together the different perspectives of strategy-makers and S&T managers.[4]

INTEGRATING TECHNOLOGY AND STRATEGY

The current conventional wisdom that emerges from the literature contends that technology should be viewed as a strategic asset, hence become an integral part of any strategic decision.[5] Figure 16.1 shows some of the reasons for integration of technology and strategy.

But how will such integration be achieved? The literature is replete with recommendations for organizational, structural, and process steps that managers should execute. For example, Arthur Chester (1994)[6] has proposed four processes for integration: (1) organize the central laboratory by technical specialty, (2) apply core competencies, (3) promote technical

Figure 16.1
Reasons for Integration of Technology and Strategy

- Technology is involved in every activity in the value chain.
- Technology and strategy need to follow same direction.
- Need for congruence of goals.
- Need to achieve strategic balance.
- Technology can have crucial effect on cost or differentiations by components of competitive advantage.
- Technology has crucial impact on efficiencies and cost of activities.
- Similar market forces impact technological changes and comparative position, hence need for congruence of direction, to defend from and adapt to these forces.
- Technology affects linkages among components of value chain, hence affects choice of options and alternative directions and allocation of resources.

This list is illustrative, and not in any order of importance.

networks, and (4) establish and encourage "research account executives." In a similar vein, Adler, McDonald, and MacDonald (1992)[7] proposed a Technical Function Strategy (TFS) process of four steps, in which policies are constructed, leading to integration. The policies include processes, resources, and linkages.

Figure 16.2 provides examples of some approaches that have been proposed for the technology-strategy alignment or integration.[8] The approaches are categorized by (1) structural/organizational actions, (2) personnel actions, and (3) managerial actions.

Although some of these approaches have been adopted by companies, much of the literature remains prescriptive. Successful American companies such as General Electric, TRW, Allied-Signal, and Allen Bradley have made various improvements in the nexus between their S&T activities and business strategy.[9] But seamless integration is a goal only partially achieved, regardless of the many models and frameworks that have been proposed over the years.[10] The long road from prescription to implementation is fraught with the nature of the phenomenon (where business and S&T belong to different cultures) and the reticence with which managers on both sides are willing and able to understand each other and to actively support and adopt integrating policies and mechanisms.

Figure 16.2
Illustrative Approaches to Technology-Strategy Alignment
or Integration

A.   STRUCTURAL ORGANIZATIONAL APPROACHES
- Organize the S&T activity by technical specialty.
- Identify and enhance "key" technologies related to core competencies.
- Encourage matrix organization.
- Promote networking and communication.
- Encourage monitoring, tracking, and evaluation of S&T
- Promote decentralization of S&T function in proximity to other components of the value chain, such as manufacturing.
- Establish technology-business committees and similar linking mechanisms.
- Create the portions of technology liaison officers
- Benchmark organizational architectures.

B.   PERSONNEL ACTIONS
- Create systems of rewards for activities that enhance strategic orientation for technologists.
- Establish systems of accountability for both business and S&T managers, with goals, milestones, and sponsorship of strategic convergence of technology and business.
- Integrate such rewards and accountability into individual performance evaluation for managers at all levels.
- Establish and foster a supportive culture that promotes and rewards orientation strategic aims.

C.   MANAGERIAL ACTIONS
- Provide senior management support to the cultural changes in favor of thinking and acting strategically.
- Elevate the chief technology officer or equivalent positions to the inner-circle of the chief executive and to an active role in establishing and implementing overall corporate strategy.
- Create and promulgate a unified S&T mission, vision, and achievable goals.
- Increase the effort to better understand the role of S&T in corporate strategic objectives.

This figure is not exhaustive, nor in any order of ranking or importance.

EVALUATION AND METRICS

The consensus among scholars and managers seems to favor integration and confluence of S&T and organizational strategies. How do we measure such a desired state of affairs? Goodman and Lawless (1994), for example, proposed an "innovation audit," based in part on Arthur D. Little's "technological competitive analysis."[11] The analysis identifies four categories of technology—base, key, pacing, and emerging—which are so named in light of their strategic relation to the competitive position and objectives of the organization.

The technology audit proposed by Goodman and Lawless is primarily a comparative analysis of the focal company *vis-à-vis* its leading competitors.[12] There are seven criteria or categories of items in the comparison: (1) track record (measured by, for example, new product introductions, success of new products, and contributions of new products to sales); (2) capability of staff (size, disciplinary distribution, reputation); (3) strength of R&D organization (flexibility, ability to execute long term projects); (4) idea generation (robustness of new ideas, mechanisms to evaluate new policies); (5) time to commercialize; (6) cost-benefits of R&D; and (7) relations among functional areas.[13]

These criteria are illustrative of the measures usually applied to assess the success of the technology-strategy integration or confluence. Partly, this is an evaluation of two distinct yet congruent programs, each with its own strategic framework. As commonalities are identified, an assessment becomes feasible of how these occur in reality. Figure 16.3 summarizes the key metrics of S&T and their use in evaluating the technology-strategy connection.

Some of the key metrics are used to assess the traditional outcomes from S&T, which happen to also be of strategic nature (e.g., contribution to sales and profits). But these metrics were not designed to evaluate the alignment of two systems of strategic plans and objectives. Such an alignment represents a different phenomenon, in which *organizational* frameworks are matched. Part of this matching is artificial, part of it relates to the establishment of stakeholders, supporters, and sponsors for S&T strategy, in its move toward alignment with corporate strategy. Measures that would capture this phenomenon would include a better assessment of the organizational processes and the participants, their motives, and the factors that drive such a movement alignment.

Figure 16.3
Key S&T Metrics and the Technology-Strategy Connection

METRIC	USE IN ASSESSING TECHNOLOGY-STRATEGY CONNECTION
Economic/Financial	• Used to assess track record of technology strategy, such as contribution to sales and profits. • Cost-effectiveness measures of "before" and "after" integration.
Bibliometrics	• Reputation of the technical personnel.
Co-word & Mapping of S&T	• Mapping used to chart the links between technology strategy and business objectives
Patents	• Used to serve as measurable milestone and benchmark for mapping the link.
Peer Review	• Subjective assessment by members of committees and similar mechanisms. • Assessment of changes in capabilities (technical & commercial)
Process Outcomes	• γ-type organizations are more likely to have a robust technology-strategy nexus & systems to evaluate it.

These are potential and actual uses, drawn from the literature and my own analysis.

The Case of Information Technology

Information technology is a special case in the need to align with corporate strategy. The literature offers a variety of models and frameworks. Busch (1999) illustrates this prescription.[14] He argues that "IT's primary role is starting to migrate from one of firefighter to that of strategic adviser" (p. 29). Henderson and Venkataraman (1999) also argue for alignment.[15] They propose a model that has IT and business strategies and IT and business infrastructure and processes. They contend that "IT is transcending its traditional 'back office' role and is evolving toward a strategic role with the potential not only to support chosen business strategies, but also to shape new business strategies" (p. 472).

But how strategic is information technology in business corporations? The issue becomes more crucial in the case of companies in the service sector. To these companies information is the key ingredient in their business. Therefore, information technology is critical to their sustained performance, competitiveness, and survival. If indeed IT-business alignment is so desirable, it may be doubly so in service companies.[16]

Despite the continuous prescriptions for strategic alignment of information technology, particularly in service companies, Geisler (1990) has found few companies that considered IT a strategic asset and evaluated IT in this fashion.[17] These findings emerged from a comprehensive study of over 100 companies in the banking, insurance, transportation, and health care industries. Geisler employed a methodology that assessed the *evaluation criteria* for IT actually used by the companies. Most frequently used were "efficiency" type criteria, such as cost-savings and improved productivity. Few companies used "strategic" criteria such as "contribution to competitiveness."[18]

These findings may be explained by several possibilities. Senior executives lack adequate understanding of the role that IT plays as a strategic asset. They treat IT as a cost and a support activity, in the same mode as R&D. Second, IT managers are seldom part of the inner circle of the chief executive, again similar to R&D. Third, there is a lack of acceptable and adequate evaluation models that explain the strategic role of IT. Finally, many executives are still captivated by the traditional role that IT used to play as an automated accounting and data processing tool, and as primarily a "back-room" operation. To view IT otherwise, as a strategic asset of consequence to the market position of the organization requires a "paradigm shift" in top management perception.[19] In this regard, a study by the Gartner group found that most companies allocate 85% of their IT to utility functions, 12% to enhance productivity, and only 3% to activities that may lead to competitive advantage.[20]

SUMMARY

The tension between S&T and administration (strategy) is the key to understanding the difficulties that organizations face in their attempts to "align" S&T strategy and business strategy. A good illustration is the application of technology in the sphere of the military and war.

With the introduction in the late 16th century of military firearms, a revolution appeared in the *organization* of the infantry in West European armies.[21] Firearm technology was implemented at the *tactical* level of the infantry company formation. Because of the effective firepower it became very popular; but the technical shortcomings of rapid reloading and unreliability and dispersion of the weapons, a high degree of coordination, drill, and intensive training became a necessary condition to the effective utilization of this technology in large formations. Thus, the availability of large groupings of highly trained and coordinated companies with mobility and destructive firepower in turn made it possible for field generals to devise different strategies of attack.

Such technology "push" sometimes encountered resistance on the part of the entrenched strategists, as was the case of the introduction of tank warfare during the 1919-1939 period. Tactical and strategic perspectives had a different goal at alignment and integration.

The S&T metrics described in this book do not directly nor adequately measure the S&T-strategy alignment. They measure attributes of the outputs from S&T and its successful application in the business aspects of the organization. Hence, by attribution, the inference is that such success is assumed to be generated by the integration between S&T and corporate strategy (among other factors).

However, this alignment is an organizational/structural phenomenon, requiring different metrics to assess its successful competition. S&T metrics are limited in their scope to the outputs generated by the activity and their potential contributions to the organization. As in previous examples, the process-outcomes model may be better suited to track the transformations of S&T outputs and their relative integration with downstream business strategies. This stagewise approach may assist in answering the question whether *strategically relevant S&T* has been practiced, in light of S&T outputs that had been generated. This, in short, is the purpose of the alignment.[22]

NOTES

1. This is a very broad topic, with an extensive literature. The brevity of this chapter is due to my desire to concentrate on metrics and evaluation. Much of the extant literature deals with the managerial, organizational, and overall corporate planning. See, for example, Burgelman, R., M. Maidique, and S. Wheelwright, *Strategic Management of Technology and Innovation,* 2nd ed. (Chicago: Irwin Publishing, 1996). Also see Tushman, M., and P. Anderson, *Managing Strategic*

Innovation and Change (New York: Oxford University Press, 1996); and Porter, M., *Competitive Advantage* (New York: The Free Press, 1985). Also see Adler, P., "Technology Strategy: A Review of the Literatures," *Research on Technological Innovation, Management, and Policy* 4(1), 1989, 25-152.

2. See, for example, Andrews, K., *The Concept of Corporate Strategy* (Homewood, IL: Dow Jones-Irwin, 1971). Also see Miller, D., "Matching Strategies and Strategy Making: Process, Content, and Performance," *Human Relations*, 42(3), 1989, 241-260; Mintzberg, H., *The Rise and Fall of Strategic Planning* (New York: The Free Press, 1994); and Schwenk, C., "Strategic Decision-Making," *Journal of Management*, 24(3), 1995, 471-493. More recently see Mintzberg, H., and J. Lampel, "Reflecting on the Strategy Process," *Sloan Management Review*, 40(3), 1999, 21-30 (40th Anniversary Issue on "In Search of Strategy"). Mintzberg and Lampel reviewed the various research schools on strategy and concluded that "we need to ask better questions and generate fewer hypotheses...better practice, not neater theory...give more attention...to strategy formation as a whole" (p. 29). Also see Luherman, T., "Strategy as a Portfolio of Real Options," *Harvard Business Review*, 76(5), 1998, 89-101. The author suggested that business strategies should be analyzed as "chains of real options" (p. 89). He also argued that "by building option pricing...we gain financial insight earlier rather than later to the creative work of strategy" (p. 99). From the metrics perspective, the more organizations quantify their strategy in financial terms, the more difficult it will be to integrate technology into this scheme, unless dramatic advances are made in the financial valuing of science and technology. See, for example, Shank, J., and V. Govindurajan, "Strategic Cost Analysis of Technological Investments," *Sloan Management Review*, 33(1), 1992, 39-51. The authors proposed a Strategic Cost Management Framework that incorporates value-chain analysis, cost-driven analysis, and competitive advantage analysis.

3. Goodman, R., and M. Lawless, *Technology and Strategy: Conceptual Models and Diagnostics* (New York: Oxford University Press, 1994).

4. See, for example, Frohman, A., and D. Bitondo, "Coordinating Business Strategy and Technical Planning," *Long Range Planning* 14(6), 1981, 58-67. Also see Williams, J., "Technological Evolution and Competitive Response," *Strategic Management Journal*, 4(1), 1983, 55-65.

5. The term "technology" is most prevalent in the literature. Although some authors distinguish between research (science) and technology, the term "technology" generally encompasses all the scientific and technical activities of the organization. See, for example, Senker, J., "Evaluating the Funding of Strategic Science: Some Lessons from British Experience," *Research Policy*, 20(1), 1991, 29-43.

6. Chester, A., "Aligning Technology with Business Strategy," *Research-Technology Management*, 37(1), 1994, 25-32.

7. Adler, P., W. McDonald, and F. MacDonald, "Strategic Management of Technical Functions," *Sloan Management Review*, 33(3), 1992, 19-37.

8. This figure benefitted from Berman, E., E. Vasconcellos, and W. Werther, "Executive Levers for the Strategic Management of Technology," *Business Horizons*, 37(1), 1994, 53-61, particularly Figure 2, page 59.

9. See *ibid.*

10. See, for example, Roussel, P., K. Saad, and T. Erickson, *Third Generation R&D: Managing the Link to Corporate Strategy* (Boston: Harvard Business School Press, 1991). These authors proposed several linking mechanisms in the form of joint committees. Also see Bean, A., and J. Guerard, *R&D Management and corporate Financial Policy* (New York: John Wiley & Sons, 1998). The authors propose integration of R&D into corporate financial plans, hence devising S&T policies that are anchored in economic and financial considerations. Also see Pant, S., and H. Cheng, "An Integrated Framework for Strategic Information Systems Planning and Development," *Information Resources Management Journal*, 12(1), 1999, 15-25. Also see proposals in the health care sector in Morrissey, J., "Integrating Business, Clinical Applications," *Modern Healthcare*, 29(7), 1999, 32-34; and Probert, D., C. Farrukh, and M. Gregory, "Linking Technology to Business Planning: Theory and Practice," *International Journal of Technology Management*, 17(1-2), 1999, 11-30.

11. See Goodman, R., and M. Lawless, 1999, *op. cit.* The A. D. Little model can be found in *The Strategic Management of Technology* (Boston: A. D. Little, Inc., 1981).

12. Goodman and Lawless, 1994, *op. cit.*, pp. 139-140.

13. These criteria are based on the "technology audit" developed by Albert H. Rubenstein. See, for example, Rubenstein, A., "Liaison Relations in Research and Development," *IRE Transactions on Engineering Management*, 4(2), 1957, 72-78; and, Rubenstein, A., *Managing Technology in the Decentralized Firm* (New York: John Wiley & Sons, 1989), pp. 330-342.

14. Busch, J., "IT Should Get More Involved in Strategic Planning Process," *Internetweek*, 75(5), 1999, 29-30.

15. Henderson, J., and H. Venkataraman, "Strategic Alignment: Leveraging Information Technology for Transforming Organizations," *IBM System Journal*, 38(2/3), 1999, 472-484.

16. See, for example, Kutler, J., "An American Banker Survey: Managing Technology, Payoff Hard to Gauge," *American Banker*, November 30, 1988, 1-6. The survey found that only half of the banks had a formal technology evaluation program. Also see Powell, P., "Information Technology Evaluation: Is IT Different?" *The Journal of the Operational Research Society*, 43(1), 1992, 29-43. The author concluded that the companies do not evaluate their IT because: (1) lack of yardsticks, (2) IT is considered "strategic" so evaluation is not necessary, (3) sharing resources increases IT, and (4) government intervention. Also see

Donlon, J., "Measuring the Value of your IT Investment," *Chief Executive*, 139(3), 1998, 70-78.

17. Geisler, E., "Strategic Management of Information Technology and Commercial Success in Service Companies: Some Initial Results," Invited paper presented at TIMS/ORSA National Meeting, Las Vegas, Nevada, May 6-10, 1990.

18. See, Geisler, E., "Managing Information Technologies in Service Companies: Strategic Versus Operational Practices," Paper presented at the International Engineering Management Conference, Eatontown, NJ, October 26-28, 1992.

19. See, for example, Agarwal, R., and J. Prasad, "The Role of Innovation Characteristics and Perceived Voluntariness in the Acceptance of Information Technologies," *Decision Sciences*, 28(3), 1997, 557-582. Also see Mousin, G., E. Remmlinger, and P. Weil, "IT Integration Options for Integrated Delivery Systems," *Healthcare Financial Management*, 53(2), 1999, 40-50.

20. See, for example, Powell, P., "Causality in the Alignment of Information Technology and Business Strategy," *Journal of Strategic Information Systems*, 2(3), 1993, 320-334. Also see Porter, M., and V. Millar, "How Information Gives You Competitive Advantage," *Harvard Business Review*, 63(4), 1985, 149-160; and, Geisler, E., and A. Rubenstein, "How Do Banks Evaluate Their Information Technology?" *Bank Management*, 64(11), 1988, 30-33.

21. See, for example, Creveld, M., *Technology and War* (New York: The Free Press, 1991).

22. See, for example, Senker, J., and P. Senker, "Gaining Competitive Advantage from Information Technology," *Journal of General Management*, 17(3), 1992, 31-45. Also see Lefebvre, L., A. Langley, J. Harvey, and E. Lefebvre, "Exploring the Strategy-Technology Connection in Small Manufacturing Firms," *Production and Operations Management*, 1(3), 1992, 269-285; and Loveridge, R., and. M. Pitt (Eds.), *Strategic Management of Technological Innovation* (New York: John Wiley & Sons, 1991).

17

METRICS AND EVALUATION
OF PUBLIC-SECTOR
SCIENCE AND TECHNOLOGY

The trend of increased cooperation between the American federal laboratories and universities and private industry is a testimony to the fact that the American taxpayers have a favorable view of public investments in science and technology. Regardless of the party affiliation in the White House or the political makeup of Congress, the United States had a consistent rate of investments in such institutions.

In the 1990s, there was a downturn in the funding of some laboratories, combined with the movement to privatize the management of certain laboratories.[1] An illustrative description of this reductionist reasoning is a list of suggestions to restructure public S&T offered by Zachary Pascal (1998).[2] He argued that "public funding of research and development delivered an impressive bounty well into the 1970s. Many contemporary technologies, notably electronics and computing, were essentially created by military patronage. And modern medicine is a creature of federal largesse" (p. 33). But he continues his argument that the federal system of S&T laboratories is mismanaged, lacks the tools to commercialize inventions, and most important, that "the government isn't a significant player in any critical field of technology" (p. 33).[3]

This chapter builds on the phenomena and trends of the late 1990s that have affected the U.S. national laboratories, but emphasizes the issues of evaluation and metrics. The chapter summarizes the issues, structure, and practices by which the federal laboratories evaluate their S&T and are evaluated by their stakeholders—and the metrics used in such evaluations.[4]

CRISIS, CHANGES, AND EVALUATION

The federal (or national) laboratories are either subordinated to a federal department (e.g., Defense, Energy, or Commerce), or stand-alone agencies in a specific area of endeavor or S&T (e.g., NASA laboratories). The overall direction of the type of S&T conducted by these laboratories has seen a "pendulum" of changes in the post-Second World War era.[5]

During the Reagan administration in the 1980s, the mandate from the administration was to avoid competition with private industry. Hence, the federal laboratories were instructed to concentrate on *basic* research, and to leave the more "relevant" or commercially oriented S&T to private industry.

Following the end of the Cold War in the 1990s, the federal laboratories were instructed to: (1) drastically increase their cooperation with other segments of the economy, particularly with private industry; and (2) restructure their S&T portfolios toward more "relevant" and commercially viable S&T projects.

This trend was supported by complementary phenomena. The first has been the succession of federal legislation outcomes in the 1980s and 1990s in which Congress lifted some restrictions on cooperation of federal entities with private companies. This was done in legislation that created the Cooperative Research and Development Agreement (CRADA) as a useful instrument for collaborative programs, and congressional acts that mandated a certain level of cooperative effort by each laboratory.[6]

The second was the end of the Cold War, and the subsequent move toward commercial applications of military-related S&T. Relevancy became the target for publicly supported S&T, coupled with increased accountability and a trend in search of added cost-efficiency, cost-cutting, and reengineering.[7]

All of these trends had a significant influence on the metrics used to evaluate the performance of the federal laboratories. As the key aspect of outcomes from the laboratories moved toward relevancy, diffusion, and commercialization, their evaluation became an assessment of the downstream inputs on the stakeholder organizations. Who were these stakeholders?

As mission-oriented organizations, the federal laboratories are the generators of dedicated S&T for the agencies to which they γbelong, and to the federal government. Figure 17.1 depicts a generalized scheme of these stakeholders.

In addition to the specific objectives dictated by the parent agency, federal laboratories are also responsible to such stakeholders as the Congress (which holds the purse strings and has oversight authority), and the welfare of the public in general. Such a situation when multiple stakeholders vie for the outcomes from the laboratories is best illustrated in the case of the Government Performance Results Act, discussed next.

Figure 17.1
A Generalized Scheme of the Stakeholders of Federal S&T Laboratories

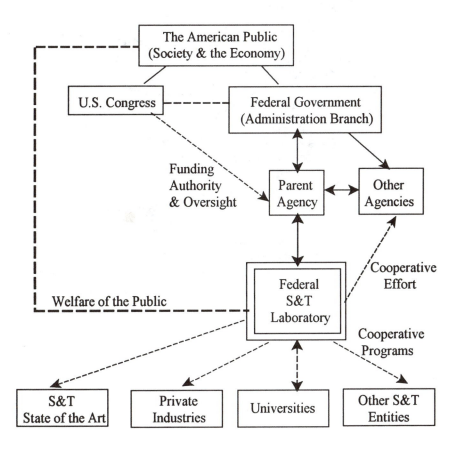

GOVERNMENT PERFORMANCE RESULTS ACT (GPRA)

GPRA is the assessment mechanism by which Congress and the federal government evaluate the performance of its departments, agencies, and laboratories. Specific strategic objectives and goals are set by each institution, and the progress in achieving them. The GPRA conceptual framework takes into account not only the direct outputs from the laboratory to the parent agency, but its impacts on the agency's goals. This is similar to the commercial complications of the industrial R&D laboratory. The emphasis in GPRA is on *quantitative* measures of progress and accomplishments of planned objectives.

But the National Science and Technology Council (NSTC) has conceded that, especially in the case of basic science, the assessment of S&T may not be quantifiable to the extent desired by the GPRA system. The 1996 report by this body also argued:

For evaluating current programs in individual agencies, merit review based on peer evaluation will continue to be the primary vehicle for assessing excellence and conduct of science at the cutting edge....

Balanced assessment of the various dimensions of program performance in an agency will require multiple sources and types of evidence. In addition to retrospective merit review, retrospective performance reports might draw on quantitative indicators, qualitative indicators, descriptive indicators or narrative text, examples of outstanding accomplishments and of more typical levels of achievement, information about context, and findings from special studies and analysis.

Because pre-existing measures of research results were developed primarily for other purposes, they have not yet been adapted for use in reporting at the agency level. Pre-existing measures capture only a subset of research outputs and outcomes. They do not map neatly or cleanly onto GPRA concepts. Consequently, these measures (e.g., publication counts, citations counts, and rate-of-return and related economic measures)...can serve only *as a starting point for agency thinking about how to design the most effective assessment strategies*[8] (emphasis added).

For applied research, development, and technology generated by federal laboratories, the pressure existed to comply with GPRA strategic goals and performance measures of accomplishment. This has led to some difficult conditions faced by federal laboratories.

Consider the case of the National Institute for Occupational Safety and Health (NIOSH). Its *vision* is to "deliver on the nation's promise: Safety and health at work for all people through research and prevention."[9] The mission: "Provide national and world leadership to prevent work-related illness, injury, and death by gathering information, conducting scientific research, and translating the knowledge gained into products and services."[10]

NIOSH has established four strategic goals to accomplish its mission:

1. Conduct a targeted program of research to reduce morbidity, injuries, and mortality among workers in high-priority areas and high-risk sectors;
2. Develop a system for surveillance of major occupational illnesses, injuries, exposures, and health hazards;
3. Increase occupational disease and injury-prevention activities through workplace evaluations, interventions, and recommendations; and
4. Provide workers, employers, the public, and the occupational safety and health community with information, training, and capacity to prevent occupational diseases and injuries.

Consider the first strategic goal. It promises to conduct research that would lead to "reduced morbidity, injuries, and mortality among workers in high-priority areas and high-risk sectors." Yet how will the outcomes from this research be measured? If NIOSH research outcomes are evaluated by the usual proximal metrics (e.g., bibliometrics and peer review), these measures fall short of assessing morbidity and mortality. The latter are measures of *downstream* outputs, as described in the Process-Outcomes approach.

It is a long way from proximal to such pre-ultimate or ultimate outputs of morbidity and mortality of industrial workers. To a large extent (as in the case of industrial R&D), NIOSH is to be evaluated by measures of phenomena that are not within its control. Much of the responsibility for reducing morbidity and mortality lies with industry's compliance with health and safety legislation and regulations.

NIOSH may be able to generate high-quality, cutting-edge, and even useful S&T, and even be able to diffuse and disseminate it effectively, but the ultimate achievement of the strategic goals depends on the actions of S&T users. These users (e.g., industry, state agencies, and the public) have a variety of agendas and timetables, as well as a plethora of incentives and barriers for the implementation of research outcomes generated by a federal organization such as NIOSH.

Therefore, the only meaningful evaluation of NIOSH S&T is by using the proximal metrics of bibliometrics and peer review. Other, downstream metrics should be used only upon an explicit understanding and mapping the progress of NIOSH outputs through the transforming organizations—as these outputs are implemented and utilized. Benefits (from NIOSH S&T) to the American working public can only be measured along the process of implementation and usage of proximal outputs.[11]

CLASH OF CULTURES

The gap between longer term "downstream" measures of performance of federal laboratories and their measurable (immediate) outputs is magnified by the dichotomy between the scientific culture and the federal requirements.

For the scientists employed in these laboratories, there emerged a culture that emphasized scientific exploration, scientific excellence, and relative academic freedom. To many federal scientists the reference group was (and is) their community of science. This meant exchange of ideas, and the timely reporting of research results.

But, in some laboratories, particularly those belonging to the Defense and Energy departments, there were strict rules and procedures for confidentiality and even secrecy, that gravely conflicted with the scientists' academic exposure. An excellent illustration of the clash of cultures was the controversy over alleged nuclear espionage at the energy weapons laboratories.

In March 1999, Wen Ho Lee, a weapons computer scientist, was fired from his job at the Los Alamos National Laboratory and accused of transferring to the People's Republic of China secret information about the U.S. nuclear program.[12] Mr. Lee argued in his defense that he transferred data from classified to unclassified computer systems at the laboratory in order to create backup copies. He contended that "it's a very common practice."[13]

Members of Congress and others in the administration have contended that there was "a culture of scientific arrogance" and lax security. Scientists in the laboratory retorted that "it's very laid-back, but very intense intellectually."[14]

Such opposite perspectives of the realities at the laboratory exemplify the conflict between the exigencies of security and the freedom to publish, to download information, and to diffuse and disseminate scientific findings.

METRICS AND EVALUATION

In the 1950s, the same Los Alamos National Laboratory and Lawrence Livermore Laboratory developed computers with the purpose of assisting them in the development of simulations and complex calculations on new generations of nuclear weapons. This was a *singular contribution* to the state of the art, and to society and the economy. As the computer technology was transferred to the civilian marketplace, it greatly contributed to the computer revolution of the 1960-1990s.

Other cases of S&T transfer from federal laboratories include the spin-offs from NASA (the Space Program), and more recently, data encryption for the Internet. Sandia National Labs (Department of Energy) have taken the lead in research and design of encryption chips.[15] Similar spin-offs and diffusion of S&T are the hallmark in medical research, as the National Institutes of Health and the Centers for Disease Control and Prevention routinely generate and transfer scientific findings in biology, medicine, and public health.[16]

But how are the natural laboratories evaluated, and which metrics are used in their evaluation? In addition to the mandated GPRA, what is the role that the metrics described in this book play in such evaluation?

Because of the peculiar nature of the national laboratories, situated among several stakeholders, there are three distinct frameworks by which the laboratories are evaluated: (1) self-evaluation, (2) evaluation by the parent agency, and (3) evaluation by others. Figures 17.2-17.4 show the role that metrics play in each framework.

Self-Evaluation for the Laboratory

Figure 17.2 shows the metrics used by federal laboratories to evaluate themselves. These include metrics to evaluate the performance of the laboratory and that of the scientific personnel.[17] Bibliometrics, peer review, and economic/financial metrics seem to be the more prevalent in self-evaluation. Depending on the type of laboratory (government-owned/government-operated or government-owned/company-operated) and the nature of the parent agency, some laboratories are more concerned with proximal measures of scientific production, whereas others are concerned with commercialization.[18]

Because of the demands of legislation, federal laboratories also evaluate their compliance with the Stevenson-Wydler Act and other legislation regarding technology transfer. In many laboratories, only 10% of the scientists are involved with transfer activities. Most regard the contributions to the parent agency and the scientific performance as the main output categories.

Figure 17.2
Metrics in Self-Evaluation of Federal Laboratories

METRIC	ILLUSTRATIVE CATEGORIES OF EVALUATION
Economic/Financial	• Cost-effectiveness computation for selected programs as background for GPRA requirement. • Returns to specific projects from collaborative programs
Bibliometrics	• Performance evaluation of scientists and research personnel • Measure of prestige and academic excellence of the laboratory • Measure of contributions to agency
Patents	• Measure of performance in some laboratories: potential for commercialization
Peer Review	• Measure of overall performance • Measure of contributions to parent agency • Measure of prestige
Mapping of S&T	• Contributions to parent agency • Cooperation with others

Evaluation by Parent Agency

The parent agency evaluates its laboratories in light of three complementary objectives. The first is a managerial and oversight function. How well is the laboratory conducting its S&T in compliance with its mission, its objectives, and its actual contributions to the agency's mission, goals, and programs.

The second evaluation objective is the assurance of the high scientific and technical quality of the laboratory, and its standing in the national and international S&T scenes. This objective supports the agency requests for funding, by pointing to the high standards of S&T that the laboratory conducts in the disciplines that are crucial at best and relevant in the very least to the agency and to the country.

The third objective is the measure of the laboratory's compliance with all the federal rules, regulations, legislation, and even expectations. Such compliance includes GPRA, technology transfer and cooperation with industry and universities, security and confidentiality, and all the other regulations regarding human resources and the management of funds and facilities within the federal structure.[19]

Figure 17.3 illustrates the use of the key metrics discussed in this book as measures in the parent agency's evaluation of its laboratories. All these metrics are utilized to some degree, relative to the objective of the evaluation.

For some parent agencies the laboratories are a crucial component of the agency's activities and mission. In the case of the National Institutes of Health, although a large portion of the funding is outsourced in the form of grants, the in-house S&T in medicine and biology allows the NIH to allocate these resources to external organs, to monitor them, and to conduct crucial research in other areas. The Centers for Disease Control and Prevention also have a critical role in the guardianship of public health. The Food and Drug Administration has laboratories that maintain the regulatory system for food and pharmaceuticals.

So, the evaluation by the parent agency is not only directed toward accomplishing the agency's mission, but also to satisfy other federal departments, with their own regulations, legislation, and procedures, hence the need to utilize multiple metrics as shown in Figure 17.3.

Figure 17.3
Metrics in Evaluation of Federal Laboratories by Parent Agency

METRIC	ILLUSTRATIVE CATEGORIES OF EVALUATION
Economic/Financial	• On-cost performance of S&T projects and programs • GPRA requirements • Ability to "downsize" budgets while maintaining S&T support to agency
Bibliometrics	• Contribution to state of the art in relevant disciplines • Contributions to agency's programs, goals, and objectives by reporting agency-relevant progress and achievements • Indication of prestige of agency's labs
Patents	• Measure of S&T achievements in quantitative terms • Measure of relevancy to industry & economy
Peer Review	• Interlaboratory comparisons & evaluation within the agency • Comparison & evaluation of labs with other labs in government & industry • Input to allocation of S&T resources
Mapping of S&T	• Measure of S&T program within GPRA and technology transfer guidelines • Measure of S&T contributions to agency's programs

Evaluation by Others

As part of the federal framework, the S&T laboratories are also evaluated by Congress and the administration, by various government organizations, by the public, and by industry, universities, the academic community, and even foreign institutions. Figure 17.4 shows some of the uses of the metrics in this book for such evaluations.[20]

Figure 17.4
Metrics in Evaluation of Federal Laboratories by Others

Metric	ILLUSTRATIVE CATEGORIES OF EVALUATION
Economic/Financial	• Measures of cost-effectiveness • Spin-offs and contributions to the economy • Comparisons with industrial and foreign laboratories
Bibliometrics	• Comparisons with productivity of industrial and foreign laboratories • Measures of prestige & achievement • Measure of cost-effectiveness • Measure of cooperation with others
Patents	• Measure of economic/scientific productivity & cost-effectiveness • Comparison with other labs, industry, & foreign
Peer Review	• Measure of achievements • Measure of standing in the scientific community • Technical achievements and spin-offs to society and the economy • Comparisons with other labs
Mapping of S&T	• Measure of technology transfer • Measure of progress and relevancy

Each of these entities has its own objectives and utilizes one or more of the metrics in Figure 17.4. In the past several decades, the evaluation by Congress and successive administrations were generally positive, as funding for the federal laboratories continued to grow, and few criticisms (other than the call for privatization of some laboratories) have been leveled against them.

COOPERATION WITH INDUSTRY AND UNIVERSITIES

In the aftermath of the Stevenson-Wydler legislation of 1980 and subsequent legislation, the federal S&T laboratories have had to transfer technology to industry, hence to increase their contributions to society and the economy. These contributions were envisioned to occur beyond the outcomes that flow from the laboratories to their parent agency. The increase in "commercialization" effort on part of the laboratories has had mixed results.

Geisler and Clements (1995) studied the commercialization of technology from a sample of 43 federal laboratories to 51 industrial companies.[21] As measures of successful transfer they utilized: (1) number of Cooperative Research and Development Agreements signed by the parties, and (2) number of technologies licensed from the laboratories to industry. The authors recognized the paucity of these two measures in evaluating all the possible dimensions of success and accomplishments of such a complex cooperative effort.[22]

Therefore, they opted for *perceived* measures of success for both the laboratory and the company. For the laboratory they employed (1) improved public image that resulted from the cooperation; (2) internal benefits to the laboratory, such as incentives to scientists and engineers, economic benefits to the laboratory, benefits accrued from exchange of scientists and engineers, and benefits from joint research projects.

The use of number of CRADAs and income from licenses may be preferred as metrics of cooperative programs because the metrics are quantitative, easily attainable, and are deemed to represent the outcomes from the complex phenomenon of public-private cooperation. Yet additional metrics should be included, so as to measure other benefits to industry and federal laboratories. Some of these benefits are not directly quantifiable, but metrics such as mapping of S&T, peer review, and process outcomes hold a promise of more detailed and comprehensive, as well as more meaningful, evaluation.

A similar topic related to the evaluation of cooperation between federal laboratories and other entities is the issue of access to publicly funded S&T by foreign companies. David Mowery (1998) argued that with the decline in federal S&T investments in the United States, and the shift from basic to "relevant" research, the U.S. government has increasingly restricted cooperation with foreign firms.[23] He contended that such restrictions (which also occurred in the European Union) are counterproductive and lead to unnecessary conflicts and loss of potential benefits to both participants.

STATE AND REGIONAL INITIATIVES

Another aspect of public-sector support and cooperative enterprise in science and technology are the initiatives by individual American states, and by regional consortia. All of the 50 states are engaged, in one form or another, in supporting S&T and in fostering cooperation between universities, industry, and state organizations.

Feller (1986) studied the interactions between state governments and universities.[24] In a series of papers Feller argued that, although relatively of a limited nature—when compared to the federal investments—state programs fostering S&T are nevertheless cost-effective.[25] The motivation for individual states to foster S&T is threefold. First, states are particularly concerned with creating and maintaining jobs in manufacturing and, especially, in emerging fields of knowledge-based industries. The strong link between politics, economics, and S&T is consistently manifested in state initiatives.[26]

Second, states are cognizant of the need to maintain a quality workforce, particularly in the technical professions. Thus, they institute initiatives to improve the S&T level of their existing workers. Third, states are also sensitive to the exodus of graduates from their institutions of higher learning. Such a "brain drain" in some states has raised alarming notes in state capitals, with the resultant action to hold and even reverse such migration trends.[27]

States usually combine a variety of measures to foster their S&T environment. The most common are grants to universities and grants for cooperative programs between universities and industry. Another popular initiative is the support given to universities for emerging companies. These are generally created within research parks and university-owned consortia. Finally, states provide different forms of support, such as consulting, patent research, economic development programs targeted to high-tech companies and start-ups, and other financial assistance in training and capital expenditures.

Performance Evaluation

In a study of New York State's Center for Advanced Technology, Feller and Anderson (1999) computed the benefits to the state from their investments in such S&T programs.[28] They considered such benefits as increased productivity, increased or retained workers in the state, and improvements in the technical quality of technical workers.

Their cost-benefit analysis yielded the result that the program generated about three to six times the amount invested by the state. Such optimistic findings may be limited by several factors, such as the nature of the distribution of state funds to the various players (universities, industry), and the always present problem of imputation—from the R&D performed by universities, for example, to the heralded economic benefits to industry and to the state.

Regional S&T Initiatives

In addition to the individual state enterprises, some states have formed consortia anchored in geography. For example, the Southern Technology Council is a consortium of 15 states, supported by "ideas" paid by member states, and other grants.[29]

The consortium has attempted to establish performance benchmarks.[30] Among the indicators used in the study were patent applications, patents awarded, active licenses, royalties, licenses to start-ups, industry-sponsored R&D, and industry outreach and training.[31]

For the most part, these regional consortia are a depository of information and research outcomes that assist state governments in developing the S&T policies.

SUMMARY

In the second half of the 20th century, the United States has developed and maintained its enormous network of public laboratories. The perennial question that seems to arise is: Are these laboratories a good public investment? Is it worthwhile for the nation to spend public funds to maintain S&T institutions?

The American public has consistently and continually agreed that this is indeed a worthwhile investment. Even in the movement to privatize the laboratories, the arguments were in the need to ameliorate managerial inefficiencies, rather than fundamentally questioning the existence or the future of the system of laboratories.[32]

So the task now boils down to ways and metrics to measure the benefits and contributions from the federal laboratories. They are, in a sense, a national patrimony that presumably generates S&T outcomes that are, in the long run, quite beneficial to the economy, the public at large, and societal institutions.

As described earlier in this chapter, such benefits are of two kinds. First, there are benefits to the parent agency. For defense agencies, the laboratories contribute proprietary and highly tailored S&T, in many instances at the cutting edge, not found in any other source. Similarly, health-related agencies fund S&T that is committed to the public health and to combating diseases and health interests that otherwise would go unresearched. These laboratories are therefore "exclusive performers" for their parent agencies. Second, there are benefits to society and industry, so that the public—who funds these activities through tax dollars—is made aware of the inventions, innovations, and overall the betterment of life.

Crow and Bozeman (1998), who conducted numerous studies of the federal laboratories, have argued that these laboratories play a complex role in the American national S&T system.[33] They approached the federal laboratories as a system, and viewed their activities and outcomes in light of those of other S&T entities, such as industry and academia. Finally, they also argued that evaluators of the federal laboratories should recognize the limitations inherent in these laboratories as engines for commercialization.

This argument is sound and it fits with my view that the national S&T laboratories conduct S&T that is *not* done by other entities in the economy. Their contributions to society and the economy are primarily by virtue of and through their fundamental function as *national* laboratories, within the mission of their agency or their federal mandate. They carry out very large projects that are beyond the capabilities of industry, and that have broad national or public significance, urgency, or repercussions. Examples include the high-energy particle accelerator, space exploration and weather satellites, and programs funded by NIH in the search for the cure for cancer and AIDS. Another marvelous example is the Internet, which owes its origins to the National Science Foundation, the Department of Defense, and other governmental agencies in the mid-1960s.[34]

To understand and measure the outcomes of the national laboratories and their societal benefits beyond normative statement, the process-outcomes approach is the last possible method. As stages are identified in the process, metrics are assigned and calculated. The national laboratories produce S&T that, through selected transformations, find themselves adopted by economic and social entities, thus creating lasting benefits. The American public has always instinctively recognized this connection and the "good" that it has derived from publicly funded S&T. It's up to federal evaluators and scholars in this area to generate and to adequately apply meaningful metrics to this phenomenon.

NOTES

1. See, for example, Galvin, R., "Forming a World-Class Future for the National Laboratories," *Issues in Science and Technology*, Spring 1994, 44-51. Also see Radosevich, R., "A Model for Entrepreneurial Spin-Offs from Public Technology Sources," *International Journal of Technology Management*, 10(7/8), 1995, 879-894.

2. Pascal, Z., "End R&D Welfare," *Technology Review*, 101(6), 33-35.

3. Pascal also argued that neither the president nor any of the congressional leaders have an understanding of technological issues. In essence, Pascal's recommendations are to trim the funding for the national laboratories by $20 billion, and to divest these funds to: (1) corporate research tax credit, (2) create citizen councils to provide direction for national S&T, and (3) increase S&T investments in developing countries.

4. Although there is a growing literature in this area, I have limited this chapter to a summary of the metrics used in the evaluation of the federal laboratories. In so doing I may have left out some topics and perspectives of scholars or managers. For the sake of brevity and emphasis I opted for a highly focused chapter.

5. See, for example, National Science Foundation, *Technological Innovation and Federal Government Policy* (Washington, DC: Office of National R&D Assessment, 1976). This report concluded that "there are no well-defined criteria with which to formulate normative judgment about the rate and duration of innovation" (p. 45). Also see Burgess, J., "The Evaluation of a Government-Sponsored Research and Development Program," *IEEE Transactions on Engineering Management*, 13(2), 1966, 84-90. Burgess argued that a federal laboratory "must be evaluated against the long-range objectives and goals of its parent organization" (p. 86). He also distinguished between what he called "in-house-creative" activities (that deal with original ideas and exploratory S&T), and "in-house-noncreative" activities (that support the laboratory's mission and objectives).

6. See, for example, Soni. S., *Techtransfer and CRADA with Federal Laboratories* (New York: Adtech Systems Research, 1994). Also see Johnson, L., and D. Schaffer, *Oak Ridge National Laboratory: The First Fifty Years* (Nashville: University of Tennessee Press, 1994). See the opinion of a former president of Sandia National Laboratories who supports the national laboratory

system, in Dacey, G., "The U.S. Needs a National Technology Policy," *Research-Technology Management*, 38(1), 1995, 9-11.

7. See, for example, Hanson, D., "NIH Leads Government in Technology Transfer," *Chemical & Engineering News*, 77(29), 1999, 40-41. Also see Wenk, E., *Making Waves: Engineering, Politics, and the Social Management of Technology* (Urbana: University of Illinois Press, 1995); and, McLean, M., J. Anderson, and B. Martin, "Identifying Research Priorities in Public Sector Funding Agencies: Mapping Science Outputs on to User Needs," *Technology Analysis & Strategic Management*, 10(2), 1998, 139-155.

8. National Science and Technology Council, *Assessing Fundamental Science* (Washington, DC, July 1996).

9. See NIOSH, *Strategic Plan 1997-2002* (DHHS-NIOSH Publication No. 98-137, 1998).

10. Although NIOSH conducts research that complements the work of the Occupational Safety and Health Administration (OSHA), which is armed with the *enforcement* capabilities of the health and safety locus, the laboratory is subordinated to the Centers for Disease Control and Prevention, so that all health-related research may reside under one agency.

11. See, for example, Burstein, C., "Introducing Reengineering to Government," *Public Manager*, 24(1), 1995, 52-54. Also see Radosevich, R., and S. Kassicieh, "Strategic Challenges and Proposed Responses to Competitiveness Through Public-Sector Technology," *California Management Review*, 35(4), 1993, 33-39.

12. See, for example, Hebert, J., "Controversy Over Nuclear Espionage Hits Bomb Scientists Hard," *The Los Angeles Times*, August 20, 1999, 5-8. Also see Pear, R., "Suspect in Atom Secrets Case Publicly Denies Ading China," *The New York Times*, August 2, 1999, 7-9.

13. Pear, 1999, *op. cit.*, p. 7.

14. Hebert, 1999, *op. cit.*, p. 6.

15. See Federal Laboratory Consortium, *Newslink*, 15(10), 1999, p. 2.

16. Another salient example is research conducted by physicists at NOAA (National Oceanic and Atmospheric Administration) who had developed a noise-detection device for early warnings of tornadoes. This device has contributed to the saving of countless lives in tornado-prone areas. See the Internet site of the agency in <http://www.outlooik.NOAA.gov/tornadoes/>.

17. Some laboratories have instituted a weighting system for performance evaluation of their scientists. In some laboratories of the Department of Defense, for example, publishing received a factor of 1.0, whereas work in cooperative research and technology transfer was valued at 0.6.

18. Patents generated by federal laboratories may be licensed by companies at nominal rates. Recent legislation has allowed for more flexible terms for proprietary rights to individual companies in these CRADA arrangements with

federal labs. See, for example, U.S. General Accounting Office, *Diffusing Innovations: Implementing the Technology Transfer Act of 1986* (Washington, DC, 1991). Also see Ross, S., "DOE's Energy Technology Program Yields Commercial Inventions," *Technology Transfer Week*, 2(12), 1998,8-9; and see Reynolds, L., "Speeding Transfer of Technology," *Management Review*, 78(2), 1989, 56-62.

19. It should be emphasized at this point that this chapter is dedicated primarily to the American realities of publicly funded S&T institutions. International examples are given in Chapter 18.

20. Each of these institutions has its own evaluation objectives and preferred metrics. The figure provides some general illustrations of metrics that may be used by any or all of these organizations. The list of metrics is not exhaustive.

21. Geisler, E., and. C. Clements, "Commercialization of Technology from Federal Laboratories: The Effects of Barriers, Incentives, and the Role of Internal Entrepreneurship," Report to the National Science Foundation, Grant #94-01432, August 1995.

22. See, for example, Furino, A. (Ed.), *Cooperation and Competition in the Global Economy: Issues and Strategies* (New York: Ballinger Publishing Company, 1988). Also see Gibb, J. (Ed.), *Science Parks and Innovation Centers: The Economic and Social Impact* (Amsterdam: Elsevier, 1985). In particular see pages 81-90, the discussion of the concept of "tecnopolis." Also see the definition of "publicness" in Scott, P., and S. Falcone, "Comparing Public and Private Organizations: An Exploratory Analysis of Three Frameworks," *American Review of Public Administration*, 28(2), 1988, 126-145. Also see Falconer, M., and. I. Lapsley (Eds.), *Accounting and Measurement: Issues in the Private and Public Sectors* (New York: Paul Chapman, 1996).

23. See, for example, Hansen, N., "Privatization, Technology Choice, and Aggregate Outcomes," *Journal of Public Economics*, 64(2), 1997, 425-442. Also see Hale, W., "Modeling a New Technology Transfer Algorithm," Paper presented at the Second International Congress on Intellectual Property, McMaster University, January 1998.

24. Feller, I., *Universities and State Governments: A Study in Policy Analysis* (Westport, CT: Greenwood Press, 1986).

25. See, for example, Feller, I., "American State Governments as Models for National Science Policy," *Journal of Policy Analysis and Management*, 11(3), 1992, 288-309. Also see Feller, I., "Evaluating State Advanced Technology Programs," *Evaluation Review*, 12(2), 1988, 232-252; and, Feller, I., "Federal and State Government Roles in Science and Technology," *Economic Development Quarterly*, 11(4), 1997, 283-296.

26. See, for example, Mowery, D., "State Government Funding of Science and Technology: Lessons for Federal Programs?" in Meredith, M., S. Nelson, and A. Teich (Eds.), *Science and Technology Yearbook* (Washington, DC: American

Association for the Advancement of Science, 1991), pp. 241-250; and see Watkins, C., and J. Wells, "State Initiatives to Encourage Economic Development Through Technological Innovation," in Gray, D., T. Solomon, and W. Hetzner (Eds.), *Technological Innovation Strategies for a New Partnership* (Amsterdam: North Holland, 1986), pp. 273-285.

27. Louis Tornatzky of the Southern Technology Council has studied the movement of these graduates among states. He found an "exodus" trend in some Eastern states. See Tornatzky, L., "Where Have All the Students Gone?: S&E Personnel Migration," Presented at the Conference of Southern Graduate Schools, February 20, 1992. Also see Krasner, J., "Study Suggests Region Losing in Best Minds," *Wall Street Journal*, April 22, 1998, p. NE1.

28. Feller, I. and G. Anderson, "A Benefit-Cost Approach to the Evaluation of State Technology Development Programs," *Economic Development Quarterly*, 8(2), 1994, 127-141.

29. The mission of this regional group is to encourage development of the region by commercializing technology, and by promoting cooperative efforts among government, universities, and industry in the region.

30. See the complete instrument used in the study in the organization's website: <http://www.csgs.org>.

31. For additional information, see the publications of the State Science & Technology Institute (ISSTI) at website: <http://www.ssti.org>. In particular, see SSTI, *Performance Assessments & Evaluation Tools: A Comprehensive Bibliography of Current Literature* (Westerville, OH, 1998). The institute is "a national nonprofit organization dedicated to improving government-industry programs that encourage economic growth through the application of science and technology."

32. Mowery, D., "The Changing Structure of the U.S. National Innovation System: Implications for International Conflict and Cooperation in R&D Policy," *Research Policy*, 27(6), 1998, 639-654.

33. Crow, M., and B. Bozeman, *Limited by Design: R&D Laboratories in the U.S. National Innovation System* (New York: Columbia University Press, 1998).

34. See, for example, Hafner, K., and M. Lyon, *Where Wizards Stay Up Late: The Origins of the Internet* (New York: Simon & Schuster, 1996).

18

METRICS AND EVALUATION OF NATIONAL INNOVATION SYSTEMS

On July 20, 1999, the 30th anniversary of the first lunar landing, Daniel Golden, NASA administrator, wrote: "But Project Apollo was much more than a national achievement or a technological feat. The successful lunar landings are an extension of the basic human imperative to explore beyond where we currently are, to see what is "over there."[1]

The Apollo Program and the NASA experience were part of the national innovation and S&T system, as are the national laboratories, industrial R&D laboratories, universities, and all other S&T entities within the boundaries of a nation.

This chapter starts with a description of the national innovation system, and then raises key issues in the evaluation of such systems. Examples from several countries are discussed, as is the role of metrics in their evaluation.

WHAT ARE NATIONAL INNOVATION SYSTEMS?

In the case of science and basic research it is difficult to assert that there are distinct national communities of science. The relative ease of flow of data and findings across national boundaries lifts some, perhaps not all, of the truly national distinctions. But, as S&T activities and their progress are the result of many and diverse institutional players, there are also possibilities that certain combinations of resources and players (e.g., industry and government), and in certain fields of science or areas of technology, may form unique systems with distinct national characteristics.

The economists Richard Nelson and Nathan Rosenberg (1999)[2] argued that "although there are many areas of similarity between the systems of countries in comparable economic settings, there still are some striking differences as well" (p. 18).

An unambiguous definition of the concept of a national innovation system is yet to be developed.[3] Although national governments tend to treat their S&T capabilities as more or less a uniquely distinct "system," the best that we may identify is a structure of organizations engaged in S&T and their capabilities (scientific and technical inventories). This structure varies by discipline as well as over time, and reflects a complex web of interrelationships that also transcend national boundaries, in many instances in a seamless manner.

Some researchers have argued that the concept is a convenient way to "provide a unit of analysis through which to explain these changes and growing interactions."[4] The said changes are the dramatic changes in technologies and their relation to the economic progress of nations. Similarly, Lundvall (1998) suggested that, whereas there is a strong correlation between the level of innovation and the strength of the national economy, as it is measured by trade, there is also the possibility of classifying innovation as a national factor.[5]

While including "knowledge" as part of the innovation structure, there is a tendency, particularly by economists, to consider the S&T "stock" of a country as a factor in the country's economic progress. Although national boundaries are largely porous to the flow of knowledge, those who search for a definition of national innovation systems consider the uniqueness of the arrangement of S&T institutions and their stock of S&T knowledge different enough to constitute a definable architecture of a unique national character.[6]

INTERNATIONAL COMPETITION AND COOPERATION

Competition among nations in S&T leads to the "brain drain phenomenon" and the imposition by national governments of restrictions on S&T exchange and on technology-embedded products. However, there are also major programs of international cooperation in S&T: for example, a joint program by the United States, the European Union, Sweden, and Japan. The International Science and Technology Centers (ISTC) has supported thousands of scientists and engineers worldwide, including nuclear weapons technologists in Russia and elsewhere, so as to divert their skills to commercial uses.[7]

International exchange in S&T helps to close gaps in technology among countries, and through R&D spillovers trade is enhanced and markets are increased.[8] Similar outcomes occur when foreign direct investments are channeled to support indigenous S&T programs and institutions.[9]

INNOVATION SYSTEMS OF INDIVIDUAL COUNTRIES

In a process similar to the evaluation of biological systems, each country (and perhaps even larger geographical regions) have developed their S&T systems in unique ways. In addition to internal characteristics, each country has had continuous interactions with other countries, over long periods of time. Hence some "genetic" interface may have occurred so that some similarities exist among the various countries.[10]

Among the factors that have contributed to the singular attributes of the S&T system in individual countries are the behavioral, historical, and political antecedents. Historically, countries have progressed through different stages, reacting differently to historical landmark cataclysms. The Second World War generated a change in public attitudes toward S&T and the end of the Cold War has brought with it the conversion of S&T to civilian uses.

Existing capabilities are another factor. Although there were mutual flows of scientific personnel and investments between countries, certain countries have developed since the late Middle Ages a solid foundation of educational institutions and even departments and units of S&T that were attached to their military or other state establishments. Hence, differences in such a foundational platform that existed in Western Europe contributed to different paces in the development of S&T systems.

Another factor is the national will (and consensus) to allocate scarce resources to S&T, whether under the rubric of "development"—as some of the developing nations have been doing—or with the purpose of providing functional social benefits such as defense, health, and education. There are distinct differences among nations in the level of urgency in public opinion and the degree to which the political and scientific establishments react to it.[11]

Among the allocation of resources at the national level there were also distinctions in the acquisition of S&T human resources. The United States has been a magnet for S&T professionals in the decades since the Second World War. Although the process differs from industry to industry, the existence of resources and opportunities in American universities, industry, and public laboratories have provided a very attractive environment to scientists and engineers worldwide.

The strengths or weaknesses of the various components of a national innovation system are also paramount in fostering different rates of growth and development. Not only was there a need for strong and well-funded universities and industrial companies, but important variables also included the positive attitudes of the political system, support of the management style in these organizations, and social, ethical, and educational attitudes that foster S&T at various levels.

In Germany, the fusion of the technology infrastructure of private companies and public S&T institutes has contributed to a strong S&T base in the case of individual federal states, as well as in the country.[12] Even when S&T institutions are modeled precisely after those in other countries, there are differences due to national unique characteristics. The case of Russian small business incubators exemplifies such a phenomenon. The Zelenograd Scientific and Technical Park (founded in 1991) has been designed to assist small electronic companies, and was modeled after American university-based incubators. But Russia's difficulties in its transition economy have made the integration of graduating companies into the general economy a very difficult task.[13]

In the case of Israel, the innovation system that has emerged in the late 1990s was influenced by a unique perspective of national security, with ramifications into the government's S&T policies. Thus, very few large firms were allowed access to publicly held technology, so that a small network of major companies has evolved, hence composing the key elements of the national innovation system.[14]

HOW TO MEASURE THESE SYSTEMS?

The complex nature of national S&T systems begs a broad measurement of its distinct structures and performance. In the case of the robotics industry in Japan, Kumaresan and Miyazaki (1999) have suggested the metrics of *patents, publications*, and *market-related data*.[15]

These metrics are illustrative of the use of some traditional measurements as bibliometrics and patents.

But there are other aspects of the national innovation system that need to be measured. Outcome measures such as patents and publications, and even some market-related measures do not offer a comprehensive measure of the strengths or weaknesses, nor of the structure of the national system. Whether implemented in the case of a single industry, or at the overall *national* level, there is a need to also assess the *structural* capabilities of universities, industry, and public laboratories—and the network and mechanisms that they form and employ in their interactions.[16]

Another model across industries assesses the benefits to society and the economy from selected innovations. Some researchers have argued that the social influences that are computed for these innovations are larger than private returns.[17] One reason may be the complexity of the national system, so that the benefits to industry are only a portion of the overall benefits to other beneficiaries such as universities, government, and the public at large.[18]

A more appropriate and much more promising model is the process-outcomes approach. In this model the progress of S&T is traced throughout the innovation continuum. By doing so, we are able to identify those organizations that transform S&T outcomes along the way, and that also *benefit from them*. Second, we are also able to compute, cumulatively, the sum total of benefits at each juncture, and at the national level.[19]

ISSUES OF GROWTH AND WEALTH

Among the difficult issues that emerge from the analysis of national systems of innovation are: (1) the relation of each system to economic growth, and (2) their relation to the differences in the wealth of nations. Economists, development scientists, and those interested in management of S&T and innovation have struggled with the manner in which they should consider innovation: as an element of wealth or simply as a factor that helps to impact the pace and the progress of growth and accumulation of national wealth.[20]

As an element of wealth, S&T and innovation are viewed in light of their contribution to the economic activity of the nation. But, as a factor in the wealth of nations, there are two salient approaches. The first explores the role of innovation in the "long waves" concept of economic cycles.[21] This approach suggests that innovations give rise to new industries, which in turn are the driving force in economic growth. The cyclical behavior of economic activity may thus be explained by the time frame for innovations to be transformed, adopted, and in their ability to create new industries or to vastly improve the efficiency of existing industries.

Rosenberg and Frishtak (1994) have eloquently summarized the topic.[22] They concluded that "none of the present day authors who work within a neo-Schumpeterian paradigm has clearly specified the causal links connecting innovation, investment, and aggregate rates of growth" (p. 83). They also argued that "the essential exercise of measuring the impact of a set of major innovations upon the economy as a whole has yet to be undertaken by any long-wave proponent" (p. 83), and that "the conceptual framework of a model of long waves in economic growth which has at its core the process of technological innovation, has still not been adequately formulated" (p. 83).

SUMMARY

A national innovation system is a construct that has been the subject of differing definitions and interpretations. A complex array of institutions, relationships, and other attributes of the national economy and society makes it very difficult to interpret the S&T/innovation phenomenon and to measure its role and impact on national affairs and growth.[23]

However we measure, and whichever metrics are employed, we are always limited in that such measures capture only a portion of the overall phenomenon. A country may have advantages in one aspect of innovation (for example, competency in basic science) but have also poor competency in other aspects (such as mechanism for technology transfer and commercialization of innovations by industry).

The emphasis should be on the "system" perspective, so that the strengths of innovation can only be construed and measured in light of the underlying competencies of the national economy, its societal dimensions, its political framework, and its dedication to S&T.

NOTES

1. *Chicago Tribune*, "Apollo's Lessons Lead Us Into Future," July 21, 1993, Section 1, p. 18.

2. Nelson, R., and M. Rosenberg, "Technical Innovation and National Systems," In: R. Nelson (Ed.), *National Innovation Systems: A Comparative Analysis* (New York: Oxford University Press, 1993) pp. 3-21.

3. See, for example, Dosi, G., C. Freeman, R. Nelson, G. Silverberg, and L. Soete, *Technical Change and Economic Theory* (London: Pinter Publications, 1988).

4. Mothe, J., and G. Paquet, "National Innovation Systems, Real Economies, and Instituted Processes," *Small Business Economics*, 11(2), 1998, p. 101.

5. Lundvall, B., "Why Study National Systems and National Styles of Innovation?" *Technology Analysis & Strategic Management*, 10(4), 1998, 407-421.

6. See, for example, Lundvall, B. (Ed.), *National Systems of Innovation: Towards a Theory of Innovation and Interactive Learning* (London: Pinter Publishers, 1992). Lundvall advanced the thesis that a *national* S&T system is dependent upon *learning*, which is an activity anchored in national and local institutions and funded by national governments with their unique attributes and programs. Also see Archibugi, D., and J. Michie (Eds.), *Trade, Growth, and Technical Change*(New York: Cambridge University Press, 1998).

7. Scott, W., "Projects Attempt to Preclude Brain Drain," *Aviation Week & Space Technology*, 146(26), 1997, 54-56.

8. See, for example, Glass, A., and K. Saggi, "International Technology Transfer and the Technology Gap," *Journal of Development Economics*, 55(2), 1998, 369-398. Also see Bayoumi, T., D. Coe, and E. Helpman, "R&D Spillovers and Global Growth," *Journal of International Economics*, 47(2), 1999, 399-428.

9. See, for example, Okamoto, H., and A. Woodland, "North-South Trade, Income Distribution, and Welfare Effects of R&D Policy," *Review of International Economics*, 6(1), 1998, 15-29. Also see Glass, A., and K. Saggi, "Foreign Direct Investment and the Nature of R&D," *The Canadian Journal of Economics*, 32(1), 1999, 92-117.

10. See, for example, Cohen, S., and J. Zysman, "The Myth of a Post-Industrial Economy," *Technology Review*, February/March, 1987, 55-62. The authors argued that "the U.S. is not shifting from industry to services but from one kind of industrial economy to another" (p. 59). Also see Pack, H., and K. Saggi, "Influence of Foreign Technology and Indigenous Technological Development," *Review of Developmental Economics*, 1(2), 1997, 81-98.

11. See, for example, Fortes, M., and A. Novais, "The Conditions for the Development of a Biotechnology Industry in Portugal: The Impact of Country Specific Factors," *Technology Analysis & Strategic Management*, 10(4), 1998, 497-509. The authors list three basic factors that influenced the development of this industry in Portugal: (1) the country's scientific capabilities; (2) the infrastructure that allows for technology transfer to industrial firms; and (3) the manufacturing foundation and its stock of knowledge. Also see the example of a

pharmaceuticals industry in Cockburn, I., and R. Henderson, "Absorptive Capacity, Coauthoring Behavior, and the Organization of Research in Drug Discovery," *The Journal of Industrial Economics*, 46(2), 1998, 157-183.

12. See, Blind, K., and H. Grupp, "Interdependencies Between the Science and Technology Infrastructure and Innovation Activities in German Regions: Empirical Findings and Policy Consequences," *Research Policy*, 28(5), 1999, 451-468.

13. See, Bruton, G., "Incubators as a Small Business Support in Russia: Contrast of University-Related U.S. Incubators with the Zeteragrad Scientific and Technology Park," *Journal of Small Business Management*, 36(1), 1998, 91-94.

14. See Veckstein, D., "Defense Conversion, Technology Policy, and R&D Networks in the Innovation System of Israel," *Technovation*, 19(10), 1999, 615-629.

15. Kumaresan, N., and K. Miyazaki, "An Integrated Network Approach to Systems of Innovation: The Case of Robotics in Japan," *Research Policy*, 28(6), 1999, 563-585.

16. See, for example, Burke, J., 'How R&D Is Shaping the 21st Century Railroad," *Railway Age*, 199(8), 1998, 55-62.

17. See, for example, Tewksbury, J., M. Cranoak, and W. Crane, "Measuring the Societal Benefits of Innovation," *Science*, 209, 8 August 1980, 658-662.

18. See, Jones, C., and J. Williams, "Measuring the Social Returns of R&D," *The Quarterly Journal of Economics*, 113(4), 1998, 1119-1135; and Donlon, J., "The Great Innovation Debate," *Chief Executive*, 134(2), 1998, 56-65. These authors discuss the issue of productivity and its link to the state of innovation. But this is a very limited view of the returns of S&T and innovation to society and the economy.

19. Other metrics described in this book are also applicable at the national level. Peer review is widely used to generate comparisons of the state of S&T/innovation among countries and regions. See, for example, Millar, A., and D. Plesch, "Pushing the Envelope Too Far?: Technology's Impact on NATO Expansion," *Journal of International Affairs*, 51(2), 1998, 641-653. Also see, Wagner, C., "International Cooperation in Research and Development," RAND Institute, Santa Monica, CA, accessible at: <http://www.rand.org>. In this report the author suggested the following metrics: (1) bibliometrics, (2) patent metrics, (3) international prizes such as the Nobel prize, and (4) consumer surplus or social rates of return from S&T. Also see Niosi, J., "The Globalization of Canada's R&D," *Management International Review*, 37(4), 1997, 387-404.

20. See, for example, Dixon, J., and K. Hamilton, "Expanding the Measure of Wealth," *Finance & Development*, 33(4), 1996, 15-18. The authors argued that agricultural land is the main natural resource, and human resources are the key component of wealth. Hence, they propose that "social capital," which may include innovation "which is difficult to both define and to measure, is an amalgam of

individual and institutional relationships that determines why one society is more effective than another in transforming a given endowment of assets into sustained well-being" (p. 16). Also see Peretto, P., "Cost Reduction, Entry, and the Interdependence of Market Structure and Economic Growth," *Journal of Monetary Economics*, 43(1), 1999, 173-195. Also see, Tassey, G., *The Economics of R&D Policy* (Westport, CT: Quorum Books, 1997). Tassey argued that those countries with the "best" combination of strategies to invest in S&T in both the private and the public sectors (with their different investment incentives) will be in a better position to survive and prosper.

21. See a summary of this topic in Ray, G., "Innovation as the Source of Long-Term Economic Growth," *Long Range Planning*, 13(2), 1980, 9-19.

22. Rosenberg, N., and C. Frishtak, "Technological Innovation and Long Waves," in N. Rosenberg, *Exploring the Black Box: Technology, Economics, and History* (New York: Columbia University Press, 1994) pp. 62-84.

23. See, for example, authors such as David Landes, who suggested that the interaction between an "open society" mode of political and economic system, and the creation and commercialization of new technology may be the key to understanding why some countries are rich and others poor. See Landes, D., *The Wealth and Poverty of Nations: Why Some Are So Rich and Some So Poor* (New York: W. W. Norton & Company, 1998). Scientific knowledge and technological capabilities are, in Landes' view, the factors that had "jump started" national economies and have provided them with the comparative advantage to grow and to accumulate wealth.

19

<u>VALUES, ETHICS, AND IMPLICATIONS</u>

Did science and technology bring us added happiness in this incredibly productive 20th century? Can we resolve the persistent issues of ethical challenges as in the continuing erosion of our privacy, and the maltreatment of our home planet brought about by S&T?

In my view, although these are valid questions, they are nevertheless the wrong questions posed by philosophers, ethicists, and environmentalists. In his book on the reasons for the schism between rich and poor nations, David Landes (1998) concluded by criticizing his critics.[1] He said:

Note that my assumption of the ultimate advantage and beneficence of scientific knowledge and technological capability is today under sharp attack, even in the Academy. The reasons for this reaction, often couched in preferences for *feeling* over *knowing*, range from disappointment at Paradise Unfound to fear and resentment by laymen of unknowable knowledge. Some of the anti's are millenarians...others are nostalgics, harking back to the mythic blessings of stateless, communal, primitive societies (p. 513).

In this chapter I have attempted to explore some of the values and ethical questions that should be asked of S&T and of the road that lies ahead. After all, this book is about evaluation of S&T, and its thesis has considered the interdisciplinary model of S&T and the role it has played (and will continue to play) in the economy, society, and in human life.

WHAT SHOULD WE ASK?

The questions that we should be asking of the state of S&T are more practical and perhaps less provocative than the usual criticisms. Those who berate S&T for the negative side effects they create (at the very least) to their destructive prowess (at worst) are well-intentioned members of society who function within the framework of our economic system. Yet they promote their criticisms while enjoying the fruits of S&T developments and progress. Even those who prefer the non-S&T lifestyle of the bucolic existence in primitive surroundings are nevertheless exploiting the S&T progress by, perhaps, reading books or toiling the soil with improved seeds. Less extremist critics surf the Internet, utilize present-day health care, and have living conditions that surpass the wildest dreams of their foreparents. All this clearly comes at a price—hence the questions we should ask.

Before we do ask, S&T is not only all around us, but it is growing in perhaps an exponential manner. In 1962, Derek de Solla Price conjured that perhaps 80 to 90% of all scientists that have ever lived are alive today.[2] In the four decades since, the number has perhaps climbed to over 90%. There is a virtual explosion in the scientific and technical output worldwide. New journals are constantly created. New patents are continually being registered. New materials, processes, innovations, and inventions are being generated and equally commercialized.

So we should first ask: "Is our life more comfortable?" This is a complex question that includes queries on: how we live, how we learn, how we keep healthy, how we move, how we raise our young, how we eat, how we dress, how we energize our homes and our machines, how we procreate, how we compute and count, how we communicate with each other, how we defend ourselves, how we work, and how we entertain ourselves.[3]

For each query we may wish to create a matrix of innovations, as shown in the example of Figure 19.1. Just a few innovations, some dating back to the early 20th century and to the middle of the century, have had tremendous influence over several aspects of our lives. They have impacted the way we learn, communicate, move, energize, and even raise our children.

Figure 19.1
An Illustrative Matrix of S&T Innovations and the Queries of Our Life

QUERIES	Illustrative S&T Innovations*				
	Transistor	Penicillin	Double-Helix	Airplane	[Future?]
•How we live	✓	✓	✓	✓	?
•How we learn	✓				?
•How we keep healthy	✓	✓	✓		?
•How we work	✓			✓	?
•How we move	✓			✓	?
•How we raise our young	✓	✓	✓	✓	?
•How we eat	✓	✓	✓	✓	?
•How we dress					?
•How we energize	✓				?
•How we procreate		✓	✓		?
•How we count	✓				?
•How we communicate	✓				?
•How we defend ourselves	✓	✓	✓	✓	?
•How we entertain	✓			✓	?
Values**	V_1	V_2	V_3	V_4	?

Future innovations that will emerge from current S&T activities
**For each cell we may wish to compute the value of the innovation to the appropriate aspect or query. This would be a measure of the benefits accrued to the aspect of our life. The sum total across the matrix would measure the total benefits of S&T for a set of innovations. Individual cells are values to the person, whereas the sum total is value to society.*

Another query we need to ask: "Do we have more answers and solutions to our problems?" S&T cannot solve every problem that society and our limitations as humans within our environment have created and continue to do so. But the issue is the relative increment to our stock of answers. S&T have helped us to find answers to questions we keep asking and to the limits of our morbidity and mortality from countless diseases. S&T, among other things, helped us to reduce the impacts from natural disasters.

"Did we extend human life?" In many countries the life expectancy has been constantly rising in this century. Diseases that once roamed the planet are now extinct.   The *distribution* and allocation of these achievements are a social and political problem in many poor countries and even in some less fortunate regions of richer countries.

Finally, "do we *know* more now than when we left the caves in search of the mysteries that resided in the outside world?" S&T have enhanced the human pool of knowledge.

The growth of S&T in the 20th century alone has been nothing less than phenomenal. We have almost come to *expect* that S&T will not only be an integral part of our lives, but will continue, indefinitely, and with renewed vigor, to furnish us with pathbreaking discoveries, inventions, and innovations in almost every facet of our existence.[4]

The average high school pupils today, at the dawn of the 21st century, have more knowledge at their disposal and are required to learn more in S&T than the most advanced scientist in the early days of the 20th century. This, of course, is disconcerting to the high-school teenager, but to society at large it is a giant step in the generation and transfer of knowledge. What a hundred years ago was the exotic knowledge of eccentric dabblers in scientific adventures, is today essential *background* knowledge for children.

Ethical Issues and the Nature of S&T

Ethical issues embedded in the role of S&T in our lives can be divided in two major categories: (1) those that are *inherent* in the nature of S&T, and (2) those that are caused by other factors. The first issue is the host of ethical questions that arise from the power unleashed by scientific discoveries and technological achievements. The potential harmful effects of nuclear radiation and nuclear weapons, and the wide range of impacts from the use of computers and automation are illustrations of both expected and unexpected consequences of S&T.[5] In many instances the scientists and engineers who explored and built such S&T have not considered the possible negative impacts.

"Disastrous Schism"

The second issue is the relation of S&T to negative consequences, but via other factors. The "disastrous schism" of S&T in human history has always been that S&T outcomes are imagined and brought to reality by scientists, engineers, and technologists. Yet these outcomes are applied, misapplied, and used/abused by leaders or managers in government and industry, who do not adequately understand them, their potential, and their power.[6]

Such a schism explains the ethical outrage of scientists on several topics and technologies and the futile attempts (such as that of physicists during the Second World War to stop the development of the atomic bomb) to influence the decisions on their inventions. The schism is one of the allocations of resources and utilization of the stock of S&T outputs and knowledge. It is also a matter of proprietorship, as the ownership of these inventions and the knowledge associated with them seldom belongs to the scientists.

A direct consequence of the schism is manifested in the current debate on patenting the sequence of human genetic material. Should such discoveries be patented by individual companies? Who does the human genome belong to: the company that decodes it? the individual human being? the scientists who did the decoding? the state or nation? or humanity at large?[7]

Each ethical decision will involve far-reaching consequences of the pace, price, and potential generation, commercialization, and utilization of S&T outcomes—those involved with the decision and future ones. Ethical answers are heavily priced. Yet each side in the debate tends to assume a position of either morality or economic necessity, while usually ignoring the possible effects on the future of S&T.

SUMMARY

In the foreseeable future we shall continue to argue with each other about the benefits and negative impacts of S&T. We will also continue to evaluate S&T with a myriad of old and perhaps new metrics.

But we must be certain to ask the right questions and to use appropriate metrics in our investigation of these questions. A more comfortable, longer, more satisfying, and more challenging life for an increasing number of human beings seems to me to be the ultimate goals of S&T. The road to these is bumpy, studded with political, social, and organizational barriers, some of which are inherent in the process and cannot be overcome.

Let us always remember that a better and happier life is due to many factors, of which S&T are only one, albeit a strong enabler of betterment of many aspects of our existence.[8] Has S&T given us more good than harm? You bet!

NOTES

1. Landes, D., *The Wealth and Poverty of Nations: Why Some Are So Rich and Some So Poor* (New York: W. W. Norton & Company, 1998).
2. Price, D. deSolla, *Science Since Babylon* (New Haven, CT: Yale University Press, 1992).
3. These queries are adapted from the Extra Millennium Issue of *Newsweek*, Winter 1997-1998.
4. See, for example, Conceição, P., D. Gibson, M. Heitor, and S. Shariq, *Science, Technology, and Innovation Policy: Opportunities and Challenges for the Knowledge Economy* (Westport, CT: Quorum Books, 2000).
5. See, for example, Brandon, K., "Science's Fantastic Growth Prompts Call for Ethics Code," *Chicago Tribune*, August 8, 1999, Section 1, p. 13. Also see Bodner, G., "Ethics in Science," *Chemtech*, May 1991, 274-280. Also see, Pacey, A., *Technology in World Civilization* (Cambridge, MA: The MIT Press, 1990), and see Coyne, R., *Technoromanticism: Digital Narrative, Holism, and the Romance of the Real* (Cambridge, MA: The MIT Press, 1999).
6. See, for example, the issue of AIDS and distribution of drugs in Dowell, W., "Ethics and AIDS Drugs," *Time*, July 12, 1999, p. 49.
7. See, for example, Yuthas, K., and J. Dillard, "Ethical Development of Advanced Technology: A Postmodern Stakeholder Perspective," *Journal of Business Ethics*, 19(1), 1999, 35-49.
8. Consider the case of the Internet. This technology has opened several avenues of radical change and progress in the ways we learn, communicate, and heal ourselves. The Internet has enabled telemedicine to develop rapidly. It also dramatically changed the face of business ("e-commerce"). In a revolution similar to that of the Sears catalog, it has provided people in remote areas the possibilities of *worldwide* shopping and worldwide access to information, knowledge, and training/education.

The Internet has brought together people from different cultures who now have a "technology" in common. It has also allowed for total communication, pictorial and verbal, across political, social, and geographical boundaries. We are yet to understand and to experience the full battery of consequences from this technology. But, whatever the negative impacts may be, the wide array of benefits will overshadow any harm the Internet may have caused. See, for example, Wilder, C., "E-Transformation," *Infomation Week*, September 13, 1999, 44-64. The author lists the radical changes that the Internet is creating in business enterprise. He argued that this change is powered by five driving factors: (1) speed, (2) knowledge, (3) culture, (4) technology, and (5) talented people. The major changes included interaction with customers, role of the technology in the business, allowing workers to solve more problems, and changeover of business processes to e-commerce.

Also see the special report on "e-life" in *Newsweek*, September 20, 1999. The magazine described the changes created by the Internet in American business, health care delivery, social relations, family affairs, politics, education, and science. Also see an interesting collection of interviews with 50 top scientists in their respective disciplines about the future of S&T: Bell, T., and D. Dooling, *Engineering Tomorrow: Today's Technology Experts Envision the Next Century* (Piscataway, NJ: IEEE Press, 2000).

EPILOGUE

The heights by great men reached and kept,
Were not attained by sudden flight,
For they while their companions slept
Were toiling upward in the night.
                    Henry Wadsworth Longfellow
                    (1807-1882)

The previous chapters may have been a dramatic consolidation of positive outlooks on S&T. I am convinced that human society is much better off with than without S&T. Knowledge and its exploitation for the common good are better than ignorance and lack of capabilities. There are of course extremes, like the use of S&T in the exterminations practiced in Nazi death camps.

But the fact remains that S&T are merely *tools* by which people extend their limited capacities—some for good, other for evil. The sum total over human history, however, has been surprisingly positive.

As I was starting this book, I began to realize the immensity of this tall order. I had to walk the fine line between simply collecting the knowledge on metrics and commenting on their use and effectiveness—and the evaluation of S&T in general, including the philosophical and ethical ramifications.

In this effort to balance the two perspectives I marveled at the unbounded growth of S&T during my lifetime, and at the promises and dangers that lie ahead. Perhaps more than in other human activities and avocations, S&T is an arduous pursuit of fleeting accomplishments. Hard work, careful planning, and enormous inputs of knowledge and perseverance are the criteria for any successful S&T endeavor. When Thomas Alva Edison argued that invention is mostly perspiration, he was only partially correct. The road to invention is littered with failures, desolation, hope, retrial, dreams, and the earthquakes of reality. But, in modern S&T it is also the sum total of the endeavors of many individuals and complex organizations.

Derek de Solla Price has argued for a convergence of S&T and the humanities, and in favor of a measured growth of S&T in line with other dimensions of society, such as size of population, its wealth, and the arts. But the consequences of S&T are sometimes so intensive as to baffle those involved in them and those who are mere spectators to the phenomenon.

On November 1, 1999, the Dow Jones Industrial Average replaced four companies among its prestigious capitalistic club of 30 member companies: Chevron Corporation, Sears Roebuck, Goodyear Tire & Rubber Company, and Union Carbide. In their place, the club accepted as members: Microsoft, Intel, SBC Communications, and Home Depot Inc. Observers have commented that these changes show a move away from companies engaged in physical capital to those that work with S&T and knowledge.

In my view, we have not just discovered the value of S&T and knowledge as critical assets in the economy. Companies such as Goodyear and Union Carbide have consistently resorted to well-funded R&D. The real change is that we, as a society, are now in a position to emphasize and recognize the role that S&T and knowledge are playing. But do we also know how to adequately measure these trends and their consequences, so that we may face the challenges ahead?

Making S&T more "humanistic" may not be the full answer. Advances in S&T have surpassed our simplistic comprehension, as Albert Einstein stated some 50 years ago. The capabilities that S&T have given us are more advanced than our moral, legal, or administrative stock of tools. An excellent example is the discoveries in the area of human genetics.

If there is one fundamental conclusion that emerges from this book, it is that S&T must be evaluated in a systemic view, with its consequences not only on the inventing person or organization, but on society and the economy. There has always been a strange, often conflict-laden relationship between scientists and those who funded and implemented their discoveries. S&T has reached a point and level of influence in our lives that it is not enough to leave it in the hands of either of the parties. Does this mean added regulations? In my view the answer lies not in additional control but in better measurement and evaluation of where S&T is heading, and with what consequences. I would like to believe that this book is a token contribution in this endeavor.

SELECTED BIBLIOGRAPHY

This is an eclectic selection of publications that are relevant to the topics in this book. This list is not exhaustive, nor a comprehensive review of the available body of work. The selected items will provide the reader with an initial perspective into the focused area of metrics of science and technology. Some of these items were previously listed in the book. All the selections reflect a broad spectrum of opinions, theses, schools of thought, and methodologies.

Adelman, L., and S. Riedel. *Handbook for Evaluating Knowledge-Based Systems: Conceptual Framework and Compendium of Methods.* Boston: Kluwer Academic Publishers, 1997.

Allen, T. *Managing the Flow of Technology.* Cambridge, MA: MIT Press, 1977.

Allison, D. (Ed.). *The R&D Game: Technical Men, Technical Managers, and Research Productivity.* Cambridge, MA: MIT Press, 1969.

Alston, J., G. Norton, and P. Pardey (Eds.). *Science Under Scarcity: Principles and Practice for Agricultural Research Evaluation and Priority Setting.* New York: CAB International, 1998.

Antonelli, C. *The Microdynamics of Technological Change.* London: Routledge, 1999.

Baiagioli, M (Ed.). *The Science Studies Reader.* London: Routledge, 1999.

Baker, E., and H. O'Neill (Eds.). *Technology Assessment.* New York: Lawrence Erlbaum Associates, 1994.

Basalla, G. *The Evolution of Technology.* Cambridge: Cambridge University Press, 1988.

Becher, G., and S. Kuhlmann (Eds.). *Evaluation of Technology Policy Programs in Germany.* Amsterdam: Kluwer Academic Publishers, 1995.

Beije, P. *Technological Change in the Modern Economy: Basic Topics and New Developments.* New York: Edward Elgar, 1999.

Betz, F. *Managing Technological Innovation: Competitive Advantage from Change.* New York: John Wiley & Sons, 1997.

Bimber, B. *The Politics of Expertise in Congress: The Rise and Fall of the Office of Technology Assessment.* Albany: State University of New York Press, 1997.

Boer, P. *The Evaluation of Technology: Business and Financial Issues in R&D.* New York: John Wiley & Sons, 1999.

Bohm, D., and D. Peat. *Science, Order, and Creativity.* London: Routledge, 2nd Edition, 2000.

Bond, J. *Science and Engineering Indicators (1998).* Washington, DC: Diane Publishing Company, 1999.

Bright, J. *Research, Development, and Technological Innovation.* Homewood, IL: Irwin, 1964.

Chubin, D., and E. Hackett. *Peerless Science: Peer Review and U.S. Science Policy.* Albany: State University of New York Press, 1990.

Crangle, R. *Technology Innovation: Research, Development, and the Patent Process.* New York: Crantech Research Publishing, 1998.

Cruishank, J., and D. Sicilia. *The Engine That Could: 75 Years of Value-Driven Change at Cummins Engine Company.* Boston: Harvard Business School Press, 1997.

Dean, B. V., and J. Goldhar (Eds.). *Management of Research and Innovation.* New York: North-Holland, 1980.

Dilts, D., D. Bialik, and L. Haber. *Assessing What Professors Do: An Introduction to Academic Performance Appraisal in Higher Education.* Westport, CT: Greenwood Press, 1994.

Dosi, G., D. Teece, and J. Chytry (Eds.). *Technology, Organization, and Competitiveness: Perspectives on Industrial and Corporate Change.* New York: Oxford University Press, 1997.

Drucker, P. *Innovation and Entrepreneurship: Practice and Principles.* New York: Harper & Row, 1986.

Duchin, F. *Structural Economics: Measuring Change in Technology, Lifestyles, and the Environment.* New York: Island Press, 1998.

Edquist, C. *Systems of Innovation: Technologies, Institutions, and Organizations.* New York: Books International, 1997.

Ellis, L. *Evaluation of R&D Processes: Effectiveness Through Measurements.* New York: ARTech House, 1997.

Elster, J. *Explaining Technological Change: A Case Study in the Philosophy of Science.* New York: Cambridge University Press, 1983.

Feenberg, A. *Questioning Technology.* London: Routledge, 1999.

Forsyth, T. *Positive Measures for Technology Transfer Under the Climate Change Convention.* Washington, DC: The Brookings Institution Press, 1998.

Fox, R. *Technological Change: Methods and Themes in the History of Technology.* London: Gordon & Breach, 1998.

Frankel, M. *Evaluating Science and Scientists: An East-West Dialogue on Research in Post-Communist Europe.* Prague: Central University Press, 1997.

Fransman, M. *Visions of Innovation: The Firm and Japan.* New York: Oxford University Press, 1999.

Freeman, C. *The Economics of Industrial Innovation.* Cambridge, MA: MIT Press, 2nd edition, 1986.

Gao Zheng, J. *Meeting Technology's Advance: Social Change in China and Zimbabwe in the Railway Age.* Westport, CT: Greenwood Press, 1997.

Geisler, E. *Methodology, Theory, and Knowledge in the Managerial and Organizational Sciences: Actions and Consequences.* Westport, CT: Quorum Books, 1999.

Ginn, M. *The Creativity Challenge: Management of Innovation and Technology.* Stamford, CT: JAI Press, 1995.

Ginzberg, E. (Ed.). *Technology and Social Change.* New York: Columbia University Press, 1964.

Goel, R. *Economic Models of Technological Change: Theory and Applications.* Westport, CT: Greenwood Press, 1999.

Gold, B. (Ed.). *Technological Change: Economics, Management, and Environment.* New York: Pergamon Press, 1975.

Griliches, Z. (Ed) *R&D, Patents, and Productivity.* Chicago: University of Chicago Press, 1984.

Griliches, Z. (Ed.). *R&D and Productivity: The Econometric Evidence.* Chicago: University of Chicago Press, 1998.

Grupp, H. *Methodology for Identifying Emerging Generic Technologies: Recent Experiences From Germany, Japan, and the USA.* Karlsrutte: Fraunhofer Institute for Systems and Innovation Research, 1992.

Gu, S. *China's Industrial Technology: Market Reform and Organizational Change.* London: Routledge, 1999.

Guerard, J., and A. Bean. *R&D Management and Corporate Financial Policy.* New York: John Wiley & Sons, 1997.

Harmon, R. *Reinventing the Business: Preparing Today's Enterprise for Tomorrow's Technology.* New York: The Free Press, 1996.

Harvard Business Review Staff. *Technology Fountainheads: The Management Challenge of R&D Consortia.* New York: McGraw-Hill, 1996.

Hensley, O. *The Classification of Research.* Lubbock: Texas Tech University Press, 1988.

Hiskes, R. *Democracy, Risk, and Community: Technological Hazards and the Evolution of Liberalism.* New York: Oxford University Press, 1998.

Holton, G. *Science and Anti-Science.* Cambridge, MA: Harvard University Press, 1993.

Irvine, J. *Evaluating Applied Research.* New York: St. Martin's Press, 1988.

Jackson, D. *Technological Change, the Learning Curve, and Profitability.* New York: Edward Elgar, 1998.

Johnson, S. *Interface Culture: How New Technology Transforms the Way We Create and Communicate.* New York: Basic Books, 1999.

Jolly, V. *Commercializing New Technologies: Getting From Mind to Market.* Boston: Harvard Business School Publishing, 1997.

Kanter, R. *The Change Masters: Innovation and Entrepreneurship in the American Corporation.* New York: Simon & Schuster Trade, 1985.

Kanter, R., F. Wieserma, and J. Kao. *Innovation: Breakthrough Ideas at 3M, DuPont, GE, Pfizer, and Rubbermaid.* New York: Harper Business, 1997.

Kasper, R. (Ed.). *Technology Assessment: Understanding the Social Consequences of Technology Applications.* New York: Praeger Publishers, 1972.

Kleinfield, I. *Engineering Economics: Analysis for Evaluation of Alternatives.* New York: John Wiley & Sons, 1997.

Lacey, H. *Is Science Value Free?* London: Routledge, 1999.

Link A., and J. Scott. *Public Accountability: Evaluating Technology-Based Institutions.* Boston: Kluwer Academic Publishers, 1998.

Little, L., and P. Hollis. *Motivation and Performance of Older Australian Academics: A Pilot Study.* Camberra: Australian Government Publishing Service, 1991.

Mackenzie, D. *Knowing Machines: Essays on Technical Change.* Cambridge, MA: MIT Press, 1988.

MaLecki, E. *Technology and Economic Development: The Dynamics of Local, Regional, and National Change.* Reading, MA: Addison-Wesley-Longman, 1996.

Mankin, D., T. Bikson, and S. Cohen. *Teams and Technology: Fulfilling the Promise of New Organization.* Boston: Harvard Business School Press, 1996.

Mansfield, E. *The Economics of Technological Change.* New York: W W. Norton, 1968.

Mar, B., W. Newell, and B. Saxberg. *Managing High Technology: An Interdisciplinary Perspective.* Amsterdam: North-Holland, 1985.

Matheson, D., and J. Matheson. *The Smart Organization: Creating Value Through Strategic R&D.* Boston: Harvard Business School Press, 1997.

McKenney, J., R. Mason, and D. Copeland. *Waves of Change: Business Evolution Through Information Technology.* Boston: Harvard Business School Press, 1995.

McLaughlin, J. *Innovation, Organization Change, and Technology.* New York: International Thomson Publishing, 1998.

Metcalfe, S. *Evolutionary Economics and Creative Destruction.* London: Routledge, 1998.

Michie, J., and D. Archibugi (Eds.). *Trade, Growth, and Technological Change.* New York: Cambridge University Press, 1998.

Moran, G. *Silencing Scientists and Scholars in Other Fields: Power, Paradigm Controls, Peer Review, and Scholarly Communication.* San Francisco, CA: Ablex Publishing Corporation, 1998.

Morella, C. (Ed.). *Patent System and Modern Technology Needs: Meeting the Challenge of the 21st Century—Hearing Before the Committee on Science, U.S. House of Representatives.* Washington, DC: Diane Publishing Company, 1998.

Mowery, D., and N. Rosenberg. *Paths of Innovation: Technological Change in 20th Century America.* New York: Cambridge University Press, 2000.

National Research Council. *Plasma Science: From Fundamental Research to Technological Applications.* Washington, DC: National Academy Press, 1995.

National Research Council Staff. *Industrial Research and Innovation Indicators: Report of a Workshop.* Washington, DC: National Academy Press, 1997.

National Research Council Staff. *1999 Assessment of the Office of Naval Research's Air and Surface Weapons Technology Program.* Washington, DC: National Academy Press, 1999.

Parayil, G. *Conceptualizing Technological Change: Theoretical and Empirical Explorations.* London: Bowman & Littlefield Publishers, 1999.

Pearce, R. *Global Competition and Technology: Essays in the Creation and Application of Technology by Multinationals.* New York: St. Martin's Press, 1997.

Perrow, C. *Normal Accidents: Living with High Risk Technologies.* Princeton, NJ: Princeton University Press, 1999.

Popper, S., E. Larson, and C. Wagner. *New Forces at Work: Industry Views Critical Technologies.* Santa Monica, CA: Rand Corporation, 1999.

Reppy, J., J. Rotblat, and V. Avduyevsky (Eds.). *Conversion of Military R&D.* New York: St. Martin's Press, 1998.

Rivette, K., and Kline, D. *Rembrandt in the Attic: Unlocking the Hidden Value of Patents.* Boston: Harvard Business School Press, 1999.

Rogers, E. *Diffusion of Innovations,* 4th ed. New York: Simon & Schuster, 1996.

Ryan, M. *Knowledge Diplomacy: Global Competition and the Politics of Intellectual Property.* Washington, DC: The Brookings Institution Press, 1998.

Sahal, D. *Patterns of Technological Innovation.* Reading, MA: Addison-Wesley, 1981.

Sato, R. *Theory of Technical Change and Economic Invariance.* New York: Edward Elgar, 1999.

Savage, J. *Funding Science in America: Congress, Universities, and the Politics of Academic Pork Barrel.* New York: Cambridge University Press, 1999.

Seeley Brown, J. (Ed.). *Seeing Differently: Insights on Innovation.* Boston: Harvard Business School Press, 1997.

Sellen, M. *Bibliometrics: An Annotated Bibliography, 1970-1990.* New York: Macmillan Publishing Company, 1993.

Shapin, S. *The Scientific Revolution.* Chicago: University of Chicago Press, 1998.

Shapira, P. *The R&D Workers: Managing Innovation in Britain, Germany, Japan, and the United States.* Westport, CT: Quorum Books, 1995.

Shaw, L., and F. Papatheofanis. *Outcomes and Technology Assessment in Nuclear Medicine.* Washington, DC: Society of Nuclear Medicine, 1999.

Sigurdson, J. *Measuring the Dynamics of Technological Change.* New York: St. Martin's Press, 1990.

Skinner, D., A. Webster, J. McLaughlin, and P. Rosen. *Valuing Technology: Organizations, Culture, and Change.* London: Routledge, 1999.

Smith, B., and C. Barfield (Eds.). *Technology, R&D, and the Economy.* Washington, DC: Brookings Institution Press, 1996.

Sox, H. *Assessment of Diagnostic Technology in Health Care: Rationale, Methods, Problems, and Directions.* Washington, DC: National Academy Press, 1989.

Stokes, D. *Pasteur's Quadrant: Basic Science and Technological Innovation.* Washington, DC: Brookings Institution Press, 1997.

Stone, M., and J. Wolf (Eds.). *Proper Ambition of Science.* London: Routledge, 2000.

Stoneman, P. (Ed.). *Handbook of the Economics of Innovations and Technological Change.* London: Blackwell Publications, 1995.

Tassey, G. *The Economies of R&D Policy.* Westport, CT: Quorum Books, 1997.

Thorenson, J., and J. Blankenship. *Information Secrets: Metrics and Measures for Valuing Information.* New York: Valuable Information Limited, 1996.

Tidd, J., J. Bessant, and K. Pavitt. *Managing Innovation: Integrating Technological, Market, and Organizational Change.* New York: John Wiley & Sons, 1997.

Torrisi, S. *Industrial Organization and Innovation: An International Study of the Software Industry.* New York: Edward Elgar, 1998.

Tushman, M., and P. Anderson. *Managing Strategic Innovation and Change.* New York: Oxford University Press, 1996.

Tushman, M., and W. Moore (Eds.). *Readings in the Management of Innovation.* New York: Harper Business, 1986.

United Nations. *Technology and Economic Assessment Panel Report: April 1998.* New York: United Nations, 1998.

Van Raan, A. F. J. (Ed.). *Handbook of Quantitative Studies of Science and Technology.* Amsterdam: Elsevier Science, 1988.

Vig, N., and Paschen, H. (Eds.). *Parliaments and Technology: The Development of Technology Assessment in Europe.* Albany: State University of New York Press, 1999.

Wailoo, K. *Drawing Blood: Technology and Disease Identity in Twentieth-Century America.* Baltimore: Johns Hopkins University Press, 1999.

Weiss, C. *Evaluation.* Englewood Cliffs, NJ: Prentice-Hall, 1999.

Zell, D. *Changing by Design: Organizational Innovation at Hewlett-Packard.* Ithaca, NY: Cornell University Press, 1997.

INDEX

Academic institutions, 23, 166-167
Academic science, 283-293; job involve-
    ment, 285-287; measuring, 283-284,
    287-292; strengths and weaknesses,
    286-287; 288-290
Academic spin-offs, 290-292
Allen, T., 319
American Medical Association (AMA),
    209, 231
Amplitude, concept of, 40-41
Argonne National Laboratory, 304

Balachandra, R., 302
Bibliometrics: analysis, 155-156; best uses,
    166-169; definition, 154; evaluation
    tool, 157-159, 336, 338, 339; how
    bibliometrics work, 155-156; journals,
    157; key bibliometric organizations,
    156-157; measures, 162; publications,
    157-160; science and technology, 169-
    170; strengths, 162-164; weaknesses
    and problems, 164-166
Blalock, H., 62
Bozeman, B., 343
Bradford's Law, 155
Brockhoff, K., 312, 314
Business Week, 288

Callon, M., 180
Campbell, D., 61, 62, 213, 265
Caterpillar, Inc., 305, 313
Citation analysis, 82, 154-157, 159, 169
Citation index, 156, 166
Civilian applications of innovations, 22
Cook, T., 61, 109
Cooperative programs with industry, 290,
    291
Cooperative Research and Development
    Agreement (CRADA), 330
Core indicators, 253-255
Co-Word Analysis: 180, how co-word
    analysis works,181; strengths and
    benefits, 181-182; weaknesses and
    problems, 180-181
Crow, M., 343

Data mining (DM): commercial
    applications, 183; evaluation, 188;
    knowledge management, 183-184;
    S&T evaluation, 186-188; techniques
    used, 182-183; weaknesses, 187; what
    it can do, 184-186
Database tomography (DT), 82, 179, 187,
    188
Davenport, T., 153

Distant covariation, 245
Dual ladder, 285-286

Economic/financial measures, 123; best
    uses,103-106, 140-142; strengths and
    benefits, 140; weaknesses and
    problems, 141
Environmental Protection Agency, (EPA),
    24
Ethical issues, 292, 359-364

Federal R&D laboratories, 24-25, 330-331,
    335-339
Fiske, D., 62
Food and Drug Administration (FDA), 337
Franklin, B., 6, 11
Freeman, C., 56
Fulton, R., 6

Garfield, E., 156, 171
Geisler, E., 1, 115, 118, 119, 133,
    162, 211, 243, 246, 255, 257, 262,
    323, 340
General Electric (GE), 142, 143, 210, 319
Goodman, R., 318, 321
Government Performance Results Act
    (GPRA), 55, 331, 332-334, 336, 337,
    338
Griliches, Z., 60, 130, 131, 135, 144, 205

Hauser, J., 76
Henry the Navigator, 5
High-technology industries, 270

Indicator imperative, 47-48
Indicator selection, 50-51
Industrial Revolution, 8-10
Industrial science, 299-310
Industrial scientists and engineers, 306-307
Input measures, 104-105
International Business Machines (IBM),
    168

Jain, R., 13
Japan, 50
*Journal of the American-Medical
    Association* (*JAMA*), 231-232

Katz, R., 76
Knowledge discovery in databases (KDD),
    179

Kostoff, R., 70, 86, 199
Krugman, P., 16, 133

Lawless, M., 318, 321
Liberatore, M., 314
Link, A., 131
Leyesdorff, L., 64, 109
Los Alamos National Laboratory, 334, 335
Lotka's Law, 160, 161
Luukkonen-Gronow, T., 283

Mansfield, E., 130
Marginal productivity, 130-131
Martin, B., 67, 108, 198, 238, 345
Measurement: biases and distortions, 46-
    47; classification scheme, 36;
    conversion and aggregation, 46;
    indicators, 41-48; instruments, 36-40;
    issues, 34-36, 44, 51-54; levels, 40;
    principles, 34-41
Medici, Cosimo de, 5
Metrics: academia, 284; bibliometric, 42,
    82; commercial and business, 81;
    definition, 34, 69-70, 74-75;
    economic/financial, 42, 80, 130-136,
    140-142; evaluating academic
    institutions, 286-290; evaluation, 321-
    323, 335-339; fundamentals, 72-73;
    industrial S&T, 300-307, 309; inputs/
    expenditures, 98-103; organizational,
    strategic, and managerial, 83; peer
    review, 42, 83, 218, 227, 233, 234;
    pool, 80-86; projects, 307-309; S&T,
    41, 42, 268-273, 300-307, 309;
    selection, 75-80, 86-89; self-
    evaluation, 335-336; single parameter,
    70-72
Mission-oriented agencies, 24-25
Mokyr, J., 15
Motorola, 25, 191, 192
Mowery, D., 340
Multiple indicators, 44-46
Mumford, L., 16

Napoleon I, 5, 8
Narin, F., 157, 169, 270
National Aeronautics and Space
    Administration (NASA), 5, 84, 330,
    335, 349
National innovation systems, 50, 105-106,
    349-354; competition and cooperation,

350-351; countries, 351-352; definition, 349-350; evaluation, 349-354; growth, 353-354

National Institute for Occupational Safety and Health (NIOSH), 333, 334

National Institutes of Health (NIH), 76, 156, 160, 223-226, 335, 337, 343

National Science Board (NSB), 23, 22, 48, 49, 53, 98, 156

National Science Foundation (NSF), 24, 49, 102, 222, 224, 225, 235, 290, 297, 343

National Science and Technology Council, 332

Nelson, R., 15, 112, 125, 213, 214, 346, 350, 355

New England Journal of Medicine (NEJM), 232,233

New Product Development (NPD), 142

Organization for Economic Cooperation and Development (OECD), 48, 50, 99

Organization-specific indicators, 253, 255-257

Outputs: bibliographic, 121-123, 187; categories, 121-123; definition, 113-114; direct, 119-120; immediate, 85, 250, 253, 254, 256, 259; intermediate, 85, 250, 254, 256, 259; measuring, 114-116; pre-ultimate, 85, 254-256; quantitative, 118-119; science and technology, 114-116; ultimate, 85, 251, 254, 256

Patents: best uses, 210-211; count, 40, 42, 44, 82, 169, 170, 201-203, 211; definition, 201-203; impacts on performance, 205-206; law, 212; link between R&D and economic outcomes, 204; measures of S&T, 201-206; metric, 201-212, 322, 336, 338, 339; peer review, 209-210; strengths and benefits, 206-207; weaknesses and problems, 207-208

Peer review: attributes and dimensions, 218-220; criteria, 222-227; definition, 217-218; desirable attributes, 218-220; external, 228-232; features, 221; metric, 218-235; process, 220-222; scientific journals, 228-232; strengths

and benefits, 232-233; weaknesses and problems, 233, 234

Performance: measures, 269; factors, 272-273

Price de Solla, D., 154, 170

Principles of measurement. *See* Measurement

Process-outcomes: best uses, 262; clustering and indexing, 257-260; indicators, 253-257; metric, 243-262, 322; model, 246-249; problems, 244-246; stages, 250-251; strengths, 260-261; transformation and diffusion activities, 251-253; weaknesses, 261

Productivity paradox, 131-135

Public sector, 229-344; initiatives, 341-342; metrics and evaluation, 335-339

Reliability, 40-41

Research and development (R&D): federal, 19, 20, 22, 24-26; impacts, 137-140; intensity, 99, 270-271; outputs, 105; productivity, 137-140; spillovers, 136-137

Richelieu, Cardinal, 5

Roach, S., 276

Roadmaps: Motorola, 192-193; Phillips, 193; strengths and benefits, 190-191; weaknesses and problems, 191-192

Rosenberg, N., 3, 106, 350, 354

Rubenstein, A. H., 115, 118, 119, 170, 226, 274, 275

Science and technology (S&T): academic, 286; American, 20, 24; audit, 273-275; Cold War, 19-21; evaluation, 186-188, 300-307, 330-331, 335-339; impacts, 120; industrial, 300-307, 309; institutional, 21-23; investments, 80; laboratories, 168-169; mapping, 189-193; measures, 269; outcomes, progress, and threats, 9-11; output categories, 116-118, 121-123; outputs and metrics, 123-124; performance, 267-273; phenomenon, 12, 26; popular support, 12-13; productivity, 130-131, 159-160; projects, 307-308; public awareness, 11-12; strategy, 317-324; support, 6-9, 12, 13; transformation, 251-252; typology, 272-273

Science: communities, 161; indicators, 48-
    54, 59-60; maps, 189-193
Second World War, 17-19, 48, 330, 351,
    352
Social indicators, 55-60
Solow, R., 130, 133
Souder, W., 69, 86
Stevenson-Wydler legislation, 336, 339
Synergy effect, 106

Technology: ancillary, 271; audit, 273-275;
    contributions, 116-120; corridors, 25-
    26; information, 322-323; public
    support, 6-9, 12-13; public opinion, 13;
    resistance, 10; society, 4-6; transfer,
    116; value pyramid, 73-75

Technology-strategy: alignment, 320;
    connection, 322; evaluation and
    metrics, 321-323; integration, 318-321
Teece, D., 61
Tennessee Valley Authority (TVA), 18, 22
Textual Data Mining (TDM), 179, 188
Triandis, C., 13

United Nations Educational, Scientific, and
    Cultural Organization (UNESCO), 48-
    49, 50
U.S. National Science Board, 49
U.S. News & World Report, 288

Van Raan, P., 189

Westinghouse, 304

About the Author

ELIEZER GEISLER is Professor of Organizational Behavior at the Stuart Graduate School of Business, Illinois Institute of Technology. Dr. Geisler is author of more than 70 scientific articles in technology management and related topics, and of four books, including two from Quorum: *Managing the Aftermath of Radical Corporate Change* (1997), and *Methodology, Theory, and Knowledge in the Managerial and Organizational Sciences* (1999).